Work Stress

LORNE SULSKY
Wilfrid Laurier University

CARLLA SMITH
Formerly of Bowling Green University

THOMSON
™
WADSWORTH

Australia • Canada • Mexico • Singapore • Spain • United Kingdom • United States

Publisher: Vicki Knight
Senior Editor: Marianne Taflinger
Editorial Assistants: Lucy Faridany and Justin Courts
Marketing Manager: Chris Caldeira
Adverstising Project Manager: Laurel Anderson
Art Director: Vernon Boes
Print Buyer: Lisa Claudeanos

Project Manager, Editorial Production: Catherine Morris
Permissions Editor: Chelsea Junget
Copy Editor: Mary Anne Shahidi
Cover Designer: Tessa Avila
Cover Image: PhotoDisc
Compositor: Brian May
Printer: Webcom

Printed in Canada
1   2   3   4   5   6   7   08 07 06 05 04

For more information about our products,
contact us at
Thomson Learning Academic Resource Center
1-800-423-0563

For permission to use material from this text or product,
submit a request online at
http://www.thomsonrights.com.

Any additional questions about permissions
can be submitted by email to
thomsonrights@thomson.com.

Library of Congress Control Number: 2004112871

ISBN: 0-534-57576-5

Thomson Wadsworth
10 Davis Drive
Belmont, CA 94002-3098
USA

Asia
Thomson Learning
5 Shenton Way #01-01
UIC Building
Singapore 068808

Australia/New Zealand
Thomson Learning
102 Dodds Street
Southbank, Victoria 3006
Australia

Canada
Nelson
1120 Birchmount Road
Toronto, Ontario M1K 5G4
Canada

Europe/Middle East/South Africa
Thomson Learning
High Holborn House
50/51 Bedford Row
London WC1R 4LR
United Kingdom

Latin America
Thomson Learning
Seneca, 53
Colonia Polanco
11560 Mexico D.F.
Mexico

Spain/Portugal
Paraninfo
Calle/Magallanes, 25
28015 Madrid, Spain

AUTHOR'S NOTE

As this book was entering the stages of production, Carlla Smith passed away on July 11, 2002. Carlla had been battling cancer for almost two years. Through her writing and teaching, Carlla touched the lives of thousands of students and colleagues. She developed an international reputation as an outstanding scholar. She was a fellow of APA, and was a member of a number of editorial boards for scholarly journals in her field.

As much as I will miss the opportunity to work and collaborate with her in the future, I will miss her friendship even more. Carlla was a remarkable human being, whose zest for life and her flaming spirit were always sources of inspiration for me and her many friends. It is still extremely difficult to believe that the phone will no longer ring, with the Texas twang of Carlla's voice reaching out to warm an otherwise cold and dreary day. To say she will be missed is an understatement. May she find eternal peace in her final resting place, and may we all learn from her undying spirit that life is to be lived to its fullest while we are here.

BRIEF CONTENTS

CONTENTS

PREFACE

All sectors of society have become increasingly aware, and interested in the topic of work stress over the past couple of decades. Decreasing work stress has become a national priority at personal, organizational, and societal levels. To educate undergraduate and graduate students on this timely and important topic, we have both taught undergraduate and graduate courses on job-related stress at our respective universities for several years. However, the issue of locating appropriate textbooks for such courses has repeatedly frustrated us. Many popular press books deal with life and work stress (just glance at the self-improvement and/or psychology sections in your local bookstore), but they mostly lack the rigor, content, and focus required by a serious treatment of the topic. Experts in organizational behavior have written some excellent books on work stress, but their target audience has typically been managers and administrators, not work psychologists or psychologists-in-training. Of course the burgeoning academic and professional literature on work stress was an option, but alone, that can prove to be overwhelming, especially for undergraduates. We wanted a source book that was written by work psychologists focused at the level of the individual worker. This book needed to critically review the literature across the broad domain of work stress in a fairly nontechnical manner, while retaining scientific integrity. Over the years, our class notes and discussions with other academics and students paved the way for such a book.

Both the topics covered and the depth in which they are covered were issues that we debated over the life of this project. Some decisions reflected our own backgrounds and expertise, as well as our assessments of critical and emerging topics in the field. As psychologists, we considered background material, beyond just the work environment, to be important in understanding the historical context and scope of job-related stress. Therefore, the first three chapters discuss topics that often preceded but heavily influenced the development of research and practice on stress in the workplace. Given the enormity of the topic, we never attempted to provide comprehensive coverage of any topic. If we have neglected to include an important topic or piece of research, we apologize for the omission. Some interesting and timely research had to be dropped due to page limitations and publication deadlines. However, we take full responsibility for the content included in this book.

We present a conceptual model of work stress in Chapter 1—a model conceptualizing work stress as a process. This model serves not only as an organizing framework for the book but also to integrate a variety of research streams within a unified "conceptual umbrella." This model has both scientific and practical utility because it attempts to organize/consolidate a vast and varied research literature, while providing a practical and strategic approach to stress management at work.

We are certainly cognizant of the dynamic nature of the workplace and the significant changes in the very nature of the work that have occurred over the past several years. These changes, resulting from technological advances and a myriad of economic, social, and other factors, have direct implications for the quality and quantity of potential work stressors. This complexity creates challenges when preparing a book like this, given that the study of work stress becomes a "moving target." By conceptualizing stress as a process, our model can accommodate these changes. In addition, and more importantly, we have attempted to introduce some of the emergent stress-related issues accompanying the changing workplace.

The work stress literature is not only a moving target but it is also multidisciplinary and, as a result, somewhat disjointed. In combination, these factors made the writing of this book a significant challenge, but a real pleasure at the same time. We sincerely hope the reader finds our approach to be both informative and interesting. Tackling such a multifaceted and complex topic does not obviate us from the responsibility of writing a well-informed and interesting text. We hope the reader agrees we have delivered on both counts.

We would like to thank all of our colleagues and students for their tangible and meaningful assistance throughout the process of writing this book. We extend our thanks to the I/O graduate students at our home institutions who reviewed the text and provided both editorial and substantive suggestions for improvement. We extend an extra measure of thanks to our research assistants who helped us with countless hours of library work so we could spend more time writing. In addition, our appreciation is extended to the following reviewers for their encouraging feedback and helpful suggestions: Arla Day, St. Mary's University; Paul Lloyd, Southeast Missouri State University; Lawrence Murphy, Xavier University; Terry Beehr, Central Michigan University; John Mueller, University of Calgary; and Daniel Ganster, University of Arkansas Finally, we very gratefully acknowledge the assistance provided by the editorial staff at Wadsworth, especially the Senior Psychology Editor, Marianne Taflinger.

Last but not least, our families including our "furry" family members, offered emotional support despite the neglect they suffered while we toiled on this project. For that, they have our eternal gratitude.

AN INTRODUCTION TO THE STUDY OF STRESS

Most people would agree that stress is an important and pervasive component of contemporary life. If asked, almost everyone would say that their lives, both work and nonwork, are very stressful and that they often do not handle stress very well. If probed further, many would probably also say that they think the stress in their lives has negatively affected their physical and emotional health and performance at work. In particular, the deleterious effects of work-related stress are increasingly cited as a key concern for both workers and the organizations employing them.

The concerns about stress appear to be well founded. Health professionals have estimated that 60–90% of all visits to health-care professionals are for stress-related disorders, such as headaches, gastrointestinal disease, back pain, and cardiovascular disease (Cummings & VandenBos, 1981). Experts claim that stress-related disorders cost U.S. industry in excess of $150 billion/year and that stress-related claims account for more than 14% of all insurance compensation claims (Pelletier & Lutz, 1989, 1991). Estimates also indicate that U.S. industry loses approximately 550 million working days annually due to stress-related absenteeism (Danna & Griffin, 1999). Not surprisingly, researchers recently found that stressful demands and low perceived control in the workplace predict increased employee health-care costs over a 5-year period (Ganster, Fox, & Dwyer, 2001). One survey even illustrated that 48% of workers react to their work-related stress by cutting corners, lying about sick days, and covering up incidents that should be reported (Boyd, 1997).

Stress has also been implicated in many serious health-related behaviors, such as smoking and substance abuse. Moreover, as we will see in detail throughout this book, the relationship between stress and a wide variety work-related variables, including human error, withdrawal behaviors (e.g., absenteeism), and work performance, are both obvious and disturbing. Accordingly, the management of work stress has become a major preoccupation of both major corporations and small business, both of which view stress as a severe and pervasive problem that is growing bigger and more troublesome over time. Overall, then, it might not be an understatement to characterize stress as an epidemic—or even a pandemic. A number of avenues of attack can be identified that attempt to curtail this epidemic.

Like any life-threatening epidemic, stress has been attacked at various levels. At a personal level, people of all walks of life have tried to manage their stress through jogging, meditation, diets, counseling, support groups, and even the adoption of new lifestyles. At an institutional and governmental level, stress has been acknowledged as a critical social issue (Hatfield, 1990; Levi, 1990). This acknowledgment has taken the form of several professional journals devoted exclusively to stress research (e.g., *Stress Medicine, Work and Stress*) and professional conferences dealing only with stress and its effects (e.g., the American Psychological Association and National Institute for Occupational Safety and Health's international conferences on work and stress).

At an organizational level, industry leaders have openly expressed alarm over the astronomical costs they believe their organizations have incurred from stress-related absenteeism, turnover, accidents, decreased productivity, and medical expenses (Danna & Griffin, 1999). In response, organizations have offered stress management workshops, "wellness" or health prevention programs, sabbaticals from work, and exercise facilities to their harried employees (Gebhardt & Crump, 1990; Ivancevich, Matteson, Freedman, & Phillips, 1990).

A more insidious cost that organizations increasingly face is the specter of lawsuits filed by workers who claim stress-related injuries (Earnshaw & Cooper, 1994). Indeed, a potential watershed case involved Digital Equipment Corporation, which was forced to pay $6 million dollars to three employees claiming physical injury from the use of company keyboards (Estrers, 1997). Physical stress can be extremely difficult to prove beyond a reasonable doubt; psychological stress is even more difficult to prove. Nonetheless, the potential for lawsuits is real and organizations are increasingly sensitive to the legal ramifications relating to work stress.

It is obvious that at personal, institutional, and organizational levels, we need to decrease the amount of stress in our lives. To eliminate or even reduce stress, however, we need to understand exactly what it is. Unfortunately, this seemingly simple task has eluded stress researchers for years and has prompted lively discussions on the topic (Ivancevich & Matteson, 1980; Mason, 1975a & 1975b; Monat & Lazarus, 1985; Schuler, 1980), even to the point of questioning why we have such a concept (Fleming, Baum, & Singer, 1984).

The purpose of this chapter is to introduce some common perspectives on stress and, from this information, develop a simple heuristic framework to use throughout the balance of the chapters. Although this book is about work-related stress, much of the foundation material in the first few chapters draws from other disciplines, such as medicine and clinical psychology. This synergism nicely illustrates the multidisciplinary nature of stress research, a synergism that has contributed to the variety and richness of the topics covered in the pages to come.

WHAT IS STRESS?

CHAPTER I

If asked to define stress, how would you respond? You might say stress is simply anxiety, tension, or pressure. Regardless of the exact content, chances are that at least one of those words would be included in your definition. You probably would not add the words challenge, excitement, and stimulation. However, if asked whether you consider both undergoing surgery and obtaining a coveted job promotion as stressful, you would probably answer in the affirmative. Would you also consider both receiving a parking ticket and being involved in a serious accident as stressful? Again, you would undoubtedly say "yes," although one incident would obviously have far more serious implications in your life than the other.

So, what is stress? Is it something good or bad, minor or major? The answer is yes! It can be (and usually is) all of those things. Before we offer a more precise definition, it would be helpful to examine some popular misconceptions about stress (Quick & Quick, 1984; Selye, 1974).

1. *You should strive to eliminate all stress in your life.*

This statement is absolutely false! If your life were stress-free, you would not study for final exams, accept a tough job assignment, or jog an extra mile. Stress with positive implications is often referred to as *eustress* (Selye, 1976). If you rise up to meet the challenges of life, growth, maturation, and adaptability can result. The right amount and type of stress can make life exciting; in fact, stress has been called the "spice of life."

2. *Stress is just "in your head." It cannot really harm you.*

This misconception, so common in the past, is less prevalent today. Although few realize how pervasive its influence is, most people now acknowledge that stress is linked to mental and physical illness. One of the major goals of this book is to demonstrate the association between stress, especially work-related stress, and illness.

3. *Stress is really just anxiety or nervous tension. If you could calm down, then you would not be stressed.*

This statement is an oversimplification. Anxiety or nervous tension can be a response to the experience of stress. However, stress is *much* more than anxiety or tension (or frustration or conflict). In fact, people (and animals) can exhibit a physiological stress reaction, for example increased heart rate and blood pressure, while asleep or unconscious.

4. *Stress only implies excess, such as too much work or stimulation.*

This misconception does not consider that being bored or understimulated can also be very stressful. Some jobs require workers to sit idle for long periods of time, waiting for some event, such as aircraft on a radar screen. Many of these workers report that such activities are very stressful.

DEFINITIONS OF STRESS

Now that we have discussed what stress is not, the stage is set to discover what stress is. Ivancevich and Matteson (1980) drew a clever analogy between stress and sin. They said that both mean different things to different people and that both are short words with emotionally charged content representing complex concepts. This mindset has given rise to a variety of definitions of stress (Appley & Trumbull, 1967; Cox, 1978; Ivancevich & Matteson, 1980; Lazarus, 1966; Mason, 1975a & 1975b; Schuler, 1980; Selye, 1974). The most common definitions have focused on the stressful stimulus, the stress response, or the interaction between the stimulus and the response (Ivancevich & Matteson, 1980; Jex, Beehr, & Roberts, 1992).

Stimulus Definitions

Stimulus definitions define stress in terms of the event or situation in the environment that contributes to or causes a noxious or disruptive experience (Appley & Trumbull, 1967); the event or situation is called a *stressor* (Selye, 1950). This type of definition has been labeled an engineering or human factors definition of stress because it focuses on the external forces or demands applied to an object. Engineers often refer to the amount of stress (external force) applied to objects, such as molecules or metal bars, necessary to produce a change in the object. In organizational research that has emphasized stimulus definitions, Caplan, Cobb, French, Van Harrison, and Pinneau (1975) defined stress as "any characteristic of the job environment which poses a threat to the individual." Cooper and Marshall (1976) stated that, "by occupational stress is meant negative environmental factors or stressors associated with a particular job." Although these researchers certainly acknowledged other factors in the stress experience, their emphasis definitely was on the stressor itself.

The implication of the stimulus definition is that stress can be defined using objective or external criteria, which has also been the reason for its popularity: Focusing on external sources can suggest direct targets of change. When applied to humans, however, this definition suffers from some obvious flaws. First, no two people respond to a stressor identically (or necessarily even agree that it is stressful), whether that stressful stimulus is a poisonous snake or an angry boss. One person's response to a single stressor may even change over time. This perspective also generally assumes that no stress is best, which, as we said previously, is usually not true.

Response Definitions

Response definitions focus on the reaction the organism (human or animal) has to the stressor. Selye's (1956) definition of stress as "... the nonspecific response to any demand" is an example of a response definition. Responses can take a myriad of forms, from immediate, reflexive, physiological reactions to chronic changes in behavior or health. Long-term or chronic changes in response to a stressor are often called *strains*. Some stressor is presumed to have precipitated the response, although the nature of the stressor is unimportant. The response to the stressor is always internal (physiological changes in the body), but it may or may not have overt manifestations, for example trembling hands or diarrhea. Longer-term responses (strains) could include an unfortunate outcome such as coronary heart disease. Although researchers who use the response definition may acknowledge the influence of other factors, their emphasis is always on the stress response.

Because of the focus on the organism's reaction, response definitions are often associated with medical or biological perspectives of stress (Alexander, 1950; Selye, 1956; Wolff, 1953). The importance of response definitions has been underscored by the critical role stress is presumed to play in the development of chronic and life-threatening diseases.

Response definitions, however, also suffer from some obvious flaws. As we will discover in the pages ahead, different responses may be associated with different stressors, and these responses may change over time. Also, the body may undergo a response very similar or identical to a stress response when no stressful stimulus is present. For example, the administration of certain drugs, such as adrenaline, can cause the body to experience a "stress response." The response definition therefore seems to be inadequate because the source of the stress (stressor) cannot be ignored. Finally, knowledge about the stressor is important if any type of intervention is desired.

Stimulus-Response Definitions

Stimulus-response (interactive) definitions conceive of stress as resulting from interactions between environmental stimuli (stressors) and individual responses (often, although not always, in the form of strains). This type of definition is more complex than the other two because the stressor-response interaction can take a variety of forms, depending on both the nature of the stressor and the response. Lazarus and his colleagues (e.g., Lazarus & Folkman, 1984) referred to this type of definition as a *relational* definition because it deals with the "... relationship between the person and the environment (stimulus) that is appraised by the person as taxing or exceeding his or her resources and endangering his or her well-being (response)" (p. 19). Due to its broader focus, the stimulus-response definition can also accommodate the influence of factors such as perceptions or appraisals (see Lazarus & Folkman's definition) about specific stressors and individual, group, and situational differences (e.g., personality style, work group support, access to medical care).

This type of definition has been very popular among organizational stress researchers. For example, McGrath (1976) defined stress as involving "an interaction of person and environment." Beehr and Newman (1978) conceived of "stress as a condition wherein job-related factors interact with the worker to change (disrupt or enhance) his/her psychological or physiological condition such that the person (mind and/or body) is forced to deviate from normal functioning" (p. 670).

The definition of stress that we adopt falls out of the stimulus-response tradition, and is very similar to Beehr and Newman's (1978) perspective, among others (Ivancevich & Matteson, 1980; Schuler, 1980). Specifically, we define *stress* as any circumstance (stressor) that places special physical and/or psychological demands on an organism leading to physiological, psychological, and behavioral outcomes. If these demands persist over time, long-term or chronic undesirable outcomes or strains may result. Thus, for example, if an individual learns that his employment may soon be terminated, he may experience a short-term increase in blood pressure (physiological outcome), become anxious (psychological outcome), and his work performance may suffer (behavioral outcome) as he finds it difficult to focus on his work responsibilities. If the psychological demands introduced do not abate over time, he may begin to experience longer-term outcomes such as serious illness and clinical depression.

For most stressors, the stress response must be preceded by the perception that the stressor is indeed threatening or stressful. In short, a psychological appraisal occurs that determines the severity of the stressor. This appraisal may then lead to specific short-term outcomes and (eventually) chronic outcomes or *strains,* and the appraisal and outcome(s) (as well as the stressor) may be affected by characteristics of the person, group, and/or situation. These characteristics are often referred to as stress modifiers or *moderators* (cf. Viswesvaran, Sanchez, & Fisher, 1999).

Specifically, a person's stress response and outcome(s) may depend on personal, group, and situational characteristics, or moderators, such as the person's age, work group cohesiveness, and the availability of medical services. Even whether the stressor is perceived as stressful can be a function of these moderators, such as one's anxiety level and previous encounters with the stressor.

The key to understanding the stimulus-response definition is to realize that some stressor, typically in the environment, provokes an immediate psychological appraisal determining whether and the extent to which the stressor is determined to be stressful. Both the stressor and the outcome of the psychological appraisal can be frustratingly diverse. This complexity is further compounded by the influence of any number of personal and situational characteristics. (We will devote much space in the pages ahead to examining this diversity.)

Using our definition, stress is a function of the stressor(s), psychological appraisal, short-term stress outcome(s), strains, and stress moderators. Any reference to the term "stress" henceforth will refer to this total experience. Our definition is consistent with the current conceptualization of stress as a dynamic process (Beehr & Franz, 1987; Ganster & Schaubroeck, 1991). Figure 1.1 presents a preliminary and admittedly overly simplistic process model of stress that will serve as a guide for the remainder of the discussion in this chapter. Process models that are more detailed and well developed are introduced in Chapter 2.

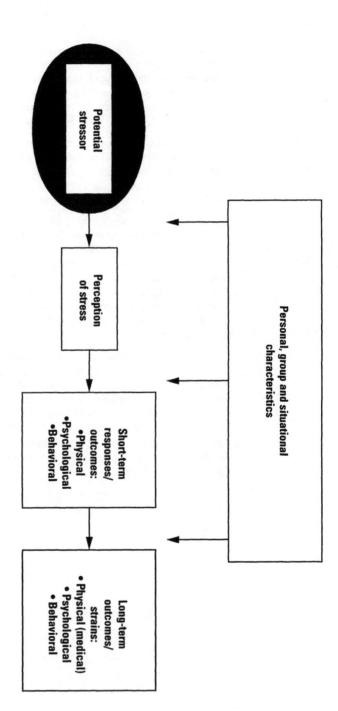

Figure 1.1 General Stress Model

Inspection of Figure 1.1 reveals that there are a number of components to the stress process. For example, a person experiences the wrath of an irate coworker. Whether and the extent to which this "stimulus" is perceived as stressful and becomes a "stressor" depends on the person's psychological appraisal of the stimulus.

This is one point at which moderator variables such as individual differences have an impact: Some people may have a propensity to find many stimuli stressful while others may be bothered only by specific types of stimuli. Are you stressed by having to wait in line at the grocery store checkout? Some people "go crazy" while waiting; others do not seem to be bothered at all—it seems they may even enjoy having some enforced idle time!

As another illustration, individuals who are considered to exhibit the Type A Behavior Pattern (Chapter 6) typically like to complete things in a hurry and thus may perceive waiting for a coworker to complete a piece of work as stressful and anxiety provoking. The same Type A individual, however, may not interpret a time deadline as stressful, and, in fact, may thrive when a deadline is imposed.

There is potentially a second point of impact (see Figure 1.1): Once stress is perceived to exist, the quantity and quality of the stress outcomes may also vary depending on these individual differences. For example, individuals who exhibit a propensity to be hostile tend to experience greater levels of illness in the face of work stress (Kivimaeki, Vantera, Koskenvuo, Uutela, & Pentti, 1998). Additionally, individuals deemed to be highly conscientious have been shown to exhibit lower levels of psychological distress in the face of certain stressors (Miller, Griffin, & Hart, 1999).

As noted earlier, the moderators of the stress process can function at a personal, group, or situational level. Although Type A is an example of a personal moderator, an example of a group and a situational moderator would be low group morale and inadequate equipment or machinery, respectively. So, if an air traffic controller must deal with low work-group morale and equipment that does not function properly, both factors would increase his perceptions of work stress and his subsequent development of stress outcomes, such as tension headaches. Of course, the low group morale and faulty equipment may be more than just moderators: they may also be considered by the air traffic controller as additional stressors! However, after several years of job tenure, the air traffic controller may eventually view his job as substantially less stressful. In this case, his coworkers' attitudes and the poor working conditions would have considerably less impact on the relationship between the air traffic controller's work stress and stress outcome (headaches).

The issue, then, is that a stimulus typically becomes a stressor only when perceived as such, at which point any number of personal, group, and/or situational modifiers can influence the link between the stressor and some type of outcome. Once perceived as stressful, the stimulus triggers a series of short-term physiological, psychological, and behavioral outcomes. As our definition indicates, if the stressor remains over time, these short-term outcomes can culminate in more serious, enduring outcomes. As an example, experiencing some stressor may quickly trigger an upset stomach (short-term outcome). Experiencing the same or other stressors over several years may produce gastrointestinal disease (long-term outcome or strain). Therefore, our definition of stress implies a process that includes both a set of short and (potentially) long-term outcomes.

The distinction between short-term and long-term outcomes naturally leads us to consider another important distinction for the stress process: stressors may be either *chronic* or *acute* in nature (Cambronne, Shih, & Harri, 1999). When a stressor is first appraised as stressful, we characterize it as an acute stressor. If the stressor persists over time, however, the stressor is considered to be a chronic stressor. Chronic stressors typically evoke the long-term outcomes. In some rare cases, an acute stressor can lead to a response/outcome normally associated with chronic stress (e.g., a suicide attempt) if the stressor is perceived to be unusually severe.

No clear dividing line exists that determines when an acute stressor becomes chronic. An individual faced with an irate coworker may consider a given altercation to be an acute stressor. If, however, altercations with the individual persist over time and are deemed to be bothersome, we would characterize the stressor as chronic. When workers indicate that their jobs are stressful, they are generally referring to persistent or chronic stressors, such as continually facing too many work demands or an ongoing fear of being laid off. Sudden or acute stressors (e.g., a machine suddenly malfunctions, a coworker commits an error, which causes difficulties for others) are also undoubtedly common and may or may not become chronic. The chronicity of the stressor will depend on whether the stressor is either removed entirely or at least attenuated to the point that it is not considered to be bothersome.

Before turning to a more detailed discussion of the stress process, we must consider a fundamental question that has direct relevance to our discussion and was alluded to in the example of the air traffic controller. Simply stated, do stimuli become stressors only when interpreted as such? Consider, for instance, a noxious chemical released on the factory floor. The odorless chemical penetrates the nostrils and lungs of unsuspecting workers. If this chemical is considered to be a stressor that leads to a physiological response, was any cognitive processing first necessary to properly label the stimuli as a stressor before the physiological reaction?

This illustration captures a debate (Lazarus, 1984; Zajonc, 1984) that has enamored behavioral scientists for decades: Do people who see an attacking tiger, for example, cognitively process the stimulus (big teeth, loud roar, etc.)

and become physiologically aroused? Alternately, is the arousal "hard-wired" such that an automatic response to the stimulus occurs without the need for intervening cognition? This latter scenario would probably have some survival value. The milliseconds saved from automatically reacting to the stimulus without the need for interpretation may be the difference between life and death! The cognitive realization of the attacking tiger, then, would likely come after the physiological response.

The fact is that some stimuli, particularly physical or environmental stressors (e.g., the noxious chemical fumes in the factory, temperature extremes, loud noise), can probably automatically elicit a response without the need for mediating interpretation. For example, up to 30% of office buildings may have severe indoor air quality problems, termed sick building syndrome (Frazer, 1998), and illness can result without any awareness that there is an environmental stressor. Most work-related stimuli that may become stressors, such as a tedious job, time pressures, or an irate boss, however, are likely not hard wired. That is, the intervening cognitions that interpret whether and the extent to which stimuli are bothersome or stressful are probably fundamental and necessary. It would be difficult to imagine that human beings are genetically predisposed to any type of automatic hard wired reaction—for example, to a dull and boring job—unless the jobs as a source of stress is first interpreted as such.

THE PSYCHOLOGY OF STRESS: THE ROLE OF APPRAISAL

In this section, we outline some of what is known about how people psychologically process stimuli that might be labeled as "stressors." As we indicated previously, many work-related stimuli will become stressors only if they are perceived as such.

Suppose you are working unprotected outside on a scalding August afternoon. What would your almost immediate response be to that environmental stressor? First, you would undoubtedly begin to perspire, which is your body's physiological cooling mechanism. If you are exposed to extreme heat for an extended period, your body might be unable to sustain its cooling action, resulting in a heat stroke; continued heat exposure would inevitably lead to death. Fortunately, such extreme outcomes are rare because so many adaptive responses are readily available (e.g., consuming large quantities of fluid, moving to a cooler environment).

Now, consider a stressor that is more typical of modern urban life, such as a demanding job. Your concern about your job might make you anxious and disrupt your sleep; you might consequently start drinking alcohol to relax yourself. If your situation continues unchanged for weeks, months, or years, you might develop a host of strains, such as poor job performance, alcoholism, and, finally, cirrhosis of the liver. Liver disease, of course, could be fatal.

How are these two scenarios different? The tragic end points are certainly identical. The first involves an environmental stressor, heat, which emanates from the natural environment. The eventual outcome of experiencing this type of stressor is well understood and fairly predictable; the effects of heat stress are universally experienced by all human beings. The second scenario, however, involves a very different type of stressor, one influenced by several personal and situational factors. Unlike heat stress, a demanding job is not a universal stressor for all humans. For some, a demanding job may be viewed as a challenge and not a threat. In addition, although prescribed responses are available for coping with heat stress, coping responses for dealing with a demanding job (e.g., asking coworkers for assistance) may be as varied and as differentially successful as the people who experience this stressor. Another distinguishing feature between the two scenarios is that the person coping with a demanding job may be just as likely to develop cardiovascular disease or ulcers as liver disease (or even no disease at all!).

Responses to an environmental stressor such as heat depend on factors like the overall number and strength of the stressors encountered and the person's ability to cope with them. For example, suppose a worker in a chemical plant must breathe highly toxic fumes while enduring heat exposure from the chemical process. Also, suppose her general health is poor. She will not cope as successfully with the multiple stressors in her work environment as someone who is in excellent health and must endure only occasional exposure to either the fumes or heat.

Beyond physical or environmental stressors, workers are potentially faced with an array of stimuli that might be perceived as stressors. Although responses to these stimuli may depend on their number and strength, the psychological interpretation of these stimuli is critical for predicting whether and the extent to which stress is perceived.

Richard Lazarus (1966) coined the term *cognitive appraisal* to describe this evaluative process. For stimuli such as a demanding job, the situation must be appraised as being stressful. So, unlike stressors such as extreme heat, psychosocial stressors must be appraised as stressful before they are truly stressors. For psychosocial stressors, stress is indeed in the eye of the beholder.

Lazarus believed that an appraisal occurs at two different points in the stress experience: when the situation is perceived as being stressful and when some type of response to the stressor is consciously chosen. The former is called *primary appraisal* and the latter is called *secondary appraisal*. Specifically, primary appraisal asks, "Is this situation stressful?" and, if the answer is "Yes," secondary appraisal asks, "What can I do about the stressful situation?" *Reappraisal* can occur based on feedback from primary and secondary appraisals. For example, a person must first decide that the job is demanding (primary appraisal) and then decide how to cope with it by, for example, asking for assistance (secondary appraisal). At some point, perhaps because the person has effectively coped with the situation, he no longer perceives it as stressful (reappraisal; remember our harried air traffic controller earlier in the chapter).

This two-part appraisal process can have profound effects even beyond direct experiences with psychosocial stressors. For example, a person may perceive the existence of a stressor that most people would agree does not exist in objective reality—for example, imagining your supervisor dislikes you. In this case, the stressor has reality only in your imagination. The effects of an environmental stressor, however, can also be compounded by stressful appraisals associated with it: The chemical worker may become very agitated and fearful about her exposure to fumes and heat, thus exacerbating her stress responses beyond those triggered solely by the environmental stressors. In addition to the appraisal process, other personal factors can affect the experience of stress. We will discuss some of these factors (e.g., personality type, gender) in later chapters.

It would be helpful now to incorporate the concepts we have discussed into the heuristic framework in Figure 1.1. Suppose a worker, in response to labor shortages caused by layoffs in his organization, is transferred to another department. He immediately has problems interacting with his new supervisor, and therefore perceives his supervisor to be a job-related stressor (primary appraisal). Based on repeated interactions with the supervisor, he develops an upset stomach and anxiety while on the job (short-term outcomes). Over time, his relationship with his supervisor deteriorates, and he develops even more severe anxiety and stomach problems. He feels increasingly more stressed by his supervisor (reappraisal) and consequently decides he must act to change the situation by, among other tactics, openly discussing these problems with his supervisor (secondary appraisal). His attempts to cope with the situation repeatedly fail, and he perceives that the situation continues to escalate (reappraisal). Eventually, given few alternate employment opportunities, he remains in his position and, over time, develops serious stomach problems and depression (i.e., long-term outcomes or strains).

Fortunately, not all stressful job-related encounters have such an unhappy ending. However, the scenario presented here serves to illustrate how the stress process can evolve for a very typical psychosocial stressor at work. If the stressor is environmental, such as exposure to toxic chemicals, the stressor may not be perceived as such, although the body responds to it as a stressor. Of course, in those situations in which an environmental stressor is perceived as a stressor, the person must cope with both the physical and psychological outcomes of such encounters.

THE PHYSIOLOGY OF STRESS

Up to this point, we have not discussed about the specifics of a very critical component of the stress model, the "stress response," which follows from the perception of a stimulus as a stressor. As soon as a stimulus is psychologically perceived as stressful, or perhaps as soon as some physical stressor (e.g., noise, heat) is encountered, the body undergoes what is now a well-established sequence of physiological reactions. Short and longer term psychological and behavioral reactions are also expected to occur as well. The physiological reactions are assumed to be qualitatively highly similar (although not identical), regardless of the stimuli that provoked them. The psychological and behavioral reactions are likely to be more variable and depend on many factors, including the quality and quantity of the stressful experience and individual or situational differences. With this as a general backdrop, we now turn to a discussion of the short and longer term physiological reactions during the stress process.

The Fight or Flight Response

The intricate chain of physiological events that occurs when an organism (human or animal) encounters a stressor was first investigated in the early twentieth century by a famous American physiologist, Walter Cannon. In his Harvard University laboratory, Cannon exposed dogs and cats to a variety of stressors, but found that their responses, regardless of the source, always followed the same pattern. Cannon (1929, 1932, 1939) called this response pattern the *fight or flight response* because, when faced with a threat (stressor), the organism's body prepares for combat or flight to safety.

The fight or flight response, a chain of changes in nerves and glands in the body, maps out a sequence of events that, scientists believe, is the result of millions of years of evolution. When the organism perceives a stressor, that message is sent to a part of the brain called the hypothalamus. The hypothalamus is a complex structure, approximately the size of the end of a human thumb, deeply seated in the brain. The hypothalamus instantaneously activates the autonomic nervous system (the part of the nervous system that regulates the involuntary activities in the body and the functions of the internal organs). Specifically, the sympathetic branch of the autonomic nervous system is triggered, which galvanizes the body into an aroused state. The sympathetic nerve fibers release a hormone (a chemical that regulates body functions) called *noradrenaline* (also called norephinephrine). Sympathetic activation through noradrenaline raises the heart rate, increases brain alertness, and elevates blood pressure through constriction of blood vessels, among many other effects.

Almost simultaneously with the sympathetic activity, the hypothalamus activates an inner layer of cells in the adrenal glands, one of which rests on each kidney. The inner layer, or medulla, of the adrenal glands, in response to stimulation from the hypothalamus, produces two hormones. These hormones are *noradrenaline* (or norephinephrine) and *adrenaline* (or epinephrine); collectively, they are referred to as *catecholamines*. Although both the sympathetic nerve fibers and adrenal medulla secrete noradrenaline, 80% of the catecholamine secretion in humans is adrenaline. As Figure 1.2 illustrates, activation of the sympathetic nervous system and the adrenal glands to synthesize noradrenaline and adrenaline produces a host of changes, physiologically and biochemically, in the body. These changes (e.g., increased heart rate, elevated blood pressure, increased air flow to the lungs (rapid breathing), hair erection (goose bumps), dilated pupils of the eyes, increased metabolism), are commonly associated with the experience of stress. Even those reactions that are not obviously related to the stress response, such as decreased digestive activity and vasoconstriction of the blood vessels in the skin, are oriented toward limiting the biological activities that are not absolutely necessary to deal with the stressor. The biochemical and physiological changes of the fight or flight response occur immediately on encounter with the stressor and dissipate very rapidly. Therefore, they are all associated with acute threats or stressors.

Cannon recognized that the stress experience requires the organism, animal or human, to make an unusual or adaptive response (recall our definition of stress on p. 6). In fact, Cannon (1922) first introduced the concept of homeostasis, or stability, and acknowledged the dysfunctional consequences of upsetting the stability or balance of the organism. The immediate stress/arousal response considered by Cannon was also identified by Yerkes and Dodson (1908), who developed the Yerkes-Dodson Law of arousal. Simply, the law states that the quality of an organism's performance increases as arousal increases, but only to a point. As arousal increases beyond an optimum amount, performance then begins to decrease. (Also see Chapter 6.) People who participate seriously in athletics will tell you that they like to increase their arousal level before the "big event". Similarly, students talk about getting "pumped up" for an upcoming exam. Indeed, this arousal, which is sometimes mistakenly called anxiety, can be beneficial in moderate amounts for galvanizing the organism for optimal action/performance—the concept of eustress we introduced earlier. Too much arousal, however, may be harmful in that performance efficiency begins to decrease, as any athlete or test taker, "paralyzed" by the stress of the moment, can confirm.

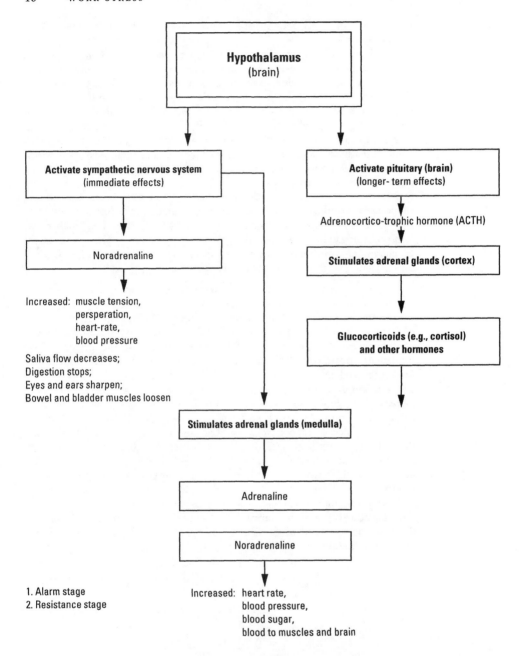

Figure 1.2 Physiology of the Stress Response

The General Adaptation Syndrome

Some years after Cannon had mapped the biochemical sequence called the fight or flight response, a young medical researcher named Hans Selye conducted experiments on rats in hope of discovering a new sex hormone. Instead, he made what many scientists consider to be an infinitely more significant discovery by extending Cannon's work on the stress response (Selye, 1956, 1974, 1976). In addition to the role the hypothalamus plays in the fight or flight response, Selye discovered that the hypothalamus activates the pituitary gland, located adjacent to the hypothalamus, to produce a very powerful hormone, adrenocorticotrophic hormone (ACTH). ACTH stimulates the outer layer or cortex of the adrenal glands to produce several hormones associated with the stress response. The class of hormones called *glucocorticoids* is the most well known and important product of this adrenal activation. The glucocorticoids include steroids such as cortisol.

The glucocorticoids' short-term function is primarily to facilitate the conversion of food substances other than sugar, particularly proteins and fats, into sugar (glucose) for energy and tissue repair. However, they also act synergistically with the catecholamines (that is, reinforcing their effects; Figure 1.2). In the short term, glucocorticoids such as cortisol promote the metabolic adaptation of the body to stressful situations by providing an increased store of blood glucose for energy and tissue regeneration. Moderate levels of glucocorticoids are even essential on a daily basis to sustain life because tissue repair and regeneration cannot occur without them.

Although glucocorticoids are essential to life, they can be very harmful to the body at the high concentrations often present in situations of prolonged or chronic stress. Sustained, elevated levels of these hormones can wreak havoc on the body by inhibiting the immune system, weakening muscle tissue, and promoting vascular disorders. One indirect effect of elevated cortisol levels has direct implications for cardiovascular health: Sustained elevations of cortisol in the body trigger lipid (fat) production, particularly cholesterol. Abnormally high levels of cholesterol in the body are widely believed to be associated with vascular blockage and cardiovascular disease.

The biochemical and physiological changes investigated by Selye begin a short time (although not instantaneously) after encounter with the stressor and dissipate slowly, even if the stressor disappears. For these reasons, they are typically associated with enduring or chronic stress.

From activation of the hypothalamus, the pituitary also stimulates the thyroid glands to produce another hormone implicated in the stress response, thyroxin (not shown in Figure 1.2). Elevated levels of thyroxin result in such changes as increased mental activity, blood pressure, respiration, and gastrointestinal activity. Like cortisol, thyroxin amplifies the effects of the catecholamines and serves as a longer term stress hormone. Although further detail is beyond the scope of this chapter, several other biochemical and physiological pathways in the body are associated with the stress response. For instance, the pituitary-insulin system also regulates blood glucose levels; and the mineralocorticoids, steroids synthesized by the adrenal cortex, are involved in blood pressure regulation through the maintenance of blood sodium levels. However, stress researchers believe that sympathetic nervous system activation and involvement of the adrenal medulla and cortex are the most important, consistent, and widely acknowledged components of the stress response (Cox, 1978).

The implications of Cannon's and Selye's discoveries present a paradox, and demonstrate very well that the short and longer term effects of these biochemical reactions can differ. As illustrated in Figure 1.2, one of the effects of sympathetic activation and the release of catecholamines is to increase the tendency for arteries to constrict and for blood to clot or coagulate. Of course, in stressful encounters, this process prepares the body to defend against injury and blood loss. Under chronic stress, the excess blood cells build up in the arterial walls. Blood pressure consequently increases and the potential for life-threatening arterial blockage rises. Arterial constrictions also have the effect of narrowing the arteries, making it more difficult for blood to flow to the heart. Additionally, one of the effects of pituitary-adrenal activation is to stimulate the immune system through increased white blood cell production. The enhanced immune response provides extra protection for the body in case of injury. However, steroid hormones can build up as a result of stress-related adrenal activation, and concentrations of steroids in the body over time can suppress immune system functioning. It therefore seems obvious that, paradoxically, how our bodies adapt to stress in the short term can be very detrimental in the longer term.

For example, your first responses when experiencing a near-miss collision with a semitruck (e.g., wildly beating heart and rapid breathing) are the result of the fight or flight response, which Selye also called the *alarm stage*. Selye labeled the chain of events initiated in the pituitary gland, which culminates in glucocorticoid production, the *stage of resistance*. The stage of resistance occurs shortly after the alarm stage. According to Selye, the body, at this point, seems to be recovering, but if the stressor is not eliminated, this recovery is only illusory. As discussed earlier, the costs of longer term adaptation are high.

Eventually, the body enters the *stage of exhaustion*, which is associated with the development of long-term or chronic strains, such as heart disease, immunodeficiency, and chronic high blood pressure. At least initially, the stage of exhaustion mimics the alarm stage, with the body rallying its last round of defenses. Of course, if the stressor remains or returns too frequently, the eventual outcome might be the death of the organism. Autopsies that Selye performed on his experimental animals revealed some of the effects of this progression of biochemical and physiological events:

adrenal glands enlarged from overstimulation, lymphatic (immune system) tissue shrunken from the effects of the steroids, and bloody, ulcerated stomach tissue from excessive acid secretion in the stomach and intestines. Selye called this total sequence of events, identified as the alarm stage, the stage of resistance, and the stage of exhaustion, the *General Adaptation Syndrome (GAS)*. We will have more to say about the GAS and Selye's theory of stress in the next chapter.

It is important to realize that the GAS is not necessarily a linear process. For example, while in the alarm stage for a given stressor, a person may be simultaneously coping with or resisting the same stressor from an earlier encounter, or perhaps resisting entirely different stressors. In short, a person may be going through a number of these stages simultaneously and/or in different sequences. It is therefore not surprising that the human body can sustain serious and or permanent injury as the stress process takes its toll over time.

It is indeed bitter irony that responses so adaptive for our primitive ancestors are so maladaptive for modern humans. Without the fight or flight response or stage of resistance, our ancestors could not have escaped from predators or speared their four-footed dinner entrees. In a confrontation with an irate client, however, an elevated heart rate or rapid breathing does not aid today's Homo sapiens. For many organizational situations, instead of flight or fight, one must "smile and take it." Workers typically have neither the option to fight or to flee. Consequently, all too often, modern humans must endure their stressors over time, resulting in a variety of dire consequences.

As the preceding paragraphs indicate, the physiology of stress presents a complex array of events for the stress researcher to consider. Complicating matters further, however, is that a series of psychological and behavioral outcomes are believed to covary with the physiological outcomes. For instance, a psychological reaction that we might observe during the alarm stage is acute anxiety. If the stressor is not removed or attenuated, however, chronic anxiety might persist in some individuals. Similarly, short-term behavioral responses might run the gamut from nonwork behaviors (e.g., alcohol consumption) to work-related behaviors (e.g., tardiness, safety infractions, loss of concentration). In the longer term, more serious behavioral outcomes are thought to arise, including self-destructive behaviors such as drug addiction, and a host of potentially serious behaviors affecting both the individual and the employing work organization (e.g., absenteeism, industrial accidents, turnover).

CONCLUSIONS

So, what is stress? Clearly, stress is a complex phenomenon composed of external stimuli (stressors), cognitive appraisal, and short- and long-term outcomes (strains), all of which can be affected by a host of contextual, group, and personal factors (moderators). Stress is really a process consisting of several stages. The physiological underpinnings of the process are fairly well understood (fight or flight response; GAS), a fact underscored by the considerable biological and medical heritage of stress research. Less well understood but undoubtedly no less significant are the psychological components of stress (appraisal processes) and their interrelationships with the physiological ones. This complex interplay provides an intriguing, if sometimes frustrating, puzzle for the stress researcher.

Conceptualizing stress as a process affords one with both theoretical and practical advantages. From a theoretical standpoint, viewing stress as a process allows us to integrate and consolidate what would otherwise be an unwieldy mass of disconnected research—all considered to be stress research. For example, research examining short-term physiological arousal can now be understood as a component of a larger stress process without any confusion about whether or not the research is actually examining the concepts of either stress, arousal, or both. Research on individual differences can be tied directly to relevant aspects of Figure 1.1; for example, research examining personality can be understood in the context of moderator variables.

From a practical standpoint, viewing stress as a process presents a systematic framework for developing stress management interventions. Although a discussion of stress management must wait until the final section of the book, suffice it to say that the process model provides a "blueprint" whereby intervention strategies can be targeted at any or all steps of the process.

At this point, you have no doubt begun to appreciate the enormous task facing the student of stress: that making sense of the complex interactions among stressors, stress responses, moderators, strains, and the appraisal process can be a tricky proposition indeed. For that reason, researchers have developed theories or models of stress that attempt to organize this knowledge in systematic and meaningful ways. Chapter 2 examines some well-known stress models.

MODELS OF STRESS

Statements such as "organizational stress is negatively related to job satisfaction" and "women and men do not differ in their levels of reported stress" are perhaps interesting and informative. However, such statements do not explain the basis for the relationship, or difference, respectively. To better understand the processes they study, researchers often systematically organize knowledge in a particular area. A systematic organization of knowledge on some topic is frequently referred to as a *theory* or *model*. Some researchers use the terms theory and model interchangeably; others reserve the term model for a picture that represents a "best-guess" or blueprint given the state of knowledge at the time of model development. This implies that models are not developed to present a definitive statement about reality—a position we endorse. Rather, models merely serve to provide a framework for organizing thought and directing research in a systematic fashion. The model of the stress process presented in the previous chapter would be an example of such a framework. In sum, stress models are developed to organize systematically what is known about stress.

Models combine both elements of structure and process. That is, structural components are included, such as environmental stimuli and personal characteristics (See Figure 1.1). Additionally, the process through which components are thought to interact is also considered. Models attempt to specify the interrelationships among components. The interrelationships can be simple (e.g., stress is related to cardiovascular disease), or quite complex (e.g., stress is related to cardiovascular disease in males who are extreme Type A personality types in high pressure jobs).

Many stress models have been proposed. Some of these models extend beyond job stress and consider life stress in general. They vary in structure, focus, and boundary conditions (what they do and do not specify). In this chapter, we explore some of the more well known stress models. The coverage is admittedly selective; an entire book could be devoted to the plethora of models! The selections represent a cross section of proposed models from different perspectives.

The models covered in this chapter can be roughly categorized as either biological/medical models or behavioral science models. The two categorizations reflect the dual nature of stress research—both as a biological and a psychological phenomenon—and the professional orientations of different stress researchers. As the reader shall soon discover, however, these different orientations frequently overlap or complement each other. Before considering specific models of work stress, it is instructive to examine models from both categorizations that consider stress more generally. Our decision to examine these more general models is based on the fact that many current work stress models draw heavily from them.

BIOLOGICAL/MEDICAL STRESS MODELS

Selye's General Theory of Stress

In Chapter 1, we discussed in some detail Selye's extension of Cannon's work on the physiological basis of the stress response and the development of the General Adaptation Syndrome (GAS). To summarize, Selye extended Cannon's investigation of the activation of the hypothalamus-sympathetic nervous system and the hypothalamus-adrenal medulla pathways to produce catecholamines during the initial phase of stressful encounters (fight or flight response or alarm reaction). Selye documented the activation of the pituitary-adrenal cortex pathway to produce the glucocorticoids (e.g., cortisol), which aid the body in longer-term and/or chronic adaptation to stressors (stage of resistance). If the stressor remains and/or increases in intensity, the body's adaptive capabilities are depleted over time. The eventual result is that the body suffers *diseases of adaptation*, such as cardiovascular disease, hypertension (high blood pressure), and gastrointestinal disorders. After all adaptive resources are depleted in the resistance stage, a resurgence of biochemical and physiological activity occurs that mimics the original alarm reaction; if unabated, this situation results in death of the organism (stage of exhaustion).

Selye found that this triad (alarm reaction, stage of resistance, and stage of exhaustion) was consistently present in the body (animal or human) after exposure to a wide range of toxic agents (e.g., hormone extracts, chemical irritants, heat). In experiments with his laboratory animals, Selye repeatedly discovered evidence of the triad in shrinkage of the thymus gland (a glandular organ in the chest, which influences immune reactions in the body), enlargement of the adrenal glands, and ulceration of the gastrointestinal tract. The most significant aspect of the triad was, according to Selye, its total nonspecificity: that is, all stressful stimuli, regardless of type of origin, elicited the same responses.

Selye proposed a general theory of stress that centered around this nonspecificity and the GAS. Selye's (1976) theory of stress has some general implications (Fleming et al., 1984). Specifically, the effects of stress are cumulative over time, and are related to morbidity and pathology if not abated. In other words, the outcomes of stress are aggravated by the passage of time and the number and severity of stressors experienced; the eventual result will inevitably be serious disease and/or death of the organism.

According to Selye, the nonspecificity of the stress response is exactly what makes the effects of stress so potent: Because each stressor an organism encounters essentially has the same physiological impact, every stressful experience chips away at the organism's finite store of adaptive resources. Consider, for a moment, the number of stressors a typical person experiences over several years and the implications of Selye's theory become quite sobering!

Mason (1971, 1975a, 1975b) challenged Selye's strong notion of nonspecificity. He demonstrated that some physical stressors, such as exercise and fasting, do not produce the typical GAS responses, and, in fact, may have positive effects. Mason (1971) also noted instances in which some of the symptoms of the GAS appear and some do not. Specifically, his research indicated that reactions to uncertainty or ambiguity were followed by increases in catecholamines (adrenaline and noradrenaline) and cortisol, whereas anger and fear were typically followed by increases in only nor-adrenaline and cortisol in the body (Mason, 1975a, 1975b).

Other researchers (Ax, 1953; Gray, 1978) have also noted biochemical differences between fear and anger responses. In general, fear seems to be more dependent on adrenaline secretion and anger on noradrenaline secretion. Some observable differences between these two emotional states can also be attributed to these biochemical differences: The red flush of anger and the pallor of fear are influenced by relative differences in biochemistry (adrenaline and noradrenaline). Similarly, exposure to psychological stressors tends to elicit more adrenaline relative to noradrenaline, whereas exposure to environmental stressors tends to elicit more noradrenaline relative to adrenaline (Funkenstein, 1955; Gray, 1978).

Selye (1975) answered these criticisms of the nonspecificity hypothesis by asserting that different stressors vary only in their specific effects; however, they all have a common core of nonspecific effects. For example, exposure to cold environments leads to behaviors such as shivering, while exposure to hot environments leads to sweating (specific responses). However, exposure to either cold and hot environments is associated with cathecholamine excretion by the adrenal cortex (a nonspecific response; also see Cox, 1978). In addition, Selye (1976) claimed that only mild stress, which was not sufficiently severe to activate all of the biochemical and physiological responses, is associated with specificity.

Selye's critics, in discussing the role of strong emotions such as fear and anger, pointed to yet another weakness in the notion of nonspecificity. By dealing only with the body's biochemical and physiological stress responses, Selye ignored the role of psychological factors. If, in fact, differential effects are observed for various emotional states associated with stressful situations, then stress responses must be influenced by psychological states more than the actual presence of the stressor (Cox, 1978, Mason, 1975a, 1975b). In some of his later work, Selye (1975) acknowledged the impact that certain "conditioning" factors, such as age, personality, learning, and diet, could have on the stress response.

Mikhail (1985) even suggested that Selye's theory of stress is, at least in any systematic sense, untestable because few demands (stressors) are stressful to all organisms. This point should sound familiar: Remember the debate raised in Chapter 1 about whether cognition precedes the physiological reaction? Mikhail argued that the stressfulness of most stressors, even environmental stressors, realistically depends, at least to some extent, on the perception of the threat. Consequently, stress can never be reliably manipulated in the laboratory for many situations: that is, manipulated to such an extent so that the researcher can ensure that the GAS occurs.

Today, little doubt exists among stress researchers that an important component of the stress response to any stressor is nonspecific. However, every stress response is also presumed to be associated with a variety of specific components. The major (as yet unanswered) question, according to stress researchers, is the degree of nonspecificity for any given stress response (Mason, 1975c).

Contemporary Biological Models

Within the past 25 years, Cannon and Selye's work have spawned considerable biological research on the stress response. These studies largely attempted to link the experience of stress to either catecholamine or cortisol excretion. As such, this work represents an extension and elaboration of Cannon and Selye's research to a variety of human life circumstances.

During stressful encounters, the excess catecholamines produced by the adrenal medulla and sympathetic nerves are excreted fairly quickly in the urine. These free-floating catecholamines can be estimated quantitatively through standard laboratory procedures on urine or blood plasma samples

(Chapter 3). Using catecholamines as an index of the stress response, many laboratory and field studies have attempted to link stressful encounters with this biochemical measure of the fight or flight response.

Increased levels of cathecholamines in humans have been observed in a large variety of life circumstances, such as space flight, university examinations, dental treatment, routinized industrial work, public speaking, laboratory tasks, and combat (see Froberg, Karlsson, Levi & Lidberg, 1971; Kagan & Levi, 1975; Levi, 1972). In addition, a number of ordinary organizational situations have been linked to catecholamine elevations, such as office workers on a piece-rate pay system (or paid by the quantity produced), supermarket workers during rush hour, and shift workers in a paper mill. In many studies, stronger conclusions could be drawn about cathecholamine excretion under stressful circumstances because comparisons were made between stressful and nonstressful circumstances for the same or similar groups of workers (Cox, 1978).

Perhaps the most well known laboratory studies of cathecholamine excretion have been conducted at the University of Stockholm by Marianne Frankenhaeuser and her colleagues. These studies have rather conclusively demonstrated that psychosocial stressors such as situational control (Frankenhaeuser & Rissler, 1970a), over- and understimulation (Frankenhaeuser, Nordheden, Myrsten, & Post, 1971), and anticipation/uncertainty (Frankenhaeuser & Rissler, 1970b) can produce measureable elevations of catecholamines in the body. For example, in the experiment involving anticipation and uncertainty, subjects in the anticipation and uncertainty condition were wired up so their heart rates could be recorded and were told that if their heart rates changed, they would receive painful shocks. In the relaxation condition, subjects were allowed to relax and read magazines in the laboratory. Not surprisingly, higher levels of adrenaline excretion were recorded in the anticipation and uncertainty condition.

More recently, Frankenhaeuser and her colleagues have focused on gender differences in work stress (e.g., Frankenhaeuser, 1991; Frankenhaeuser, Lundberg, & Chesney, 1991; Frankenhaeuser, et al., 1989; Lundberg & Frankenhaeuser, 1999). For instance, Frankenhaeuser et al. (1989) investigated gender differences in stress and work in a sample of Swedish male and female middle managers. They reported that both groups showed classic stress (biological) reactions at work. However, after work, the female managers returned to a baseline (low stress) level more slowly than the male managers. Lundberg and Frankenhaeuser (1999) also examined work and family issues in a sample of male and female executives. They found that the female executives, especially if they had children, were more stressed and had higher norepinephrine levels than the male executives.

Of particular interest to applied researchers is the research on steroids (cortisol) because of cortisol's association with chronic stressors. Increased cortisol production in the body can be measured both with urine and blood plasma samples and has been documented for a variety of stressors, such as medical exams (Bliss, Migeon, Branch, & Samuels, 1956), hospitalization (Mason, Sachar, Fishman, Hamburg, & Handlon, 1965), combat (Elmadjian, 1955), flying (Hale, Kratochvil & Ellis, 1958), chronic work stressors (Lundberg & Frankenhaeuser, 1999), and work–nonwork conflict (Luecken et al., 1997). From the results of these and many other studies, researchers are confident that a wide variety of psychosocial stimuli elicit the alarm reaction, as assessed by elevated catecholamine levels, and the stage of resistance, as assessed by elevated cortisol levels in the body.

Biological stress models with a more applied orientation can be found in the area of psychosomatic or behavioral medicine. This area of research emphasizes the link between the experience of stress and the subsequent development of pathology or illness (Lachman, 1972), and, as such, are more "macro" applications of Selye's perspective.

Behavioral Science Stress Models

Although biological models were extremely helpful in providing an initial framework for stress research, they ultimately raised more questions than they answered. These models typically focus on stress responses or outcomes and are largely unconcerned with what constitutes a demanding stressor, or what specific situational and personal variables influence the process. Because these unanswered questions seem to be within the domain of behavioral scientists, especially psychologists, much stress research within the past few decades has originated from that discipline. We will examine two general approaches, which target the stress experience across several life domains, and a number of job-related approaches, which focus specifically on the experience of stress in the work environment.

In discussing these models, we do not intend to imply that other general life models (e.g., Elliott & Eisdorfer, 1982; Mechanic, 1978) and job-related models (e.g., Beehr & Newman, 1978; Ivancevich & Matteson, 1980) have not made contributions to stress theory and research. Rather, our goal here is to be synoptic rather than comprehensive in reviewing the literature.

General Life Models

Cognitive-Transactional/Phenomenological Model.   Until the 1960s, the biological (largely Selye's) view of stress predominated. However, the appearance of Richard Lazarus's seminal work, *Psychological Stress and the Coping Process,* in 1966 marked a change in the focus of stress research. Lazarus's major theme in 1966 and in later works (Lazarus, 1976) was that, for stress to occur, cognitive appraisal of the situation must first be experienced; and this appraisal must result in the perception of an imbalance between the demand and the capability of the organism to deal with it. Unlike the biological approaches, Lazarus's view of stress emphasized the stimulus-response definition of stress, which he labeled a relational definition (Chapter 1). That is, Lazarus and his colleagues were more interested in what provoked the perception of stress (the stressor) and how individual characteristics might interact with the cognitive appraisal of the stressor to produce undesirable outcomes.

The cognitive-transactional or, as it is often called, the cognitive-phenomenological model of stress (Lazarus & Launier, 1978), assumes that stress is "neither an environmental stimulus, a characteristic of the person, nor a response but a relationship between demands and the power to deal with them without unreasonable or destructive costs" (Coyne & Holroyd, 1982, p. 108). The implications of this stress model represent a dramatic departure from the earlier biological models: The cognitive-transactional model assumes that a stressor cannot be labeled as such unless it is perceived to be a stressor. The perception of the stressor varies across persons and, within each person, across occasions and time. Changes in psychological states and situational factors may dictate how a potential stressor is evaluated. For example, if a person is very anxious or in an unfamiliar environment, she may interpret a situation, such as meeting new people, to be stressful; however, if relaxed and in a familiar environment, she may interpret such a situation quite differently. The use of the term "potential stressor" instead of the term "stressor" in our model (see Figure 1.1) underscores the importance of subjective evaluation.

Because of the centrality of cognitive appraisal in this model, Lazarus examined the role of the appraisal process in depth. He proposed three types of cognitive appraisals: primary appraisal, secondary appraisal, and reappraisal (Chapter 1). As already described, primary appraisal refers to the initial evaluation; secondary appraisal refers to the process of deciding how to deal with the stressor; and reappraisal refers to the reevaluation of the situation after primary and secondary appraisal occur.

Lazarus proposed three types of primary appraisal: irrelevant, benign-positive, and stressful. If a person views the situation as being irrelevant or benign-positive, no stress appraisal will result. If the situation is perceived to be stressful, two types of stressful primary appraisals can occur: harm-loss and threat. *Harm-loss* appraisals usually involve the potential (real or imagined) loss of something or someone important to the person making the appraisal. This loss can take many forms, such as the loss of a relationship through death or separation, or, in a more tangible sense, the loss of money or personal possessions. *Threat* appraisals usually occur when a person perceives that his or her ability to deal with the demands of the situation is inadequate. The demands may be extremely high, or the person's ability to deal with the demand may be very low, or both. Lazarus also acknowledged the existence of *challenge* appraisals, which are situations perceived to be very demanding but within the capabilities the person. When situations are perceived to be challenging, the outcomes may be quite positive.

The difference between threats and challenges may not always be clear (Coyne & Holroyd, 1982), although the former is probably associated with classical stress reactions whereas the latter with growth and development. Individual differences also undoubtedly play a role in the distinction. For example, a person with high self-esteem may view a promotion as a challenge; a person with low self-esteem may view it as a threat.

According to Lazarus, both person and situation factors can influence the initial appraisal process (Lazarus & Folkman, 1984). The person factors include both commitment and beliefs. If a person is committed to a course of action because the outcome is important to him and has a strong belief in his ability to control events related to the valued outcome, he will probably appraise a stressor as a challenge rather than a threat. Lazarus believes that, in addition to personal control beliefs, existential beliefs—particularly faith in God or a higher power—are critical in forming appraisals. Several situation factors are also hypothesized to have an impact on appraisals, such as available resources, ambiguity of harm, and imminence of harm. Although a more imminent event is typically judged to be more stressful than a distant event, the influence of ambiguity of harm is more difficult to specify. Ambiguity generally intensifies threat if potential harm is perceived. However, ambiguous situations, by their very nature, also allow person variables to shape the meaning of the situation: A person who possesses a strong belief in her mastery (control) over her environment is less apt to appraise an ambiguous situation as threatening.

The other components of the appraisal process, secondary appraisal and reappraisal, are also important in Lazarus's cognitive transactional model of stress. Secondary appraisal is a complex evaluative process that considers what coping options are available, whether such options can successfully ameliorate the stressful situation, and the probability that they can be applied effectively (Lazarus & Folkman, 1984). Reappraisal is a changed appraisal that results from new information from the environment and/or a person's own reactions. As such, reappraisal is merely an appraisal that follows an earlier appraisal, and therefore both are guided by similar processes.

As these definitions imply, the interactions between the different types of appraisals can be quite complex and dynamic. For example, a benign appraisal may be reappraised as a threat appraisal. Consequently, secondary appraisal kicks in, and coping options are assessed. Another reappraisal indicates that the threat is increasing and the selected coping option is ineffective, which results in the selection of a new coping option, and so on.

Lazarus and his colleagues illustrated the relationships between the aforementioned variables in Figure 2.1 (Lazarus, Delongis, Folkman, & Gruen, 1985). Both person and environment variables are hypothesized to influence the appraisal process, leading to both immediate and long-term effects. In terms of Lazarus's model, a person who perceives little control over his environment and little social support will probably appraise a demanding job as highly stressful. Consequently, he may believe that he will be unable to cope with his job requirements through typical means (e.g., working overtime, obtaining assistance from her coworkers and supervisor) and decide to quit. This decision may lead to feelings of depression and migraine headaches, which can affect her psychological and physical health over time. The model also considers the effects of multiple encounters with the stressor and the effects within a single encounter, both of which may exacerbate the outcomes and lead to changes in appraisals. Although not directly indicated in Figure 2.1, Lazarus believed this process to be dynamic and recursive; that is, "The system is dynamic in that appraisal and coping processes continuously change, and it is recursive in that outcomes can influence antecedent variables...." (Lazerus et al., 1985, p. 777).

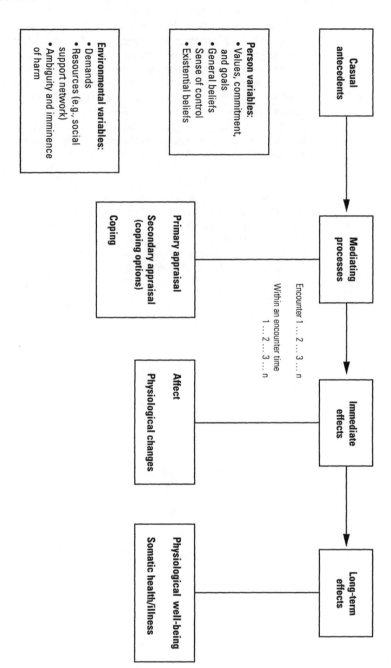

Figure 2.1 Illustrative System Variables for the Stress Rubric

Lazarus's model, with its emphasis on cognitions and psychological processes, has had a tremendous impact on stress research in general and organizational stress research in particular. One of the model's primary attractions is its generality and universality. The major components of the model are broadly applicable across a range of life stressors, which differ in type, context, and severity. For these reasons, the model has been adopted in some form by most contemporary stress researchers.

Although Lazarus's model has clearly influenced current work stress models, it has been criticized for its focus on the individual (Brief & George, 1991). Specifically, Lazarus (1991) argued that his model can be applied to the workplace; however, Brief and George (1991) pointed out that the model fails to consider that a potentially stressful event may be common to a group of individuals or workers. This point implies that researchers should seek to develop models that consider how potential stressors are evaluated by groups of people, and their focus should not be too restrictive so that stress is evaluated only at the individual level.

Finally, whereas the Lazarus formulation was designed to be general in its scope, other theoreticians have typically conceived of stress in a more restricted fashion, such as concentrating on one type of stressor or context. Next, we briefly discuss another behavioral scientist's conceptualization of stress in the post-Selye era, which was influenced, at least to some extent, by the cognitive transactional perspective.

Conflict-Theory Model. Irving Janis's seminal text *Psychological Stress* (1958) was influential in shaping the path of stress research. Janis began his research on stress during World War II by studying the fear reactions of soldiers in combat and civilians in air raids (Janis, 1951), and extended his work by studying the stress reactions of surgical patients in hospitals (Janis, 1958). He later generalized this earlier research on traumatic life events to include many life situations in which people have encountered difficulties in making important decisions (e.g., divorce, natural disasters, and career; Janis & Mann, 1977a).

One of the major conclusions Janis drew from his research was that people can tolerate stress better if they are provided with realistic warnings and preparations about the potential impending stressor, regardless of the nature of that stressor. Janis believed that this preparation stimulated the "work of worrying," or mentally rehearsing the onset of the potential threat and its implications. Janis formalized the results of his research in a conflict-theory model of stress (Janis & Mann, 1977b). This model assumes that stress itself is a frequent cause of faulty decisions in life because people display premature closure, or the termination of the decision process, before a careful deliberation of the situation is conducted. This fact is especially true when stress levels are extremely high.

The major components of the model are antecedent conditions, mediating processes, and consequences. The *antecedent conditions* include information about the impending danger (stressor) from the environment and any factors relevant to the stressor. The *mediating processes* are the psychological states the person experiences while anticipating and coping with the stressor. These processes involve a series of sequential questions (Are the risks serious if I don't change? Are the risks serious if I do change? Is it realistic to hope to find a better solution? Is there sufficient time to search and deliberate?) that the decision maker asks to determine the stressfulness of the situation. Depending on the level of perceived stress, the person will use one or more coping patterns. Four *coping patterns* (unconflicted inertia, unconflicted change, defensive avoidance, and hypervigilance) are associated with increasing levels of stress, whereas one (vigilance) is typically associated with sound decision making. The *consequences* refer to the outcomes of the person's anticipation of and interaction with the stressor.

To illustrate, a person facing an impending hurricane in his hometown gathers information about the potential disaster, such as the nature and severity of the storm (antecedent conditions). Armed with this information, he asks himself the questions posed in the previous paragraph, which increases his stress level about the potential destructiveness of the storm. Consequently, he determines that he has too little time to avoid the storm and decides not to think about it (defensive avoidance) or panics (hypervigilance) (mediating processes). The result of this process may be that our decision maker suffers loss of property and personal injury from engaging in maladaptive coping and resulting behaviors (consequences).

Janis's model of stress was developed from his observations of people in a variety of stressful situations, and while intuitively appealing, it has some deficits as a decision-making model. For example, people are neither rational, predictable, nor sequential decision makers (Stevenson, Busemeyer, & Naylor, 1990); that is, they do not follow a systematic train of thought under stress. Relatedly, Janis and Mann's (1977b) model is really a decision-making (not a stress) model that treats stress as an interference or nuisance factor. Finally, although Janis has broadly supportive empirical research (see Janis & Mann, 1977a) for predictions generated from his model, it has mostly been applied to the extreme traumas of life, such as illness and other life-threatening situations, and not to common work stressors.

Job-Related Model

Like the general life stress models, there are several approaches to describing and explaining job-related stress. These models also differ in the degree they emphasize certain facets of the stress experience at work. In our opinion, two theoretical models have influenced contemporary organizational stress research more than others; we first present those two models, person-environment fit and job demands-job decision latitude. Our discussion then follows with brief descriptions of several other theories and perspectives that have had an impact on how job-related stress has been conceptualized.

Person-Environment Fit Model (or P-E fit). This model has historical roots in the work of such eminent psychologists as Lewin (1951) and Murray (1938). Lazarus's transactional model of stress implicitly used the P-E fit concept in cognitive appraisal, in which an assessment is made regarding the correspondence between environmental demand and the person's resources to cope with it. The concept of P-E fit has also appeared in some form in many contemporary theories of organizational stress (e.g., Karasek, 1979; McGrath, 1976; Schuler, 1980), as well as other areas of organizational behavior, such as job satisfaction (Locke, 1976) and selection (Chatman, 1989; Schneider, 1987).

Very generally, P-E fit treats stress as a lack of fit or correspondence between characteristics of the person (individual needs and abilities) and characteristics of the environment (environmental demands and supplies). This lack of fit is presumed to be associated with all the traditional responses and strains related to the stress process.

The most well known and comprehensive treatment of P-E fit in organizational stress was presented by French and his colleagues (Figure 2.2; French, Caplan, & Harrison, 1982; French, Rodgers, & Cobb, 1974). French's version of P-E fit distinguishes between two types of fit: First, the fit between the needs and values of the person (p) and the environmental supplies and opportunities to meet them (e), is called the *supplies-needs fit.* For example, a worker who has a high need for affiliation would not fit well with a job that offered few opportunities for interpersonal interactions. Second, the fit between the demands of the environment (e) and the abilities of the person to meet those demands (p), is called the *demands-abilities fit.* A worker with poor typing skills would not fit well with a job that required considerable typing and word processing.

Another distinction in fit is between objective and subjective fit. According to French and his colleagues, fit in terms of P and E components can be assessed either subjectively or objectively. *Subjective fit* is measured by assessing the person's perceptions. *Objective fit* is measured independently of the person's perceptions, usually through external sources (e.g., supervisors' or coworkers' reports, personnel files). The association between the objective and subjective person (P) measures is labeled *accuracy of self assessment* and the association between the objective and subjective environment (E) is labeled *contact with reality.* A misfit between the subjective components of P and E is assumed to be more closely related to strains (specifically, illness) than objective misfit. French also defined attempts to resolve misfits between objective components as coping, which implies active behaviors targeted toward changing E or P, and between subjective components as defense, which implies avoidant or palliative attempts to manage the stress generated by the misfit between e and p (Figure 2.1).

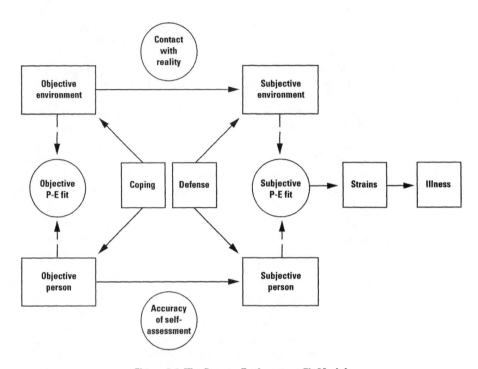

Figure 2.2 The Person-Environment Fit Model

French's version of P-E fit involves measuring both P and E (usually only the subjective variety). The P and E components, unlike other versions of P-E fit (see Bowers, 1973) are phrased with commensurate (parallel) content, such as "How much discretion would you like in your work activities?" (P) and "How much discretion do you have in your work activities?" (E). Responses are typically made on a 5–7 point Likert-type scale.The fit measure is then calculated with a difference or discrepancy score (P–E) (French et al., 1982; McGrath, 1976), although interactive or multiplicative (PxE) (Cherrington & England, 1980) and proportional forms (P/E) (Stokols, 1979) have also been used. Alternately, Edwards (1996) advocated the use of response surface methodology to assess fit. He adopted this approach due to measurement problems with difference scores and the fact that it reduces the three-dimensional relationship between P, E, and strain to two dimensions. Regardless of form, the purpose of all of these complex measures is to assess fit by determining how much the person (P) dimension differs from the environment (E) dimension.

The relationships between the fit measure and some type of strain (e.g., job dissatisfaction, depression, somatic complaints) are then determined. These relationships have varied from monotonic (linear) ones in which strain increases as fit decreases to curvilinear (nonlinear) ones in which strain increases/decreases up to a point and then decreases/increases or levels off (asymptotes). French et al. (1982) reported both types of relationships in their data: The relationship between the fit for overtime and strain indicated that excess overtime (compared with individual preference) was related to somatic complaints, whereas the fit for workload and strain indicated that when workload was either too low or too high (compared with preference) job dissatisfaction was more likely to occur.

Major tests of French's model of P-E fit in organizational settings have been reported by a number of investigators (Blau, 1981; Caplan, Cobb, French, Harrison, & Pinneau, 1980; French et al., 1982; Harrison, 1978; Kaldenberg & Becker, 1992). The most extensive test of P-E fit in organizations was conducted by researchers at the Institute for Social Research at the University of Michigan using data on 23 occupations (Caplan et al., 1975). This and other studies (for example, Caplan, Cobb, French, Van Harrison, & Pinneau, 1980; Harrison, 1985) have reported strong support for some of the theory's predictions (Figure 2.1), illustrating that the fit measure (P-E) has significant relationships with several types of strain (e.g., job dissatisfaction, depression, boredom) beyond the components themselves (P and E individually, or what people report they desire or need and they report they have, respectively).

Although the initial studies showed impressive support for some of the P-E fit predictions, the explanatory power (amount of variance explained) of the fit measure itself has typically not been very large in the Caplan et al. (1975) and subsequent research. Also, some studies have failed to support P-E predictions. For example, Blau (1981) did not find expected relationships between stress and job performance, although the relationships between stress and job dissatisfaction were in accord with predictions. In answer to some problems with the original model, Caplan (1983) proposed an extension of the traditional model in which he considered past and anticipated (future) fit as well as present fit. This dynamic model should enhance the prediction of strain beyond the traditional model.

Despite its intuitive appeal and extensive theoretical base, P-E fit has been widely criticized by stress researchers in recent years (Edwards & Cooper, 1990; Eulberg, Weekley & Bhagat, 1988; Ganster & Schaubroeck, 1991). Ganster and Schaubroeck (1991) maintained that the value of the theory has been limited because of its focus on the processes whereby strain occurs rather than specific work characteristics (stressors) that produce strain. Therefore, researchers have used only a small number of P and E dimensions to assess fit. They also criticized P-E fit researchers for an almost total reliance on self-report measures to the exclusion of the more objective measures implied by objective P-E fit (see Chapter 3 for a discussion of problems with self-report measures).

Edwards and Cooper (1990) provided an even more detailed examination of problems with the P-E fit model. First, they noted that empirical work on P-E fit has not differentiated between the supplies-needs and the demands-abilities fit measures, which questions the validity of these two dimensions. More recently, however, Edwards (1996) found support for the two different types of fit measures: Although the supplies-needs (values) fit was mostly associated with job dissatisfaction and the demands-abilities fit with tension, both types of fit were related to both strains in a large graduate (MBA) student sample. Second, Edwards and Cooper criticized P-E fit researchers for erroneously equating theoretically and methodologically different forms of fit (that is, the discrepancy, interactive, and proportional forms discussed earlier). For example, the discrepancy form implies E is judged against a standard (P) and that larger deviations between P and E are associated with greater strain, whereas the interactive form only implies that P influences the relationship (acts as a moderator; Chapter 7) between E and strain. (See Edwards & Cooper, 1990, for a complete discussion of the different forms of fit.) Third, they acknowledged other statistical and methodological difficulties, such as the use of difference scores, which have been criticized for their often assumed lack of reliability and validity.

Although Ganster and Schaubroeck's (1991) and Edwards and Cooper's (1990) reviews were quite critical, the jury is still out on P-E fit theory. French's original formulation of P-E fit in organizations, as detailed in the previous discussion, has not been completely operationalized or adequately tested. Edwards's (1996) investigation of the validity of the supplies-needs and demands-abilities dimensions of the model is an encouraging step in the right direction. Some of the most stringent criticisms, however, have historically been methodological, not theoretical, and have focused on the use of difference or discrepancy measures. Difference scores (P-E) have been roundly criticized for not being reliable or useful measures, at least compared to their individual component measures (P and E) (Edwards & Cooper, 1990; Johns, 1981). In answer to these criticisms, some research (C. S. Smith & Tisak, 1993; Tisak & Smith, 1994) has shown that theoretically and methodologically well developed difference scores can be both reliable and useful measures.

Job Demands–Job Decision Latitude Model. Another organizational stress model that has been highly influential is the job demands–job decision latitude model developed by Robert Karasek (1979) (Figure 2.3). This model has generated an impressive body of empirical research (cf. Kinicki, McKee, & Wade, 1996) and has been called the the most important model of organizational stress in the latter part of the twentieth century. The model hypothesizes that psychological strain develops from the joint effects of job demands and the decision latitude available to the worker.

Job demands are defined as psychological (not physical) stressors present in the work environment, primarily heavy workload (overload). *Decision latitude* is defined as a measure of discretion in decision making or job control; this variable has been operationalized in various ways, such as the worker's authority to make job-related decisions and the variety of skills workers use on the job.

Karasek's model draws its framework from a large body of research in experimental psychology (Averill, 1973; Rodin & Langer, 1977; Seligman, 1975), which has reliably demonstrated the importance of personal control for both animals and humans. Further, the evidence is rather compelling that perceptions of personal control are related to positive health-related outcomes and lack of personal control to health-related decrements across many types of subjects and settings (e.g., Bosma, Stansfeld, & Marmot, 1998; Folkman, 1984; S. M. Miller, 1979; Shirom, Melamed, & Nir-Dotan, 2000).

According to the demands-control model, job strain occurs when job demands are high and job decision latitude (control) is low; conversely, growth and development occur when job demands are high and job decision latitude is high. Karasek (1979) explored other combinations of job demands and decision latitude (Figure 2.3); for example, a job that is high in decision latitude but has few stressors (demands) would be relatively unstressful and therefore a "low strain job."

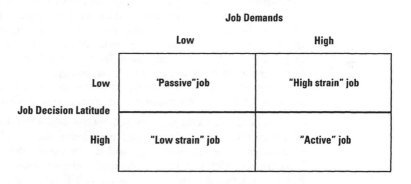

Figure 2.3 The Demands-Control Model

The general premise behind Karasek's model is that high demands produce a state of stressful arousal that, if paired with conditions of low control, cannot be adequately dissipated or managed. Karasek tested these propositions on data from large national surveys of workers in the United States and Sweden. (The Swedish data were longitudinal—that is, collected at two points in time on the same subjects.) He claimed support for the model in both countries. Specifically, he found that jobs high in demands and low in control were associated with strain—specifically exhaustion—and dissatisfaction (life and job) in the American data and depression in the Swedish data. Karasek (1979) stated that "... most working individuals in countries with advanced economies, such as the United States and Sweden, find that the requirement of using intellectual skill or making decisions represents an opportunity to exercise judgment. This enhances the individual's feelings of efficacy and ability to cope with the environment; it is not a source of stress" (p. 303). Karasek concluded by noting that the most important implication of his results was that it may be possible to reduce strain without compromising productivity by simply increasing the amount of control available to workers in their jobs.

Empirical support for the demands-control model falls into two categories. The most supportive research has included epidemiological (disease-related) studies, both longitudinal and cross-sectional, which relied on large-scale or national samples aggregated by occupational level (e.g., Alfredsson, Karasek, & Theorell, 1982; Karasek, 1979; 1990). The epidemiological studies have typically focused on the development of coronary heart disease and related risk factors (e.g., smoking and hypertension) in different types of workers. Other research has been conducted at the individual level and has used primarily self-report measures of demands, control, and strains collected from workers in a single or few organizations (e.g., Spector, 1987; Tetrick & LaRocco, 1987). Relative to the large scale studies, the individual level studies have used mostly small homogeneous (similar in personal and/or situational characteristics) samples and have generally found less support for the model's propositions, although there are a few notable exceptions (e.g., Fox, Dwyer, & Ganster, 1993).

Despite the fact that the demands-control model has dominated the field of occupational epidemiology and provided a theoretical basis for much organizational stress research within the past decade (Ganster & Schaubroeck, 1991), it has not escaped widespread criticism. Ganster and Schaubroeck outlined two general flaws with Karasek's approach (see also C. S. Smith, Tisak, Hahn, & Schmeider, 1997). First, job decision latitude has not been operationalized in a consistent manner; for example, control measures have included repetitous or monotonous work (Karasek, 1979), skill utilization (Sauter, 1989), and dealing with customers and the public (Haynes, LaCroix, & Lippin, 1987). In his initial study, Karasek (1979) used very different operationalizations of decision latitude in the American and Swedish samples. In the American sample, the decision latitude variable included the job characteristics components of autonomy, skill complexity, creativity, and the ability to learn new things; in the Swedish sample, decision latitude was measured with a composite of the education level required to perform the job and the repetitiveness of work activities. Such a broad conceptualization of the control construct across research that has tested the demands-control model makes one question exactly what is being measured. Carayon & Zijlstra (1999) also distinguished between three different types of control: task control, decision control, and resource control. This further underscores the complexity inherent in the control construct.

Second, little evidence exists of an interactive effect between demands and decision latitude, as predicted by the model; that is, strain is hypothesized to develop primarily from situations of both high demands and low control (de Rijk, Le Blanc, Schaufeli, & de Jonge, 1998). Rather, evidence is stronger for an additive or main effect of demands and control: Specifically, both high demands and low control individually predict strain (Fletcher & Jones, 1993; Ganster & Fusilier, 1989; Kasl, 1989). Even when significant interactions have been documented, Ganster (1989) claimed that inappropriate statistical analyses were performed on the data. Karasek (1989) replied that the standard statistical tests are too restrictive. At this point, however, the controversy has not been resolved.

Critics have also charged that the large scale studies confounded sociodemographic differences in jobs with control (Ganster, 1989; Payne & Fletcher, 1983). That is, job/occupational level is related to the amount of control, with higher status jobs conferring more control. This confound makes unambiguous interpretation of much of the epidemiological research difficult.

Yet another criticism is that the model is conceptually very narrow in that it considers only two constructs, worker control and decision latitude. Extensions of the model to include different approaches in assessing the effects of demands and control represent perhaps a promising area of contemporary research. For example, Landsbergis, Schnall, Schwartz, Warren, and Pickering (1995) reported that participants in an ongoing prospective (longitudinal; Chapter 3) study who scored in the lowest third of decision latitude and the highest third of job demands showed higher systolic blood pressure readings than the other groups of participants; blood pressure readings also decreased over a three-year interval for those individuals in the study who moved from high strain (high demands, low control) to low strain (low demands, high control) jobs. Relatedly, a study investigating the effects of job characteristics (demands and control) on immune system functioning (Meijman, van Dormolen, Herber, Rongen, & Kuiper, 1995) found that suppression of immune variables (Chapter 1) was associated with reports of higher demands and lower control in 37 white male shift workers. The authors cautioned, however, against overinterpreting these results with such a small sample size. Radmacher and Sheridan (1995) also attempted to validate Karasek's model through independent assessments of jobs using the EEOC's "Description of Occupational Classifications"; they reported agreement between these assessments and the job characteristic patterns (demands-control) predicted by the model in data from several hundred participants collected at two points in time (1991 and 1992).

The most fruitful research on extensions of the demands-control model has considered the impact of other theoretically relevant variables, such as locus of control (Schmieder, 1994) and social support (J. V. Johnson, 1989; Parkes, Mendham, & von Rabenau, 1994). This latter variable was considered sufficiently important that it was included in Karasek and Theorell's (1990) elaboration of the original model. Parkes et al. (1994) examined the role of social support in the context of the demands-control model in two studies. In both studies, they found that reports of high levels of somatic symptoms were associated with high demands–low control only when support was low. Social support was an important moderator variable in both studies, while the pattern of demands and control predicted by Karasek's model was not found. The authors interpreted their results as suggesting that failure to consider a critical third variable or moderator (social support) may account for inconsistent findings in prior research.

Much recent research has explored the boundary conditions under which the model's predictions do and do not hold up, resulting in more support for the model, especially in specific situations (see van der Doef & Maes, 1999, for a review). For example, de Jonge, Dollard, Dormann, Le Blanc, and Houtman (2000), using improved measures of demands and control, found that jobs characterized by high demands and low control are associated with ill health but only in some occupational groups. Schaubroeck, Jones, and Xie (2001) discovered that job demands are positively related to ill health and decreased immune functioning among efficacious (i.e., high self-efficacy) workers who perceived low control, which supports the predictions of the model. However, for inefficacious workers who perceived that they had high control, job demands are also related to ill health and decreased immune functioning. The researchers reasoned that workers who are low in self-efficacy might find control debilitating because they cannot use it effectively to cope with demands. Therefore, following the prescriptions of the demands-control model may actually exacerbate stress and strain for some workers!

Despite the criticisms of the demands-control model, it continues to guide much contemporary research and practice (e.g., stress managment programs that increase worker control and social support; Landsbergis & Vivona-Vaughn, 1995). The model's focus primarily on the work environment, not the worker, as the locus of stress and strain encourages the creation of healthier workplaces. However, research such as Schaubroeck et al.'s (2001) study imply that a "one size fits all" approach to work stress is often overly simplistic and inappropriate.

Process Model of Task Performance. Another theoretical model that has influenced organizational stress research is the process model of task performance (McGrath, 1976; Figure 2.4). Overall, this model is generally not as well known as the previous models we have considered. McGrath developed the process model to explain the stress related to task performance, particularly work-related task performance.

The model is based on the premise that task performance is a function of perceived stress and actual task ability and difficulty. Perceived stress depends on the perceived consequences (importance) of task performance and the perceived uncertainty of being able to perform. Actual task difficulty depends on the objective or "real" situation (stressor), which affects perceptions of perceived task difficulty (perceived situation or stressor). In turn, this appraisal process results in a perception of the stressfulness of the task. The person then engages in a decision process to determine the needed coping responses to deal with the task stressor. These responses result in the performance process, in which selected behaviors are evaluated on quality, quantity, and speed. The last link is the outcome process, which indicates whether the selected behaviors produce the desired outcome. The outcome process feeds back into the original situation (task stressor), and the cycle may repeat itself (see Figure 2.4).

The following illustration of the process model may be helpful. A worker is asked by his supervisor to handle a project for an important client (the situation). The worker perceives successful completion of the project within the required time frame to be difficult, although probably attainable; he also knows that failure may adversely affect his future in the organization (perceived situation). The worker then decides on the appropriate course of action to achieve project completion (response selection), such as recruiting coworkers and working overtime. These activities (behaviors) result in the successful completion of the project by the deadline, which may influence the worker's role in future projects.

McGrath's model differs substantially from those discussed previously in that it deals only with the stress related to task performance. The process model is also different in another way: It distinguishes performance from outcome. Often performance does not match the outcome, and the outcome affects future situations. If, in the preceding example, the worker successfully completed the project but was demoted to a lesser position in the organization or terminated, his performance would not match the outcome. This situation is unfortunately all too familiar to workers who have been victims of recent organizational mergers and downsizing.

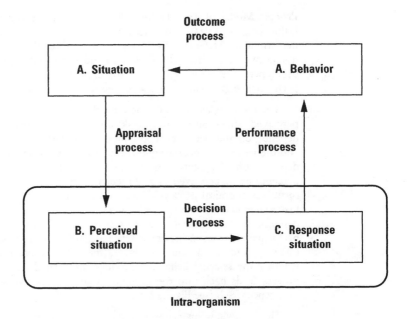

Figure 2.4 McGrath's (1976) Process Model of Task Performance: Analysis of the Stress Cycle

McGrath's process model has not stimulated as much research or as much controversy as the person-environment fit or demands-control models of work stress. It has, however, received accolades in a critique of some common stress models (Eulberg, Weekley, & Bhagat, 1988). Eulberg et al. (1988) criticized many models for their extremely broad focus and lack of specificity. Such models, they maintained, are difficult to test empirically because of their generality; consequently, these frameworks give little guidance concerning how constructs should be operationalized and what predictions should be offered. They praised the process model for its focus on task performance and the specific predictions that could be generated from its constructs. However, there is a negative aspect to the process model's parsimony: Although cognitive appraisal occupies a central role, the influence of other personal and situational factors (e.g., personality, culture) is not acknowledged. This deficit undoubtedly stems from the general experimental paradigm upon which the model was based and its reliance on a very limited set of constructs (arousal, task difficulty, and task ability). Also, other than some research by McGrath and his colleagues (McGrath, 1976), the validity of the model has not been demonstrated empirically.

Integrative Transactional Process Model.   The integrative transactional process model incorporates environmental stressors, perceptions, the stress response, and stress outcomes, plus a host of moderator variables (Figure 2.5). Beehr and Schuler's (1982) model is in accord with Lazarus's conceptualization of stress by focusing on the role of cognitive appraisal (individual perception). Time (duration of stress) is incorporated through the separation of the immediate perception of stress and longer term responses or outcomes, plus an explication of Selye's GAS in the response segment of the model. The authors indicated that the name of the model (integrative transactional model) implies that its relationships are reciprocal, happen across time and/or stressors, and integrate diverse areas of theory and research. Indeed, the relationships implied in Figure 2.5 could accommodate virtually every perspective we have discussed in this chapter.

This model has contributed to organizational stress theory through its acknowledgment of the importance of time in the stress process. We echo the sentiments of other stress researchers (Eulberg et al., 1988; McGrath & Beehr, 1990) in criticizing many stress models for their cursory or nonexistent treatment of the role of temporal factors. Most perspectives either ignore or only implicitly acknowledge the dynamic nature of the stress process.

Another strength is that individual and contextual differences, such as organizational changes, job qualities, personal experience, and individual needs/values, are given a central role in the model. Many other models, such as the demands-control and the process models, do not formally acknowledge the role of individual or contextual differences in the stress process, a deficit that has been criticized (Bacharach & Bamberger, 1992).

Eulberg et al. (1988) criticized a model similar to the integrative transactional process model for being too general, vague, and nonfalsifiable. As they noted, "the number of direct and indirect hypotheses which can be generated by this model are numerous, and there is a strong possibility of creating inner contradictions among hypotheses" (pp. 340–341). The same criticism could easily be levied against the integrative transactional model. Unfortunately, in an attempt to be comprehensive, Schuler's model fails to provide enough specificity to allow researchers to generate concrete, testable hypotheses. So, this model is generally not testable (or falsifiable), although it does provide a useful heuristic framework (much like our general stress model in Chapter 1) to help organize information about work stress. Thus, the model provides a blueprint for organizing current research findings and directing future research; and, as noted at the beginning of this chapter, this is the reason researchers develop models in the first place. As models are continually tested and refined, theories of work stress may ultimately emerge that can stand the test of empirical scrutiny and falsifiability.

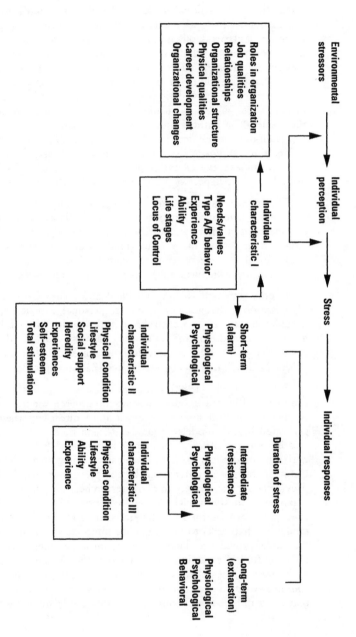

Figure 2.5 Integrative Transactional Process Model of Stress in Organizations

Conservation of Resources Theory. Hobfoll (1988) proposed a new stress theory, the conservation of resources (COR) theory. The main thesis of this theory is simple and elegant: "... People have an innate as well as learned desire to conserve the quality and quantity of their resources and to limit any state that may jeopardize the security of these resources" (p. 25). According to Hobfoll (1988, 1989), if one is threatened by a possible loss in resources, fails to obtain expected resources, or experiences an actual loss in resources, she will experience stress.

In COR, resources are conceived of as falling into one of four categories: objects, personal characteristics, conditions, and energies. *Objects* are material possessions, such as food, housing, and clothing. *Personal characteristics* describe a person. For example, traits such as self esteem, attitudes, and career-orientation are personal characteristics. *Conditions* refer to states of being that one considers desirable and worth seeking, such as social support or interpersonal relationships. *Energies* are the means or way in which resources are obtained (e.g., knowledge, skills).

This theory incorporates stress as a process (Chapter 1). Specifically, the stress process begins if a person actually loses resources, is threatened by resource loss, or fails to obtain expected resources. The evaluation of resource availability can take a cognitive, unconscious, or biophysiological form. For instance, the cognitive evaluation of resources is very similar to the notion of cognitive appraisal (Lazarus & Folkman, 1984).

Hobfoll initially conceptualized his theory as a general theory of life stress, of which work is only one domain. Within the past decade, for example, COR has been used to explain how people cope with a natural disaster (e.g., Benight, Swift, Sanger, Smith, & Zeppelin, 1999), pregnancy (Wells, Hobfoll, & Levin, 1997), work-related burnout (e.g., Hobfoll & Shirom, 2001), and work-family conflict (e.g., Grandey & Cropanzano, 1999).

Hobfoll's theory, however, has been particularly useful in explaining certain types of work stress. Lee and Ashforth (1996) used COR as a guiding framework to examine how demand and resource components were related to three job burnout dimensions (emotional exhaustion, depersonalization, and lack of personal accomplishment; Chapter 6) in their meta-analysis. They found that the burnout dimension of emotional exhaustion (the feeling of being drained or used up, unable to face a day's work, totally unenthusiastic) was most strongly related to the resource and (especially) demand components, suggesting that workers with burnout are most sensitive to resource loss. Grandey and Cropanzano (1999) also developed a conceptual framework based on Hobfall's theory; using COR, they maintained that work-family conflict exists because one loses resources while attempting to perform both work and non-work roles. Using a sample of 326 university professors, they assessed the impact of work and family stressors on personal and work-related strain within a longitudinal design and generally found support for their model.

Based on its considerable theoretical development and broad applicability to multiple life situations, COR shows great promise as a theory of life and work stress (Hobfoll, 2001; Quick & Gavin, 2001; Schwarzer, 2001; Thompson & Cooper, 2001), although some theorists disagree with Hobfoll's emphasis on a resource-based, as opposed to an appraisal-based, conceptualization of the stress process (e.g., Lazarus, 2001; Schwarzer, 2001; Thompson & Cooper, 2001). The implication that people make assessments based on what they had in the past, currently have, or expect to have in the future shares some conceptual similarities with the theory we discuss next.

Cybernetic Theory of Stress. Edwards (1992) proposed yet another model of organizational stress, a cybernetic theory of stress, coping, and well-being in organizations. This interesting approach is built on cybernetics, or control theory, one that concerns the functioning of self-regulating systems (Ashby, 1966). The core of this model is the negative feedback loop, which serves to minimize differences between environmental characteristics and referent criteria. Although control theory has been extensively incorporated in theories of mental and physical health (e.g., Hyland, 1987) and organizational behavior (e.g., Campion & Lord, 1982; Taylor, Fisher, & Ilgen, 1984), Edwards maintained that its influence has previously been implicit only in organizational stress theory. For example, both the person-environment fit theory and the process theory of task performance assume that workers evaluate environmental conditions relative to their own internal referents (abilities, needs, or desires); the degree of this discrepancy determines stress levels, coping efforts, and the eventual development of strain.

In his model, Edwards defined stress as a discrepancy between the worker's perceived state and desired state, only if that discrepancy is judged by the worker to be important. Stress then affects well-being and activates coping attempts. This model also views the experience of stress as a process in a dynamic system of multiple discrepancies experienced over time.

Although other research on stress and coping (e.g., Frone & McFarlin, 1989; Kivimaeki & Lindstroem, 1995; Latack, Kinicki, & Prussia, 1995) has incorporated the notion of control theory, many of the specific predictions proposed by Edwards (1992) remain to be tested. He has, however, developed a Cybernetic Coping Scale (Edwards & Baglioni, 1993) and validated it using a sample of MBA students. Because all biological systems (including the human system) require feedback loops to function appropriately, the cybernetic theory has logical appeal. On the other hand, primarily cognitive or "rational" theories of human behavior often have not been very successful in explaining human behavior (Nisbett & Ross, 1980). The significant emotional component of the stress experience may far outweigh the cognitive component, a limitation of the cybernetic approach that Edwards (1992) acknowledged.

Stressor and Response-Specific Models. A wide variety of work stress models have been proposed that specifically focus on particular stressors, groups of stressors, or select responses (see Sparks & Cooper, 1999, for evidence supporting situation-specific models). As one example, a model was developed that considers the effects of shift work on various strains (Colquhoun & Rutenfranz, 1980). We will examine this model in Chapter 4 when the topic of shift work is discussed. We also consider additional models throughout the text where relevant. What follows are just a few examples of these types of models.

Given the current interest in downsizing and layoffs, a really salient stressor for many individuals in today's economy is layoffs (see also Chapter 5). Two models have been proposed that outline the process through which layoffs adversely affect individuals (Harris, Heller, & Braddock, 1988; Leana & Feldman, 1988). For example, Leana and Feldman (1988) proposed that, in the face of a job loss, people attempt to determine the cause of the layoff and undergo cognitive appraisal, which includes an assessment of severity and likelihood of reversibility. Thus, if a worker is laid off but disliked his job anyway, severity may be judged as low. If the probability of being rehired is high, he will perceive a high likelihood of reversibility. Of course, assuming he is independently wealthy or has other job options, he may not even care about reversibility!

The influence of Lazarus here is clear and direct, which underscores the utility of the more general stress models (e.g., Lazarus, 1976) for providing a theoretical base from which more specific models may be explicated. The influence of the biological perspective is also evident inasmuch as physiological reactions and psychophysiological disorders are acknowledged. The model also incorporates moderator variables (e.g., locus of control, self-esteem), which influence the type of coping strategies chosen. Leana and Feldman's model culminates with the possibility of reemployment, underemployment, or continued unemployment following the coping efforts. If underemployment or continued unemployment persists, health is predicted to suffer along with deteriorations in family and social relations.

Other models consider a restrictive but defined set of work stressors. For instance, Cooper and Cartwright (1994) proposed a model listing seven potential stressors, including relationships at work and problems with the work itself. First, they considered factors intrinsic to the job itself, such as poor working conditions, long hours, fear of injury, poor illumination, and excessive noise (also see Chapter 4). Second, the model incorporates role stressors, such as conflicting demands at work and lack of clarity in how to complete job tasks (Chapter 5). Third, the model includes relationship-oriented stressors, such as mistrust of coworkers. Fourth, job insecurity, a common stressor for workers affected by corporate downsizing, mergers, and layoffs, is included as another stressor category. Fifth, organizational-level variables—for example, poor organizational communication and culture—

are incorporated as potential stressors. Finally, they included the dimension of the work–nonwork interface. Attempting to manage this interface may lead to several stressors, such as lack of time for family activities or interference of family problems in work activities (Chapter 5).

These models propose stressors or stressor categories that cut across a variety of potential jobs or occupations. However, some models have been developed that specifically focus attention on stressors unique to particular occupations. Consistent with this approach, Hart, Wearing, and Heady (1995) developed and tested a model unique to police officer stress (Chapter 4). They surveyed 507 police officers across two related studies. Their results suggest that, surprisingly, police officers did not find the work of policing inherently stressful. Most people who are not in the law enforcement profession would probably assume that dealing with criminal activities and interpersonal disputes is stressful! On the other hand, the researchers found that dealing with the organizational (police department) bureaucracy was a consistent source of perceived stress. One possibility, of course, is that the law enforcement profession attracts and retains certain types of people who actually thrive in situations that many would find stressful, such as arresting a drunk driver. This point underscores the importance of individual differences in the stress process and raises a point that is worth repeating: Many stimuli become stressors only if they are perceived as such.

Finally, some models have been developed that consider particular responses or consequences of stress. An example is a model proposed by Murphy, DuBois and Hurrell (1986). The primary focus of this model is on unsafe behavior and accidents. As illustrated in Figure 2.6, their model traces the process by which work and nonwork stressors lead to potential accidents through the intervening stages of acute reactions, decreased capacities, and unsafe behaviors.

Murphy et al. noted that their model is incomplete in that it does not capture some of the possible antecedent conditions that lead to accidents and injury. For instance, several factors may contribute to job-related accidents, including poor lighting, inadequate job training, and selecting workers who do not have the requisite skills to perform their job properly and safely. Nevertheless, the intent of the model is to highlight the notion that stress may be an important antecedent of industrial injuries. Perhaps even more importantly, their model emphasizes the idea that stress management interventions can be vital in reducing injury rates in certain situations.

In summary, organizational stress models have proliferated over the past decade or so. Many of these models draw from the biological perspective, the life stress literature (most notably the work of Lazarus), or both. As concerns about work stress continue to grow, expect to see the development of further formulations and, perhaps, the development of "meta-models" that attempt to consolidate the various approaches.

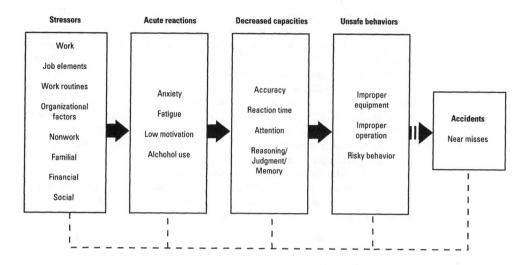

Figure 2.6 Model of Stress and Accidents

Conclusions

Eulberg et al. (1988) voiced four general negative trends or criticisms of current models in organizational stress research. First, they maintained that most models are too broad in scope and content, attempting to account for too many themes. Second, they criticized most models for focusing on the objective environment when the subjective environment (individual perceptions) is so crucial to the experience of stress. Third, they discussed the cursory treatment that stress theory has traditionally given temporal factors—which is surprising given that the chronic nature of stress is widely acknowledged. Fourth, they called for more process and fewer "variance" theories, or more theories that attempt to explain the stress process and not examine simple relationships among stressors and strains. Using Eulberg et al.'s (1988) four negative trends, we can evaluate the status of some of the models we discussed in this chapter.

In terms of the first criticism, some models, such as Lazarus's cognitive-transactional model and Schuler's integrative transactional process model, are clearly unfocused and overly comprehensive. Others, such as McGrath's process model and the stressor and response-specific models, cover more limited domains. A number of the models reviewed here followed the second trend by not acknowledging the central role of subjective factors and individual perception in the stress process. In Selye's general theory,

Karasek's demands-control theory, and Hobfoll's COR, the subjective environment (appraisal) does not occupy a central role. Individual perceptions, however, are very important concepts in Lazarus's cognitive transactional model, Edwards's cybernetic theory, and Schuler's integrative transactional process model. The third criticism, the disregard of temporal factors, is applicable, at least in an explicit sense, to all theoretical models except Schuler's process model and Edwards's cybernetic theory. However, some models, like Selye's (GAS), Hobfall's COR, and Leana and Feldman's (1988) model of job loss, make an implicit assumption about the passage of time. Some of the models discussed here, specifically Selye's general model, French's person-environment fit, Hobfoll's COR, Edwards's cybernetic theory, and McGrath's process model, disagree with the fourth trend by taking a process approach. Other models, for example, Janis's conflict-theory model, are more descriptive. Such approaches are less apt to generate testable hypotheses and future model-building.

Overall, the models presented in this chapter illustrate some of the divergence in the way stress is conceptualized in the research literature. However, the various theoretical approaches do share conceptual linkages and similarities. For example, according to Lazarus, individual perception is critical in determining reactions to environmental events. These perceptions are also central to both the "P" and "E" components of the P-E formulation in that people are thought to compare perceptions of the environment with perceptions about what they desire from the environment. Personal perceptions are also at the heart of Edward's and McGrath's models in that they predict that people compare their perceptions of what they want (i.e., needs, desires) with the state of the environment. More specific models such as Leana and Feldman's model of job loss also assume that cognitive appraisal is central to the overall stress process.

In addition, the models are all similar in that they focus on the individual as the unit of analysis. Future theoretical developments may benefit from considering other levels of analysis (i.e., group, organization) when conceptualizing work stress (cf. Bliese, & Jex, 1999). Thus, for example, what is the process leading to the experience of stress in a work group?

In summary, although the models are obviously distinct in various respects, a process-orientation and cognitive appraisal as central features of the stress process appear to permeate most perspectives. These common themes suggest that stress researchers view the experience of stress largely as the end product of a cognitive process. Whether and the extent to which this process occurs within the province of conscious awareness is not broached (cf. Hobfoll, 1988, 1989). Is cognitive appraisal a conscious deliberate activity, or does it occur automatically outside of conscious awareness? This interesting but fundamental question, among others, should inspire future theoretical developments as scholars attempt to better understand the experience of work stress.

Stress Methods and Measures

In Chapter 2, we discussed some models of stress; some of them were global stress models while others focused directly on the workplace. Each of these models has served to provide a springboard for future research, which is a major goal of any model. By studying models such as the ones we examined in Chapter 2, researchers can develop testable hypotheses to investigate in future research; indeed, this point was one of the major criteria on which we evaluated each model. The results of such empirical or data-based research provide the fuel for future model or theory building, and so the cycle of scientific inquiry continues.

The primary purpose of this chapter is to investigate how empirical or data-based stress research is conducted. First, we examine the methods of stress research, or how stress research is designed. An examination of the measures of stress, or the variables that are assessed in the study of stress, follows next. Much of this section is devoted to the physiological and biochemical measures of stress because considerable interest and controversy currently surround the use of these measures. Then, some examples of stress research are provided. Finally, some current "hot" methodological topics in stress research, such as the influence of common method variance, are discussed.

STRESS RESEARCH METHODS

All empirical research can be classified as either experimental or nonexperimental. *Experimental* studies have an independent variable (what is being manipulated or changed) and a dependent variable (what the independent variable is changing, or what is being measured). Many experimental studies have a comparison or control group, as well as experimental groups. The control group does not receive the manipulation but is assessed on the dependent variable. A true experiment also has random assignment of subjects (persons) to experimental and control conditions, which simply means that every person in the study has an equal chance of being in any condition.

Nonexperimental studies may or may not meet some of the criteria that are necessary for experimental research (e.g., identifiable independent and dependent variables or random assignment to conditions). However, nonexperimental research always lacks some form of rigorous control that is associated with experimental research. This implies that is more difficult (if not impossible) to make any causal inferences about the effects of the independent variable(s) on the dependent variable(s). For example, assume two groups of workers are studied whereby only one group receives training on how to reduce stress and the stress levels of the two groups are then compared. If the stress levels are lower in the group receiving training, it might be tempting to conclude that the training was the cause of the lowered stress in the treatment group. However, if workers were not randomly assigned to conditions (as they would be in a true experiment) and the groups were simply chosen from two different areas of the plant, it is possible that the group receiving the training already had lower stress levels before training! Thus, it would be incorrect to conclude that training had any causal impact on stress levels.

Empirical research can also be classified as either laboratory or field research. Most experimental studies are conducted in the *laboratory* because laboratory settings allow a much greater degree of control over the independent and dependent variables. Also, conducting experiments (or any type of study) in *field* settings presents a host of logistical and practical problems, including time and monetary costs. For example, it can be quite expensive from both a time and monetary standpoint to ask employees to leave their work stations to participate in a research study. Even if the study requires only that employees participate for a brief time, they may not want to lose their scheduled breaks or remain after their shift. Ultimately, shutting down a production line or other disruptions may become necessary, which might discourage the organization from participating in the research project at all. Nonetheless, there are some examples, albeit few, of field experiments on organizational stress. An example of such an experiment is provided later in this chapter.

The greater control of the laboratory environment is frequently offset by its artificiality. People in an experiment know they are being studied, and so they may behave in unusual or unnatural ways. Also, many of the tasks subjects perform in laboratory experiments are not similar to their normal, routine activities. Their behavior in the experiment, therefore, may not in any sense reflect their typical or everyday behavior. For these reasons, researchers are often concerned about the generalizability (external validity) of the results of laboratory studies to behavior in the real world.

Most nonexperimental research is conducted in the field, not the laboratory. For the stress researcher, this means going out into actual work settings to collect data. This type of design is often termed an *"ex post facto"* or *correlational research design.* The latter name is not really precise, however, because a correlation is actually a statistic that may be computed for a variety of research designs, including experimental designs. The confusion probably stems from the fact that correlational statistical analyses are most often performed as part of ex post facto research.

One feature of the ex post facto design is the lack of experimental controls. In such a design, the researcher is often unable to control for nuisance (confounding) variables that may affect the dependent variable. For example, in a study examining the effects of stress management on job satisfaction, it would be important to ensure that the group receiving the intervention is not qualitatively different from the control group at the start of the experiment. If the control group members are, on average, "more stressed" than their experimental counterparts from the beginning, any group difference in job satisfaction after the intervention may be attributed to the initial differences rather than to the manipulation (the intervention). For this example, initial group differences in stress levels is a confounding variable because it provides an alternative explanation for differences in the outcome (dependent variable) across the two groups.

By controlling for these confounding variables (through equal treatment of groups other than the manipulation, random assignment, etc.), any differences in the dependent variable between groups or conditions can be causally attributed to the independent variable, which is the primary goal of any experimental research. An important caveat here is that because we can never be certain all confounds have been controlled, causal inferences should always be made with some degree of caution. Alternately, the ex post facto design affords no design features that control for confounds. In fact, here we use the terms *predictor* and *criterion* in place of the experimental terms, independent and dependent variable, respectively, to underscore the idea that one variable (criterion) may not be "dependent" on another variable (predictor).

To compensate for the lack of controls inherent in the ex post facto research design, researchers sometimes invoke special statistical techniques (e.g., analysis of covariance, hierarchical regression) that purport to statistically control for confounding variables. However, these analytical techniques offer no guarantees that all confounding variables have been identified and thus statistically controlled. In sum, the ex post facto design can establish predictive relationships (e.g., increasing stress predicts lowered job satisfaction) without allowing us to infer that the predictor (stress) causally affected the criterion (job satisfaction).

To establish whether and the extent to which the predictor variable is related to the criterion variable, statistical analyses are used. The *correlation coefficient* is a statistic that provides an index of the association between two variables, such as perceived stress and job satisfaction. The bivariate correlation coefficient and its multivariate (three or more variables) analog, the multiple correlation coefficient, are often used in field research to assess naturally occurring relationships.

It may seem that the lack of experimental rigor associated with the ex post facto design would inevitably make it a poor cousin to the controlled experiment. Of course, the situation is not quite that simple. Real world data obtained from ex post facto research are typically much more representative of everyday life; what is lost in (experimental) control is often gained in generalizability.

The relative merits of laboratory versus field studies are typically not at issue in stress research. For ethical reasons, researchers are not able to "stress" groups of workers simply to measure the effects. Also, organizational stress usually reflects an ongoing or chronic situation, which is extremely difficult (although not impossible) to simulate in the laboratory. For these reasons, organizational stress researchers usually study stress as it naturally occurs in the work environment.

When conducting field research, sometimes the stress researcher can *almost* satisfy the requirements of an experiment. The deficit frequently involves the researcher's inability to establish random assignment to the experimental (and control) groups. This situation is not uncommon when stress management programs in industry are assessed (see Chapter 8). Workers are usually assigned to such programs based on their membership in a specific group or department or their expressed interest in participation. Therefore, comparisons between the group that received the stress management program and the one that did not are biased because the groups may have been fundamentally different before the introduction of the independent variable.

When research fulfills *some* of the requirements of an experiment (e.g., manipulation of an independent variable) and not others (e.g., random assignment to conditions), it is called a *quasi-experiment* (see Cook, Campbell, & Peracchio, 1990, for a detailed explanation of quasi-experiments). Although the nonexperimental field study is by far the most commonly used method of studying organizational stress (for all the reasons just discussed), there are some notable exceptions, which we will examine later in this chapter.

STRESS MEASUREMENT CRITERIA

Ivancevich and Matteson (1980) classified stress measurement as either the medical research approach or the behavioral science approach (Duff & Lipscomb, 1973). In the *medical research approach*, the subject reports to a medical clinic or hospital, where a medical history is taken, along with routine laboratory tests and medical examinations. The laboratory tests are assessed by a trained group of medical technicians. The attending physician aggregates information from all of these sources to arrive at a diagnosis.

The *behavioral science approach* to stress measurement also involves the collection of relevant data from a subject or subjects. These data, as in the medical approach, may involve self-report measures, such as medical history and biochemical (laboratory) and physiological (medical) tests. However, behavioral scientists typically assess stress with a wider variety of different *types* of measures than the medical specialist; these measures are often more indirect and difficult to use effectively. The behavioral scientist is also as likely (or more likely) to collect these data in the field (work or other environments) than in the laboratory.

More recently, Kasl (1989) proposed the *occupational epidemiology approach,* which could identify relationships between the objective work environment and health outcomes. This perspective would enable researchers to link toxins, hazards, and disease in the work environment to health decrements. For example, investigators may discover that a recent increase in eye injuries in an industrial facility was due to decreased mandatory safety training for new employees. Unfortunately, this broad-based approach has not been adopted in the years since Kasl's proposal (Kasl, 1996).

Reliability

Regardless of the type or types of measures used, all must satisfy a few fundamental measurement criteria. The most important criteria are reliability and validity. *Reliability* refers to the consistency of any measurement or diagnostic instrument or the absence of random error of measurement. As the amount of random error in measurement increases, reliability decreases accordingly. Random error may be introduced because of a variety of possible factors, including some characteristics of the person being measured, situational variables, and characteristics of the measure itself. But what is meant by random error?

As an illustration, consider a man who completes a questionnaire asking him to indicate the coping strategies he used in the past to deal with a stressor. If he is suffering from the flu at the time, he may be tired and therefore not pay close attention to the questions. If he then completes the same questionnaire again at a later date when his health has recovered, his responses the second time may be quite different. This inconsistency across time resulting from the illness captures the essence of random error: Scores are sometimes affected by unpredictable chance factors like illness or a noisy testing environment. These chance factors introduce error into measurement.

Because several factors can introduce random error into stress measurement, various statistical strategies have been developed to diagnose these factors. For example, to distinguish random error from chance factors occurring over time (such as illness), the same measure can be administered to individuals at two different points in time and the degree of relationship assessed between the two sets of scores. This approach is called the *test-retest* approach and assesses whether any degree of temporal stability exists in the measurements.

In stress research, however, a high degree of temporal stability is not necessarily expected because stress levels may change over time. A more common type of reliability assessed in stress research is *internal consistency* reliability. Internal consistency reliability examines the existence of random error introduced due to the specific items selected for the measure and the extent to which the items are similar in nature.

To illustrate how item similarity affects this type of reliability, consider a 10-item measure designed to assesses perceived stress across a variety of issues (e.g., interpersonal stress, stress associated with work scheduling, overload). A consistent or similar pattern of responses across this rather varied set of 10 items may not be expected. If, however, all 10 items assess the same issue, such as interpersonal stress, a given respondent would probably be more consistent in her ratings across the 10 items. For example, the respondent tends to give the vast majority of items high ratings. With 10 similar items, internal consistency reliability should be relatively higher because respondents are more likely to respond consistently across similar types of items.

Because more than one source of random error exists, a measure can be reliable in one sense (e.g., little random error due to characteristics of the person completing the measure) and unreliable in another sense (e.g., high random error due to the specific items selected for the measure). Thus, an examination of test-retest reliability may indicate high levels of reliability while the opposite is true when internal consistency is examined.

In sum, the total amount of error variance or random error in a measure can be determined by adding up the error across sources. Figure 3.1 illustrates this relationship for two potential sources of random error using some hypothetical error variance percentages: Chance factors over time and the selection of particular items. As additional sources of error are discovered, the percentages in Figure 3.1 may change accordingly.

Many of the analyses examining measurement reliability involve the computation of correlation coefficients. Because the magnitude of the correlation coefficient ranges from minus 1 to 0 to plus 1, larger values (i.e., further from 0) indicate higher levels of reliability. Reliability estimates, however, are only interpretable as positive relationships. For example, in a test-retest study, a high positive correlation (e.g., .8 or higher) between scores on the test administered at two points in time indicates that random error occurring over time is not a serious problem; reliability with respect to consistency over time has been achieved.

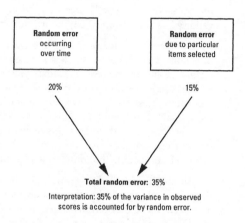

Figure 3.1 How Random Error Functions

Validity

The other criterion, *validity*, is often considered to be the measurement property that is the most difficult to attain. Validity of measurement simply refers to whether valid inferences can be drawn from scores on a measure (Binning & Barrett, 1989; Landy, 1986). For example, if a measure such as a stress questionnaire purports to assess stress levels, with higher scores indicating greater stress levels, can you correctly infer that as people's scores on the measure increase, their levels of stress also increase?

A measure can be perfectly reliable and yet have little or no validity. As an example, if a person measures the circumference of his head five times in the next 15 minutes, he will undoubtedly obtain the same value. Consequently, this measurement is quite reliable. However, if the person asserts that the size of the circumference of his head is an index of intelligence, few would agree that this is a valid inference!

There are multiple strategies used to establish the validity of inferences. Moreover, a preponderance of the evidence approach is typically used to validate inferences. In a criminal trial in which there is no hard evidence of guilt, the prosecuting attorney will attempt to provide multiple sources of evidence to substantiate guilt. In the same way, researchers who examine validity will collect a variety of sources of information to "make their case."

One piece of evidence is reliability evidence. Although reliability is not sufficient for validity, it is nonetheless necessary. In other words, knowing that the measure is relatively free of random error does not by itself imply that validity has been established, but it is nonetheless an essential precondition.

Other strategies for validating inferences have traditionally been called "types" of validity, but they are really just strategies for validating inferences about scores on a measure of interest. The first type is the *construct* approach. Behavioral scientists use constructs to describe intangible concepts, such as intelligence, motivation, or stress. If a new stress questionnaire is statistically related to a second more established questionnaire (i.e., individuals with high scores on one measure have high scores on the other), this evidence suggests that valid inferences might be drawn from scores on the new measure. In other words, the new measure would seem to be measuring the construct it was intended to measure.

Although a detailed exposition of other strategies is beyond the scope of our discussion, we should briefly mention two other general strategies: The content approach and the criterion-related approach. The *content approach* essentially involves a nonstatistical, rational demonstration that the items on the measure represent the domain of interest. For instance, if we ask people to complete a measure in which they indicate those stressors they actually experienced from a list of job stressors, the measure (list) should include all relevant stressors. If a number of stressors are omitted, some people with low scores on the measure might have had higher scores if additional or different items had been included. In this case, it would be dangerous to infer that people with lower scores experienced fewer stressors than those with higher scores.

The *criterion-related approach* involves demonstrating that scores on the measure of interest predict scores on some other measure (the criterion). Identical to the construct approach, this approach involves the computation of correlations. For example, assume scores obtained from a device measuring heart rate are used to predict scores on a measure of adrenaline secretion. If the heart-rate scores predict the adrenaline scores (they are significantly correlated), this relationship helps to substantiate the inference that the heart-rate measure permits valid inferences to be drawn about adrenalinee levels across people.

Although the *criterion* approach may appear to be operationally identical to the *construct* approach—insofar as they both involve the computation of correlations—a subtle difference exists between them. In the construct approach, two measures that purport to measure the same thing (e.g., two questionnaires both designed to assess perceived stress levels) are typically correlated. Alternately, the criterion approach involves choosing two measures; one measure, called the predictor (e.g., a stress questionnaire), is used to predict a criterion of interest (e.g., a measure of heart-rate). The predictor and criterion are not measuring the same construct; one simply needs to establish whether and the extent to which valid inferences can be drawn about the criterion from scores on the predictor. Thus, we may ask if increasing levels of perceived stress allow us to infer increasing levels of heart rate?

Two specific strategies that fall within the criterion approach (with many specific variations) can be identified: the *concurrent* and *predictive approaches*. If the responses on the heart-rate and adrenaline test are measured at the same time, then a concurrent strategy is being used. If the responses on the heart-rate measure are used to predict adrenaline levels at some future time, then a predictive strategy is being used. Although we have discussed these strategies separately, in practice, the preponderance of the evidence approach implies that more than one strategy should ideally be employed. Collectively, these different strategies combine together to assist in validating whatever inferences are drawn from scores obtained from any measure in question.

With a brief discussion of measurement issues now completed, we now turn to three general types of diagnostic procedures or measures that are typically used by behavioral scientists to collect data on job-related stress: self-report (interview and surveys), behavioral (archival and observed behaviors), and medical (physiological and biochemical). All of these measures are subject to the measurement criteria of reliability and validity discussed here.

Types of Stress Measures

Self-Report Measures.   Self-report measures, which include surveys or questionnaires and interviews, require people to report on their experiences, feelings, or attitudes. In stress research, self-report measures can inquire about the nature of the stressors, how people cope with perceived stressors, the short and longer term stress responses, and various personal and contextual factors that may play a role in the stress process. Generally, these types of stress measures assess the affective, somatic, and cognitive aspects of perceived stress. Self-report measures of stress have a high degree of face validity (or the outward appearance of measuring stress). They also make a lot of sense: The best way to find out if someone is stressed is to ask!

One of the earliest data collection techniques used in organizational stress research is the *interview* (see Kahn, Wolfe, Quinn, Snoek, & Rosenthal, 1964); the interview's popularity undoubtedly originated from the its widespread use in clinical psychology as an assessment tool. Interviews can be unstructured or structured. Unstructured interviews usually ask the interviewee to state his or her feelings or experiences concerning some topic (in this case, stress). In structured interviews, however, the interviewer usually asks the interviewee a set of specific questions determined prior to the interview.

The limitations of the interview are that it is time-consuming, potentially costly, and provides highly subjective data that are often difficult to summarize. An example should clarify these limitations. A stress researcher desiring to interview employees about stress in their organization typically arranges to interview one or a few employees away from their workstations. Depending on the amount and type of information the interviewer collects, each interview usually lasts from 30 to 60 minutes. If several interviews are conducted, the process becomes time-consuming for the interviewer and the employees and potentially costly for the organization, particularly if the workers are absent from their workstations during working hours. Primarily for these reasons, the interview is rarely the primary data collection technique of choice today. The interview's real utility, however, often lies in the rich source of information it provides in the preliminary stages of data collection. The information gained from the interview can be used as source material for developing questionnaires and surveys.

Questionnaire or survey measures of stress have taken a bewildering variety of forms, both in terms of format and content. Structured questionnaires usually ask people to indicate if the stressor or stress response/outcome applies to their situation, and/or how frequently or intensely they experience it. The content may be very general, such as asking about overall stress levels at work, or very specific, such as reactions to specific types of organizational stressors. These responses are usually made on checklists or Likert-type scale formats (Table 3.1). (Several of the most widely used stress questionnaires will be introduced when we discuss specific research areas in the next two sections of the book.)

Structured questionnaires have been used more than any other data collection technique in contemporary organizational stress research. Their widespread use is not surprising given that, unlike the interview, they are relatively inexpensive and easy to administer to large groups of people. In addition, structured questionnaire responses are easily quantifiable and are therefore amenable to statistical analyses. Such analyses can allow the researcher to explore her data more completely and therefore be more confident in the interpretation of the results. The information provided by statistical analyses (e.g., results in the form of percentages and average values of stress levels across departments in an organization) is also easily communicated to both workers and management.

Although questionnaires are typically used in stress research to ask respondents a series of closed-ended questions with some type of rating response, there exists a second type of questionnaire called the *unstructured questionnaire*. In some instances, questionnaires may take the form of a series of open-ended questions (e.g., What do you see as some of the emerging sources of stress in your organization and why?). Here, respondents are free to respond by writing their responses. Because respondents can provide qualitative responses (i.e., they do not simply provide numerical ratings for each question), the questionnaire is deemed to be unstructured.

TABLE 3.1   EXAMPLES OF TWO COMMON TYPES OF ORGANIZATIONAL STRESS SELF-REPORT SCALES

Listed below are some situations that often bother people in their jobs. Think about your present job. How well does each of the following words or phrases describe it?

Circle: 1 for "Yes" if it describes it
                 2 for "No" if it does not describe it
                 3 for "?" if you cannot describe

	Yes	No	?
1. Too little recognition for work	1	2	3
2. Receive contradictory instruction	1	2	3
3. Too little feedback about my performance	1	2	3

*Note: Items adapted from *The Job Stress Index*. Perrysburg, OH: Smith, Sandman, and McCreery.

Listed below are statements that represent possible feelings people might have about their jobs. For each statement below, circle the response (from 1 to 5) that best indicates how you feel about your job.

	Extremely false	Somewhat false	Neither true nor false (neutral)	Somewhat true	Extremely true
1. I have to do things that should be done differently.	1	2	3	4	5
2. I work with two or more groups who operate quite differently.	1	2	3	4	5
3. I work on uneccesary things.	1	2	3	4	5

Analysis of the qualitative data may involve examining the responses across respondents for common themes, and this can be accomplished through visual inspection or through the use of special computer software designed for the analysis of qualitative data. Of course, the data are open to the subjective interpretation of the individuals who code the responses and extract the themes. Although this type of questionnaire data may provide a rich source of information, it can be very time consuming to analyze, and the reliance on subjective interpretation is considered by some stress researchers to be a serious limitation of the approach.

Despite their general appeal, both interviews and questionnaires have some common shortcomings. All self-report measures are subject to various response biases. People may respond in socially appropriate ways. For example, someone who perceives the admission of feeling stressed to be a sign of emotional weakness may report he experiences no stress in his life. When working with law enforcement officers and firefighters in stress management workshops, it has often been our personal experience that the most significant breakthrough is the actual admission by these professionals that they even have any job-related stress!

Even if individuals are motivated to provide accurate responses, they may not be able to do so. For instance, asking people to rely on their memory of past events through retrospective reports invites forgetting and a host of potential cognitive biases, such as reliance upon cognitive schemas (Sulsky & Smith, 1995). Schemas may be understood as clusters of information stored together in memory. For example, if Paul is asked to provide self-report data on how he previously coped with a particular stressor, he will discover these coping activities all stored together in a "coping schema." When asked to retrieve these coping activities from memory, however, he may erroneously retrieve activities that he attempted for a stressor other than the one he actually considered. Because all of the coping activities are clustered together in memory, the potential for falsely recalling or recognizing items on the self-report measure and consequently providing incorrect responses, is a real concern.

Jex, Beehr, and Roberts (1992) identified a potential problem in using the word "stress" in self-report instruments. They found that when study participants were asked about their stress at work, they interpreted "stress" as "strain", not "stressor." Therefore, the word "stress" appears to be associated with physical or psychological strains, such as headache or anxiety, not with the stressor that produced them (e.g., a difficult supervisor). Given this point of confusion, Jex and his colleagues recommended that the term "stress" not be used in self-report scales; rather, the word should be avoided completely or substituted with other words, such as "frustration" or "bother."

Recently, Schwartz (1999) highlighted additional problems associated with self-report measures. Specifically, Schwartz pointed out that the ways in which questionnaire items are worded and formatted can greatly alter the resulting responses. Changes in the response scales used can also have dramatic effects on the results. For example, respondents might be asked to rate a series of work stressors on either "severity" or in terms of how "bothersome" each stressor is perceived to be. This subtle difference in the rating scale may elicit quite different response patterns due to differential interpretations of the two types of scales.

Although there definitely are biases inherent in the use of self-report measures, they do allow for individual perceptions to influence responses. Individual perceptions, as already discussed, are a critical component of the stress process. The perception of stress can (and often is) more predictive of strains than any true "objective" stressor. In sum, because they allow individuals to express their perceptions, the measures capture an important component of the overall stress process.

Behavioral Measures. Behavioral measures usually involve the measurement of actual behavior. In a laboratory setting, this might mean that the experimenter rates the subject's persistence on a task (number of minutes or hours) and his performance decrement (number of errors) under stressful conditions. In field studies, such measures could include job-related absences (number of days lost from work), number of accidents or injuries at work over the past year, or number of cigarettes smoked per day. These data may be collected by asking people to report their behaviors, consulting records, files, or archives, and observing and recording behaviors as they occur. The latter option, recording behaviors as they occur, can be very useful when the researcher doubts that people are able (or willing) to accurately report their own behaviors. For example, people may be unaware of the number of cigarettes they have smoked in one day or how many times they have been late for work in one month.

Researchers sometimes assume that because behavioral measures assess actual behavior, they are necessarily reliable and valid. But like any other type of measurement, behavioral measures can lack reliability and validity. Drawing from some of the foregoing examples, a subject's persistence on a task may not reflect the degree of stress he experienced (validity), and the number of job-related absences collected at one point in time may not present a consistent picture of a worker's overall absenteeism levels (reliability).

Medical Measures. *Physiological stress measures* can include any index of sympathetic nervous system activation, such as electrodermal response (sweating), respiration, heart rate, blood pressure, and muscle tension. Because these variables demonstrate large individual differences, it is preferable that each subject serve as his or her own control for any within-subject study.

For example, blood pressure readings from each subject should be collected before and after exposure to a stressor and the two readings compared. Comparisons among different people on their blood pressure readings can be problematic because individual variability among people is so great. Natural, constant fluctuations in many physiological variables also reinforce the need for multiple readings from each subject. The mere act of having one's blood pressure taken may even increase readings. The term "white coat hypertension" refers to a person's anxiety and the resulting reactivity of his blood pressure in response to a medical environment. To complicate the measurement process even further, physiological variables are often influenced by posture, physical activity, caffeine intake, nicotine levels, dietary sodium (salt), and heredity (Balick & Herd, 1986; Schneiderman,

Weiss, & Kaufmann, 1989). Because of these confounds, physiological stress measures, especially the cardiovascular measures, are especially prone to problems with *specificity*, or the ability to identify those persons with a particular condition relative to those who do not. In sum, the existence of error may permeate these types of measurements. We have more to say about this later.

Blood pressure and heart rate are among the most common physiological stress measures. Both provide rapid and sensitive assessments of responses to both physical and psychological stressors. Under ideal conditions, blood pressure and heart rate are assessed repeatedly, with subjects resting comfortably several minutes prior to and during measurement. In situations where reactions to chronic stressors are being measured (the work environment), ambulatory (portable) monitors are preferable. In such situations, participants should record their activities at the onset of each measurement so that multiple measurements can be compared (Fleming & Baum, 1987; Katkin, Dermit, & Wine, 1993).

The instrumentation used to assess physiological stress responses can be expensive and require considerable training to correctly operate them. Some techniques require intrusive and novel procedures, such as the placement of electrodes on the body (e.g., in the measurement of electrodermal responses). When these constraints are considered with the limitations discussed in the preceding paragraph, the use of physiological measures in stress assessment may lose some of its appeal.

Another method of assessing stress relies on *biochemical measures*, the most common of which are the catecholamines, adrenaline and noradrenaline, and the glucocorticoids, such as cortisol. Increased levels of catecholamines in blood and urine have been reliably linked to both psychosocial and environmental stressors (Chapter 2). Although accurate estimates of catecholamines can be obtained with either blood or urine samples, blood samples are generally more appropriate for examinations of reactions to acute stressors, while urine samples are more appropriate for research on reactions to chronic or recurrent stress (Fleming & Baum, 1987). The implication, of course, is that blood sampling is typically more suited to laboratory experimentation, and urine sampling to field studies. This issue is often referred to as *sensitivity*, or the extent to which a test identifies people with a certain condition. Biochemical measures are also affected by specificity, or the extent to which a test can identify those who have the condition relative to those who do not. (See earlier discussion.) Biochemical measures may lack validity because of sensitivity and specificity issues.

Collection of blood samples for catecholamine extraction, however, can be quite tricky. Catecholamines in the blood have a very short half-life, typically less than 2 minutes after exposure to the stressor, and exist only in minute quantities. Also, catecholamine levels can be quite sensitive to venipuncture (drawing blood). For these reasons, multiple samples of blood should be drawn over the interval being studied. This requirement necessitates such invasive and potentially dangerous procedures as using an indwelling catheter inserted in a vein (Fleming & Baum, 1987), which makes close medical supervision mandatory. In addition, once obtained, catecholamines in blood samples deteriorate very rapidly. The blood samples therefore must be preserved immediately and then processed for analysis within two hours or frozen at very low temperatures.

Fortunately, the collection of urine samples for catecholamine extraction is, compared to blood sampling, quite simple and noninvasive. Given the difficulties inherent in field research, this is indeed fortunate! The issue of precise timing in sample collection is not nearly as critical because urinary catecholamine levels change slowly compared to blood plasma levels and typically reflect catecholamine output over the previous few hours. Because, however, chronic reactions are being assessed and any one sample may not be a reliable indicator of catecholamine levels, multiple urine samples are required during the time interval being studied (Fleming & Baum, 1987). In addition, catecholamine concentrations naturally vary over the 24-hour day, so multiple samples should be taken over a 24-hour interval or the sampling time controlled in some other way. Catecholamines typically peak in the early afternoon and trough (reach their lowest point) during the night or very early morning. Although urine samples do not degrade as rapidly as blood samples, the urine samples also need to be processed shortly after sampling. Both blood and urine samples for catecholamine extraction must be analyzed by a trained laboratory technician using standardized assay techniques.

In addition to catecholamines, glucocorticoids, specifically cortisol, are excreted by the body in response to a wide variety of psychosocial and environmental stressors (Chapter 2). Cortisol even seems to be more sensitive to the effects of psychosocial stressors than catecholamines (Fleming & Baum, 1987). Unfortunately, the relationship between cortisol levels and stressor exposure is more complex than the direct relationship between catecholamines and stressors. Psychosocial stressors can influence the increase or decrease of cortisol depending on such factors as the specific type of stressor and whether the stressor is acute or chronic. For this reason, some experts maintain that catecholamines may be preferable indices of stress reactions (Fleming & Baum, 1987).

Like catecholamines, estimates of cortisol levels in the body can be obtained from both blood and urine samples. To ensure accurate assessments of cortisol levels, multiple samples of either blood or urine should be obtained from each subject over the sampling interval. It is especially critical for multiple samples to be collected over a 24-hour period due to the natural fluctuation of cortisol levels in the body over the 24-hour day; for most people, cortisol levels peak between 5 a.m. and 10 a.m. and trough (reach their lowest point) between 4 p.m. and 8 p.m. These normal changes in the body's concentration of cortisol occur because of cortisol's role in several important physiological processes, such as carbohydrate metabolism. The blood and urine samples obtained for cortisol extraction also must be analyzed by a trained laboratory technician using standard assay techniques.

The newest method of cortisol measurement uses salivary cortisol, or the assessment of cortisol with samples of saliva. This technique shows promise as an assessment tool because most people consider it to be noninvasive relative to urine and blood samples. Researchers who have compared salivary cortisol with serum cortisol reported strong evidence that the measures will produce similar results (Burke et al., 1985; Vining, McGinley, Maksvytis, & Ho, 1983). Other advantages of using salivary cortisol are that it is relatively easy to obtain in work settings and reduces the risk of infection and trauma relative to blood drawing.

In addition to diurnal or time-of-day effects, both catecholamines and cortisol are affected by physical activity, changes in posture, diet, and medication. Cortisol, in particular, is sensitive to oral contraceptive intake. All of these potential nuisance factors must be controlled or at least accounted for when assessing biochemical measures of stress.

The last biochemical measures we discuss here are those associated with lipid metabolism in the body, such as free fatty acids, triglycerides, and most importantly, cholesterol. As mentioned in Chapter 1, elevated levels of cortisol trigger increased lipid (fat) production in the body. The role of lipid responses, particularly cholesterol, in the development of cardiovascular disease has been widely acknowledged. Researchers believe that the measurement of lipids in the blood provides a valid index of the body's response to both psychosocial and environmental stressors (Balick & Herd, 1986). All of the potential confounding factors discussed in relation to other biochemical measures are also applicable to lipids.

Similar to the other biochemical measures, some types of lipid measures are more sensitive to acute stressors and some to chronic stressors. For example, fatty acid levels tend to be associated with exposure to acute stressors (Dimsdale & Herd, 1982), while triglycerides and cholesterol are associated with chronic stressors. Cholesterol, in particular, is sensitive to the effects of chronic stress over periods of months or years (Balick & Herd, 1986).

Similar to the behavioral measures, researchers sometimes assume that physiological and biochemical measures are necessarily reliable and valid because, on the surface, they appear to be "scientific" and objective, divorced from human judgment and perception. However, the reliability and validity of these measures is often suspect because of the many potential sources of error discussed previously (see also Hurrell, Nelson, & Simmons, 1998), Kasl (1996) has even suggested that researchers abandon some of the common biological markers, such as cortisol and blood pressure, and focus on lipid compounds and some types of behavioral measures (e.g., smoking).

Fried, Rowland, and Ferris (1984) voiced the same concerns and more in their critique of research on the physiological and biochemical measurement of work stress. They pointed out the rather obvious fact that, except perhaps for cardiovascular symptoms, insufficient research existed to establish a valid link between physiological/biochemical symptoms or measures and work stress specifically: The data were definitely very suggestive, but not definitive (i.e., the construct validity evidence was weak). They also criticized researchers for selecting specific physiological or biochemical measures in a seemingly cavalier manner. In many of the studies they reviewed, invalid measures were selected to assess the research questions being investigated. One of the most flagrant violations was the use of measures inappropriate for the assessment of acute versus chronic work stressors. Such distinctions, as we discussed previously, are extremely important if the research results are to be interpretable. In addition, they criticized prior research for controlling few or no confounding factors, such as diet and posture, in their physiological and biochemical measurements.

Table 3.2 summarizes some of Fried et al.'s (1984) data for the studies they reviewed that assessed cardiovascular measures (mostly heart rate and blood pressure), catecholamines, and (blood) serum cholesterol. It is indeed surprising that fewer than 50% of some of the most important and widely acknowledged confounding factors were controlled in these studies. (The *only* factor that was consistently measured was gender.) The omission of these factors introduces potential *systematic error,* which can be assessed and controlled a priori. In this case, for example, age is a potential source of systematic error because health decrements typically accompany the aging process. Unfortunately, in the 20 years since Fried et al.'s article, our review of the current research literature on work stress gives us no reason to refute their overall criticisms.

TABLE 3.2   SOME POTENTIAL CONFOUNDING FACTORS CONSIDERED IN THE PSYCHOLOGICAL AND BIOCHEMICAL MEASUREMENT OF WORK STRESS

Type of measure	Number of Studies Reviewed	Family Tendency	Health	Posture	Consumption of Caffiene and /or Nicotine	Diet	Time of Day	Physical Activity
Cardiovascular Measures (mostly heart rate and blood pressure)	23	13%	26%	17%	4%	*	*	*
(Serum) Cholesterol	15	27%	20%	7%	7%	13%	*	*
Catecholamines	9	44%	*	44%	44%	*	44%	11%

*Not applicable

SELECTED EXAMPLES OF ORGANIZATIONAL STRESS RESEARCH

Having discussed some common stress research methods and measures, we are now ready to combine this information to examine three different types of organizational stress research. These studies include a laboratory experiment, a field experiment, and an ex post facto field study. In all three cases, only parts of each study are discussed; please refer to the original articles for further details.

The Laboratory Experiment

Sales (1969) was interested in whether he could capture a common type of job-related stressor, work overload, in the laboratory and determine whether that stressor produced physiological and psychological stress responses. He randomly assigned 73 undergraduate men to one of three experimental groups, an overload condition, in which subjects were assigned more work than they could possibly finish in the allotted time, and an underload condition, in which subjects could easily finish the work in the allotted time. The experimental task involved solving anagrams, or rearranging letters to produce a meaningful word. One dependent variable was serum cholesterol levels as assessed with blood samples taken prior to and immediately after the experiment.

Sales found that, in the overload condition, blood cholesterol levels increased during the experiment, while in the underload condition, cholesterol levels decreased. Subjects also reported that they felt more stressed in the overload condition compared to the underload condition. Because Sales randomly assigned subjects to conditions and exercised experimental control by manipulating the independent variable (workload), he could assume that changes in workload caused changes in the dependent variable (blood cholesterol levels).

One obvious criticism of this research, and much laboratory research in general, is the potential lack of generalizability; we simply cannot determine if similar results would occur in real life. However, Sales countered this criticism by asserting that, if such measurable changes could occur during a relatively innocuous laboratory experiment, imagine what potentially occurs in the many threatening situations people encounter in the real world! We add yet another comment: The strong results of this experiment are indeed unexpected, given that blood cholesterol is not a particularly good indicator of responses to short-term stressors (see earlier discussion). Sales's research was also notable in that he attempted to systematically examine the effects of a job-related stressor, work overload. Although the physiological and biochemical effects of this type of psychosocial stressor have been investigated in the laboratory by other researchers, such as Frankenhaeuser (Chapter 2), laboratory experiments on organizational stressors are unusual.

The Field Experiment

Jackson (1983) wanted to determine whether increasing workers' participation in job-related decisions would reduce perceived stress and strains. The subjects in her study were 126 hospital staff and nursing personnel. She collected premeasures on the variables of interest, such as perceived stress (a self-report measure), job satisfaction (a self-report measure), and job-related absence frequency (a behavioral measure) before the experimental manipulation. Subjects were then randomly assigned to experimental or control (no treatment) conditions. The independent variable was whether they received the intervention: increased participation through increases in the number of staff meetings from once to twice per month. (Although Jackson tested a model of worker participation using a complex experimental design, we discuss only a small portion of her study here.)

Outcomes were assessed both at 3 and 6 months. After 6 months, Jackson found that the increased participation in the group receiving the intervention caused decreases in perceived stress and absence frequency and increases in job satisfaction. She therefore concluded that participation in job-related decision making was an important causal factor through its influence on workers' levels of perceived stress and strain measures (job satisfaction and absence frequency). Because Jackson manipulated an independent variable and randomly assigned subjects to experimental conditions, any changes in the dependent variables, the perceived stress and strain measures, were probably caused by the effects of the manipulation.

The experimental field study is a rare phenomenon in organizational stress research because real-world conditions rarely allow the researcher to exercise any degree of control over subjects and experimental conditions. Even though Jackson was able to assign workers randomly to experimental treatments, her results really cannot be interpreted as rigorously as Sales's results. One reason is that subject attrition (dropout) occurred between the manipulation and multiple assessments of the dependent variables. This means that a somewhat different set of workers experienced the manipulation and assessments. Another reason is that all subjects who participated in the study had opportunities to discuss the research with each other, which may have biased the results.

Regardless of its weaknesses, however, Jackson's study remains an unusual and striking example of controlled field research. Also, similar to Sales's conclusions, the fact that Jackson's relatively weak manipulation (i.e., increasing staff meetings from once to twice per month) produced measurable changes in employee perceptions and behaviors provides compelling evidence of the positive effects of worker participation.

The Ex Post Facto Field Study

Sutton and Rafaeli (1987) were interested in whether the characteristics of workstations (i.e., where people actually do their work) were stressors for a sample of 109 clerical employees. They investigated whether atmospheric conditions, such as temperature, lighting, and intrusions from other people, such as noise and crowding, affected workers' reactions (job satisfaction and somatic or health complaints, both self-report measures).

Sutton and Rafaeli used a varied data collection procedure. They interviewed employees at their workstations and also asked them to answer a survey; these two data collection procedures were used to assess workers' reactions and also some of the subjective workstation characteristics, such as the perceived amount of noise and quality of lighting. Behavioral and physical observations of workstations were collected by the researchers to determine objective factors of the work environment (e.g., room density or the number of people in room/room size and actual room temperature). Behavioral and physical observations were desirable in this case because characteristics such as room density and temperature can be accurately assessed by external observers.

Overall, the researchers found that characteristics of workstations were only weakly related to the worker reactions of job satisfaction and somatic complaints. Interestingly, they also discovered that employees who reported being overloaded with work were even more oblivious to these physical stressors than those who reported less work overload. The implication, of course, is that the overload experienced by these workers distracted their attention from other, perhaps less serious, stressors.

Sutton and Rafaeli's study is an example of the most common type of job-related stress research, an ex post facto field study. Their study qualifies as an ex post facto field study because no subjects were assigned to conditions, and there was no experimental manipulation. The data collected from these clerical employees simply reflected the natural, ongoing conditions in their work environment. Another way of thinking about this design is that the environmental conditions and outcome variables such as job satisfaction existed prior to the study. In other words, the researchers simply collected the information "after the fact," as opposed to manipulating and creating levels of environmental conditions or satisfaction during the study—hence, the name expost facto for this design. Unfortunately, with such data, one cannot assume that workstation stressors cause employee reactions, nor discount the fact that other factors, such as organizational policies and practices, may have affected the results.

CURRENT METHODOLOGICAL TOPICS IN ORGANIZATIONAL STRESS RESEARCH

A few methodological and statistical issues have captured the interest of organizational stress researchers in recent years. The topics covered here include the relative merits of subjective versus objective measures, the impact of structural equation modeling (SEM) and meta-analyses, the effects of common method variance, the role of negative affectivity in research, and the importance of longitudinal studies.

Subjective versus Objective Measures

One of the most controversial of the methodological issues in organizational stress research is the debate over the relative merits of subjective versus objective measures of stress (Kasl, 1987; 1996), a debate that is no closer to resolution now than a decade ago (e.g., Frese & Zapf, 1999; Perrewe & Zellars, 1999; Schaubroeck, 1999). Organizational stress researchers have long acknowledged that, at best, a weak relationship often exists between perceptual or self-report stressors and strains (job-related and general), and physiological and biochemical indicators of stress, such as blood pressure and catecholamine levels (Frew & Bruning, 1987; Ganster, Mayes, Sime, & Tharp, 1982; Howard, Cunningham, & Rechnitzer, 1986; Steffy & Jones, 1988). This argument can also be extended to include behavioral measures, such as absence frequency or accident rates, and other source measures, such as supervisory ratings (Frese & Zapf, 1988; C. S. Smith & Tisak, 1993; Spector, Dwyer, & Jex, 1988).

The assumption, of course, is that those individuals who report experiencing organizational stressors with greater frequency or intensity should also demonstrate elevated physiological, biochemical, and/or behavioral responses to stress (recall the general stress model in Chapter 1). This assumption, however, has not been strongly supported. One possible explanation for the lack of support is that, because stress is a dynamic process, researchers are simply tapping different points on the stress continuum (Cox, 1985). Specifically, the psychological perception of stress may occur earlier or later than the measurable physiological or behavioral symptoms in the context of any stressful experience. Single or only a few measurements of any type over time may fail to detect significant relationships (A. K. Johnson & Anderson, 1990). Alternately, unreliablity in any of the measurements (self-reports, physiological indices, or behavioral outcomes), will also attenuate the relationships among them. Indeed, potential biases in measuring or recording physiological indices may render them nonobjective.

Ganster and Schaubroeck (1991) reviewed job-related research that had used self-reports of stressors and some type of physiological or biochemical strain. They found only a few supportive studies (e.g., Mathews, Cottington, Talbott, Kuller, & Siegel, 1987). More recently, this list has been extended to include, for example, studies by Shirom, Westman, Shamai, and Carel (1997) and Carrere, Evans, Palsane, and Rivas (1991).

The studies with positive findings mostly had used highly standardized data collection procedures with multiple assessments and modalities (i.e., a mixture of multiple subjective and objective measures; see also Ivancevich & Matteson, 1988); these researchers had also carefully controlled the numerous confounding variables that can affect physiological or biochemical measurement, such as physical activity and nicotine intake.

Frankenhaeuser's work (Chapter 2), in which some psychosocial stressor, such as work overload, is typically manipulated in the laboratory, and biochemical and/or physiological measurements are taken, exemplifies this type of research. Ganster and Schaubroeck admitted, however, that the primary limitation of this type of research is that longer-term or chronic effects of exposure to these stressors are unknown. Of course, this limitation severely decreases the generalizability of laboratory research to real work settings.

Frese and Zapf (1988) provided some insightful comments about the problems presented by the lack of convergence between subjective and objective (particularly other source) measures. They contended that researchers have not been very systematic in differentiating between objective and subjective dimensions. For example, because all types of data are typically collected and/or assessed by human beings, variables such as absence or performance ratings may be subjectively biased. Even typical self-report or questionnaire measures can be more or less biased depending on their content and format: Consider the difference between these two questions: "How overloaded are you with work each day?" versus "How much work do you accomplish each day?" They maintained that researchers rarely have access to the worst work environments; therefore, existing data are probably fairly restricted to the more productive and humane workplaces. They also discussed the fact that researchers typically observe workers for only limited time periods, and that the presence of the researcher in the work setting may have a reactive effect on worker behavior. These factors, among others, led Frese and Zapf to conclude that measured or assessed relationships between subjective and objective measures would be small or underestimates of the true relationships!

Today, researchers such as Schaubroeck (1999) have argued that the major focus of research attention should be the objective environment for a very practical reason. Specifically, knowledge of the objective environment is more helpful in designing worksite stress management interventions and thereby creating more healthy work environments.

Statistical Advancements: Structural Equation Modeling (SEM) and Meta-Analyses

A contemporary extension of multivariate correlational analyses is *structural equation modeling (SEM)*. Using special computer programs such as LISREL (Joreskog & Sorbom, 1989), these complex statistical techniques take a matrix of correlations (or covariances) among variables, examine the relationships among them, and compare these relationships with the relationships hypothesized by the researcher.

SEM has become a standard tool in stress research for model testing within the past decade or so (Hurrell, Nelson, & Simmons, 1998). Suppose a researcher wants to test the model of stress and accidents proposed by Murphy, DuBois and Hurrell (1986; Figure 2.5) in Chapter 2. First, data are collected on the variables in the model (e.g., work routines, fatigue, reaction time, risky behavior) from some sample of interest. The model hypothesizes that these variables have both direct and indirect relationships with other variables. For example, certain types of work routines, such as shift work, directly lead to fatigue, which in turn directly reduces reaction time, which directly increases risky (unsafe) behavior, which directly influences accident occurrence. Notice that some variables are only indirectly related to others: The effects of shift work affect reaction time only through the influence of fatigue. The computer program LISREL provides several tests of statistical fit that show how closely the relationships hypothesized by the researcher agree with the relationships found in the data.

SEM does have some limitations. For instance, SEM allows researchers to draw weak causal inferences from tests of their models because the technique can control for measurement error. However, a strong inference test of any model still requires the manipulation of variables within a controlled laboratory experiment. At best, all anyone can really say is that the model tested appears to be consistent with the pattern of data collected: Cause and effect inferences cannot be unambiguously made. Moreover, alternative models that were not tested may delineate alternative causal relationships among our variables; these models may be equally (or even more) consistent with the pattern of data. In sum, no substitute exists for experimental design from the standpoint of formulating causal inferences, and a technique such as SEM cannot overcome the fact that the data were nonexperimentally generated.

Regardless, SEM has had an enormous impact on the status of theory in organizational stress research (as well as many other disciplines): Rather than relying on the accumulated weight of indirect evidence over time, SEM has allowed researchers to directly test and revise their stress models (Hurrell et al., 1998).

Another fairly recent advancement has been achieved through the use of *meta-analyses,* or the quantitative accumulation of research results for the purpose of summarizing or integrating the findings in some area (see Hunter & Schmidt, 1990, for a detailed treatment of this topic). Previously, researchers qualitatively assessed the outcomes of several empirical research studies and voiced an educated guess regarding the status of research on a topic. For instance, considering the results of several studies on gender differences in job-related stress, does such a difference really exist? If so, what is the magnitude and direction of that difference? The meta-analyst uses the results of individual studies as data points for a statistical assessment of research questions such as this one. Meta-analysts have also refined the technique such that measurement can be assessed and controlled (Hunter & Schmidt, 1990), thus permitting an even more precise assessment of overall effects. We will discuss several important meta-analyses in later chapters, for example, the meta-analyses of gender effects in job-related stress (Chapter 6) and the relationship between role stressors and organizational and personal outcomes (Chapter 5).

Although meta-analysis has taken much of the subjectivity out of expert opinion and literature reviews, permitting a relatively unbiased assessment of research results, it has been criticized on several grounds. For example, the outcome of any meta-analysis is heavily influenced by the specific studies included; consequently, two meta-analyses on the same topic may reach different conclusions because different studies were included in each. This situation occurred with two different meta-analyses of role stressors published in the 1980s, each of which reached quite different conclusions about the status of research in this area (Fisher & Gittleson, 1983; Jackson & Schuler, 1985; see Chapter 5). Meta-analysts have also disagreed about the statistical corrections (tests) that have been used to assess the effects calculated from meta-analyses. These criticisms aside, the statistical approach of meta-analysis has allowed for a more objective assessment of the status of research than was possible with purely qualitative reviews, permitting researchers to more rapidly and accurately identify important areas for future study.

Common Method Variance

A frequent argument among behavioral scientists involves caveats against the use of all self-report (questionnaire or interview) measures, such as self-reports of stressors and strains. Many researchers assume that relationships among self-reports are at least somewhat inflated from what has been called common method variance (Frese & Zapf, 1988; Ganster & Schaubroeck, 1991). *Common method variance* simply refers to the assumption that the relationships among variables are influenced more by the method of measurement (in this case, self-reports) than by any real or true relationships among constructs (D. T. Campbell & Fiske, 1959). A hypothetical example involves the (inflated) relationship between a person's responses on stress items and job satisfaction items on a questionnaire. This type of response bias might occur because the person reasons that, because he feels stressed at work, he must not be very satisfied with his job regardless of his true level of job satisfaction. He therefore responds accordingly.

Reviews of stress research (Ganster & Schaubroeck, 1991; Jackson & Schuler, 1985) have generally found greater relationships between self-reports of stressors and strains than any other type of measure, thus lending credibility to the effects of method variance. Kinicki, McKee, & Wade (1996) found that 68% of the studies examined in their review of the stress literature used common measurement methods for both predictor and criteria (generally self-report measures), which suggests that method variance may indeed be a pervasive issue for work stress research. However, Jex and Beehr (1991) argued that if the relationships between self-reports of stressors and strains reflect mostly method variance, then these relationships, regardless of the study variables or context, should always be large in magnitude. Of course, this is definitely not true! They also observed that method variance, which is a type of measurement bias or error, occurs more frequently in measures with poor measurement properties (low reliability and validity).

The debate has not been resolved, with some researchers asserting the pervasiveness of method bias in research using self-report measures (Schmitt, 1994; Williams, Cote, & Buckley, 1989), and others asserting that the problem has been overstated (G. S. Howard, 1994; Spector, 1994; Spector & Brannick, 1989). Researchers have recently taken a more balanced approach by proposing methods to assess and adjust for any method variance within the context of individual study analyses (e.g., Lindell & Whitney, 2001).

Interestingly, method variance concerns have not been raised in connection with other methods of stress measurement, such as physiological measures. However, method variance may infiltrate any measurement procedure (Spector & Brannick, 1989). Thus, method variance is a concern not only for self-report measures, even though the method variance problem has primarily targeted self-report measures.

Negative Affectivity (NA)

Researchers have identified another potential methodological bias in organizational stress research in the dispositional construct: negative affectivity. *Negative affectivity (NA)* is simply a stable personality trait that reflects individual differences in negative emotionality and self-concept (Watson & Clark, 1984). Regardless of their objective situations, people high in NA tend to focus on the negative aspects of their environments and generally express high levels of distress relative to low NA people. When Brief, Burke, George, Robinson, and Webster (1988) statistically controlled for NA in their sample of 497 managers and professionals, the magnitude of the relationships (correlations) between stressors and strains was reduced. From these results, they suggested that stressor-strain relationships may be largely due to NA, given that much work stress research relies on self-report measures. Brief et al. claimed that NA may function both as a correlate of stressors and strains and as a methodological "nuisance" variable; this simply means that NA represents both an individual difference in how people respond to stressors and strains and a source of variance that must be controlled or accounted for when examining the relationships between stressors and strains.

Jex and Beehr (1991) pointed out that the Brief et al. (1988) study had a few methodological weaknesses, however. First, Brief et al. used an unusual measure of job stressors, a work-related life events scale (Chapter 5), which assesses acute, rather than chronic, organizational stressors; chronic stressors are, by far, more commonly studied. Second, they used a measure of NA, the Taylor Manifest Anxiety Scale, which has items that are similar to items in many health-related strain measures (e.g., self-reported health or anxiety). Therefore, controlling for NA would affect the stressor-strain relationship, particularly for some types of strains.

Chen and Spector (1991) attempted to replicate Brief et al.'s research using different measures of NA and work stressors. They found little evidence that NA functioned as a methodological nuisance in the relationships between stressors and strains (although it was a correlate of both). Very recently, Spector, Chen, and O'Connell (2000), using a strong inference (longitudinal) design, replicated their 1991 findings. In addition, other studies (Jex & Spector, 1996; Tombaugh & White, 1989) have failed to replicate Brief et al.'s original results. Schaubroeck, Ganster, and Fox (1992) used SEM to analyze data on stressors, strains, and NA from a sample of 311 fire and police department workers. Their sophisicated data analyses also failed to support NA as a methodological nuisance variable. However, they suggested that NA should be measured in self-report stress research to examine its influence as a possible biasing individual difference variable.

Brief et al.'s original findings and their subsequent re-analyses (see M. J. Burke, Brief, & George, 1993) are still open to debate. Indeed, a major research journal recently published a very lively debate on this issue (Judge, Erez, & Thoreson, 2000; Payne, 2000; Spector, Zapf, Chen, & Frese, 2000). Regardless of the eventual outcome, the question about the role of NA, however, has sparked considerable interest over dispositional variables in organizational stress research (e.g., Iverson, Olekalns, & Erwin, 1998; Parkes, 1990).

Cross-sectional versus Longitudinal Research

The last methodological topic is one that is commonly raised in many areas of psychological research, but is particularly important in organizational stress: the issue of longitudinal research. From our previous discussions, it is obvious that stress, particularly organizational stress, is a dynamic process. Yet, much organizational stress research employs single measurements of stressors and strains at single points in time. Why, for example, should a single measurement of cortisol levels be related to chronic health measures or job performance within the past year for a group of workers?

According to Frese and Zapf (1988), there are many plausible ways in which stressors can contribute to ill health over time. A few of the different models they discussed are the exposure time model, the accumulation model, and the adjustment model. The *exposure time model* predicts that the longer a person endures a stressor (or stressors), the higher the rate of dysfunction or illness. For example, a person who endures a stressful situation for 5 years will be more prone to the development of strains than if she had endured the same stressor for 6 months. The *accumulation model* predicts that illness develops from enduring an accumulation of stressors over time and does not disappear even if the stressors are reduced or removed. The fact that people who have developed cardiovascular disease often continue to be afflicted even after making lifestyle changes (reducing or removing life and work stressors) provides an example of this model. The *adjustment model* predicts that initially illness develops in proportion to the duration of exposure to the stressor (or stressors); however, after a certain point, the person adjusts to the stressor and illness decreases, although the stressor remains. An example is the shift worker, who initially feels physically distressed by changes in his sleeping and waking schedule, but seems to adjust over time, even though he remains on shift work.

To complicate matters further, Frese and Zapf (1988) asserted that different types of stressors and strains (illness) may follow different models. They

> ...*suggest a completely different way of thinking about this problem: it is not the small correlation (effects) that should make us skeptical but rather the large correlations (effects). Given the complexity of the measurement problems, the complexity of different kinds of causal models involved in a longitudinal study... and the fact that the workplace is only one (albeit an important) area of stress in the life of people, one should only expect small correlations (effects). (p. 398)*

Very recently, Garst, Frese, and Molenaar (2000) followed up Frese and Zapf's earlier theoretical paper. They tested various stressor-strain models in a longitudinal design using data from East German workers. Their results are quite complex, but they did find some support for a stressor-strain trend model and a short-term reaction model. The reaction model assumes that stressors immediately and directly affect strains, which is consistent with the short-term effects implied by our general stress model (Figure 1.1). The trend model states that chronic, slow-moving changes (e.g., increases) in stressors will be accompanied by slow-moving changes in strains. The trend model shares some characteristics with the exposure time model just discussed.

Overall, the choice of cross-sectional versus longitudinal research strategies is a fundamentally important one that has not been adequately addressed in the years since Frese and Zapf's article appeared. Although admittedly more difficult from a logistical standpoint, longitudinal studies afford us a potentially richer and more dynamic array of data than would otherwise be obtainable. We revisit this issue in Chapter 7 when we consider methodologies used to assess how people cope with stress at work.

CONCLUSIONS

What, then, is the organizational stress researcher (or even a serious consumer of stress research) to do? The morass of measurement caveats, potential confounds, and outright practical problems inherent in the study of stress, particularly organizational stress, make the business of stress research a seemingly frustrating (and sometimes impossible) enterprise. What, you may ask, can be done? Quite a bit, actually. Following is a list of a few fairly simple suggestions.

1. Measures (self-report, behavioral, biochemical, and physiological) should be used that have tested and acceptable measurement properties (reliability and validity). At least in part, two of the methodological nuisance factors we discussed (common method variance and negative affectivity) could more easily be attributed to measures possessing less than optimal measurement properties. In the same vein, careful thought should be given to the selection of the most appropriate measures. Is acute or chronic stress of interest? Depending on the answer to this question, the choice of measures may differ considerably.

   After the measures are chosen, the problems involved in using them (e.g., diet, physical activity, response bias) should be, to the extent possible, controlled. Results of research studies that failed to use measures with acceptable measurement properties and control relevant confounding factors should be suspect.

2. Studies that measure stressors and strains with a single type of measurement, such as all self-report, at a single point in time may not tell us anything new or useful. Stress, including organizational stress, is a dynamic, multifaceted process. Consequently, longitudinal research, which has the capacity to examine dynamic changes in stressors and strains over time, is needed. These studies may use any one or combinations of the research designs and measures discussed earlier. Exploratory (or simple descriptive) studies may be necessary initially to develop the groundwork for systematic, hypotheses-driven research. However, important theoretical questions that involve cause-and-effect issues (e.g., do some types of stressors directly influence the development of some types of strains?) can ultimately be answered only with strong inference studies that exercise experimental control and manipulation of variables.

3. The statistical innovations of the 1980s and 1990s—structural equation modeling and meta-analyses—can help us understand the morass of often conflicting research results in organizational stress research. However, it must be realized that these techniques are not panaceas, but have limitations that can affect their usefulness. So, it is prudent to be a cautious consumer of any research incorporating SEM or meta-analytic techniques.

4. Appreciation for what is known and patience for what must yet be learned are requisites for both the researcher and consumer of stress research. Jex and Beehr (1991) summarized our sentiments exactly: "Slow progress in work stress research may simply be the price for studying a complex phenomenon...." (p. 355).

THE NATURE OF
JOB-RELATED STRESS

The material covered in the first part of this book took a somewhat broad perspective by considering the topic of stress in general without restricting attention solely to stress at work. In this section, the focus is specifically on the experience of job-related or organizational stress. We examine each aspect of stress at work in detail: the several sources of job stress (the stressors); the short and long-term outcomes (the strains), and the intervening individual, group, and situational characteristics that influence relationships between stressors and outcomes (the moderators). Although the third section of this book is devoted to coping with stress and stress management (Chapters 7 and 8), in this section, we will also consider specific coping strategies that have been applied to certain types of job-related stressors where appropriate. To an extent, we cannot separate out discussions of stressors, outcomes/strains, and moderators because, as discussed in Part I, they are all part of the continuum we call the stress process (Figure 1.1). However, each chapter focuses primarily on one or more of these three parts of the experience of job-related stress.

In Chapter 4, we concentrate on select stressors,specifically as they relate to work on a more global or macro-level: the total job or occupation as a stressor, followed by environmental or traditional blue-collar (industrial) stressors (e.g., noise, routinized work). Shift work and alternative work schedules as organizational stressors are also considered.

In Chapter 5, we deal with micro-level stressors; that is, stressors that do not emanate directly from the work itself or the surrounding physical environment. Specifically, we consider the voluminous literature on role-stressors. We also investigate some contemporary sources of job-related stress such as work-family conflict, computers and automation, and downsizing and unemployment.

The last chapter in this section, Chapter 6, examines the outcome/strain end of the stress continuum: specifically, the effects of stress on job attitudes and performance, and especially on personal health. The important role of individual differences (e.g., personality, gender) as stress moderators in understanding the total stress process is also discussed.

MACRO-LEVEL WORK STRESSORS

CHAPTER 4

*The Occupation and
Physical/Organizational
Environment*

THE JOB OR OCCUPATION

Most people are guided by the implicit assumption that some jobs are more stressful than others. For example, you probably agree that the job of a demolitions expert is more stressful than that of a janitor. If pressed to give a reason for your answer, you would undoubtedly say that the demolitions expert faces the threat of injury or death in the performance of his or her job whereas the janitor typically does not. However, jobs are often considered to be stressful for a variety of reasons other than threat to life or limb.

From a study of the health records of 22,000 workers in 130 occupations, the National Institute for Occupational Safety and Health (NIOSH) compiled data on stress-related disease incidence by occupation (M. J. Smith, Colligan, & Hurrell, 1977). Twelve occupations out of a top 40 list with a very high incidence of health care admissions and mortality were identified: laborers, secretaries, inspectors, clinical laboratory technicians, office managers, managers/administrators, foremen, waitresses/waiters, machine operatives, farm owners, mine operatives, and painters (Table 4.1). Some other occupations that showed a higher than average incidence of health-care admissions and mortality were health care (e.g., registered nurses, nurses aides and dental assistants), skilled blue-collar work (e.g., machinists, electricians), public services (e.g., social workers, police), and sales (e.g., sales managers and representatives).

TABLE 4.1   OCCUPATIONS WITH HIGH INCIDENCE OF STRESS-RELATED
DISEASES

Occupation	Rank	Mean z-scores for Death Certificates*	Mean z scores for Meantal Health Admissions*	Mean z scores for General Hospital Admissions
Laborers	1	216.84	97.97	44.85
Secretary	2	-2.40	42.64	25.95
Inspector	3	5.76	10.71	17.80
Clinical Laboratory Technician	3	0.57	5.87	17.46
Office Manager	3	0.57	0.16	14.48
Foreman	4	0.84	-9.50	12.07
Manager/Administrator	4	4.26	-13.76	20.03
Waitress/Waiter	5	0.13	26.15	-1.13
Operatives	5	-13.74	16.52	0.25
Farm Owner	6	35.30	-3.60	-8.50
Mine Operative	6	21.97	0.33	-2.16
Painter (not artist)	6	15.09	-0.38	-2.71

*Note: High positive scores indicate high (above average) levels; scores close to 0 indicatae average or normal levels; high negative scores indicate low (bleow average) levels.

In another NIOSH-sponsored study, L. Murphy (1991) examined the association between job types and disability from cardiovascular disease in a 1978 U.S. health interview survey of almost 10,000 workers. Across 2,485 occupations, he found that the job dimensions associated with cardiovascular disability were hazardous situations, responsibility for others, exchanging information, and attention to devices (equipment, machinery). Occupations with high scores on these dimensions were transportation jobs (air traffic controllers, truck drivers, airline pilots/attendants, bus drivers, and locomotive engineers), teachers (preschool and adult education), and craftsmen/foremen (machinists, carpenters, and foremen).

According to the NIOSH-sponsored research that has investigated stress-related occupational differences across thousands of American workers in several hundred different jobs, many of the jobs at the bottom of the organizational ladder (e.g., laborers, secretaries, and machine operators) are among the most stressful. The NIOSH studies identified a few common stressors across many of these jobs: for example, a fast work pace, long working hours, repetitive and boring job tasks, physical hazards, and dealing with equipment or machinery.

Despite the common themes across occupations identified by NIOSH researchers, they and others have noted distinct occupational differences, both in the amount and type of stress experienced (Sparks & Cooper, 1999). For example, French, Caplan, and Harrison (1982) reported that the administrators in their sample identified very different job-related stressors than the scientists or engineers.

In addition, Grosch and Murphy (1998) examined over 8,000 employees across diverse jobs and discovered that workers whose occupations involved the use of machines or transportation equipment reported higher levels of depression and lower levels of health compared to managerial and professional occupations. These results suggest that there may be systematic differences across occupations in terms of both the quality and quantity of work stressors.

The identification of occupationally specific stressors has been particularly important in targeting areas for change or intervention. If stressors unique to a particular job or class of jobs can be identified, interventions can be developed that potentially attenuate or even eliminate the stressors in question. This is akin to "curing the disease" rather than treating the symptoms through individual-level stress management techniques like meditation or structured relaxation exercises. We will return to the issue of stress management when we consider it in detail later (Chapter 8). We now examine some specific occupations and consider what is known about the stressors that are frequently associated with these occupations.

Police and Firefighters

The law enforcement profession has long been universally recognized as stressful. Hans Selye (1978) even stated that, "Unlike most professions, it (police work) ranks as one of the most hazardous, even exceeding the formidable stresses and strains of air traffic control" (p. 7). Research on the stress of police work has proliferated in recent years, a testimony to the increasing awareness that police work is inherently stressful (e.g., Beehr, Johnson, & Nieva, 1995; Hart et al., 1995; Stephens & Long, 2000). Increased job stress, unfortunately, has been linked to increased police violence (Kop, Euwena, & Schaufeli, 1999).

Besides the obvious physical dangers often associated with this profession, police officers have identified excess paperwork, red tape, dealing with the court system, coworker and supervisor conflict, shift work, and lack of support from the public as job-related stressors (Greller, Parsons, & Mitchell, 1992). Because of the erratic nature of police work, officers often report both work overload (too much to do) and work underload (too little to do).

A study of occupational stress in a group of police officers in the midwestern United States found that the following stressors: (a) underutilization of skills, (b) quantitative work(over)load, and (c) job future ambiguity, were related to individual psychological strain (Kaufmann & Beehr, 1989). These police officers were not only stressed by having too much to do that was too easy or routine, but they also feared for their future employment. The stressor job future ambiguity (i.e., uncertainty about one's continued or future employment prospects) is unfortunately an increasingly common occupational stressor, particularly in corporate America. We will have much more to say about the topic of job loss and downsizing in Chapter 5.

Many occupational stressors associated with police work, especially shift work, exposure to physical dangers (Beaton & Murphy, 1993), and psychological trauma (Corneil, Beaton, Murphy, Johnson, & Pike, 1999), are shared with firefighters. In fact, firefighters' 1990–1991 rates of occupational injury and illness were the highest of any group of U.S. workers (U.S. Bureau of Labor Statistics, 1990). Police work, as well as firefighting, has frequently been glamorized in the media, so it is indeed surprising to people that many facets of both professions are considered to be boring and unstimulating (Davidson & Veno, 1980; Mitchell & Bray, 1990). Added to these stressors, firefighters must rely heavily on teamwork and spend many hours at the station, both of which can aggravate administrative and coworker conflicts (Beaton & Murphy, 1993). High rates of divorce (Hurrell, 1977) and alcoholism (Heiman, 1975), common strains among police officers and firefighters, underscore the potentially devastating effects of these job-related stressors.

Before we leave this discussion, we thought we might share an observation from our applied work with firefighters. Specifically, one common theme that emerges is that triggering the fire alarm appears to set in motion another type of alarm—Selye's alarm reaction—as firefighters undergo the beginnings of the General Adaptation Syndrome ,or GAS (also see Beaton, Murphy, Pike, & Jarrett, 1995). What many of them report as very stressful, however, is the uncertainty and the related feeling of no control over what awaits them at the scene. Often, this surge of adrenaline proves to be of no use because the problem turns out to be either a false alarm or relatively minor. The uncertainty about whether a serious fire or hazard awaits is often reported as a salient stressor for many firefighters. We expect that a similar type of uncertainty likely leads to perceived stress in police officers as well.

Social Workers and Teachers

Some people-oriented service professions, such as social work and teaching, have job stressors in common with both the police and health-care professions. Social service workers report little positive feedback from their jobs or the public, unsafe work environments, frustration in dealing with bureaucracy and excessive paperwork, a sense of personal responsibility for clients, and work overload (Eaton, 1980; Ross, 1993).

Teachers indicate that excessive paperwork, lack of adequate supplies/facilities, work overload, and a lack of positive feedback are salient stressors (Kyriacou & Sutcliffe, 1978; Phillips & Lee, 1980; Starnaman & Miller, 1992). Urban teachers have also complained of the stress of dealing with vandalism and physical violence from students (Dworkin, Haney, & Telschow, 1988; Phillips & Lee, 1980). Burnout, a special type of stress response often associated with the human service professions (Chapter 6), appears to occur all too frequently in the teaching profession as well (e.g., Bakker & Schaufeli, 2000; Friedman, 2000).

Data obtained from a recent inventory of teacher stress called The Teacher Stress Inventory (Fimian & Fastenau, 1990), indicate that professional investment is a particularly salient issue for teachers. Professional investment refers to a number of specific stressors, including a lack of opportunities for promotion, lack of control over job-related decisions, and a lack of emotional/intellectual stimulation. Clearly, we applaud attempts to develop surveys specific to particular occupations or jobs. Such specialized surveys allow stressors unique to the job or occupation in question to be uncovered.

Finally, Richard and Krieshok (1989) were interested in the possibility that coping moderates the relationship between stress and strain in university faculty. Moreover, they were interested in examining whether gender and academic rank (e.g., assistant vs. associate professor) are important variables to consider when investigating the associations among stress, strain, and coping. Eighty-three faculty members from a large university completed a number of questionnaires assessing levels of stress, strain, and coping activities. Although coping, gender, and rank did not function as hypothesized in their data, they reasoned that academic rank might be an important variable for understanding the stress process in university faculty. Specifically, in terms of reported strains, men tended to suffer less from the effects of perceived stress as they moved up in academic rank while the opposite was true for women.

Health-Care Workers

Medical personnel, particularly nurses, have been studied in much contemporary stress research, although research has also considered other workers in the health-care profession (e.g., Arsenault, Dolan, & Van Ameringen, 1991; Landsbergis, 1988). Nurses have reported that work overload, heavy physical work, shift work, patient concerns (dealing with death and medical treatment), and interpersonal problems with other medical staff, particularly physicians, are common stressors (Hipwell, Tyler

& Wilson, 1989; C. L. Lee, 1987; Marshall, 1978). A study of 171 nurses across five hospitals also found that some of these identified stressors—work overload, little support from supervisors, and negligent or incompetent coworkers—were sources of stress related to depression and decreased work performance (Motowidlo, Packard, & Manning, 1986).

In a sample of 252 nurses, Hemingway and Smith (1999) found that characteristics of the organization predicted the onset of stressors, which, in turn, predicted outcomes such as absenteeism. These results suggested that researchers need to more closely examine organizational characteristics (e.g., the amount of support; the nature of formal/informal relationships) as antecedents of stressors and perhaps attempt to alter characteristics deemed to be detrimental to employees. Another implication of their study is that context-driven or organizationally specific theory may prove to be superior to the more general approaches (Chapter 2) in guiding research and practice.

Many of the job-related stressors reported by nurses are experienced to an even greater degree by medical doctors, who also suffer from high rates of depression and alcoholism (Firth-Cozens, 2001). For example, early research (Caplan et al., 1975) found that physicians encountered the highest levels of workload, job complexity, and responsibility for people. Revicki and May (1985) reported that dealing with suffering, fear, death, and difficult patients were very salient stressors for medical doctors. Kirkcaldy, Trimpop, and Cooper (1997) also found that German physicians working over 48 hours per week experienced a greater number of driving accidents and higher job-related stress.

Revicki and Whitley (1995) investigated the occupational stress of emergency medicine residents. They reasoned that emergency medicine residency should be a particularly stressful position because of the unpredictable and often extreme nature of the job itself and the relative inexperience of many workers. Over a three-year period, the researchers followed a large sample of emergency medicine residents; they comprised 20–37% of that job category in the United States. Their results confirmed previous cross-sectional research (e.g., Revicki, Whitley, Gallery, & Allison, 1993) in demonstrating the importance of task and role clarity in defusing the effects of job-related stress: Emergency medicine residents who reported a great deal of ambiguity regarding their roles and responsibilities and little task clarity also reported more depression than their peers who reported less ambiguity and more clarity. We will have a good deal more to say about these very important role-based stressors in Chapter 5.

One medical professional who has attracted the attention of stress researchers is the dentist. C. L. Cooper (1980) attempted to identify dentists' job-related stressors by interviewing a group of American dentists gathered for a professional meeting. He found that coping with difficult patients, building a practice, administrative duties, and public opinion of the dentist as an inflictor of pain were identified as salient stressors. Cooper also found that the dentists most bothered by these stressors showed increased blood pressure and abnormal heart rhythms (electrocardiograms). Cooper and his colleagues (Cooper, Watts, Baglioni, & Kelly, 1988) replicated many of these findings several years later with a sample of dentists in Great Britain. In addition, lack of respect for practicing dentistry and having too little professional and personal time were identified as occupational stressors in a longitudinal study of 108 American dentists (DiMatteo, Shugars, & Hays, 1993). One common theme cutting across these studies is that dentists are distressed by their poor public image, at least relative to other medical professionals. Perhaps the media could help out by televising programs that portray dentists in a positive light!

A common theme linking occupational stressors across different types of medical professions is difficulty with interpersonal interactions and/or interdependency on others (coworkers or patients). Medical professionals are trained to be skilled scientists and clinicians but are often woefully unprepared to deal with people-oriented issues. These types of issues are also quite frequently beyond individual control; for example, some patients are dissatisfied regardless of the quality of care they receive. Lack of control over the work environment also undoubtedly contributes to the stress experienced by these professionals.

Another area of concern is workplace violence, which has increasingly caught the attention of the media, as well as organizational researchers and practitioners (Braverman, 1999). This violence has often resulted in assaults on health-care workers (Schat & Kelloway, 2000). Much of the documented violence has been against nurses (Arnetz, Arnetz, & Petterson, 1996) and more specifically, psychiatric workers in hospitals (Carmel & Hunter, 1991). Although few statistics exist on the incidence of violence against health-care workers in outpatient settings, the meager evidence does suggest that assaults are underreported (Bloom, 1989). In an exploratory survey of 108 psychologists, Fong (1995) found that 17% of her sample had experienced some type of assaultive incident by a client or patient. These incidents ranged from threats to actual attacks against person or property.

Air Traffic Controllers

In addition to the occupational stressors common to many jobs, behavioral scientists believe that the reported stressfulness of contemporary jobs is due, in large measure, to the small amount of control that workers perceive they have over their daily work activities and working conditions (S. Fisher, 1985; Sauter, Hurrell, & Cooper, 1989). A perceived lack of control is reported to be one of the most potent stressors for air traffic controllers, a profession that is legendary for its stressfulness. Air traffic controllers (ATCs), who monitor air traffic through electronic devices in airport facilities, often have little control over potential crisis situations and workload (Zeier, 1994).

One study compared occupational stressors reported by Canadian and New Zealand air traffic controllers and found high agreement regarding the top job-related stressors: equipment limitations, peak traffic situations, general work environment, and fear of causing an accident (Shouksmith & Burrough, 1988).

More recently, Zeier (1994) found a positive relationship between subjective and objective workload and saliva cortisol levels in a sample of air traffic controllers in Switzerland. For each ATC, subjective workload was measured through questionnaire responses; objective workload was measured with a composite index of the average number of aircraft controlled, number of radio communications, and duration of radio communications during successive 10-minute intervals. These results are consistent with previous research that has shown a link between work (traffic) load and health problems in ATCs (Cobb & Rose, 1973; Laurig, Becker-Biskaborn, & Reiche, 1971). Although Zeier estimated that only 10–15% of his sample were at risk for serious stress-related problems, he claimed that complaints from ATCs about excessive work stress should be taken seriously.

Office and Managerial Workers

Another surprisingly high-stress occupation is clerical and secretarial work. A national study that examined the relationship between coronary heart disease and employment (Haynes, Feinlieb, & Kannel, 1980) found that the incidence of heart disease was much higher in female clerical workers than in any other group of women studied. The women at highest health risk reported they had little control over their job mobility and nonsupportive supervisors. Additionally, Narayanan, Menon, and Spector (1999) found that compared to select other occupations, clerical workers suffered from higher levels of work overload and a perceived lack of control.

An occupation that has been identified as quite stressful but that is typically characterized by considerable control and discretion is managerial work (Cavanaugh, Boswell, Roehling, & Boudreau, 2000). Some important stressors for managers are work overload, conflict and ambiguity in defining the managerial role, and difficult work relationships (R. J. Burke, 1988; Glowinkowski & Cooper, 1986). Managers who experience these stressors have also reported increased anxiety and depression (Cooper & Roden, 1985), alcohol consumption (Margolis, Kroes, & Quinn, 1974), and propensity to leave the organization (Bedeian & Armenakis, 1981).

Gender differences may be important when considering stress and managerial work. Research conducted in Sweden, for example, suggests that male managers' catecholamine output dropped at 5 p.m., although this was not true for female managers. For females, norepinephrine levels actually increased after work (Frankenhaeuser et al., 1989). These results suggest that, for females, the work–home spillover of managerial stress to their personal life is a potentially serious problem. Compared to males, female managers appear to have greater difficultly leaving their problems at the office when they go home. (Also see Chapter 5.)

Interestingly, some occupations are considered stressful not because they require too much in work quantity from workers but because they require too much in quality. This aspect of work overload is called *qualitative overload,* as opposed to the *quantitative overload* typically reported by managers. Qualitative overload has been identified as an occupational stressor for workers in highly technical jobs, such as science and engineering (French & Caplan, 1973).

This short exploration of stressful occupations has revealed that stressful jobs span the organizational hierarchy. We focused on the diversity of stressors across occupations because such information is useful in designing stress management interventions or employee development programs for different types of workers. However, many of these high-stress jobs share some common stressors. Some of these stressors, (e.g., exposure to physical hazards and use of machinery and equipment), are frequently associated with industrial or blue-collar occupations, a topic to which we now turn our attention.

THE PHYSICAL WORK ENVIRONMENT

The stressors faced by workers in industrial settings, such as foundries or factories, are often qualitatively quite different from stressors faced by office workers or managers. In a sense, all stressors emanate from the physical environment (unless, of course, they are simply figments of one's imagination!). However, white-collar workers rarely must endure excessive noise or temperature extremes as part of their daily job-related activities. As we discussed in Chapter 1, environmental stressors are also quite unique in that they can result in direct physical trauma regardless of workers' perceptions. The perception of elements of the physical environment as stressful or harmful may even compound the trauma induced by the environment. For these reasons, the effects of such stressors can be particularly devastating. We now examine some specific physical stressors.

Noise

Foundry and factory workers are often exposed to noise created from the operation of equipment or machinery, such as jackhammers or drill presses. The most obvious concern with such noise in work environments is the potential for hearing loss. After initial exposure to high-intensity noise, some temporary hearing loss occurs, which is recovered a few hours or days following exposure. However, after repeated exposure to high-intensity noise, recovery decreases over time, resulting in permanent hearing loss. This type of deafness is particularly insidious because it is caused by damage to the auditory receptors in the inner ear, and, consequently, nerve impulses cannot be transmitted to the brain. Hearing loss caused from nerve damage to the inner ear is usually not correctable surgically or with a hearing aid. Some nerve deafness also naturally occurs with the deterioration associated with the aging process, so the effects of occupational deafness may be compounded in older workers.

Because of the serious health implications of noise exposure, the Occupational Safety and Health Administration (OSHA) has set standards for noise exposure times of workers at different noise intensities (Table 4.2). A permissible noise exposure for a sound (noise) intensity level of 110 decibels (dB), which is equivalent to being 6 feet from an amplifier at a rock concert, is only 30 minutes. Anyone who has attended a rock concert while sitting near the speakers would probably agree that the 30-minute window is definitely exceeded! However, workers with ear protection can lengthen their permissible exposure times.

Besides hearing loss, it seems logical that occupational noise may also affect work performance, as anyone who has tried to concentrate on a task in a noisy environment can attest. However, the effects of noise on performance are not clear-cut. In general, task performance is impaired only at very high noise intensities (over 95 dB). Performance on simple or well-learned tasks may even show performance improvements in slightly noisy settings. This enhancement probably occurs because the noise acts to focus a person's attention on the task at hand or because the noise acts as a stressor, raising the person's arousal level and therefore overcoming the boredom associated with the task (Broadbent, 1976; Poulton, 1978).

An exception to the enhancement effect seems to be the performance of verbal tasks, particularly the comprehension of written material, in a noisy environment (A. Smith, 1989). Such performance decrements are presumed to occur because the noise masks the "inner" speech associated with reading and/or contributes to overarousal (Broadbent, 1976, 1978; Poulton, 1977, 1978). Performance deterioration under noisy conditions has also been noted when tasks are performed continuously without rest pauses (Davies & Jones, 1982) and when tasks are very difficult, especially in terms of information processing requirements (Eschenbrenner, 1971). There is even some evidence that changing or intermittent noise levels affect task performance to a greater extent than constant noise levels. Intermittent noise seems to act as a distractor, preventing any adaptation to the noise (Teichner, Arees, & Reilly, 1963).

Recently, Evans and Johnson (2000) performed an interesting experiment, designed to simulate open-office noise levels. They randomly assigned 40 female clerical workers to either a low-intensity noise exposure condition or to a control condition. Compared to the control condition, subjects in the noise condition experienced elevated urinary epinephrine (adrenaline) levels, made fewer attempts to solve difficult tasks (puzzles) after exposure, and were less likely to make necessary postural adjustments in their computer workstation (a risk factor for musculoskeletal disorders). Given the deficits that were found after only 3 hours of noise exposure, the researchers emphasized the potential health effects of chronic exposure to low-intensity noise in the workplace.

Unfortunately, most of the evidence about task performance in noisy conditions comes from laboratory experiments. The tasks in such experiments are typically simple or short in duration (e.g., arithmetic and reaction-time tasks), and the subjects are students (cf. Persinger, Tiller, & Koren, 1999) or military personnel. The conclusions from these studies may not be very generalizable to older workers who perform a variety of tasks and who have been subjected to noisy work environments for years (Sanders & McCormick, 1993).

Temperature

Heat. As anyone who has worked near a blast furnace in a steel or glass mill can confirm, exposure to extreme temperature conditions can be very stressful. Under conditions of extreme heat stress, the body absorbs more heat than it can expel, body temperature rises, and illness or death can eventually result. Some industries are notorious for heat-related illness, for example, construction (Jensen, 1983) and the iron and steel industry (Dinman, Stephenson, Horvath, & Colwell, 1974). NIOSH has estimated that between 5 and 10 million workers in the United States may be exposed to levels of heat at work that represent both a safety and health hazard (Hancock, & Vasmatzidis, 1998).

Because of the potentially serious health effects of extreme heat exposure, various professional and government agencies have proposed heat exposure limits in workplaces. These recommended limits are multidimensional, simultaneously considering several factors that can influence heat tolerance. For example, NIOSH's guidelines (National Institute for Occupational Safety and Health, 1986) consider energy expenditure (workload), degree of heat acclimatization, and work–rest cycle (frequency of work breaks). Other obvious heat-reduction strategies can also be implemented, such as the use of air conditioners, fans, and protective clothing (Wasterlund, 1998). Under extremely hot conditions, medical supervision and protective clothing are mandatory.

Similar to the effects of noise on performance, the effects of heat on task performance are complex, varying with the type of task. Performance on simple or routine tasks, such as reaction time, short-term memory, and arithmetic laboratory tasks, shows little or no deterioration under physical tolerance limits (Ramsey & Kwon, 1988). In fact, brief exposure to heat stress may even improve performance on these simple tasks. An arousal mechanism is again believed to account for this effect: The physical arousal produced by the heat compensates for the boredom created by the task, thus enhancing performance.

Performance on complex tasks, (e.g., vigilance and dual or multiple tasks), begins to deteriorate at about 86° F. Although various explanations have been proposed for this decrement, one interesting perspective is that complex task performance is affected by brain temperature, which is extremely sensitive to heat stress (Ramsey & Kwon, 1988). Similar to the noise research, the research on heat stress is largely composed of short-term laboratory experiments with young subjects. The generalizability of these findings to older adults who chronically endure heat stress at work is unknown.

Cold.   Although job-related cold exposure is less common than heat exposure, some workers must endure exposure in winter weather and refrigerated chambers. The industry that leads in cold injuries is oil and gas extraction (particularly in Arctic climates), followed by transportation, warehousing, and protective services (Sinks, Mathias, Halpern, Timbrook, & Newman, 1987). Cold stress, unlike heat stress, is usually not severe and rarely results in death. This is fortunate, because human beings are not able to cold acclimatize in the same way they can heat acclimatize (Astrand & Rodahl, 1986). The use of heaters and insulated clothing, particularly gloves, seems to be quite effective in protecting against cold stress.

Apart from the health risks associated with cold exposure (e.g., frostbite), little is known about performance under frigid conditions. The effects of cold stress on performance are influenced by several factors, such as air temperature, humidity, air flow, type of task, and length of cold exposure. Manual performance is most affected by cold exposure: Finger dexterity decreases at temperatures below 55° F, with much greater decreases at lower temperatures (Riley & Cochran, 1984). Performance data on complex cognitive tasks under cold conditions are limited and inconclusive. Cold exposure seems to be associated with apathy and motivational decrements (Payne, 1959), which could definitely affect task performance. Again, the scanty data on performance under cold stress are mostly limited to laboratory experiments, which may have only limited generalizability to actual work settings.

Interaction Effects of Environmental Stressors

Our discussion has previously focused only on the effects of different single types of environmental stressors, although we alluded to more complex effects when we mentioned that noise or heat can raise a person's arousal level sufficiently to overcome the boredom associated with the task. Indeed, coping with multiple stressors is the norm for many contemporary workers, so it makes little sense to examine stressors in isolation (Danna & Griffin, 1999). One of the most well-known interactive effects deals with noise and sleep loss. Wilkinson (1963) examined the effects of noise and sleep deprivation on performance in a laboratory reaction time task. He found that both noise and sleep loss individually resulted in task performance errors. However, for those subjects who were sleep deprived, task performance actually improved under the noise condition relative to the quiet condition. The two stressors, noise and sleep loss, cancelled out each other because the noise increased arousal sufficiently to overcome the lethargy associated with sleepiness.

Stressors can also produce effects that linger after the stressors are no longer present. Glass and Singer (1972) provided evidence of the after-effects of an environmental stressor in their classic experiment on the effects of intermittent and unpredictable noise on laboratory task performance (solving puzzles). They found that subjects exposed to unpredictable noise (i.e., noise presented at seemingly random time intervals) performed worse, after the noise was removed, relative to subjects exposed to predictable noise. Further, those who had experienced the unpredictable noise tended to show motivational, as well as performance, deficits by making fewer attempts to solve the experimental tasks. (Also see the experiment discussed earlier that examined task performance under low-intensity noise; Evans & Johnson, 2000).

A recent longitudinal field study by Melamed, Fried, and Froom (2001) also illustrates the potent interactive effects of chronic stressors. The researchers followed 1,831 industrial employees in Israel over a 2–4 year interval. They found that, among workers exposed to high noise levels, those with complex jobs (i.e., high task complexity and variety) showed two-fold increases in blood pressure levels relative to those with simple jobs. Workers in complex jobs also reported lower job satisfaction under high, compared to low, noise exposure. Overall, under low noise conditions, job complexity appeared to have beneficial effects. The researchers concluded that those workers who perform complex jobs under high noise exposure (common scenarios in many modern industrial facilities) are at considerable risk under high noise exposure.

The Wilkinson (1963), Glass and Singer (1972), and Melamed et al. (2001) studies illustrate the complexity by which environmental stressors undoubtedly operate in real life. Not only are workers simultaneously exposed to multiple stressors (e.g., noise, heat, cold) that may have both individual and interactive effects among themselves (e.g., noise and heat), attributes of the person (e.g., sleep loss),and the job (e.g., job complexity), but these effects may linger long after the stressors have disappeared. Small wonder that researchers have frequently been frustrated in their attempts to document the individual impact of specific job-related stressors in both work and nonwork domains!

As we noted in Chapter 1, one very real problem in modern workplaces that is undoubtedly influenced by the interaction of multiple stressors is "sick building syndrome" (SBS; Danna & Griffin, 1999; Frazer, 1998). SBS is a collection of symptoms of general malaise associated with the habitation of some work environments. These symptoms include irritation of the skin, eyes, nose, and throat, neurotoxic complaints (e.g., headache, nausea, drowsiness, fatigue), congested eyes and nose, and reports of unpleasant or unusual odors or tastes (Molhave, 1989). SBS is frequently associated with air-conditioned working environments and poor indoor air quality

(Bourbeau, Brisson, & Allaire, 1996; Hedge, 1984; Mendell & Smith, 1990). However, many studies have failed to find specific environmental stressors associated with reports of SBS.

Hedge, Erickson, and Rubin (1992) investigated a possible relationship between SBS and personal and occupational factors. Of the 18 office buildings they surveyed, all met acceptable standards for indoor air quality, although more than 70% of the workers reported at least one symptom of SBS. Those workers who reported the greatest number of symptoms were also women who reported high job stress, low job satisfaction, and VDT (video display terminal) use. The researchers concluded that the mystery of SBS will be solved only by considering a complex pattern of environmental, occupational, and personal factors, some of which have yet to be determined from future research.

Recent studies have reconfirmed the impact of multiple personal and occupational factors, as well as the obvious environmental ones, on SBS. For example, stress and lack of social support (Mendelson, Catano, & Kelloway, 2000), and problems in organizational structure and communication patterns (Thoern, 2000) have all been implicated in the development of sick building syndrome.

TABLE 4.2   DESCRIPTIONS OF NOISE LEVELS AND EXPOSURE LIMITS ACCORDING TO OSHA

Sound Level, dBA		Permissable Time, hours
80		32
85		16
90	Subway train (20 feet)**	8
95		4
100		2
105		1
110	Riveting machine (operator)**	0.5
115		0.25
120*	Rock concert with amplifier (6 feet)**	0.125*
125*		0.063*
130*		0.031*

*Exposures above 115 dBA are not permitted regardless of duration, but should they exist, they are to be included in computations of the noise dose.

** Specific noise sources.

THE ORGANIZATIONAL ENVIRONMENT

Routinized Work

In addition to the effects of noise and extreme temperature stress, other environmental characteristics of industrial work are considered stressful, such as the repetitive, routinized tasks associated with many assembly-line jobs in factories. This type of work is commonly experienced as boring and monotonous. In fact, behavioral scientists have long known that boredom is associated both with decreased physiological arousal and negative attitudes toward work, which leads to perceptions of repetitiveness, unpleasantness, and constraint (Barmack, 1937; Kivimaeki, & Kalimo, 1996; Melamed, Ben-Avi, Luz, & Green, 1995).

Workers report that job-related boredom often results from quantitative and qualitative underload (i.e., not having enough work and work that is too easy, respectively; Fisher, 1993). However, because industrial work is largely defined by technology and therefore not easily amenable to change, researchers have concentrated their efforts on identifying particular types of workers who are more or less suitable for machine-paced work. In general, more intelligent and extroverted individuals become easily bored (Fisher, 1993), and many probably self-select out of such jobs.

The jobs that are totally machine-paced, such that a machine totally controls the work flow, are considered to be the most stressful. In these jobs, workers have no control over their tasks and often have difficulty consistently pacing themselves properly with the machine. Workers in these types of machine-paced jobs have shown high levels of physiological stress (adrenaline), anxiety, depression, somatic (physical body) complaints, and job dissatisfaction (M. J. Smith, 1985).

A weakness of most research on job-related monotony is that the existence of routinized work has simply been inferred from incumbents' job titles. Few studies have obtained objective assessments of routinized work and both subjective (perceived) and objective measures of work monotony. Melamed et al. (1995) asked blue-collar workers in 21 manufacturing plants in Israel to respond to self-report measures of subjective monotony (i.e., the job descriptors "routine," "monotonous," and "varied enough"), job satisfaction, and psychological distress. Sickness and absence data were collected from personnel records. From job analysis data, worker's jobs were classified as having a short work cycle (less than 1 minute), a medium work cycle (1–30 minutes), a long work cycle (30 minutes–1 hour), or varied work (no predetermined order of activities). Work cycles refer to the work activities that must be performed repetitively during the course of a work day.

The researchers found that workers in short-cycle repetitive jobs perceived the highest levels of subjective monotony. Repetitive work was also related to job dissatisfaction and psychological distress, particularly for workers in short-cycle jobs who reported lower job satisfaction and higher psychological distress compared to workers engaged in varied work. Satisfaction and distress were mainly related to subjective monotony, whereas the absence data were related to both subjective and objective monotony. Interestingly, the subjective and objective measures of monotony were only moderately related; Melamed and his colleagues speculated that the indirect manner in which the job analysis data were collected could have influenced this relationship. These results confirm that repetitive work, measured both from the worker's perspective and from independent assessments of the work environment, are directly related to important personal and organizational outcomes. The results also make a case for collecting different types of repetitive work variables, given the lack of convergence between them.

Of course, some routinized work may suffer from the opposite of boredom: namely, a high requirement for constant attention. The need for constant attention is a feature of many blue-collar jobs where attention to detail in the manufacturing process is critical (e.g., assembling circuit boards). For example, Martin and Wall (1989) conducted two studies with alternative methodologies to investigate the effects of attentional demand and cost responsibility on psychological strains. Specifically, they investigated the hypothesis that psychological strain is the end result of an interaction between attentional demand and high-cost responsibility. In the first study, a field experiment, operators of computer-based equipment experienced each of four different job conditions that varied in attentional demand and cost responsibility. As predicted, the job condition that was highest on both dimensions was associated with the highest level of strain. However, because their design did not include a low-demand, high-cost responsibility condition, it was not possible to rule out the possibility that cost responsibility alone was responsible for the results.

The second study was conducted in the same electronics plant. However, this study used survey methodology to assess the variables of interest in the first study across a wide variety of shopfloor jobs. Overall, the survey results suggested that high attentional demands, combined with the knowledge that errors will be costly, predict both health and job attitudes. Thus, support for the interactional hypothesis was obtained, although the nonexperimental design of the second study did not permit causal inferences about the effects of demands and responsibility on strains. The authors echoed a point we emphasized earlier: the need to consider how stressors interact to produce various outcomes.

Recent studies on repetitive work have examined the impact of stress and psychosocial factors on worker health, especially musculoskeletal disorders (Lundberg, 1999). For example, Rissen, Melin, Sandsjo, Dohns, and Lundberg (2000) found that supermarket employees who reported high stress levels also had elevated muscle activity (sEMG). Increased muscle activity is often implicated in the development of musculoskeletal disorders.

In sum, routinized work is inherently stressful. Not only do workers often find these types of jobs boring, but the nature of the work, which usually requires some type of pacing with machine output, can be quite demanding. Unfortunately, technological advances can exacerbate the demands and therefore further increase the stressfulness of these jobs. New technology has not only increased the requirements of many jobs but has also enabled management to continuously monitor workers' activities. We will examine electronic performance monitoring (EPM) as a contemporary stressor in the next chapter.

In discussing job-related noise, temperature extremes, and repetitive or routinized tasks, we have by no means exhausted the list of macro-level stressors. Poorly designed equipment, machinery, and workstations (e.g., an uncomfortable chair or work surface) can create considerable joint and muscle pain, not to mention the possible accompanying perceived stress; all of these stressors will eventually have implications for worker health, performance, and attitudes. However, the study of such stressors usually falls under the domain of engineering or human factors psychology and will not be directly addressed here.

Another macro-level stressor that has been historically associated with certain types of work (e.g., nursing, policing) but can have pervasive effects throughout the organization, is shift work (Parkes, 1999; C. S. Smith et al., 1999).

Shift Work

If you have ever pulled an all-nighter cramming for an exam, tending a sick child, or making the rounds of New Year's parties, you probably remember how you felt the next day. Do you think your performance at work or school the next day was below average? If you took a nap in the afternoon or evening, were you groggy and unable to function well afterward? Did you sleep poorly throughout the night after napping earlier? The answer to all of these questions is probably "yes." The lost night's sleep both deprived you of a night's sleep and disturbed your body's normal sleep-wake cycle.

Circadian Rhythms and Stress. Human beings, unlike some other mammals such as the bat, are day-oriented creatures. Our society and our personal lives are typically geared toward daytime activity and nighttime inactivity (mostly sleep). It is therefore not surprising that many other human functions are oriented toward this type of cycle. The most well-known are physiological variables, such as body temperature, heart rate, and blood pressure, although nonphysiological variables, notably self-rated alertness and some types of task performance, also follow this trend. Concentrations of many of these substances in the body usually reach a peak during the day and a trough, or low level, during the night. This cyclic activity repeats every 24 hours; such 24-hour cycles are called *circadian cycles* or *rhythms*. Theoretically, these 24-hour cycles will change if the sleep-wake period is altered for 10–14 days. For example, if you decided to consistently alter your waking hours to include 1 a.m.–6 a.m. and your sleeping hours to include 9 a.m.–3 p.m., the peaks and troughs of your 24-hour temperature cycle would change accordingly.

This information about circadian rhythms should clarify why people generally do not function well at night: Many bodily processes are at their lowest ebb at night, much like an idling automobile. So it is not surprising that people who try to work at night and sleep during the day often report that they cannot do either very well. Shift workers, who comprise approximately 20–25 percent of the workforce, must chronically cope with changing work and sleep schedules. Shift work is defined broadly here, and refers to any regular employment outside the 7 a.m.–6 p.m. interval (Monk, 1989). The costs of adjusting to shift work can be high, affecting every aspect of a person's life from personal relationships to work performance. The extreme importance of this facet of organizational life has even been recognized by the federal government in a recent publication by the Office of Technology Assessment (1991).

As a job-related stressor, shift work has been conceived to function similarly to other stressors. In fact, shift work researchers have argued that stress theory has conceptually guided the development of much shift work theory (E. Taylor, Briner, & Folkard, 1997). For example, Colquhoun and Rutenfranz (1980) proposed a "stress and strain" model (Figure 4.1) to describe the process whereby the detrimental effects of shift work arise. Note that their model is similar to our heuristic model in Chapter 1, although some researchers believe that shift work functions quite differently from other types of job-related stressors (Cervinka, 1993). In their model, stress develops from the disruption of the shift worker's circadian rhythms created by shifting working and sleeping hours. The shift work strains, such as performance and health problems, are shaped by intervening variables (or moderators, e.g., personality characteristics and organizational policies).

Monk (1988) also proposed a model to explain how strain arises from shift work. As well as the disruption of circadian cycles just discussed, his model emphasizes the influence of sleep interruption and deficit, and social and domestic problems.

More recently, C. S. Smith et al. (1999) extended prior research to propose a process model of shift work and health. This model attempts to explain how personal and situational factors (e.g., age and workload, respectively) influence the development of sleep and social and domestic disturbances in shift workers. In turn, active and passive coping responses affect the manner in which these disturbances negatively or positively affect the progression of both proximal and distal strains (e.g., anxiety, gastrointestinal symptoms). They found preliminary support for the model across three samples of shift workers. However, because C. S. Smith et al. (1999) used cross-sectional, self-report data to test their model, their results should be viewed with caution.

Performance. Task performance has been widely investigated by shift work researchers, although most studies have been conducted in the laboratory. Compelling real-world evidence for the influence of circadian factors on work performance draws from some widely publicized nuclear power plant accidents, such as those at Three Mile Island and Chernobyl. The Three Mile Island mishap occurred at 4 a.m., when the nuclear power plant operators were halfway through their night shift. The shift workers who committed the almost fatal errors were on a weekly rotating shift schedule (or a shift schedule that changed every 7 days). Knowing that shift work disrupts cyclic physiological functions and sleeping patterns, it is obvious why shift workers often perform worse than comparable permanent day workers. However, the impact of shift work, particularly night work, is not simply to adversely affect all task performance. The nature of the performance differences is complex and seems to depend on the type of work or task being performed.

Scientists have long known that levels of arousal in the body parallel the 24-hour temperature cycle. The performance trends (over 24 hours) of many simple tasks, (e.g., simple reaction time and visual search) also parallel the body temperature and arousal cycles. Therefore, performance on simple tasks, such as monitoring and inspection in assembly-line work, would be expected to reach their lowest levels during the late night and early morning hours (Folkard, 1990; Monk, 1989). These performance decrements, of course, would be further exaggerated by sleep loss.

Paradoxically, some complex mental tasks involving short-term memory may be performed fairly well at night, assuming they are not accompanied by severe sleep deficits. Monk and Embrey (1981) studied workers who operated a process control refinery in a large automated chemical plant and were on a rapidly rotating shift schedule (3 days on rotating shifts followed by 2 rest days). Because the shift cycle rotated so rapidly, these workers retained their day orientation. Their job activities were relatively complex cognitively, requiring the aggregation of information about plant operations. Because these tasks were performed on the computer, performance could be objectively monitored. The researchers measured the shift workers' actual work performance over a 1-month interval. As predicted, job performance was better on the night shift than on the day shift. However, the researchers concurrently measured the shift workers' performance on a simple visual search task, which required the identification of a specific target (a certain number or letter). Also as predicted, simple task performance was worse on the night shift relative to the day shift.

Although it is widely accepted that simple task performance is tied to the body's temperature and arousal cycle, the process underlying complex task performance is unknown at this time. To further complicate this issue, some studies have not shown the night superiority in complex task performance found by Monk and Embrey (1981). Researchers currently believe that the complex task performance cycle is itself very complex, varying widely with the type of complex task. Evidence also exists suggesting that the biological clock underlying complex performance adjusts more readily (less than 10–14 days) to changes in sleep schedules than the clock underlying simple task performance (Folkard, 1990).

The implications of these task-based performance differences for scheduling shift work in industry are enormous. For example, routine, highly learned, or monotonous work should be automated or closely monitored at night. Slowly rotating or fixed shifts would also aid simple task performance, assuming workers also adjusted their sleeping hours accordingly. Complex tasks, requiring judgment and decision making, might be more effectively performed at night and on rapidly rotating (every 2 or 3 days) shift systems, assuming workers retained their day orientation and were not sleep-deprived. Unfortunately, industry has largely neglected to consider these issues when designing shift systems (Monk, 1989; C. S. Smith et al., 1999).

Health. A paradoxical finding in shift work research is that shift workers often report fewer health complaints than comparable day workers. Workers who are the most distressed frequently leave shift work early, and those who remain in shift work undoubtedly comprise a select group (Angersbach et al., 1980). Frese and Okonek (1984) maintained that published statistics are probably biased because they do not distinguish among the reasons workers left shift work and therefore underestimate the number of workers who left specifically for health reasons. "Reminiscence" data from former shift workers (retired police officers) even indicated that, in retrospect, they perceived their health and well-being as being worse than they realized at the time (Spelten, Barton, & Folkard, 1993).

Gastrointestinal disorders are the most prevalent health problems associated with shift and night work (Angersbach el al., 1980; Koller, 1983; Vener, Szabo, & Moore, 1989). Rutenfranz, Knauth, and Angersbach's (1981) review of health statistics for over 30,000 workers reported the incidence of gastric ulcers to be .3–7% for day workers, 5% for shift workers with no night work, 2.5–15% for shift workers on the night shift, and 10–30% for shift workers who left shift work. More recently, Costa, Folkard, and Harrington (2000) estimated that 20–75% of shift and night workers, compared to 10–25% of day workers, complain of irregular bowel movements and constipation, heartburn, gas, and appetite disturbances. In many cases, these complaints eventually develop into chronic diseases, such as chronic gastritis and peptic ulcers (Costa, 1996).

Night work, not just shift work, appears to be the criticial factor in the development of gastrointestinal disease (Angersbach et al., 1980). A review of 36 studies covering 50 years of data and 98,000 workers indicated that disorders of the digestive tract were two to five times more common among shift workers who experienced night work than among day workers or shift workers who did not work at night (Costa, 1996).

Tucker, Smith, Macdonald, & Folkard (1998) also found that the length of shifts and the timing of the changeover from night to morning shifts predicted self-reports of physical health. Specifically, they found that shift workers' reported health was poorer (e.g., digestive problems) for relatively longer shifts (i.e., 12 hours vs. 8 hours) and relatively early changeovers (i.e., 6 a.m. vs. 7 a.m.).

Shift work researchers have often speculated that gastrointestinal problems may be greater for shift workers because they have more limited access to healthy food than day workers (i.e., restaurants and stores are often closed at night), and their irregular hours encourage inconsistent dietary habits. Although no confirming studies have been reported (e.g., Tepas, 1990), Lennernas, Hambraeus, & Akerstedt (1994) investigated a large number of nutritional variables across both shift workers and day workers. They found no differences in nutritional intake among the groups. Other factors, such as circadian disruption or sleep deficits, may be the culprit in this case (Vener et al., 1989).

Despite years of debate, most researchers now acknowledge that a relationship between shift work and cardiovascular disease exists (e.g., Tucker, Barton, & Folkard, 1996). In a controlled study, Koller (1983) found that 19.9% of shift workers suffered from some form of cardiovascular disease compared to 7.4% of day workers. Using data from a longitudinal study spanning 15 years, Knutsson, Akerstedt, Jonsson, & Orth-Gomer (1986) also reported an increased risk of cardiovascular disease in shift workers. In a recent review of the epidemiological literature on cardiovascular disease and shift work, Boggild and Knutsson (1999) calculated that shift workers have a 40% increase in risk in cardiovascular mortality or morbidity over day workers.

Similar to our discussion on the origin of gastrointestinal disorders in shift workers, the etiology of cardiovascular disorders is unknown (Akerstedt & Knutsson, 1997). The risk factors for cardiovascular disease are consistent with many of the problems associated with shift work, such as gastrointestinal symptoms, sleeping dysfunction, and smoking. Shift work can also function as a stressor, thus exacerbating the stress response over time and resulting in increased blood pressure, heart rate, and cholesterol (Costa, 1996).

Attitudes and Social Factors. Shift workers' job-related attitudes have not been widely researched, but existing data suggest that shift workers are more disgruntled than their day-working counterparts. In general, shift workers report lower job satisfaction (Agervold, 1976; Furnham & Hughes, 1999; Herbert, 1983), need fulfillment, and emotional well-being (Frost & Jamal, 1979) than their day-working counterparts. These negative attitudes can probably be attributed, at least in part, to the personal problems that seem to be associated with shift work.

The negative effects of shift work are most pronounced in shift workers' nonwork lives. The most frequent complaint voiced by shift workers is that shift work interferes with their personal lives, particularly their marital and parental roles (Jackson, Zedeck, & Summers, 1985; Staines & Pleck, 1984). The interference is most strongly felt when shift work schedules require night and weekend work that conflicts with family activities. In a rare study of the views and feeling of shift workers' partners, L. Smith and Folkard (1993) reported that shift workers' spouses were unhappy with their partners' shift work and felt that their lives were substantially disrupted by it. This sentiment was echoed in a survey of over 1,400 hourly workers, in which divorces and separations were reported to be 50% more frequent in night workers than in other groups of workers (Tepas et al., 1985).

In addition to the disruption associated with unusual or changing schedules, shift work can impose excessive domestic load: Shift workers, and particularly women, frequently work at night and tend to domestic and child-rearing duties during the day. This type of schedule does not allow sufficient time for sleep and leisure activities. As evidence, female night workers with two children sleep on the average 9 hours less per week than unmarried female day workers (Gadbois, 1981). Men who work the night shift sleep approximately 8 hours less per week than their day-working counterparts.

Whether married or unmarried, shift workers often complain that they are unable to become involved in social, community, and religious activities because of their work schedules (Folkard, Minors, & Waterhouse, 1985; Monk, 1989). A survey of British shift workers in the steel industry found that their major complaint was their work schedule's effect on their social life. This social isolation undoubtedly contributes to the fewer friends and more leisure time spent in solitary pursuits reported by shift workers compared to day workers (Herbert, 1983; Walker, 1985). Similarly, Bohle & Tilley (1998) found that night shift workers expressed negative attitudes toward shift work and a primary expressed explanation was the social isolation resulting from sleep during the daytime.

Shift workers' relationships and life outside of work appear to be almost universally negatively affected by their hours of work. Their employing organizations and the shift workers themselves can accomplish much toward alleviating these effects, which is a topic we turn to next.

Shift work Coping Strategies. The preceding discussion has presented a bleak picture indeed: Shift workers suffer greater health problems, more negative attitudes, decreased job performance, and increased personal problems relative to comparable day workers. In addition, roughly 20% of all workers who attempt shift work are unable to successfully adapt to its demands (Monk, 1988). These problems will not diminish in the future as the percentage of shift workers grows with increased automation and computerization, continuous manufacturing operations, and 24-hour service facilities. Fortunately, there are a number of personal and organizational strategies to aid adaptation to unusual and changing work schedules (Table 4.3).

TABLE 4.3   SUMMARY OF RECOMMENDATIONS FOR SHIFT WORKERS

1. Keep a set or ROUTINE sleeping schedule as much as possible. Sleep the same number of hours each day or night. While on one shift, go to sleep the same time each day or night.

2. Eat meals at the same or similar times of the day and night. While on one shift, adopt an eating schedule and stick to it.

3. If you're hungry eat a light snack before going to sleep.

4. Exercise regularly but not within 2–3 hours before sleeping.

5. Limit use of caffeine and alcohol. Don't take caffeine within 4–5 hours of bedtime.

6. While sleeping during the day: (1) Pick the quietest room, and reduce light and noise as much as possible; (2) Encourage family members to recognize "quiet times."

7. Relax before going to bed, and regard the bedroom as only a place to relax and sleep.

8. Focus on ADAPTATION. Shift work can be difficult, but it can also be an acceptable, alternative way to schedule work.

From an organizational perspective, shift systems should be designed with some regard for human circadian functioning. From a circadian perspective, a fixed shift allows workers to adapt fully to his or her specific schedule and is therefore potentially the best type of shift schedule. However, on days off, shift workers often revert back to a day schedule and must re-adapt to their shift schedule when they return to work. This situation is equivalent to a self-imposed rotating shift system. Because rotating shift systems do not restrict shift workers to evening or night work, such schedules are becoming increasingly popular in America, and they are already common in some European countries.

Because of the popularity of rotating shift systems, shift work researchers have debated which variation of the rotating shift is optimal. All experts agree that the weekly rotating system, which is very common in the United States, most likely has negative effects on worker health and performance because the body only partially adapts to the new schedule within the 7-day interval (Czeisler, Moore-Ede, & Coleman, 1982; Monk, 1989). Beyond the agreed admonition against weekly rotating schedules, shift work researchers are divided on the best type of rotating system, with some advocating a rapidly rotating system (Akerstedt, 1985) and some a slowly rotating system (Czeisler et al., 1982). Regardless of type, however, every shift system should be implemented only after a detailed analysis of the specific situation, which may consider such factors as the type of worker and job tasks (Monk, 1989).

At the individual level, two factors, circadian type (C. S. Smith, Reilly, & Midkiff, 1989) and age, seem to influence adjustment to shift work. You are undoubtedly familiar with people who feel best in the early morning hours and prefer to arise and retire early: They are often called *larks* or *morning types*. Conversely, other people feel best in the evening or night hours and prefer to arise and retire late: They are called *owls* or *evening types*. Extreme morning types especially seem to experience difficulty coping with night work and changing shifts (Hildebrandt & Stratmann, 1979; Moog, 1993). Age also affects adaptation to shift work because, as people age, their circadian rhythms become more morning-oriented and less flexible; shift workers in their 40s and 50s often experience sleeping difficulties and decreased well-being (Foret, Bensimon, Benoit, & Vieux, 1981; Monk & Folkard, 1985). Consequently, organizations should counsel both morning types and older shift workers about the potentially negative effects of night work for them.

In addition to designing shift systems to be consistent with human circadian functioning and monitoring certain types of high-risk shift workers, organizations can generally improve adaptation to shift work by providing education and counseling. Information about the effects of changing sleep–wake cycles and coping with such lifestyles should be incorporated into existing employee orientation and development programs (e.g., Monk, 1988; Monk & Folkard, 1992; C. S. Smith, Reilly, Moore-Hirschl, Olsen, & Schmieder, 1989; Table 4.3).

Blue-Collar versus White-Collar Work

Based on the stressors just discussed, it might be tempting to draw a simple distinction between blue-collar and white-collar work, such that the macro-level stressors we examined pertain more to blue-collar occupations. After all, stressors like excessive noise and shift work are often (although not always) associated with industrial work or trade occupations. Thus, from an organizational standpoint, should stressors be classified as either "blue-collar stressors" or "white-collar stressors"? In this section, we would like to point out that such a simple distinction is misleading.

Wallace, Levens, and Singer (1988) offered some thoughts about the concept of blue-collar work. Wallace noted that researchers have not been able to agree on exactly what constitutes blue-collar work. The term historically implied unskilled, manual work performed for an hourly wage, but has been widely applied to many types of service work, such as the jobs of janitors, waiters (food servers), and beauticians (hairstylists). Other definitions have included both skilled and unskilled work in service or production jobs, or any work that is not professional or managerial.

One of the problems in classifying blue-collar work is that occupation is closely related to social class, which is itself related to housing options, leisure pursuits, diet, access to medical care, and educational attainment, among other things. Of course, all of these factors individually and collectively greatly affect individual lifestyle (Sorensen et al., 1985). For example, smoking, alcohol consumption, and unhealthy eating appear to be more prevalent among blue-collar workers than white-collar (especially professional and managerial) workers (Badura, 1984; McMichael & Hartshorne, 1980; Wallace et al., 1988). The link between lifestyle (especially the health risk factors just mentioned) and medical or health outcomes has long been acknowledged. Therefore, not only are blue-collar workers exposed to environmental risk factors at work (e.g., extreme heat, loud noise), their lifestyle exposes them to additional risk factors.

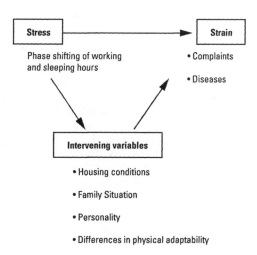

Figure 4.1 Model of Stress, Intervening Variables, and Strain associated with Shiftwork
(adapted from Rutenfranz et al., 1981)

The lower echelons of white-collar work and the upper echelons of blue-collar work are also often undistinguishable. The classification of certain service occupations, (e.g., police, firefighters, and nurses) has been particularly perplexing; these jobs have even been labelled as nonprofessional white-collar. One of the reasons for the definitional confusion between white- and blue-collar work is that the traditional boundaries are disappearing in contemporary organizations. Advances in automation and technology, particularly computer technology, have eased the physical demands of many blue-collar jobs and elevated their status (Briner & Hockey, 1988; Howell, 1991). Computerized production workers, for example, operate keyboards and read technical material from computer screens. They often have computer access to information, such as equipment costs and specifications, formerly available only to management.

Conversely, computer technology has resulted in the de-skilling of many white-collar jobs (Charmot, 1987). Office workers seated in front of a computer screen for 8 hours every day often find that computerization has resulted in work tasks that are simpler, fractionated, and more boring than before. White-collar work, in this case, has assumed many aspects of assembly-line or production work, including specialization and higher speed and accuracy requirements. Added to the "routinization" of their job tasks, many workers at all levels are having to adapt to some form of computer monitoring of work performance (see Chapter 5).

These new white-collar jobs may benefit from the broader view of job-related boredom provided by C. D. Fisher (1993). Fisher extended prior conceptualizations of boredom, which focused primarily on a limited number of task- and person-specific issues (see previous discussion), to include attributes of the task, environment, person and person-environment fit. For example, she hypothesized that strengthening perceptions of internal control of worker behavior (e.g., greater autonomy through relaxation of rules and work procedures) and implementing goal setting programs may alleviate job-related boredom. In both cases, workers should perceive greater personal investment, and, consequently, increased involvement, in their work activities.

S. Fisher (1985) claimed that, even though the gap between white- and blue-collar work may be narrowing, the blue-collar worker still endures greater industrial (environmental) hazards and less comfortable physical working conditions than the typical white-collar worker. Blue-collar work also frequently commands less pay and status than white-collar work. All of these factors add up to the blue-collar worker perceiving high demands (stressors) and reduced control at work. According to Karasek's job demands-control theory of work stress (Chapter 2), individuals who work in high-demand, low-control jobs are more likely to experience job-related stress and stress-related illnesses. Thus, we expect that the blue-collar worker would incur higher work distress with the resulting consequences.

Nevertheless, Wallace et al. (1988) asserted that "a division into blue- and white-collar groupings is no longer a meaningful exercise" (p. 56). Indeed, Wallace and her colleagues' in-depth assessment of blue– white-collar differences collected from 919 workers randomly drawn from a large data bank found surprisingly few differences between the two groups. In the years ahead, blue- and white-collar workers may share the same job stressors or they may develop entirely new sets of stressors. For example, a production worker who formerly enjoyed physically active work may find sitting at a computer screen highly stressful. Regardless of the outcome, future discussions specifically of blue-collar stress may be meaningless or, at the very least, quite different from the current ones.

CONCLUSIONS

In this chapter, we adopted a macro-perspective by examining occupations or job types and the work environment (physical and organizational characteristics) as sources of stress. We reported that, although many stressors are specific to certain occupations, many jobs share a common set of stressors. Numerous lower-level or industrial jobs also require workers to adapt to environmental stressors, routinized work, and night and shift work. Researchers have discovered a great deal about the parameters of human functioning under noise and temperature stress in the laboratory. However, the generalizability of their findings to workers who are chronically exposed to several of these environmental stressors over years is unknown. Conversely, from both laboratory and field studies, researchers have amassed considerable knowledge about routinized work and shift work, although little of that information has been directly applied to organizations.

To conclude this chapter, we would like to pose a series of questions arising from the material presented in this chapter and offer our responses accordingly.

1. *From a practical standpoint, should individuals be assessed on a common set of stressors, or should stress assessments be tailored to particular occupations or jobs?*

On the one hand, some commonalities in stressors across occupations do seem to exist. On the other hand, however, specific occupations are associated with stressors that do not generalize across occupations. Perhaps the solution is to consolidate stress assessment measures by including both generic items as well as items tailored to specific occupations. We will consider the issue of stress assessments more fully in our discussion of stress management in Chapter 8 (also see Chapter 2).

2. *Should one assume that physical stressors, such as noise or heat, have equal effects across individuals, thus directly leading to unwanted outcomes?*

There is no question that excessive noise or heat can directly lead to unwanted and potentially dangerous physiological outcomes, such as hearing damage or heat stroke, respectively. However, the role of cognitive appraisal should not be discounted; even if the stressor is physical and can lead to strains.

The key point is that the process of cognitive appraisal will directly influence the outcomes of the stress process. For example, a loud air conditioner may be perceived by some individuals as an extreme nuisance and stressor, affecting their concentration, making them anxious, and raising their blood pressure. Other individuals exposed to the same sound may not be bothered by it nearly as much (or at all). Similarly with heat, individuals vary in terms of their subjective appraisals of how hot it actually is. In sum, cognitive appraisal is an important component of the stress process for both physical and nonphysical stressors; and the appraisal process has direct implications for psychological, behavioral, and physiological outcomes.

3. *Should job enrichment programs be uniformly applied to reduce or alter jobs commonly viewed as monotonous or boring?*

Clearly, technological constraints may limit the ability to reconceptualize some jobs to render them less routine and boring. Nonetheless, for at least some work commonly perceived as monotonous, it is possible to reconfigure the work to make it more challenging and interesting. One example is the use of autonomous work groups in a manufacturing setting (Wall, Kemp, Jackson, & Clegg, 1986).

Although it might seem logical to equate the enrichment of a job with job improvement, improvement is in the eye of the beholder. Indeed, a recent review of job-redesign studies provided by Briner and Reynolds (1999) suggests that generally these interventions lead to somewhat mixed reviews: Some improvements are realized (e.g., job satisfaction) while some negative consequences result as well (e.g., increased absenteeism). An implicit assumption underlying these interventions is that all employees would like a job with more challenge and responsibility. However, there are individual differences across employees in terms of their receptivity to an enriched job (Hackman & Oldham, 1980). Some employees would rather have a routine, boring job and would see an increase in responsibility as a serious stressor. This point underscores the challenge organizational psychologists face when introducing an organizational-level intervention: How does one accommodate the almost inevitable variability across employees exposed to any intervention? At a minimum, any intervention such as job enrichment must be carefully considered and the implications—both positive and negative—anticipated before actually enacting the intervention.

4. *When selecting applicants for hire in a job involving shift work, should screening tests be developed, such that adaptability to shift work is considered as a selection criterion?*

Clearly, one may be able to determine that some applicants are more likely to be stressed by shift work than others. One may even be able to determine that some applicants will more likely be effective on day shifts compared to night shifts. However, no evidence exists suggesting that adaptability to shift work (as we currently measure it) will predict job performance beyond other more traditional selection predictors, such as selection interviews and cognitive ability tests. For a shift work predictor to be useful and, perhaps legally defensible, the predictor must forecast job performance beyond other predictors already in use. The idea is arguably a provocative one and worthy of future research. Of course, as we discussed previously, these predictors have been successfully used in shift worker counseling and development programs for some time.

MICRO-LEVEL WORK SRESSORS

CHAPTER 5

*Role-Stress and Contemporary
Sources of Stress*

ROLE-STRESSORS AT WORK

In Chapter 4, we explained that macro-level stressors often involve characteristics of the physical environment (e.g., noise, heat) or the work itself (e.g., machine-paced tasks). Micro-level stressors, however, are usually more related to the worker's role in the organization, or the tasks, duties, and expectations that identify his or her position in the organization. For example, a clerk-typist's work role might be defined by such tasks and duties as typing correspondence, filing papers, sorting mail, and making ledger entries. The clerk-typist has her own expectations about which tasks are most critical in the performance of her job. However, her coworkers and supervisor also have expectations about these aspects of her work role often have very different perceptions not only about how critical certain job duties and tasks are, but even whether they should be performed at all!

The Role Episode Model: The Birth of Work-Role Stressors

Much organizational stress research in the last 30 years has investigated what happens when workers experience difficulties with their work-role demands. Work-role demands result both from the specific responsibilities associated with formal job descriptions and the informal responsibilities that grow with jobs. For example, typing correspondence is undoubtedly a formal work-role responsibility for the clerk-typist,

113

although greeting clients or making coffee may be informal responsibilities that developed over time. Those individuals who directly interact with a worker in the performance of his or her job-related activities are often referred to as that worker's *role set;* supervisors and coworkers are the most obvious members of a worker's role set, although people outside the organization (e.g., clients, customers, suppliers) can also be part of the role set. In role theory terminology, the clerk-typist is called the *focal person* and the supervisors and coworkers who directly interact with her the *role senders;* the focal person and role senders collectively define the role set.

The concepts embodied in role theory began in the 1950s with the work of Parsons (1951), Merton (1957) and Gross, Mason, and McEachern (1958). However, the birth of organizational role stress research really occurred in 1964 with the publication of Kahn et al.'s book entitled *Organizational Stress: Studies in Role Conflict and Ambiguity.* It was the first major publication to inspire sustained interest in the topic of work stress. Although previous theoreticians like Selye mentioned the workplace in their writings, this book really made the topic of job-related stress an area of serious, scientific inquiry.

Kahn et al. provided a theoretical basis for the study of organizational role stress with their Role Episode Model (Fig. 5.1), in which a focal person and role senders interact while being influenced by organizational factors (e.g., structure, size), personality factors (e.g., values, motives), and interpersonal relations (e.g., personal and group influence). *Role pressures* result from role senders' expectations for the focal person's role performance. These role pressures, whether evaluated subjectively by the focal person or objectively by role senders or others outside the role set, were classified by Kahn et al. (1964) as different forms of either role conflict or role ambiguity.

Role Conflict and Role Ambiguity. *Role conflict* occurs when role demands clash. Kahn et al.'s typology of role conflict includes four different forms of role conflict. *Intrasender conflict* occurs when one role sender communicates conflicting or incongruent messages to the focal person. For example, a department manager asks his subordinates to increase productivity but cut overtime. *Intersender conflict* arises when two or more role senders send conflicting or incongruent messages to the focal person. This type of role conflict is commonly found in organizations when a worker has two or more supervisors; often, satisfying one supervisor neglects or conflicts with the demands of the other. *Interrole conflict* occurs when two or more roles conflict for the focal person. A common example is the conflict that frequently occurs when a working woman juggles the different role demands of work and family. This particular form of interrole conflict has generated considerable interest in recent years, and we will address it separately in a later section examining work-family conflict. *Person-role conflict* arises from incongruities between the needs and values of the focal person and the expectations of role senders. This type of conflict can occur when role

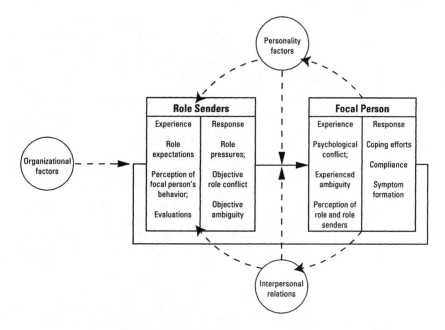

Figure 5.1 Kahn, Wolfe, Quinn, Snoek, and Rosenthal's (1964) Role Episode Model, Including Factors Involved in Adjustment to Role Conflict and Role Ambiguity, pp. 26, 30.

requirements violate the focal person's moral values; for instance, her superiors may expect an executive to pad the expenses billed to a client although such practices violate the executive's personal code of ethics.

Beyond the four types just described, Kahn et al. (1964) also realized that other, more complex forms of conflict may arise. *Role overload* occurs when the focal person cannot meet all of his or her role demands within a given time frame. Kahn et. al. thought this role pressure frequently results from a complex combination of intersender conflict (i.e., conflicting expectations from multiple role senders) and person-role conflict (i.e., conflicting priorities). Role overload is a very common form of role conflict in contemporary organizations, where downsizing has often shifted more responsibility to a shrinking workforce.

Role ambiguity results whenever the focal person perceives that role demands are ambiguous or unknown. Kahn et al. (1964) defined role ambiguity either as task ambiguity or socioemotional ambiguity.

Task ambiguity results when inadequate or confusing information exists concerning how to perform certain tasks related to the focal person's role.

Task ambiguity covers three specific forms: ambiguity regarding the scope of one's work-role responsibilities, how these responsibilities should be fulfilled, and which role senders must be appeased. In other words, these three forms translate into the questions: What should be done, how should it be done, and who cares whether it is done?

Socioemotional ambiguity refers to ambiguity regarding the consequences of the focal person's work role behaviors. This type of ambiguity considers the uncertainty about how one's behavior affects him or herself, the role set, or the total organization. As an example, a manager may be uncertain if his employee development plan will reflect well on him in his next performance review, if his subordinates will perceive the plan positively, and if the plan is consistent with the long-term goals of the organization.

An application of several of the components of the theoretical model (Fig. 5.1) might be helpful. Suppose Samantha works for Acme Automobile Corporation as a design engineer. Her supervisor expects that Samantha will complete the laboratory and road testing of a new truck model (role expectations) so it can be marketed. Samantha is experiencing (role) pressure to complete the test battery because the company believes that sales generated from the new truck will increase its third-quarter profits (organizational factors). Samantha experiences this pressure as conflict because she believes that rushing the new truck to market will compromise the rigorous quality control program every new product must undergo (person-role conflict). She worries that a hastily marketed truck may prove to be unsafe. Samantha's tendency to always see things in a negative light (personality factor) and her poor relationship with her supervisor (interpersonal relations) further increase Samantha's sense of conflict and her negative perceptions of Acme and her supervisor. She deals with this demand by working overtime to complete the project (response: coping efforts). Unfortunately, these pressures also prompt Samantha's migraines to flare up, causing her considerable discomfort (response: symptom formation). Samantha's difficulty in complying with these organizational demands results in displeasure in the corporate office and lower expectations for future projects (feedback loop).

To test hypotheses generated by the role episode model, Kahn et al. (1964) conducted two major studies, an intensive study and a national survey. In both studies, data were collected using a structured interview format. In the intensive study, approximately 50 focal persons and their role set (immediate supervisors, subordinates, and coworkers) were identified and interviewed. In the national survey, 725 workers were identified and interviewed from a large national sample encompassing both urban and rural areas. The purpose of the intensive study was to provide detailed information on the exact processes by which role pressures develop and are acted on in organizations. The national survey was designed to complement the intensive study by enabling the researchers to determine whether the information generated in the intensive study generalized to large groups of workers in the United States. As hypothesized, Kahn et al. found that the role conflict generated by role senders' role pressures resulted in a number of negative consequences or strains (e.g., job-related tension, job dissatisfaction); role ambiguity was also associated with substantial strains (e.g., decreased self-confidence, perceptions of futility).

Kahn et al.'s (1964) findings and their implications sparked perhaps one of the largest thrusts of organization research in the second half of the twentieth century. Twenty years and several hundred studies later, Jackson and Schuler (1985) conducted a meta-analysis, or quantitative review, of the research literature on role conflict and role ambiguity. They reported that increased levels of these role stressors were associated with lower worker participation, lower organizational commitment, higher tension and anxiety, and higher propensity to leave the organization. (We will have more to say about these relationships in Chapter 6.) Thus, Jackson and Schuler directly reaffirmed the negative organizational and personal consequences of role conflict and role ambiguity that Kahn and his colleagues first documented in the early 1960s. Moreover, research suggests that role conflict and role ambiguity may interact to predict lowered levels of job performance (Fried, Ben-David, Tiegs, Avital, & Yeverechyahu, 1998). Thus, the combination of both forms of role-stress may be a lethal combination from the standpoint of work performance.

Other Work-Role Stressors.   Although role conflict and ambiguity have dominated role stress research in the last 25 years, other role-related variables are also potentially important white-collar stressors. By definition, the manager typically manages the work of employees in the organization, which implies that the manager's work role includes *responsibility for other people*. Responsibility is esteemed in contemporary society. However, the risks of failure are often great, resulting in personal and professional trauma. Surprisingly, few researchers have investigated this role stressor. Caplan (1971), who studied the risk factors associated with coronary heart disease in a group of NASA employees, discovered that those workers who had responsibility for people also smoked more heavily. (Of course, smoking is a widely acknowledged risk factor for heart disease.) Responsibility for others can be particularly stressful when it conflicts with organizational goals (e.g., maintaining services while curtailing costs; Baglioni, Cooper, & Hengley, 1990). Some occupations are also stressful because they inherently involve responsibility for other people. Air traffic control, teaching, health care, law enforcement, and social work are occupations that are considered stressful because they are associated with responsibility for people (Chapter 4).

A manager's role is characterized by constant interactions with people, both internal and external to the organization (Mintzberg, 1973). Therefore, *interpersonal problems with coworkers* is another possible work role stressor. French and Caplan (1973) reported a relationship between role ambiguity and poor interpersonal relationships at work. According to these researchers, this relationship suggests that interpersonal problems stifle effective communications, which lead to role ambiguity and other problems, such as low job satisfaction. Another study (Smith & Sulsky, 1995) reported that interpersonal problems with coworkers was a frequently cited stressor across three diverse groups of workers. More recently, Frone (2000) tested a model of interpersonal conflict at work. The major predictions of the model were supported: Specifically, conflict with supervisors was associated with organizational outcomes, such as job satisfaction and turnover, and conflict with coworkers was associated with personal outcomes, such as depression. This topic deserves more attention from researchers, especially given the prevalence of interpersonal conflict in most work settings and the methodological shortcomings of existing studies (i.e., cross-sectional, self-report data).

A Critique of Organizational Role Stress Research

Over the past few decades, behavioral scientists have intensively researched the influence of role-based stressors, particularly role conflict and ambiguity, and have consistently found that these stressors predict both personal and work-related outcomes. Some research, albeit limited, has also been conducted with the goal of establishing causal linkages between role stressors and select outcomes (e.g., Kemery, Bedeian, Mossholder, & Touliatos, 1985). However, there were some rather stringent criticisms of this research.

King and King (1990) recommended that the definitions of role conflict and role ambiguity should be clarified. Most of the research on role conflict and ambiguity has used the self-report scales developed by Rizzo, House, and Lirtzman (1970; see Chapter 3, Fig. 3.1), which measure the subjective perceptions of the focal person's role conflict and ambiguity. However, Kahn et al. (1964) conceived of role conflict and ambiguity as possessing both subjective components, as experienced by the focal person, and objective components, as reported by the focal person's role set (see Fig. 5.1). Very few studies have attempted to assess the objective components of role stressors by measuring how members of the role set perceive the focal person's role (e.g., asking coworkers or supervisors how stressful they consider the focal person's work-role activities to be).

When both subjective and objective components have been measured, they often do not agree (Smith & Tisak, 1993). This lack of agreement may simply indicate that the focal person and his or her role set are observing different aspects of the role sending and receiving process (see Fig. 5.1). For example, the focal person's coworkers may be unaware that he is experiencing conflicting expectations from two different supervisors. Or, the lack of agreement could indicate that the constructs themselves have not been adequately measured.

The possibility that the role constructs have not been adequately measured concurs with another criticism: Researchers have not attempted to determine if role conflict and ambiguity are truly multidimensional. For example, does intersender conflict exist apart from and function differently than intrasender conflict or socioemotional ambiguity? It seems logical that a worker who reports conflict with her supervisors will be hesitant to openly discuss performance issues with them. Consequently, she will also experience ambiguity about how her performance is perceived by her superiors. Most attempts to assess role conflict and ambiguity have not individually measured the different subtypes of role conflict and ambiguity. The Rizzo et al. (1970) scales, for example, do not directly measure intrasender conflict or socioemotional ambiguity (King & King, 1990). In answer to this criticism, Breaugh and Colihan (1994) developed three facet (dimentional) scales (work method ambiguity, scheduling ambiguity, and performance criteria ambiguity) to assess role ambiguity at work (see Table 5.1).

TABLE 5.1   BREAUGH AND COLIHAN'S (1994)
FACET AMBIGUITY SCALES

Work Method ambiguity: Uncertainty related to the methods or procedures for accomplishing work

"I am certain how to go about getting my job done (the methods of use)."

Scheduling Ambiguity: Uncertainty associated with scheduling or sequencing work tasks

"My job is such that I know when I should be doing a given work activity."

Performance Criteria Ambiguity: Uncertainty concerning job performance standards

"I know what level of performance is considered acceptable by my supervisor."

Whereas different subtypes of role conflict and ambiguity have not typically been assessed, research on *role overload,* which Kahn et al. (1964) conceived to be a form of role conflict, developed relatively independently of the other role constructs. Two types of overload have been measured: quantitative and qualitative. Quantitative overload results when workers report that they have too much or too many things to do (usually in a short time frame). As discussed in Chapter 4, modern managers frequently report quantitative overload. However, qualitative overload occurs when workers believe that they lack the ability or skills to perform competently, regardless of the time allotted. Technical occupations, such as science or engineering, are often associated with qualitative overload (see Chapter 4). Most of the research on overload has assessed the quantitative type and has found a relationship between quantitative overload and personal health (e.g., increased coronary risk factors; Sales, 1969) and job performance (e.g., increased absenteeism; Margolis, Kroes, & Quinn, 1974).

Figure 5.1 and the related discussion earlier in this chapter demonstrate the conceptual richness of Kahn et al.'s theoretical model. Unfortunately, that conceptual richness has never been realized in much of the role conflict and ambiguity research. For example, a typical empirical study might ask the study participants fill out several self-report measures (also see the study by Sutton and Rafaeli, 1987, in Chapter 3) that assess the frequency and/or intensity of their perceived role conflict, role ambiguity, job satisfaction, intent-to-turnover, and health complaints. Some type of correlational analysis would then be used to investigate the relationships between the role stressors and organizational and personal outcomes. The Kahn et al. model implies that data should also be collected from the study participant's role set (coworkers and supervisor) on the variables of interest. In addition, the model indicates that a variety of organizational, personality, and interpersonal factors can affect or moderate the process.

A review did examine the possibility of a moderator variable in the context of role ambiguity and strains (Frone, 1990). Specifically, using the quantitative review approach of meta-analysis, Frone hypothesized and found support for the idea that tolerance for ambiguity is an important moderator in the seven studies he considered. That is, the relationship between role ambiguity and strain is significantly greater for individuals who have difficulty tolerating ambiguity in their work roles. The results of this study are interesting; however, the conclusions were based on a limited number of studies. Thus, additional studies would be helpful to bolster the generalizability of the conclusions.

The Kahn et al. (1964) model clearly states that certain antecedent or precipitating organizational factors must provide the necessary conditions for role conflict or ambiguity (and their consequences) to occur. Although the three classes of variables have been investigated in role stress research, the inclusion of one or more variables from the three types (e.g., participation in decision making, an organizational factor, anxiety level, a personality factor) in any particular study does not seem to have directly evolved from considering the relationships implied by the model.

Finally, King and King (1990) recommended that researchers emulate Kahn et al.'s original theoretical framework by incorporating more causal or strong inference models in their research. Some studies (see Kemery et al., 1985; Kemery, Mossholder, & Bedeian, 1987; O'Driscoll & Beehr, 1994) have tested causal models (typically in the form of structural equation models; see Chapter 3) loosely derived from Kahn et al.'s model.

Kemery, Mossholder, and Bedeian (1987) used two hypothesized models of work-related stress (Beehr & Newman, 1978; Schuler, 1982) and one model of job satisfaction (Locke, 1976) to derive three competing causal models examining how role conflict and role ambiguity influence turnover intentions in organizations (see Fig. 5.2). Model A implies that the presence of role conflict and role ambiguity both influence the development of lower job satisfaction and higher numbers of physical symptoms, which lead to intentions to leave the job. Model B is essentially the same model as A except

a. Model predictions based on Beehr & Newman's model.

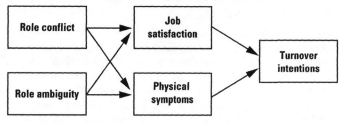

b. Model predictions based on Schuler's model.

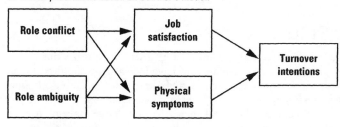

c. Model predictions based on Locke's model.

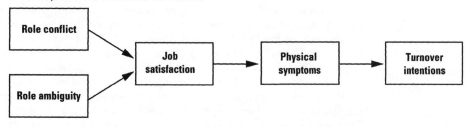

Figure 5.2 Alternative Study Predictions

that it hypothesizes that job satisfaction and physical symptoms are reciprocally related. That is, in addition to the influence of role conflict and ambiguity on satisfaction and symptoms, lower job satisfaction triggers more physical symptoms, which, in turn, triggers lower satisfaction, and so on. Of course, the end result in both models is increased intent to turnover. Model C assumes that the presence of role conflict and role ambiguity collectively contribute to the development of lower job satisfaction, which leads to increased physical symptoms, which then produces greater intent to leave the job. Although all models contain the same variables, models A and B imply that the role stressors simultaneously impact satisfaction and symptoms, which both lead to increased turnover intentions, while model C implies an ordered sequence of events (e.g., job satisfaction must first be reduced before symptoms are manifested).

Using 890 employees (faculty and staff) from a large university, Kemery et al. (1987) tested the three models. Employing structural equation modelling techniques, they found the strongest support for Model B. This model is considerably more complex than the other two because it hypothesizes that variables both simultaneously and mutually influence other variables (and are themselves influenced). Although Model B tested only selected components from Kahn et al.'s (1964) framework (psychological conflict, experienced ambiguity, and selected responses), these results support the validity of the type of complex relationships implied by the role episode model.

CONTEMPORARY STRESSORS

In the following section, we consider a variety of stressors that have become more pervasive in recent years and have increasingly captured the attention of both work stress researchers and the public at large. Although these stressors may appear to have little in common at first glance, they certainly share one commonality: All have become more salient over time as technology, job requirements, and life-demands continually evolve.

Work-Family Conflict

What is work–family conflict? Simply stated, work–family conflict is the conflict that ensues from competing role demands: the demands of work and the demands of family (Duxbury, & Higgins, 1991). For example, having to bring work home or working overtime may interfere with family-related responsibilities like child care. Family responsibilities may also interfere with work demands. Although, from an organizational standpoint, work–family conflict could be classified as a form of role conflict, we view work–family conflict as a type of stressor that is clearly on the increase in recent times. Thus we feel comfortable classifying it as a special type of contemporary stressor.

What evidence suggests that work–family conflict is on the rise? The commonly heard mantra "leaner and meaner" implies that organizations are asking more of employees as they downsize, merge, or otherwise restructure. Often, this request means a briefcase full of papers to work through in the evenings and on weekends. So, not surprisingly, a trend of working longer hours developed (Danna & Griffin, 1999; Maume & Houston, 2001), which undoubtedly has contributed to work–family conflict as well. Telecommuting ,or telework, defined as the substitution of computers and communications technology for physical travel to work on a regular basis (Olson & Primps, 1984; Van der Wielen, Taillieu, Poolman, & Van Zuilichem, 1995), has also become a recent trend, especially in jobs amenable to computerization. Telework may specifically lead to increases in family–work conflict because the individual is physically at home during working hours, and expectations among family members or friends may interfere with work responsibilities (cf. E. J. Hill, Miller, Weiner, & Colihan, 1998; Standen, Daniels, & Lamond, 1999). Finally, with the proliferation of dual-career couples (Hammer, Allen, & Grigsby, 1997; Mitchelson, & Burns, 1998), balancing work and home responsibilities has become increasingly difficult, leading to increases in work–family conflict.

What effects do family–work conflict have on satisfaction with both work and life in general? Kossek and Ozeki (1998) conducted a meta-analysis to answer this question. Overall, they found that work–family conflict negatively predicted both work and life satisfaction, and this was true for both situations where work-role demands caused difficulties meeting family-role demands and family-role demands negatively influenced the work role. However, the relationships were stronger for work-role demands affecting family-role demands, and some (albeit limited) evidence suggested that the relationships were stronger for women.

More recently, Allen, Herst, Bruck, and Sutton (2000) performed meta-analyses on the relationships among work–family conflict and work-related outcomes (e.g., job satisfaction, absenteeism), nonwork-related outcomes (e.g., life satisfaction, family satisfaction), and stress-related outcomes (e.g., depression, burnout). The relationships between work–family conflict and the stress-related outcomes, especially burnout and work-related stress, were among the strongest across all categories. These data suggest that dealing with family interferences brought on by work demands is a potent source of stress for most people. According to Allen et al. (2000), "The results of this review convincingly demonstrate the widespread and serious consequences of WFC (work–family conflict)," p. 301.

Evidence has also been accumulating that work–family conflict adversely affects mood. Williams and his colleagues (e.g., K. J. Williams & Alliger, 1994; K. J. Williams, Suls, Alliger, Learner, & Wan, 1991) have extensively studied mood in employed parents. In a study of working mothers, K. J. Williams et al. (1991) found that when juggling multiple role demands, these women reported that negative mood extended to other occasions within the same day but did not spill over to the next day.

These researchers used an interesting research method called experience sampling methodology (ESM; see also Teuchman, Totterdell, & Parker, 1999). In ESM, study participants receive signals from beepers or watches at random intervals and are instructed to answer one page of an individual ESM diary each time they hear the signal. This method allows the researcher to obtain an instantaneous record of events as they occur throughout the day or night. Williams and his colleagues reasoned that such a technique would circumvent the recall problems of retrospective self-report data because the data are recorded as they occur.

In a more recent study using data from both working mothers and fathers, K. J. Williams and Alliger (1994) confirmed that negative moods developed from work extended to family life, and negative moods emanating from home extended to work. However, the evidence for these effects was stronger for women.

Organizations are becoming well aware of the problems associated with work–family conflict. For example, one concept gaining popularity is *alternative work arrangements,* whereby employees are given some measure of flexibility in terms of both when and where they work (Powell & Mainiero, 1999). Flexible scheduling has been found to help mitigate against the stress associated with work–family conflict (Thomas & Ganster, 1995). Companies are also beginning to devote resources toward child care in the form of on-site care facilities (Thomas & Ganster, 1995). Even the government has become involved: In 1993 the U. S. Congress passed the Family and Medical Leave Act, providing parents with time off work following childbirth.

Telework and permanent part-time work are additional options some organizations are offering employees. These options hopefully may also mitigate the effects of family-role demands on work-role demands (Table 5.2). Two-thirds of *Fortune 1000* companies have telework programs, and it has been predicted that the numbers will increase over time (McClay, 1998). However, as noted earlier in this section, telework may contribute to the problem of family-role demands encroaching on work-role demands, especially if family members develop unreasonable expectations simply because Mom and/or Dad are physically at home.

TABLE 5.2   SOME ADVANTAGES AND DISADVANTAGES OF TELEWORK,
OR TELECOMMUTING

Advantages	Disadvantages
Responsiveness to Employee Needs	Alienation and Isolation from Workplace
• Family Responsiveness (Permits flexibility in arranging day care/babysitting and social commitments)	• Social Isolation (omits interactions with coworkers; no office "grapevine")
• Maternity Benefits (maintains contact woth work while on formal leave; not "gone, & forgotten" at promotion time)	• Career Development (less opportunity for skill development)
	• Exploitation (often associated with long hours and little pay; less possibility of union involvement)
• Illness and Disability (permits flexibility in assuming part-time or limited work schedules	• Burnout (promotes workaholism; greater temptation to work around the clock)

Models of Work and Family Conflict. Although behavioral scientists are beginning to understand the effects of work–family conflict for outcomes such as work and life satisfaction, how the work and family roles interact has been the subject of some debate. Alternative perspectives have been offered, such as the recent value incongruence model proposed by Perrewe and her colleagues (e.g., Perrewe & Hochwarter, 2001), which maintains that conflict may arise because important work and family values are not achieved. However, for some years, three different models, each claiming to explain how these roles interact, have dominated the research literature: the independence or segmentation model, the compensation model, and the spillover model (Wilensky, 1960).

The *independence or segmentation model* assumes that the two domains are mutually independent (P. Evans & Bartolome, 1984; Staines, 1980) and that a person's functioning in one domain has no influence on the other domain. Generally, this model specifies that work is associated with traditional masculine attributes (hard-driving, instrumental, competitive) and family/home with traditional feminine attributes (intimate, relationship-oriented, fun-loving) (Piotrkowski, 1978). The independence model is really not a type of mutual influence model, but a noninteractive or null model.

The *compensation model* postulates that people look to one domain to compensate for what is missing in the other domain (Evans & Bartolome, 1984; Liou, Sylvia, & Brunk, 1990). This compensation takes the form of differential investments people make in each domain (Champoux, 1978). For example, someone with a shattered marriage may immerse herself in her work activities because she cannot achieve a sense of efficacy in her personal life. Compensation has typically been measured as a negative relationship (correlation) between work and nonwork factors (e.g., work and family satisfaction).

The *spillover model* maintains that the influence of work on family and family on work are essentially inseparable (Liou et al., 1990; Staines, 1980). In the spillover model, the relationship between family and work are assumed to be truly reciprocal because attitudes and behaviors in one domain directly affect the other domain (Keon & McDonald, 1982; Kirchmeyer, 1992; S. R. Parker, 1967). Thus, according to this perspective, role demands from one arena (e.g., work) will have a direct and negative impact on the other role (cf. Leiter & Durup, 1996). The spillover perspective appears to be the one favored by work stress researchers in recent years because the essence of the work–family conflict construct is a negative spillover of one role to the other. This perspective has received the most research support (Kelloway & Barling, 1994; Rain, Lane, & Steiner, 1991; Rice, Near, & Hunt, 1980; Tait, Padgett, & Baldwin, 1989).

Although admittedly a bit of a digression, one should conceptually distinguish and disentangle the spillover effect from other conceptualizations of spillover (which are conceptually distinct from the spillover implicated in work–family conflict). First, spillover can be conceptualized from the standpoint of personal style. The caring parent, for example, would also become an employee-centered manager. The manager's success in motivating employees through mentoring, in turn, would reinforce those behaviors so that he becomes an even more nurturing parent.

Second, spillover can be conceptualized from the perspective that one does not necessarily leave work stress at the office (or life stress at home). The cliched scenario of the disgruntled employee who argues with his supervisor and then goes home to yell at the children and fight with her husband is an example of negative spillover.

Yet another conceptualization of spillover is the situation in which stress in one partner/spouse affects the stress levels of the other partner/spouse. Westman and Etzion (1995) examined this form of spillover in a sample of military couples from the Israeli army. Using structural equation modeling or SEM (Chapter 3), Westman and Etzion demonstrated that the experience of stress was bidirectional; stress from each spouse appeared to affect the other. Interestingly, a spouse's sense of control over his or her own life was found to affect the amount of spillover: A spouse with a high sense of personal control tended to "transmit" less stress to his or her spouse, compared to those who did not feel empowered by a sense of control.

Because potentially multiple conceptual definitions of spillover exist, the meaning of spillover must be clearly explicated in whatever context is being considered. Simply stated, one must always clearly define the constructs examined. Otherwise, both precision and understanding of the phenomena under scrutiny are lost.

Limitations of Work and Family Conflict Research. As the previous review has demonstrated, research on work–family conflict is clearly on the upsurge, and interest in the topic has grown in both the research and applied (i.e., work) communities. Nonetheless, a number of concerns can be raised regarding this area of research.

First, consensus must be reached on the precise meaning of the concept of "family." Its meaning has become more varied over the years, and little consensus exists on how precisely it should be defined (Rothausen, 1999). For example, there are two-parent families, unmarried partners with children, and so on. Any attempts to explicate conflict between work and family must do so with consideration to the meaning of the term.

Second, both Kossek and Ozeki (1998) and Allen et al. (2000) noted that much improvement is needed in how we assess work–family conflict. For example, measures should clearly specify exactly what form of conflict is being assessed: work affecting family or family affecting work (e.g., Frone, Russell, & Barnes, 1996). Some measures contain items addressing both directions of conflict, making it difficult to tease apart these two types of conflict.

Third, the issue of life stage in the study of work–family conflict should be considered. That is, the type of conflict experienced by a young married couple with young children is probably qualitatively and quantitatively different from a middle-aged married person with grown children. How the quality and quantity of conflict changes over the life span is an interesting question and suggests that a "one size fits all" approach to alleviating conflict may be impossible. Thus, for example, expending resources on child-care facilities may assist some workers, but not necessarily all of them.

Fourth, work–nonwork researchers have neglected to address some of the potentially positive consequences of having multiple roles. Prior research has focused almost exclusively on the negative effects of women's employment on children and marriage and, to a lesser extent, of family on women's employment. The positive aspects of work–nonwork roles have been mostly ignored. For example, married women, including married women with children, often report that they are more satisfied with their jobs than other groups of women (Roskies & Carrier, 1994). This research even suggests that, for women, family roles can buffer job stress and that the lack of a family may even be considered quite stressful (Gutek, Repetti, & Silver, 1988).

Fifth, researchers have focused their efforts almost exclusively on the manager or professional worker's traditional nuclear family (two parents and their children; Parker & Hall, 1992). Very little is known about work–nonwork stress in nonmanagerial workers with nontraditional families (e.g., minority industrial workers who are also single parents with extended families; Allen et al., 2000).

Sixth, the role of cognitive appraisal in the perception of work–family conflict has received little attention even though cognitive appriasal is central to most theories of work stress (Edwards & Rothbard, 1999). Accordingly, Edwards and Rothbard attempted to integrate the concept of P-E fit (Chapter 2) with the perception of work–family conflict. Their approach is welcome in that they adopted a theoretical framework to explain a phenomenon that has infrequently been grounded in established theory (Zedeck, 1992).

Finally, most work–nonwork research has used cross-sectional studies that simply examined the relationships between retrospective self-reports of such variables as work–family conflict, work and family involvement, and work and life satisfaction. Historically, few studies have used longitudinal, experimental, or strong inference (causal) designs (Allen et al. 2000). An exception is the work of Williams and his colleagues (Williams & Alliger, 1994; Williams et al., 1991; see earlier discussion), which used a research methodology called experience sampling to collect longitudinal data on mood spillover from juggling multiple roles. Some studies have also examined causal models of work–family roles (Duxbury & Higgins, 1991; Frone, Russell, & Cooper, 1992). Unfortunately, their results do not present a very optimistic picture of the plight of working parents, particularly of women in nonmanagerial or industrial jobs.

On a promising endnote, researchers have very recently begun to broaden the work–family construct, a limitation discussed earlier in this section. Most studies have included only workers who are married, have children, and/or elder care responsibilities (e.g., Frone, Russell, & Cooper, 1992; Hammer et al., 1997). As a result, workers who are single, childless, or who have no elder care responsibilities are ommitted from research studies. Yet, these workers may still perceive stress from work–nonwork conflict. To address this issue, organizations, and to some extent researchers (e.g., Fisher, Hoffman, Lin, Fuller, & Laber, 2000; E. J. Hill et al., 1998), are advocating the term "work–life balance" instead of work–family conflict. This comprehensive approach should provide a more realistic picture of all workers' struggles to achieve well-rounded lives.

Stress Associated with Managerial Work

A number of stress-related issues relevant to mangerial work has arisen as increasing numbers of women entered the managerial ranks over the past decade. With this influx, a number of questions can be raised: Given traditional gender stereotypes, do woman managers experience greater levels of stress compared to their male counterparts? Also, given the time demands inherent in many managerial positions, how do managers cope with the demands of the job and perhaps the demands of a family as well?

The manager or corporate executive of the 1970s and 80s was typically a man with a traditional wife who remained at home to care for the children. Is this stereotypical family still the norm? Given the organizational and cultural changes that have occurred in the previous 10-15 years, most people would respond "No." Brett, Stroh, and Reilly (1992) examined traditional stereotypes about the corporate manager in the 1990s by addressing seven generalizations (five of which follow) taken from the popular and research literatures.

Dual-Career Generalizations. Brett et al. (1992) used a random sample drawn from a 1990 data base of 1,000 managers transferred in 1987–1988 by twenty *Fortune 500* companies from eight different industries; these data were part of a larger study on employee relocation in the United States (Brett, Stroh, & Reilly, 1990). One of the most noteworthy contributions of Brett et al.'s (1992) research is that the breadth of their database permitted comparisons, not only between dual-career and traditional managers, but also between dual-career managers with and without children.

The first set of generalizations deals exclusively with female managers.

> **Generalization 1:** Female managers' career progression lags behind their male counterparts'. Not only were female managers progressing more slowly up the hierarchy, they also earned lower salaries than male managers. Brett et al. (1992) found that this generalization held for dual-career female managers with and without children. Interestingly, dual-career women with children were considered more frequently for relocation or transfer than dual-career women without children (although the two groups did not differ in the number of actual relocations). However, all types of male managers (dual-career and traditional, with and without children) were considered for relocation (and actually relocated) more frequently than dual-career female managers with and without children.

> **Generalization 2:** Female managers' work attitudes are as positive as those of male managers. The relocation study data agreed with this generalization on all dimensions except job involvement. Although female managers' levels of job satisfaction and organizational commitment were similar to the levels reported by male managers, female managers, especially those with children, reported lower levels of job involvement. This difference undoubtedly reflected the greater involvement of female managers in their nonwork lives.

The second set of generalizations investigated by Brett et al. (1992) pertains to male managers.

Generalization 3: Because dual-career male managers are less willing to relocate, their careers progress more slowly than careers of their traditional male counterparts. With relocation often closely related to promotion rates, this generalization makes sense. However, Brett et al. found that it applied only to dual-career male managers with children, who were being relocated and promoted at lower rates than all other groups of male managers. The salary progression of dual-career managers with children also lagged behind that of the other groups of male managers. Dual-career male managers without children were advancing at the same rate as (or faster than) traditional male managers. However, this finding did not hold for salary: The salaries of dual-career male managers without children had increased much less rapidly over several years than the salaries of the traditional male managers. One explanation offered for this effect was that the traditional male manager conformed to social expectations of the male as a sole provider and could draw on his unemployed wife to support his career advancement (e.g., the stereotype of the "country club" wife), both of which were rewarded by the organization (Pfeffer & Ross, 1982).

Generalization 4: Dual-career male managers are as satisfied with their jobs and personal lives as traditional managers. This generalization was supported by the relocation study and other studies (e.g., Kingston, 1988), and is consistent with much of the research on dual-career issues. Namely, because they are often the primary providers, with higher status jobs and higher salaries than their wives, dual-career managers are typically similar to traditional managers.

Much of this discussion has indirectly implied that children may affect the career progress of both female and male managers.

Generalization 5: Children have a negative influence on the career progress of both male and female managers. Is this indeed true? Both the relocation and other studies (e.g., Greenglass, Pantony, & Burke, 1988; Kline & Cowan, 1988) have consistently shown that, regardless of gender, managers with children are less satisfied with their lives and marriages than managers without children. This generalized dissatisfaction undoubtedly stems, at least in part, from the increased role conflict experienced by managers who are also parents. However, existing data also indicate that parents endure more than their share of corporate discrimination (Brett et al., 1992). The old adage that babies and boardrooms do not mix appears to have been taken to heart by corporate America and applied to both male and female managers.

Solutions to the Dual-Career Dilemma. Both men and women generally want families and fulfilling work. What, then, is the solution to this dilemma? Of course, one obvious solution is to enable working parents to gain access to affordable and reliable child care provided in a nurturing, enriched environment. Almost every working parent has faced the simultaneous occurrence of a sick child or an absent babysitter, and pressing work demands. For years, many European countries have acknowledged that women have as much right to paid employment as men, and have provided or largely subsidized child care for their citizens (Gutek, Repetti, & Silver, 1988). However, government involvement in child care, even in the form of sufficient state subsidies to have a real impact, seems to be highly unlikely given the fairly conservative political and social climate in America today.

Because the child-care issue is as much a work-related issue as a social or political problem, American business would seem to be the next most likely candidate for action. In the words of one business leader, "We have a nationwide shortage of decent, affordable child care. Employers are finding more parents coming to work with something on their minds besides their jobs." As we noted previously in our discussion of work–family conflict, organizations are beginning to devote resources to assist employees in this regard. The key word, however, is "beginning." The American Business Collaboration for Quality Dependent Care, composed of 156 corporations (e.g., IBM, AT&T, Johnson & Johnson, and Exxon), has invested millions in child care centers nationally. But, according to Lehman (1995), much greater corporate involvement is needed before significant progress can be achieved in improving quality child-care availability for working parents.

Computerization and Automation

In recent years, work environments from the plant floor to the office cubicle have become increasingly automated and/or computerized. What do you think your reaction would be if your supervisor told you that your job would soon be completely computerized and that your daily job duties would consist solely of sitting in front of a computer screen? Or, what if you were told that your services would no longer be needed because your job was being completely automated and would soon be obsolete? These two scenarios have been played out many times over the past decade and promise to follow the North American workforce into the future. Technological enhancement is often cited as one strategy to increase organizational effectiveness, to become more competitive in a highly competitive market. Unfortunately for both organizations and their employees, many organizational issues beyond the technical problems involved in implementing new technology (e.g., which computer hardware and software are most appropriate for specific functions) have rarely been considered.

One issue, discussed at length in Chapter 4, is the blurring of barriers between traditional white- and blue-collar work. While advances in technology, particularly computer technology, have eased the physical demands of many blue-collar jobs and elevated their status, the computerization of white-collar jobs has often produced work tasks that are simpler (less skilled), more fractionated, and more boring. The result of such changes is that many lower-level office jobs and low- to mid-level management positions have become redundant, and many office workers and managers realistically fear for their jobs (Kraut, 1987; Sinclair, 1986).

Given the widespread use of computers, another issue of concern is the alleged health problems associated with computer screens (video display terminals, or VDTs). These complaints range from skin rashes to miscarriages. In addition, one frequent complaint is the potential development of carpal tunnel or repetitive stress injury caused from the continuous act of typing on the computer keyboard.

Given the quantity of ergonomic research to determine the optimal design of computer systems, such complaints are indeed surprising. In 1983, the National Academy of Sciences appointed a panel to study the health risks associated with computer usage (Leeper, 1983). After careful study, the panel reported that there was no scientific evidence that, when designed according to current technology, computers per se were implicated in the development of health problems. However, the panel also indicated that health risks may develop from the manner in which computers are integrated into the work setting (see Korunka & Vitouch, 1999, for a recent extension of this argument).

One implication of the panel's findings is that, although we know quite a bit about the optimal design of computer systems, we know relatively little about how to appropriately introduce computerization into the workforce to ensure its acceptance and subsequent success (Turnage, 1990). Beyond the evidence that prior experience with computer technology influences attitudes toward computer usage (Rafaeli, 1986; Salanova & Schaufeli, 2000) and that these attitudes influence intentions to use computers or computer experience (Bagozzi, 1981; Hill, Smith, & Mann, 1987; Potosky & Bobko, 2001), our knowledge base about the subjective component of human-technology interaction is minimal. Unfortunately, a mystique exists about computers (Norman, 1984), such that inexperienced users often have negative, perhaps sometimes irrational, attitudes about them (Arndt, Clevenger, & Meiskey, 1985; Brock & Sulsky, 1994). These subjective components may outweigh the technical ones because, if workers have negative attitudes toward new technologies, they cannot (or will not) use them effectively.

Electronic Performance Monitoring (EPM)

One of the newest and most controversial technological innovations in contemporary workplaces is electronic performance monitoring (EPM). EPM provides management with access to workers' computer terminals through the use of computer networks. Through this access, managers can determine the pace and accuracy of their employees' online work activities. For example, computers can be programmed to monitor employee performance on a number of countable activities, such as the number of keystrokes made in a given time unit and the number of typing errors committed. In 1987 the U. S. Office of Technology Assessment reported that more than 6 million American workers experienced EPM; by 1990, that figure had grown in excess of 10 million workers (9 to 5, Working Women Education Fund, 1990). Most of the workers subject to EPM are clerical workers who perform simple, repetitive office work, although monitoring of upper-echelon employees is increasing (U. S. Congress, Office of Technology Assessment, 1987). In particular, monitoring of electronic correspondence (e.g., e-mail) represents an easy opportunity for organizations to "look in" on their workforce regardless of employees' positions in the organization.

The emergence of EPM has generated considerable interest in the research community for a number of reasons. First, EPM systems represent a viable alternative or supplement to the more typical process of using supervisors to subjectively evaluate employees. Second, EPM systems may be viewed by some as inherently more objective because the typical EPM system involves computer tracking of objective performance indicators (e.g., number of errors, time spent). These performance indicators may be perceived as more objective compared to supervisor ratings on dimensions such as leadership or creativity. Third, EPM may be seen more fair, to the extent that perceived objectivity is heightened.

In spite of some of the perceived advantages associated with EPM systems, many concerns have been raised. For example, does an EPM system bias evaluations to those aspects of performance that are most easily quantifiable? Given the emphasis placed on the quantity of performance in these systems, some employees might be tempted to sacrifice performance quality to maximize performance quantity. Additionally, some people question the ethics of EPM, especially when worker privacy is violated (e.g., monitoring the length of bathroom breaks).

Close scrutiny of individual behavior through EPM has generally been assumed to be stressful, so much that some European countries currently have laws that limit the extent of individual monitoring. Indeed, the assumed link between EPM and job-related stress appears to be a valid one: Several studies, both in the laboratory and field, have reported that EPM is associated with increased stress at work (Aiello & Shao, 1993; Amick & Smith, 1992; Davidson & Henderson, 2000; Gallatin, 1989; Irving, Higgins, & Safayeni,

1986; M. J. Smith, Carayon, Sanders, Lim, & LeGrande, 1992). For example, in a survey of over 700 telecommunications workers, M. J. Smith et al. (1992) found that monitored employees reported higher levels of tension, depression, anger, anxiety, fatigue, and anger than their non-monitored peers. In another survey of monitored workers, 81% of the respondents indicated that EPM increased their job-related stress (Gallatin, 1989).

In a laboratory study of data-entry operators, only those operators with substandard performance were selected to generate high workload demands in a numeric data-entry task performed over a 3-day period. Results indicated that those participants in the EPM condition showed more mood disturbance (e.g., irritation, tension) and musculoskeletal discomfort (Schleifer, Galinski, & Pan, 1992).

Finally, Silverman and Smith (1995) manipulated the source (computer vs. human) as well as the level of monitoring in a laboratory study of undergraduates performing a computerized mail-sorting task. Their data indicated an effect only for source on perceived (not physiological) stress: Participants reported that a human monitor was more stressful than a computer monitor! These results underscore the importance of controlled experimentation, even when field studies seem to be in agreement. On a lighter note, these results also make one give thanks that human beings will probably never be able to achieve the degree of monitoring easily achieved by a computer!

The next logical questions one may ask are: Specifically, why is EPM so stressful and is EPM worthwhile in productivity gains? EPM seems to be associated with increased stress because of the changes in job design that frequently accompany advances in technology. Monitored workers have complained about both increases in workload and decreases in personal control over the performance of their work activities (M. J. Smith et al., 1992). Other possibilities include decreased opportunities for socialization with coworkers as workers are more closely monitored and the deskilling and simplification of work in an effort to quantify it (Amick & Smith, 1992). The payback in performance is equivocal at this time. Some evidence suggests that EPM may facilitate performance only for easy tasks, and may actually hinder performance on complex tasks (see Aiello & Kolb, 1995). Beyond ethical and stress-related considerations, this represents a serious, bottom-line concern associated with EPM systems.

Given that EPM, in some form, is and will continue to be a fact of organizational life for many workers, Aiello and Kolb (1995) offered recommendations to employers, some of which we repeat here. First, to curtail the potential for an adversarial worker–management relationship fostered by EPM, efforts should be directed toward creating positive worker–management relationships through such activities as the development of shared performance goals. Second, to the extent possible, worker control should be increased through involving employees in the development of EPM systems and productivity standards (see Stanton & Barnes-Farrell, 1996). Aiello and Kolb (1995) suggested that the negative effects of EPM may be best understood using Karasek's (1979) demands–control model presented in Chapter 2. After all, EPM systems may cause jobs to be redesigned such that decision latitude decreases and demands for productivity increase.

Although much research examining the stress-related effects of EPM remains to be done, one thing is clear: EPM systems are on the increase as organizations attempt to integrate new and emerging technologies into the workplace. These systems have potentially profound implications for how work is accomplished and assessed, as well as how they affect employee attitudes and stress. As more of these systems are introduced and examined, researchers will be in a position to better appreciate what EPM can and cannot accomplish. Of fundamental importance is that the stress implications of EPM be fully understood and appreciated. The available evidence, although somewhat limited to date, suggests that EPM critics can clearly point to work stress as an unwanted outcome of the implementation of EPM systems.

ORGANIZATIONAL CHANGE AND TRANSITION

To stay competitive, organizations often adapt to the changing demands and circumstances of the marketplace and the environment. Major organizational changes—acquisitions, mergers, and downsizing—have become increasingly common as whole industries struggle for their economic survival. Such events frequently alter not only individual jobs, but also the structure and function of the organization itself.

One of the most widely publicized organizational changes was the divestiture of AT&T. Ashford (1988) studied a sample of employees in one of AT&T's marketing departments 1 month prior to and 6 months after that organization's transition to an unregulated entity. At the level of the individual employee, the change often meant a new work location, new job description, new coworkers, and new supervisors. She found that both the anticipation of the change and the change itself was perceived to be very stressful by creating uncertainty and disruption, respectively. Individual coping resources and responses proved not to be extremely useful overall in dealing with the change, probably because the situation was largely beyond personal control. Nevertheless, feelings of personal control, the ability to tolerate ambiguity, and sharing anxieties with others (social support) moderated the stressful effects to some extent prior to and 6 months after the transition.

From these data, Ashford (1988) recommended that the stress associated with organizational transitions may be defused by providing as much information as possible (i.e., increase perceived control) and encouraging social support groups. Ashford (1988) warned, however, against overinterpreting these data, given the uniqueness of the sample and the total reliance on self-report data.

Although Ashford uncovered some important variables associated with transition, such as changing job descriptions and new coworkers, one of the key stressors associated with organizational mergers and acquisitions is the possibility of a clash between the cultures of the merging organizations. By organizational culture, we refer to shared organizational values and norms. For example, there are norms for appropriate conduct (e.g., Is it okay to take work breaks whenever desired?), communication (e.g., Can employees contact upper management directly or must they go through their immediate supervisors?) and dress codes (e.g., Is it appropriate to wear jeans in the office?). In those situations in which one company either acquires or merges with a second company, it is conceivable that conflict will arise surrounding the new culture.

According to Cartwright and Cooper (1994), two factors likely account for the level of success in merging two cultures together. First, the members of each organization evaluate the attractiveness of the culture in the other organization. Second, the willingness of members from each organization to modify their original culture must be considered. Given these two factors, the possibility exists that a new, mutually acceptable culture will emerge through a blending of the two cultures.

Of course, however, the merging of the two cultures may not be desired by employees of one or both organizations. The new culture may pose difficulties for select employees, particularly when the culture is at odds with employees' value systems. Thus, in the new organization, if an employee suddenly learns that he must now report his whereabouts to the manager on a daily basis, this might be deemed to be highly stressful. Finally, the larger and more dominant organization may simply impose its culture on the smaller organization (which may have been acquired). Again, this circumstance might lead to the experience of stress in those employees from the smaller organization, if they are uncomfortable with the transition.

Before leaving the discussion of organizational transition, it is important to note that the introduction of new technologies may have a tremendous impact on the organization and its employees. Nolan and Croson (1995), for example, proposed a six-stage process of transforming an organization to maximize efficiency through the use of information technologies. Although we will not review the process here, their first stage is of direct relevance to this discussion. According to Nolan and Croson (1995), the first stage involves organizational downsizing; downsizing becomes necessary inasmuch as information technologies enable an organization to manage itself more efficiently without the need for as many layers of management. Therefore, introducing new information technologies may mean that some individuals lose their jobs. Downsizing and job loss are topic areas of increasing relevance and importance; we turn to these issues next.

Downsizing and Job Loss

In recent years, downsizing has become a fairly common occurrence, one that has had direct and pervasive effects on individual workers. *Downsizing* is defined here as the systematic reduction of a workforce by the employing organization (Appelbaum, Simpson, & Shapiro, 1987). The organizational decision to downsize usually results from acquisitions, mergers, and technological changes, all of which often reduce personnel needs. Other factors include international competition, a rapidly changing marketplace, and economic recession. Although some "downsized" organizations may eventually experience increased profitability (cf. Burton, Keels, & Shook, 1996), the short-term repercussions of downsizing can be traumatic on both a societal and individual level. On a societal level, the burden of unemployment and welfare programs has grown enormously. On an individual level, workers often experience depression, insecurity, and low self-confidence from job loss, particularly when they are unable to secure new employment in a tight labor market (Appelbaum, Simpson, & Shapiro, 1987).

Models of Job Loss. One of the most direct effects of downsizing is job loss. In Chapter 2, we noted that stress models specifically addressing the issue of job loss have proliferated given the current interest in the topic. Because the effects of job loss can be so personally devastating, particularly for the more disadvantaged segment of the workforce (e.g., V. L. Hamilton, Broman, Hoffman, & Renner, 1990), the topic would seem to be a likely target for psychological research. Strangely, however, until the mid-1980s, little research had dealt with job loss at the individual level, focusing instead on societal or economic trends associated with unemployment.

DeFrank and Ivancevich (1986) reviewed the individual level research and concluded (not surprisingly) that job loss has a deleterious effect on physical health and on psychological and social adaptation. They proposed a theoretical model of job loss, which incorporated both organizational and individual risk factors for job loss (e.g., company finances, individual skill levels), the immediate, personal impact of job loss (e.g., loss of income) or job retention for survivors (e.g., loss of colleagues), moderators of job loss (e.g., social support networks, age), individual coping attempts (e.g., job search activities, withdrawal), and the effects of job loss (e.g., boredom, depression, substance abuse). Although DeFrank and Ivancevich provided no data to test their model or the propositions generated from it, they charged other researchers with the task of using their model as a springboard for future work on job loss.

Kinicki (1985) also proposed a causal model of job loss specifically associated with plant closings. Similar to DeFrank and Ivancevich's model, Kinicki's model incorporated some individual-level variables, such as expectation of plant closing, personal employability and work orientation (ethic). These variables were hypothesized to influence affective outcomes (e.g., stressful life events, costs associated with new employment, and anxiety). The model was tested with a sample of 60 recently unemployed plant workers in the Midwest. Kinicki generally found support for the relationships hypothesized in the model, particularly for expectations of plant closing and costs associated with new employment. That is, anxiety was particularly high for those workers who reported that the cost of new employment was high because their new employment options were not as attractive (e.g., they must accept less pay, more overtime in a new position). On the other hand, some prior knowledge of the plant shutdown seemed to be beneficial in reducing stressful life events, the costs associated with reemployment, and anxiety.

From these results, Kinicki recommended that organizations should reduce the costs associated with reemployment by helping their terminated workers find suitable new employment and also by providing advance warning of plant shutdowns to allow sufficient time for planning and preparatory coping. However, Kinicki's results must be interpreted with caution because they were based on single-source, self-report data from a small sample.

More recently, Kinicki and his colleagues (Prussia, Kinicki & Bracker, 1993) expanded the theoretical assumptions of earlier job loss models by testing an attributional model of job loss and unemployment status with covariance structure analysis, a statistical technique that uses correlational data to allow causal inferences (Chapter 3). They surveyed 79 manufacturing employees 1 month prior to and 18 months after termination. Tests of the model indicated that internal and stable attributions for job loss negatively influenced reemployment prospects: Employees who believed that their own efforts were generally responsible for their job loss (i.e., self-blame) had lower expectations for reemployment.

This study illustrates the importance of cognitive factors in understanding the impact of job loss. Although such factors as financial concerns, skill levels, and market conditions are obviously related to a displaced worker's reemployment prospects, his or her mental state can have a tremendous impact on the job search process (cf. Ginexi, Howe, & Caplan, 2000, for an alternative perspective). A negative, self-deprecating mindset can prevent the displaced worker from presenting him or herself positively or even from seeking reemployment.

Interestingly, Latack, Kinicki and Prussia (1995) proposed a model of how individuals cope with job loss (see also Kinicki, Prussia, & McKee-Ryan, 2000). The model posits that people strive for a sense of psychological equilibrium. Specifically, the individual examines how the job loss adversely affects his economic, psychological, physiological, and social well-being. These adverse effects are assumed to create discrepancies. For example, a social discrepancy might be created if the individual loses some social contacts from work, yet would like to maintain the level or quantity of social contacts he enjoyed before losing the job. To restore a sense of equilibrium in terms of social relationships, she chooses specific coping actions to reduce the discrepancy and restore the equilibrium. Thus, she may decide to join a social club or seek out current friends for increased social contact.

The particular coping activities chosen are assumed to depend on a number of factors, including coping goals, coping efficacy, and coping resources. Additionally, whether the discrepancy is perceived as either a harm/loss or a threat (Chapter 1) and the intensity of the perceived discrepancy are both assumed to influence coping goals and ultimately the coping activities chosen.

Essentially, the coping-with-job-loss model assumes that individuals attempt to restore a state of psychological equilibrium in the face of job loss. The model clearly has a cognitive emphasis: A person is assumed to cognitively evaluate the situation and choose coping responses accordingly. Consistent with this model, Leana, Feldman, & Yan (1998) found that appraisal of the situation was the best predictor of coping strategy choice. We will have much more to say about coping in Chapter 7.

Survivors of Job Loss. Perhaps one of the most popular topics of psychological research on job loss has focused on the organizational *survivors*, not the recipients, of job loss (i.e., the coworkers whom the displaced employee leaves behind). A number of models have been developed examining different issues relating to survivors. For instance, Mishra and Spreitzer (1998) developed a model based on Lazarus's work (Chapter 2), which attempts to predict survivor reactions based on their cognitive appraisals of the downsizing. Saunders and Thornhill (1999) proposed a model delineating how management might best handle the downsizing to maximize survivors' organizational commitment.

Davy, Kinicki, & Scheck (1991) developed and tested a model of survivor responses to layoffs. This model hypothesized that perceived personal control over organizational activities, such as company policies, pay increases, and perceived job security, influences job attitudes (e.g., job satisfaction). Using data collected before and after the layoffs, they tested their model on 88 employees from an organization in the process of downsizing through layoffs. Results showed that those survivors who generally reported that they were allowed some control over their work activities also felt that the layoff decisions were just. In addition, those survivors who felt the layoff decisions were just and their jobs were fairly secure, reported more positive attitudes toward the organization. Davy and Kinicki's conclusions point to the importance of considering the impact of the larger organization context when studying the effects of work layoffs. They warned, however, that their results were based on a small and perhaps unrepresentative sample.

Joel Brockner and his colleagues (e.g., Bennett, Martin, Bies, & Brockner, 1995; Brockner, 1985; Brockner, Davy, & Carter, 1985; Brockner, Grover, &

Blonder, 1988; Brockner, Grover, Reed, & Dewitt, 1992; Brockner, Tyler, & Cooper-Schneider, 1992; Brockner, Wiesenfeld, & Martin, 1995) have indisputedly been the most prolific contributors to organizational survivor research. They have examined survivor responses both in simulated laboratory settings (e.g., Brockner et al., 1985) and in field settings experiencing actual layoffs (Brockner et al., 1992). The laboratory simulations typically have been created using a simulated work group with college students. Job survivor responses have been studied by dismissing one of the group members and then measuring the effects on the survivors (Brockner et al., 1985). In the field studies, Brockner and his colleagues surveyed survivors of recent organizational layoffs regarding their perceptions and attitudes both before and after the layoff (Brockner et al., 1992).

Although most of their field data has been collected in organizations, Brockner and his colleagues also replicated some of their results with a random sample of Chicago residents who had experienced interactions with the legal system (i.e., police officers and judges). In this case, the legal system was considered to be comparable to a traditional organization because both have authority figures who act according to a set of rules or guidelines. Their data indicated that those citizens who reacted most negatively to their personal experiences with the legal system were those whose prior commitment to legal authorities was high and who felt they had been treated unfairly. Field data from the layoff survivors in a financial services organization were consistent with the Chicago data: Organizational survivors who expressed the most negative attitudes toward their employing organization were those who felt highly committed to the organization prior to the layoff but felt that the organization had handled the layoff unfairly (Brockner, et al., 1992).

More recently, Allen, Freeman, Russell, Reizenstein, & Rentz (2001) examined several survivor reactions in a longitudinal research design and discovered that the initial impact was negative, as predicted by prior research. Although some variables did not change over time, organizational commitment, job involvement, and role overload decreased from the pretest (predownsizing) to the second posttest (postdownsizing). These results indicate that some of the negative effects of downsizing may persist over time if management does not intervene.

How can the results of these studies be used to help employees and organizations deal more effectively with technological and organizational change? From reviewing the research on automation, computerization, and downsizing, the overall prescription that can be offered to management is to be sensitive to the human component and involve individual workers in the process whenever possible. This message is very strong and consistent. When organizations adopt new technologies (including computerization) and consider only the optimal design of the new systems, workers may be unable or unwilling to use them.

When organizations implement change, especially downsizing, considering only the bottom-line implications of such changes while ignoring the human impact, at least two undesirable outcomes may result. First, the displaced workers may personalize the job loss, feeling personally demoralized and responsible for their plight, which could negatively influence their future employment prospects. Second, if the organizational survivors of downsizing feel that management acted unfairly in handling the terminations, they may themselves feel more negatively toward their employing organization even if they were not personally affected. Although management may consider employee involvement to be too time-consuming and frustrating during organizational change and crisis, such practices may indeed be crucial to the long-term success of these endeavors (see Appelbaum, Simpson, & Shapiro, 1987; Ashford, 1988).

Downsizing from a Management Perspective. Concerns about organizational change and transition are not only the province of salaried or lower-level employees; managers might also express concerns and experience stress during organizational change, including downsizing.

For instance, O'Neill and Lenn (1995) interviewed middle-level managers who were in the process of experiencing a significant level of downsizing in their organization. One theme that emerged was one of role ambiguity: Managers expressed concern that they were central players in the change effort, yet their actions might undermine their own futures in the organization! Managers expressed anger when downsizing was justified on the grounds that somehow the company, in its present configuration, had failed. Managers also expressed anxiety when they did not fully understand the underlying rationale for the changes. Communication is at issue here: Executive-level management must clearly articulate the strategic rationale for fundamental changes. Unfortunately, however, poor channels of communication are common in organizations. Ford and Ford (1995) argued that effective communication is a key element in successful organizational change; breakdowns in communication can lead to a variety of problems, including the possibility that the entire change effort may stall or fail altogether.

Beyond anger and anxiety, O'Neill and Lenn (1995) also found that middle-level managers expressed cynicism, resentment, and a sense of resignation. Obviously, to minimize feelings of anxiety or resentment, change must be handled carefully and thoughtfully. As Galpin (1996) noted, involving all constituents in any change effort is critical; an inclusion strategy wherein all levels of management are working together is extremely important. Such a strategy should help to mitigate the negative consequences associated with organizational change.

CONCLUSIONS

In this chapter, we examined a diverse array of stressors, from the ambiguity and conflict related to work roles, the demands associated with juggling work and nonwork roles, to the influence of automation and downsizing. Although the traditional role stressors, role conflict and ambiguity, were the focus of organizational stress research in the 1980s and 1990s, the work–nonwork stressors and the stressors associated with technological change and job loss have more recently captured the attention of researchers as well as the general public.

We raised the issue that researchers have been criticized for not developing and testing strong inference or causal models to investigate the process by which role stress develops in organizations. Although that criticism is still largely unanswered, studies such as the one by Kemery et al. (1987; Figure 5.2) have heeded the call for more process-oriented and theoretically driven research.

The development of these types of causal models in stress research and the application of sophisticated statistical techniques like structural equations modeling (SEM) for model testing represent meaningful theoretical and methodological advancements for work-stress research (Chapter 3). However, as we indicated in Chapter 3, these techniques cannot be used to unambiguously establish cause and effect relationships with any degree of certainty. Because these models are based on data obtained from nonexperimental research designs, all that can really be done is establish that a model is consistent with a pattern of data (and perhaps is more consistent than a competing model). This situation is quite different from stating the model is "true" or "correct" in any sense. Given the proliferation of these techniques in work-stress research, however, it is important that the consumer of research be at least somewhat familiar with these sophisticated analytical approaches and their limitations.

Research on role stressors is certainly ubiquitous in the work-stress literature. At this point, however, behavioral scientists cannot say with any degree of certainly that role stressors have an effect on organizational or personal outcomes. This is because the research is nonexperimental. All they can say with confidence is that role stressors are associated with or predict alternative outcomes of interest. Of course, one alternative would be to experimentally manipulate levels of role stress in a carefully controlled experimental design and then examine the potential effects of the stressors on outcomes like health. This approach, however, quicky raises a number of ethical and practical concerns that argues against it (e.g., manipulating stress to cause decreased health is highly unethical). Again, analytic techniques such as SEM cannot overcome the lack of experimental control. Although we may assume there is a causal link between role stressors and outcomes, that assumption is different from demonstrating it empirically.

Unlike the more traditional organizational role–stress research, work–nonwork is a fairly recent topic of systematic inquiry. As previously noted, however, much work remains to be done. Nonetheless, the upsurge of interest in this topic is encouraging, and we look forward to further methodological and theoretical advancement in the years to come.

Similar to the area of work–nonwork, technological change, organizational transition and downsizing, and job loss are fairly recent topics of scientific scrutiny. Also, consistent with the other topics discussed in this chapter, the knowledge gained about these contemporary work stressors has largely not yet benefited workers.

One of the most pressing problems in the area of job loss is the absence of a theoretical underpinning or a conceptual basis to guide research efforts in the spirit of Kahn et al. (1964). Aside from a few fledgling models (e.g., DeFrank & Ivancevich, 1986), the empirical (data-based) research abounds with little allegiance to any organizing framework. However, perhaps we are being overly critical, given the newness of these topics and the difficulty inherent in studying workers (and organizations) in crisis.

If one restricts oneself to the practical implications of the empirical research, does the prognosis change? We believe not. We previously gave a broad prescription for worker involvement in the change process, even in the case of job loss, because research strongly suggests that such steps are necessary for sustaining personal and organizational well-being. However, caveats about mishandling organizational change (regardless of the form) have been around for at least 15 years.

For example, Marks and Mirvis (1985) described the "merger syndrome," characterized by increased centralization and decreased communication: Management fails to inform workers about the organizational change (merger), thus fueling rumors and anxiety levels. The end result is that employees are distracted, productivity typically declines, and many workers (often the best ones) leave the organization. Sufficient data now exist to substantiate the early warning signs provided by researchers such as Marks and Mirvis, and it is incumbent on behavioral scientists to strongly communicate that message.

On a brighter note, these concerns may diminish or at least evolve as the nature of work changes in response to organizational changes. In contrast to the typical employee of the past who entered his office at 8 a.m. and worked until 5 p.m. during the work week, the "re-engineered or restructured" employee of the 21st century may work at home or at a remote worksite, keep irregular work hours as the job demands, and access advanced computer technology to replace the information formerly supplied by coworkers. He may not even be a permanent, full-time member of the organization, but a part-time employee who has been contracted solely to complete a specific job alone or with a team of other workers (Patterson, 1994).

Relatively little is known about the job-related attitudes and performance of this very new type of employee. For example, Will he miss having coworkers and an office environment? Will he be able to manage her time without constant supervision? Will he feel commitment toward her "invisible" employer? However, there is every indication that real changes in workers' attitudes and behaviors are already occurring. In the words of one contract worker, "I do a good job for them because I feel an obligation as a contractor. But I don't feel loyalty, not the old-fashioned sense of loyalty we used to have. It's the realization that it's just not going to be the same ever again" (Patterson, 1994, p. 85).

PERSONAL AND ORGANIZATIONAL STRAINS AND MODERATORS

Health, Attitudes, Performance, and Individual Differences

The model of the stress process we presented in Chapter 1 indicates that the perception of stress is followed by short- and longer-term psychological, behavioral, and physiological outcomes or responses. In addition, moderator variables, such as personality type, may affect (a) whether and the extent to which a stimulus is initially perceived as stressful and, (b) the nature and severity of the responses to the perceived stressor(s). The term "strain" is often used to capture the vast array of potential outcomes or responses. Therefore, the "strain" can be used in the collective sense to include the three general classes of responses indicated above.

The purpose of this chapter is twofold: (a) to examine a variety of different strains as studied in the life stress and job stress literatures, and (b) to consider some moderator variables that potentially play important roles in the overall stress process. First, we examine research that has investigated strains from the life stress literature, including research on the relationships between stressful life events and daily hassles and various strains. Second, we turn our attention to the work stress literature that has considered the extent to which job-related stressors predict the occurrence of various strains, including burnout—a timely topic that has captured the interest of both the research community and the general public. Finally, we focus on select individual and contextual difference variables (mainly in their role as moderator variables) that have been the focus of stress researchers in recent years.

STRESSFUL LIFE EVENTS, DAILY HASSLES, AND STRAINS

In this section, we present an area of stress research that has studied the relationship between life stressors, both common and uncommon, and the development of strains such as illness, negative attitudes, and decreased performance. These stressors cut across several life domains, including work, and have been linked to many types of strains.

Stressful Life Events (SLEs)

Defining SLEs. Early stress research was conducted primarily by medical researchers, such as Hans Selye and Water Cannon (see Chapters 1 & 2), and individual health is still the most commonly used outcome measure in stress research. Several areas of research have evolved because of their specific emphasis on health and have direct implications for understanding organizational stress.

Holmes and Rahe (1967) proposed one of the earlier attempts to link a variety of life stressors, major life events, many of which occur infrequently, to physical health problems. They examined the relationship between the number of *stressful life events(SLEs)* (e.g., "change in financial state," "divorce," "death of spouse," "retirement," "fired at work") experienced by a person and the development of physical illness. They reasoned that, by enduring multiple stressors over time, people repeatedly experience the stress response; the body is consequently subjected to the physiological changes that often culminate in illness. This perspective is very similar to Selye's notion that repeated exposure to stressors strips away the body's adaptive resources over time (Chapter 2).

Initially, only a global change score, or the total number of life events experienced in a specified time interval (usually the past year), was used to assess the impact of stressful events on health. However, Holmes and Rahe were also interested in the relative impact of each of these stressors and developed weights or mean values for each event. Holmes and Rahe subsequently revised this instrument to produce a self-administered paper-and-pencil version, the Schedule of Recent Experience. Adequate internal consistency (Skinner & Lei, 1980) and test–retest reliabilities (Rahe, 1974;,1989) have been reported for various forms of the scale, as well as evidence of predictive validity in positive relationships between illness rate and degree of life change (Rahe, Mahan, & Arthur, 1970; Ruben, Gunderson, & Arthur, 1971). However, the SRE has remained relatively unchanged since its development decades ago and compares poorly to more sophisicated measures (see following discussion; T. W. Miller, 1993).

Dohrenwend and and his colleagues (Dohrenwend, Krasnoff, Askenasy, & Dohrenwend, 1982; Dohrenwend, Raphael, Schwartz, Stueve, & Skodol, 1993) elected to retain the SLE framework but expand it to include a wider range of variables incorporating both the person (e.g., personality, coping) and the situation (e.g., social network, work environment). They held that the checklist approach to measuring SLEs (i.e., simply checking any items that apply) had largely contributed to the low predictive validity of SLEs: Checklists often have a large amount of measurement error because of large item variability. For example, serious injury and illness events have been interpreted by respondents to run the gamut from episodes of flu to heart attacks. Therefore, they decided to adopt a varied data collection method, incorporating both an interview and rating form component. The existing data for this newer approach suggests that it holds promise as a superior data collection method relative to the traditional SLE checklist (Dohrenwend et al., 1993).

SLEs and Strains.   From research spanning almost 30 years, the preponderance of evidence indicates that when people report they have experienced several events, they also frequently suffer from any number or types of illnesses. More specifically, SLEs have been examined within the context of diseases such as cancer (Levenson & Bemis, 1991), coronary heart disease (Tennant, 1987), the common cold (Totman, Kiff, Reed, & Craig, 1980), and immune system functioning (Geiser, 1989), as well as general physical health (Creed, 1985). This research has generally found a relatively small but significant relationship between stressful events and disease onset.

One particular physiological strain that has captivated the attention of the general public and media is coronary heart disease (CHD): Specifically, does stress predict the onset of CHD? CHD is a progressive disease whereby arterial walls narrow (e.g., due to plaque formation), making it more difficult for oxygenated rich blood to reach the heart muscle. When the heart is deprived of too much oxygen, a myocardial infarction or heart attack occurs.

Although a detailed examination of the link between stress and CHD is beyond the scope of this discussion, the physiological underpinnings of CHD are now somewhat well understood (Balick & Herd, 1987; Ornish, 1982). This knowledge has placed stress as one of the key precipitating agents in the development of CHD, along with diet, exercise, smoking, and heredity.

At the risk of oversimplification, the following process traces the relationship between CHD and stress. The release of adrenaline/noradrenaline during Selye's alarm stage (see Chapter 1) causes arterial constriction and the formation of platelets on the inner walls of the arteries. Collectively, the constrictions and platelets reduce the ability of blood to flow to the heart muscle. Moreover, the various physiological events during Selye's alarm and resistance stages have been implicated in the elevation of LDL (low-density lipoprotein) or "bad" cholesterol and arterial plaque (Ornish, 1982). Although the physiological chain of events is extremely complex and more is yet to be learned, scientists at least now have a clearer understanding of the causal link between stress and the onset of CHD. We will have more to say about CHD later when we discuss Type A behavior pattern.

Researchers have also studied the relationship between SLEs and psychological disorders, for example depression (Hammen, Davila, Brown, Ellicott, & Gitlin, 1992) and schizophrenia (Rabkin, 1980). Consistent with the research on physical disease, the results of these studies suggest that a significant relationship exists between SLEs and psychological health. These results should not be too surprising; after all, the role of the environment in the development of psychological disorders has been widely documented.

Turning now to behavioral outcomes, only a few studies have investigated the relationship between stressful life events and behavioral outcomes, including job-related outcomes. Vincino and Bass (1978) examined the relationship between "lifespace variables," which included SLEs, and employee performance. They reported that stressful life events predicted job success, which was measured with a composite of job grade attained, supervisor effectiveness ratings, and supervisor potential ratings.

Bhagat (1983) proposed a theoretical model examining the relationships between personal SLEs and organizational outcomes. The gist of the model is that work concerns decrease in importance as nonwork problems become the primary focus, which will eventually lead to decreased job involvement, and subsequently, lower job satisfaction and performance and higher absenteeism and turnover. To illustrate, a chronically ill child may become a primary focus in life for a working parent, diminishing her identification and satisfaction with her job. In meeting her nonwork obligations, she may frequently be absent from work and seek alternate employment that permits more time with her sick child. Bhagat, McQuaid, Lindholm, and Segovis (1985) tested a portion of this model using a sample of administrators, health-care providers, and clerical staff. They found that personal life stress was correlated with all outcomes except absenteeism and turnover. More recently, Bhagat and Allie (1989) reconfirmed these relationships in a sample of teachers.

Dohrenwend et al. (1982) also proposed a stress model incorporating SLEs, although, unlike the Bhagat model, it is not context-specific. In this model, stressful life events (e.g., death of a loved one, a new job, or financial difficulties) are jointly determined by events in the environment and characteristics of the person. This model holds to the commonsense notion that some environments and some people are simply more prone to experience stress. A very anxious person in a high-pressure advertising position, for example, would probably report a large number of SLEs relative to his easygoing counterpart in a secure government administrative job. The SLEs produce stress, which can lead to no changes or undesirable changes in functioning or psychological growth. These outcomes are presumed to also be affected by external factors, such as social support or material goods, and internal factors, such as values and biological predispositions. This model is similar to Lazarus's model (Chapter 2) in that it posits that stress occurs from an interaction between environmental events and characteristics of the person experiencing the events. It differs from other models in assuming that neutral and positive outcomes can accrue from the stress experience. However, other than the substantial data linking SLEs and health problems, the validity of this model has not been tested.

Critique of SLE Research. Undoubtedly the life events approach has enjoyed popularity because it is both intuitively appealing and elegantly simple: People often become ill after dealing with life stressors. From the admonitions of family members, friends, and physicians, coupled with personal observation, everyone has observed this relationship in themselves and others. Significant life events have indeed been shown to predict a variety of physiological, psychological, and behavioral outcomes. With respect to physical health, however, it is surprising that the total life events experienced by an individual over a specific time interval have not proven overall to be very strong predictors of health problems.

Kasl (1983) offered several reasons for the poor predictive validity of Holmes and Rahe's (1967) life events scale. Much life events research is retrospective and cross-sectional: It asks people about these events and their health after the fact. However, disease often develops in stages over time. If individuals are not followed over time, then whether they were already experiencing health difficulties is unknown. Researchers need to establish individual health status, document life changes, and then determine what health decrements follow. According to Kasl, life events are also not separable from a person's environment and stage of life. For example, alcoholics experience many SLEs due to the disruption alcoholism causes in their lives, and the elderly experience relatively few. (One aspect of aging is that, as people age, they experience fewer life changes or at least fewer new changes.) In the same vein, no change can be more stressful than change itself: For infertile married couples, not experiencing pregnancy or the arrival of a baby may well be stressful.

Finally, it is important to point out that stressful life events may play an important role in the process model of work stress (Chapter 1; Figure 1.1). That is, SLEs may serve as moderator variables in that they influence the relationship between job-related stressors and outcomes. A dull, routine job may be perceived as especially stressful when a person must concurrently deal with one or more stressful life events (e.g., a marital breakup). Moreover, the perceived stress associated with the dull job may lead to more severe outcomes if multiple stressful life events occur simultaneously.

Daily Hassles

In addition to the methodological problems just mentioned, critics of SLE research have alleged that the "positive" SLE items (e.g., "gain of a new family member," "vacation") are, compared to the "negative" items (e.g., "divorce," "trouble with boss"), relatively unimportant predictors of outcomes (Bhagat et al., 1985), and that SLE scales do not measure persisting or chronic stressors (Lazarus, 1983). Lazarus and his associates (DeLongis, Coyne, Dakof, Folkman, & Lazerus, 1982; Kanner, Coyne, Schaefer, & Lazarus, 1981) maintain that the annoying, frustrating, minor stressors that people encounter frequently or *daily hassles,* such as "physical appearance," "your children," "family-related obligations," and "investments," have stronger relationships with health problems than stressful life events.

Daily Hassles versus SLEs. In one of the early studies comparing daily hassles with stressful life events, Kanner et al. (1981) examined both types of stressors in a sample of middle-aged men and women and found that daily hassles were better predictors of psychological symptoms than SLEs. The researchers hypothesized that life events are probably too distal (i.e., far removed) to predict outcomes such as health problems, whereas daily hassles are more proximal (i.e., closer in time), expressing the immediate pressures of living. These findings have been replicated in a number of studies, not only for psychological symptoms (Flannery, 1986; Holahan, Holahan, & Belk, 1984), but also for mood (DeLongis, et al., 1988; Eckenrode, 1984; Wolf, Elston, & Kissling, 1989) and physical health (DeLongis et al., 1982; Holahan & Holahan, 1987; Holahan et al., 1984).

Only a few studies have investigated the relationship between daily hassles and organizational outcomes (Chiriboga & Bailey, 1986; Hart, 1999; Ivancevich, 1986; Orpen & Welch, 1989; Zohar, 1999). Ivancevich (1986) collected daily hassles, SLEs, and psychological health data from a sample of hourly assembly-line workers. He also collected absenteeism and performance data from personnel files. Hassles were significantly related to absenteeism and physical health, and, consistent with prior research, hassles were stronger predictors of health symptoms than SLEs. Chiriboga and Bailey (1986) reported similar results in a sample of over 1,000 critical care and medical surgical nurses in six different hospitals. Additionally, only daily hassles were significantly related to burnout; they stated that "when dealing with the burnout of staff nurses it is the distracting and annoying day-to-day stressors... that exert the major stressful impact on nurses" (p. 91).

Very recently, Hart (1999) reported that worker life satisfaction was related to nonwork and work hassles, and nonwork and work uplifts in police officers. (Uplifts are positive minor events.) Zohar (1999) also found work hassles predicted daily end-of-day mood, fatigue, and subjective workload in a sample of military parachute trainers. However, Orpen and Welch (1989) failed to find any significant relationships between daily hassles and job attitudes and performance.

Evans, Johansson, and Rydstedt (1999) devised a job-redesign intervention for urban bus drivers (e.g., installation of electronic information systems on buses, creation of separate bus road lanes) to decrease job-related hassles, such as passenger demands and traffic congestion. Compared to the pre-intervention assessment, perceived stress, heart rate, and systolic blood pressure decreased after the intervention was implemented. This study nicely illustrates the potential utility of using daily hassles to alleviate stress in the workplace.

Critique of Hassles Research. Critics have voiced some serious methodological concerns about daily hassles research. First, daily-hassle items have been confused with SLE items on stress scales (Pratt & Barling, 1988). For example, items such as "spouse begins or stops work," "change in sleeping habits," and "marital separation" were included on both the SLE scale and an early daily-hassles scale. Both daily hassles and SLEs are distinct from the more widely studied chronic stressors, which are perceived to be moderately stressful but enduring events (e.g., role conflict and ambiguity; Chapter 5).

Some recent research indicates that the confusion over the definitions of these different types of stressors may be even more serious than previously supposed. Hahn and Smith (1995, 1999) examined whether people who answer different types of stress items actually perceive daily hassles to be distinct from the more serious chronic stressors and SLEs. In a sample of over 300 health-care professionals from two hospitals, they found that her respondents neither classified hassles, SLEs, and chronic stressor items correctly, nor did they even agree among themselves which items should be hassles, SLEs, or chronic stressors. According to Hahn and Smith, these data lend strong support to Lazarus, DeLongis, Folkman, & Gruen's (1985) contention that the individual appraisal of an event is the most important component of the stress process: Stress is indeed in the eye of the beholder!

Second, the measurement of daily hassles may be confounded with psychological symptoms (Dohrenwend, Dohrenwend, Dodson, & Shrout, 1984; Dohrenwend & Shrout, 1985). To illustrate this point, Dohrenwend et al. (1984) asked 371 clinical psychologists to classify each item on the hassles scale as either a hassle or a symptom of psychological disorder. More than 75% of the 117 items on the hassles scale were rated as "more likely" or "about as likely" to be psychological symptoms as hassles! This criticism led to a lively debate in the research literature between Dohrenwend and his colleagues and Lazarus and his colleagues (Lazarus et al., 1985) and the development of a revised daily hassles scale (DeLongis et al., 1988) that attempted to address these weaknesses.

Very recent studies have been more supportive of the effects of hassles, especially in the work domain, probably because they incorporated methodological improvements. For example, Hart (1999), Zohar (1999), and Evans et al. (1999) used longitudinal designs. Zohar (1999) also collected data using a combination of well-validated self-report scales and expert ratings, whereas Evans et al. (1999) used observational data, physiological measurements, and participants' self-reports.

So, what do all of these criticisms say about the status of SLE and hassles research? The bright side of all of the controversy is that the SLE approach has stimulated much fruitful research over the past two or three decades. Today, the consensus is that both stressful life events and daily hassles have a small to moderate, but important, link with illness and other strains.

ORGANIZATIONAL STRESSORS AND STRAINS

Personal health has undeniably been the focus of much stress research and application over the past several decades. However, this research evolved primarily from the life stress perspective. Alternately, work stress research has tended to focus more on the relationships between assorted job stressors and psychological and behavioral strains.

Work-Related Stressors and Psychological Strains

The psychological strains examined by organizational stress researchers have primarily taken the form of job attitudes. Job-related attitudes of relevance here include job satisfaction, organizational commitment, job involvement, propensity (inclination)-to-leave the organization, and job-related tension or anxiety. The relationships among organizational stressors and these job-related attitudes are some of the strongest and most consistent in stress research, particularly for the stressors role conflict and ambiguity (Jackson & Schuler, 1985; Chapter 5). People who report stressful work situations also report that they are tense, anxious, dissatisfied, uncommitted, uninvolved at work, and seriously considering seeking employment elsewhere.

Models of Job Stressors and Attitudes. One of the more enduring theoretical perspectives on job-related stress and attitudes is the model proposed by Bedeian and Armenakis (1981). This model hypothesizes that greater role conflict and ambiguity lead to increased job tension, which results in lower job satisfaction. Lower job satisfaction, in turn, increases the intention (propensity) of the worker to leave the organization. In addition to hypothesizing an indirect influence of role conflict and ambiguity on propensity to leave, the model also predicts a direct influence on these two variables, in which role conflict and ambiguity directly reduce job satisfaction and increase propensity-to-leave (Figure 6.1). Bedeian and Armenakis (1981) found empirical support for their model in a sample of staff at a nursing service. Bedeian and his colleagues (Kemery, Bedeian, Mossholder, & Touliatos, 1985) reported supportive results in a replication of the 1981 study in three samples of accountants and one sample of hospital workers.

Netemeyer, Johnston, and Burton (1990) attempted to test the original model using structural equation modeling techniques (SEM; see Chapter 3). They mailed surveys that assessed variables in the model to the field sales force of a national manufacturer of consumer goods and received responses from 183 of these salespeople. Statistical analyses of the data indicated that the effects of role conflict and ambiguity were mostly indirect: That is, increased role conflict and ambiguity increased propensity to leave by increasing job tension and decreasing job satisfaction (see Figure 6.1). The direct effects of the role stressors on satisfaction and propensity-to-leave were much weaker. Therefore, the hypothesized relationships in the model were only partially supported. Finally, Lang, Wittig-Berman, and Rizkalla (1992) also used structural equation modeling to test the original model and some modifications of it. They confirmed Netemeyer and colleagues' results that the effects of role stress were mostly indirect but also reported that satisfaction was the more important intervening variable.

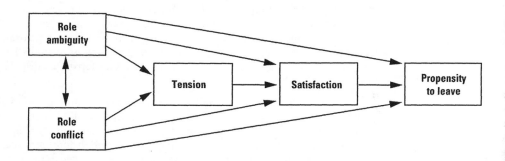

Figure 6.1 A path-analytic study of the consequences of role conflict and ambiguity

As discussed in Chapter 5, Kemery, Mossholder, and Bedeian (1987) investigated alternative theoretical models of the effects of role stress on physical symptoms and job attitudes (job satisfaction and turnover intentions). They found the greatest support for the most complex model, which hypothesized that job satisfaction was an intervening variable between role stress and turnover intentions and that job satisfaction was reciprocally related to (both a cause and an effect of) physical symptoms. Hendrix, Ovalle, and Troxler (1985) also reported more support for a complex relationship between stress and turnover intentions: In their sample of Defense Department employees, they found that work context factors (e.g., participation in decision making) were important in determining the satisfaction-turnover intention link.

When the research on job-related stressors and attitudes is examined at the level of simple correlations relative to theoretical models, very different conclusions are reached. The bivariate correlations indicate that increased levels of job-related stressors, primarily role conflict and ambiguity, are moderately related to decreased attitudes, mostly job satisfaction and turnover intentions. However, tests of the more sophisticated models demonstrate that the relationship between these stressors and attitudes is indirect and more complex. For example, the presence of role stressors appears to decrease job satisfaction (among other attitudinal effects), which increases intention to leave. The simple correlational data are not incorrect, but rather incomplete in the situations they describe. These results illustrate why Structural Equation Modeling (SEM; Chapter 3) and other contemporary statistical innovations have revolutionized research on complex systems such as organizations.

Downsizing and Job Attitudes. Much recent focus on job attitude research has been on downsizing and organizational change. In Chapter 5, we discussed in some detail Brockner's research on the attitudinal effects of job layoffs for organizational survivors. Across several laboratory and field studies, Brockner's results are quite consistent: Organizational survivors who expressed the most negative attitudes toward their employing organization were those who felt highly committed to the organization prior to the layoff but believed that the organization had handled the layoff unfairly (e.g., Brockner et al., 1992).

Another study (Begley & Czajka, 1993) examined how organizational commitment affected the relationships between perceptions of the stress related to organizational change and job satisfaction, intent to quit, and health. The researchers collected these data both from clinical staff before and after a major organizational consolidation (accompanied by a hiring freeze but no actual layoffs) within the psychiatric division of a hospital. They found that the stress associated with the change increased job displeasure (a combination of job dissatisfaction, intent to quit, and irritation) only for those workers who reported low organizational commitment. These results seem to contradict Brockner's finding that highly committed employees are the most adversely affected, although the critical difference is that no coworkers were terminated in the psychiatric hospital sample.

The one generalization that can be drawn from these studies is that the relationship between job-related stressors and attitudinal outcomes after organizational change is not a simple or direct one, which agrees with our previous summary of the more generic research on job stressors and attitudes. Interestingly, this specific pattern of relationships between stressors and attitudes does not seem to apply to stressors and behavioral outcomes, particularly performance. This is the topic to which we now turn.

Work-Related Stressors and Behavioral Strains

Although researchers (and organizations) have had a long-standing interest in the link between stress and performance, data on the relationships between job-related stressors and behavioral outcomes, such as job performance and absenteeism, are often weak. In their meta-analyses of the correlates of role conflict and ambiguity, Jackson and Schuler (1985) reported that the relationships of role ambiguity and role conflict with job-related performance are very low, especially for objective performance, such as quantity of output. These low correlations may reflect, in part, the problems that often plague objective performance measures (e.g., objective performance can be limited by situational factors, such as economic conditions and available resources). However, the weak link between stressors and behavioral outcomes also reflects the complex nature of their relationships. An alertness or arousal mechanism has been used to explain some of these relationships.

In 1908, Robert Yerkes and John Dodson demonstrated that performance increased with increasing arousal up to a point. Beyond that point, however, performance decreased with increasing arousal (Figure 6.2). Arousal here refers to a general stress response characterized by alertness or activation. This complex relationship between arousal (a stress response) and performance is often called the *inverted-U* or *curvilinear relationship,* which can generally be explained by saying that too little stress is just as detrimental as too much.

To illustrate, if you were feeling extremely stressed when you interviewed for a job you really wanted, your performance during the interview would probably not be as high as you would have achieved if less stressed. However, if you were totally relaxed, even lethargic, during the interview, you probably also would not achieve your best performance. In the same vein, workers who perform dull or monotonous tasks are often aided by the addition of a stressful stimulus, such as loud noise or music. The noise or music can increase the worker's arousal level to the point that performance level actually increases (see Chapter 4).

Becoming aroused when faced with a potentially stressful stimulus probably has some adaptive consequences. Hans Selye's alarm stage (Chapter 1) with its various physiological correlates underscores the benefits of short term arousal when faced with a stressful situation. In sum, the inverted-U relationship can be understood from the standpoint of Selye's alarm stage, in which some arousal is likely beneficial in the short term to help maximize the adaptive response(s) to the stressful situation in question.

The inverted-U relationship has received some support, especially in laboratory research (see Cohen, 1980). However, other explanations have been offered. Stress and performance may have a (1) positive, linear relationship, (2) negative, linear relationship, or (3) no relationship. If stress and performance have a positive, linear relationship, increasing levels of stress are associated with increasing performance (people perform better the more stress they experience). If stress and performance have a negative, linear relationship, increasing levels of stress are associated with decreasing performance (people perform better the less stress they experience). Of course, if stress and performance are not related, increasing (or decreasing) stress levels are not associated with any level of performance.

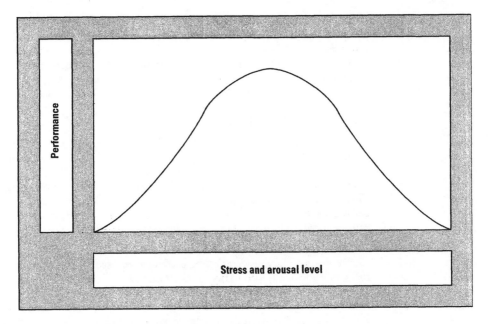

Figure 6.2 The Yerkes-Dodson Law

The empirical support for an inverted-U relationship between stress (arousal) and performance in field settings is limited, with data often revealing only a negative linear relationship between stress and performance (Westman & Eden, 1996). Jamal (1984) examined the relationship between job stressors and employee performance as assessed by the immediate supervisor and personnel records in two samples of nurses. Although most of his data supported a negative linear association between stressors and performance (higher levels of reported stressors were associated with lower performance), the stressor role ambiguity (Chapter 5) showed a nonlinear relationship with performance. A more recent study (Abramis, 1994) found only negative linear or no relationships between role conflict, role ambiguity, job insecurity, and job performance as measured by the respondent and a coworker.

These studies, however, provide "weak-inference" tests of the inverted-U model because arousal was not measured directly; rather, arousal was inferred from the levels of self-reported stressors. The relationships implied by the Yerkes-Dodson law conjure up all types of interesting possibilities in which stressors might be used to enhance performance. The addition of a stressor such as noise might increase performance on assembly-line jobs, which are often monotonous and repetitive, and when workers suffer from lack of sleep, which is frequently true for shift or night workers. Unfortunately, the optimum stress level associated with peak performance varies with people, tasks, and situations, so it is extremely difficult to specify how much of any stressor will produce a particular level of performance for a specific individual. Because multiple data points are really needed to determine complex relationships such as the inverted-U, the cross-sectional studies that have examined stress and performance cannot provide a definitive answer about the nature of the stress-performance relationship (Beehr, 1985). Given these difficulties, some researchers (Westman & Eden, 1996) have even suggested that the search for a curvilinear relationship between stress and performance in work settings be abandoned.

Work-Related Stressors and Burnout

One type of organizational strain that has behavioral, attitudinal, as well as health-related components is burnout. Burnout has been the focus of attention by researchers and the popular media in recent years. In fact, you have probably used the term to describe yourself, perhaps after final exam week or a hectic period at work. Shirom (1989) speculated why the concept of burnout has been readily integrated into contemporary society: Burnout refers to the interaction of the person with some type of stressful environment. Thus, the label of burnout does not stigmatize the person but rather the conditions to which the person is subjected.

In a more formal sense, burnout is often used in reference to the stress experienced by human-service professionals, particularly social workers, therapists, police officers, and teachers. Why does burnout most often affect human service professionals? These jobs frequently require workers to accommodate the extreme needs and dependencies of clients, patients, or students. Such extraordinary demands can be emotionally debilitating for the worker. However, burnout, at least from the perspective of stress researchers, has come to mean far more than an emotional response to "people" stress.

Defining Burnout. In the late 1970s and early 1980s, the psychological and medical community began to realize that the array of symptoms called burnout was a serious health and organizational problem beyond the normal experience of stress at work. Maslach and her colleagues (Maslach & Jackson, 1982, 1984, 1986) can be credited with the development of burnout as a scientific concept. In fact, burnout technically consists of three specific types of stress responses, usually found in individuals who work in people-intensive jobs (Maslach & Jackson, 1981).

1. *Exhaustion*, or feelings of being drained or used-up, unable to face a day's work, totally unenthusiastic. Can have intellectual, emotional, or physical components.

2. *Depersonalization,* or the act of putting psychological distance between the individual and others, creating feelings of emotional detachment, callousness, and cynicism.

3. *Decreased personal accomplishement,* or the feeling of not living up to former goals and expectations; wasted efforts including feelings of helplessness and low self-esteem.

Although empirical research has determined that burnout is indeed multidimensional (Cherniss, 1980; Leiter, 1991; Maslach, 1982), the emotional exhaustion component indisputably appears to be the most important of the three dimensions (e.g., Cox, Kuk, & Schur, 1991; Maslach & Jackson, 1981; Pick & Leiter, 1991; Rafferty, Lemkau, Purdy, & Rudisill, 1986). In fact, Shirom (1989) and Leiter (1991) have both argued that emotional exhaustion is the defining construct of the burnout syndrome.

Leiter (1991) hypothesized how exhaustion, as a central feature of the burnout process, may be related to the other two dimensions. SEM analyses (Chapter 3) of data obtained from health-care workers in a mental hospital suggested that work demands (e.g., overload, interpersonal conflict) combined with the underutilization of job skills to develop feelings of emotional exhaustion, which then led to depersonalization. Depersonalization was also influenced by a lack of coworker support and escapist types of coping. Decreased personal accomplishment, which develops concurrently (parallel to) but largely independently of exhaustion and depersonalization, was related to underutilization of skills, coworker support, and coping. This model (Leiter, 1993) contrasts with one of Leiter's earlier phase models (Figure 6.3a), which hypothesized that exhaustion occurs first, followed by feelings of depersonalization, which then lead to decreased personal accomplishment (Leiter & Maslach, 1988).

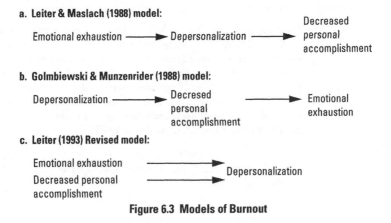

Figure 6.3 Models of Burnout

A fair amount of debate has occurred in the burnout literature over the appropriate developmental model of the burnout process (e.g., Dierendonck, Schaufeli, and Buunk, 2001). The two most popular models were developed by Golembiewski and Munzenrider (1988) and Leiter and Maslach (1988). The Golembiewski and Munzenrider model (Figure 6.3b) proposes that increases in depersonalization lead to decreased personal accomplishment, which together lead to increased emotional exhaustion. Leiter (1993; Figure 6.3c) later revised the Leiter and Maslach model to show that decreased accomplishment develops independently of but parallel to exhaustion, which is still hypothesized to lead to depersonalization. Decreased personal accomplishment is influenced by factors other than the two burnout dimensions (see previous paragraph). In a longitudinal study of a sample of social service workers, Savicki and Cooley (1994) did not find clear support for either of the models, whereas Dierendonck et al. (2001) reported that an alternative model fit their data better than the other two models. Regardless of the model, however, emotional exhaustion has consistently proven to be the most important component and has typically been closely related to feelings of depersonalization.

Because emotional exhaustion is the dimension that is the least specific to burnout, it has been argued that burnout (exhaustion) may be little more than the experience of stress, depression, or other negative affect (i.e., a new label for an old phenomenon). Although this possibility is far from resolved (see Cox, Kuk, & Schur, 1991; Maslach & Schaufeli, 1993), researchers believe that the conceptualization of burnout as the development of a multidimensional syndrome over time distinguishes it from other constructs. Research that has shown different patterns of relationships between the three dimensions of burnout and other variables also provide support for the discriminant validity of the burnout syndrome (i.e., different burnout dimensions are related to different strains) (e.g., Corrigan, Holmes, & Luchins, 1995; Jackson, Turner, & Brief, 1987; Janssen, Schaufeli, & Houkes, 1999; Savicki & Cooley, 1994). For example, Firth and Britton (1989) reported that emotional exhaustion was related to increased absenteeism and depersonalization to turnover.

R. T. Lee and Ashforth (1996) conducted a meta-analyses (Chapter 3) of the three burnout dimensions. From the 61 studies included in the review, they concluded that the burnout dimensions were differentially associated with strains: Emotional exhaustion was positively correlated with turnover intentions and negatively correlated with organizational commitment; depersonalization was negatively correlated with organizational commitment and job satisfaction; and personal accomplishment was positively correlated with control (active) coping behaviors. This quantitative review provides rather compelling evidence for the construct (discriminant) validity of the burnout dimensions.

The experience of burnout has traditionally been studied within the context of specific types of jobs or occupations. Therefore, one of the side benefits of burnout research has been the accumulation of knowledge about the stressors and strains in numerous occupational groups. Burnout research has been conducted with nurses (Carson et al., 1999; Firth & Britton, 1989; Garden, 1989; Ogus, 1995), physicians and dentists (Gorter, Albrecht, Hoogstraten, & Eijkman, 1999; Lemkau, Rafferty, Purdy, & Rudisill, 1987), teachers (De Haus, & Diekstra, 1999; Greenglass, Fiksenbaum & Burke, 1995; Maslach, 1999; Russell, Altmaier, & VanVelzen, 1987), social-service workers (Savicki & Cooley, 1994), lawyers (Jackson, Turner, & Brief, 1987), and managers (Dolan, 1995; Garden, 1989; R. T. Lee & Ashforth, 1993).

The prevalence of burnout in people-intensive jobs, such as social work and medicine, has been well documented. However, a related and very important question is "Who burns out within these jobs or occupations?" Maslach (1982) examined some demographic characteristics of workers who had experienced burnout. She found that although no gender differences existed in the incidence rate of burnout, women experienced more emotional exhaustion and men more depersonalization. These effects are probably attributable to gender-role differences between men and women. Workers who are younger, Caucasian, unmarried, and childless are also more likely to experience burnout. This profile is not surprising: Young workers are probably more idealistic in their expectations of life, and workers without families lack a significant source of social support.

Measuring Burnout. Early burnout studies bore little resemblance to the sophisticated quantitative assessments of multiple theoretical models that characterize much current research. Burnout originally developed out of clinical or non-empirical observations of phenomena in the real world. Consequently, burnout constructs (definitions; dimensions) and related theory developed post hoc. This sequence of events (unsystematic or changing construct definition and development) often presents measurement problems, and burnout research was no exception.

Consistent with its unscientific roots, early measures of burnout included case studies, single-item (How burned-out do you feel?) inventories, and self-report items developed only for a single study (Maslach, 1993; Schaufeli, Enzmann, & Girault, 1993). Only two self-report measures have been used in multiple studies across time, the Maslach Burnout Inventory (MBI; Maslach & Jackson, 1981, 1986) and the Burnout Measure (BM; Pines & Aronson, 1988).

The Burnout Measure has 21 self-report items that express exhaustion and are scored from "never" to "always." According to its developers, the BM is suitable for self-diagnosis, and therefore test score interpretations are provided. Test norms have been used to classify people at risk for burnout (Astrom, Nilsson, Norberg, Sandman, & Winblad, 1991), although the validity of these norms has not been established (Schaufeli et al., 1993). Published reliabilities (test–retest and internal consistency) of the BM are adequate (Pines & Aronson, 1988). BM scores have also demonstrated validity in relationships with work and life satisfaction (Pines, Aronson, & Kafry, 1981), intent-to-leave the job (Pines & Aronson, 1988), actual turnover (Weinberg, Edwards, & Garove, 1983), and self-reported physical health (Pines & Aronson, 1988).

An apparent weakness of the BM is that it was constructed to have a single dimension, despite the widespread belief that the burnout construct is multidimensional. However, this single dimension measures a person's level of exhaustion, which is also perceived to be the defining component of burnout.

The Maslach Burnout Inventory is the most widely used burnout measure. The inventory describes burnout as a three-dimensional syndrome composed of emotional exhaustion (e.g., "I feel like I'm at the end of my rope"), depersonalization (e.g., "I treat some students as if they were impersonal objects"), and reduced personal accomplishment (e.g., "I feel I'm positively influencing other people's lives through my work"—reverse scored) (Maslach & Jackson, 1981, 1986). Unlike the BM, the MBI was constructed to be used in the human-services professions and must be reworded (e.g., substitute "student" for "client") for use in other contexts. The current form of the MBI has 22 items scattered across the three dimensions. These items are scored according to their frequency of occurrence, from "a few times a year" to "every day" (Maslach & Jackson, 1986).

The reliability of the MBI has proven to be adequate (Corcoran, 1995; Maslach & Jackson, 1986). Evidence for the validity of MBI scores has been demonstrated in relationships with job satisfaction (see Schaufeli et al., 1993) and depression (Meier, 1984). In both cases, emotional exhaustion was the strongest correlate of the three dimensions. The factorial validity (i.e., dimensionality) of the MBI has also been investigated, with the three-dimensions being confirmed across several studies, although none attempted to use the appropriate confirmatory techniques (see Schaufeli et al., 1993). The results of at least one study, however, have suggested that the MBI may be unidimensional (Corcoran, 1995).

Overall, both the BM and the MBI appear to be reliable and valid measures of burnout. The emotional exhaustion dimension (i.e., the single dimension of the BM and one of three dimensions of the MBI), however, has very consistently been the most robust, reliable, and valid.

Today, the scientific concept of burnout as a specific type of stress response in human-service jobs has been extended to new occupations, such as industrial workers (Demerouti, Bakker, Nachreiner, & Schaufeli, 2001). Definitions of burnout have been expanded to include such concepts as increasing disillusionment and psychological erosion (Schuafeli & Enzmann, 1998). Researchers have examined some of the most important causes (e.g., workload, time pressure) and consequences (e.g., depression, psychosomatic complaints) of burnout in detail. They have also developed diverse theoretical models of the burnout process (e.g., burnout as a mismatch between person and job, Schaufeli & Enzmann, 1998; burnout as an outcome of job demands and lack of job resources, Demerouti et al., 2001). And, although the longitudinal studies of burnout have not been as supportive as the cross-sectional ones (Schaufeli & Enzmann, 1998), researchers today agree that burnout is a viable syndrome, one that is undoubtedly more pervasive in many work settings than previously believed (Demerouti et al., 2001; R. T. Lee & Ashforth, 1996).

Given the personal and organizational implications of burnout, interventions to alleviate the effects of burnout for different groups of workers have been developed. Some of the more common interventions that have been used include counseling, skills training, and social support groups. These burnout interventions will be discussed in detail in Chapter 8 (Stress Management).

MODERATORS OF THE STRESS PROCESS: INDIVIDUAL AND CONTEXTUAL DIFFERENCES

We have now examined a variety of stressors originating from both within and outside the organization. We have also examined a number of potential personal and organizational outcomes or strains. However, our understanding of the stress process will, at best, be incomplete if our explorations are limited to the stressor-strain relationships. Everyone knows people who lead stressful lives and yet rarely become ill or perform poorly; yet, other people seem to crumble at the mere suggestion of adversity. For these two types of people, the stress process appears to function quite differently. What distinguishes these two types?

Individual difference variables are variables that permit the distinction among people on such factors as gender, race or ethnicity, age, social status, past experience, heredity, intelligence, and personality types. Individual difference variables play a central role in the stress process (see Payne, 1988). More technically, these variables can change, or *moderate*, the stressor-strain relationship (see Chapter 3 for a discussion of moderator effects). For example, you may have a hypothesis that women perceive stressors differently and respond differently from men. If this prediction is true, then gender moderates the stressor-strain relationship. As another example, the relationship between time waiting in lines at the grocery store or bank and the degree to which waiting is perceived as stressful may be greater for certain personality types. We also briefly examine one contextual variable, culture, that has recently captured the attention of organizational stress researchers.

One recent example from the research literature nicely illustrates the concept of a moderator variable. Jex and Elacqua (1999) examined whether self-esteem moderates the relationship between role stressors and both physical and psychological strains. Overall, their results provided some support for moderator effects such that the positive relationship between stress and strains was stronger, as expected, for individuals low in self-esteem.

In the following sections, we take a closer look at some of the more widely studied individual difference or moderator variables in stress research. Before continuing however, we believe it is useful to distinguish between a moderator variable and a *mediating variable*.

A mediating variable is an intervening variable that "transmits" the effects of one variable onto another. For example, if we hypothesize that an environmental event (e.g., noise) causes cognitive appraisal of the stressor, which, in turn, causes increased heart rate, cognitive appraisal is deemed to be a mediating variable between noise and heart rate increase. Alternately, if we hypothesize that increasing levels of noise predict increasing heart rate more strongly when cognitive appraisal is highly negative compared to when it is slightly negative, the appraisal would be considered to be a moderator (Chapter 1).

Gender

Gender is one individual difference that may distinguish how people perceive and respond to stress. From birth, females live in a different world from males. They are taught to behave differently and to have different expectations in life than their male counterparts. It would therefore not be surprising if women experience stress differently from men.

An interesting finding reported by some researchers (Davidson & Cooper, 1987; Jick & Mitz, 1985) is that women tend to develop psychological stress responses, such as depression and fatigue, whereas men tend to develop physiological or physical stress responses, such as high blood pressure or heart disease. A meta-analysis (Chapter 3) of gender differences in occupational stress, however, found no evidence of gender differences in either psychological or physiological stress across 19 studies (Martocchio & O'Leary, 1989). More recently (and consistent with the meta-analytic findings), Jamal (1999a) and Vermeulen and Mustard (2000) found little evidence of gender effects in stressor-strain relationships. Finally, in a large cross-cultural study of occupational stress and gender, K. Miller, Greyling, Cooper, Lu, Sparks, and Spector (2000) reported no gender differences in work stress within each country (South Africa, the United Kingdom, the United States, and Taiwan) and limited support for an interaction between gender and stress across countries.

A few studies have reported some gender differences, particularly in blue-collar jobs, although those differences are quite minor (Terborg, 1985; U.S.

Department of Labor, 1974, 1978). Gender differences also appear to exist for some health outcomes: Working women report more psychosomatic ailments (e.g., tiredness, irritation, and anxiety; Cooper & Davidson, 1982), mental distress (Piltch, Walsh, Mangione, & Jennings, 1994), and depression (Murphy, Beaton, Cain, & Pile, 1994) than men. Some research has shown that females experience higher levels of burnout (Pretty, McCarthy, & Catano, 1992) and job discrimination (Murphy et al., 1994) than their male counterparts. Two large-sample studies in the United States (Piltch et al., 1994) and Canada (Trocki & Orioli, 1994) also reported that women experienced higher levels of some work and personal stressors and stress-related symptoms than men.

Currently, one of the most salient, gender-related stressors is sexual harassment in the workplace. Widespread incidents of harassment, mostly with men as perpetrators and women as victims, have caught the attention of both the media and organizational researchers. Fortunately, this trend has spawned a surge of empirical research (e.g., Dekker & Barling, 1998; Goldenhar, Swanson, Hurrell, Ruder, & Deddens, 1998; Piotrkowski, 1998). Unfortunately, the existing studies have almost universally confirmed the existence of sexual harrassment and its negative consequences for women in the workplace.

So, the question of whether women really experience stress differently than men has not been resolved. In sum, we do know that women experience some unique stressors, and that some of their stress responses, particularly in the area of mental health, differ from men's responses. Based on the mixed pattern of results across studies, however, the degree to which gender is a significant moderator in the stress process is still open to question.

Ethnicity

People who are members of ethnic minorities may perceive and respond to stress differently because they may have different lifestyles and experiences than the white majority. However, scant research exists on racial differences in job-related stress. Ford (1985) believes this deficit has occurred because most stress researchers belong to the majority group.

The research on job-related stress and ethnicity that does exist largely suggests that minority groups suffer greater stress than the white majority. Ramos (1975) studied 202 minority professionals (both ethnic minorities and women) at an aerospace organization and found that minority professionals experienced more job-related stress than their nonminority counterparts. In another study of minority professionals in a large manufacturing and sales organization, Ford (1980) found that Black subordinates of Black supervisors were less stressed than Black and Hispanic subordinates of White supervisors. Hispanic women also reported even higher levels of stress than their Hispanic male peers. Interestingly, Gutierres, Saenz, and Green (1994) reported that being in a numerical minority at work was more stressful for White workers than Hispanic workers in a sample of university employees. They interpreted these results to mean that Hispanic workers had become accustomed to such situations, whereas, for White workers, being in the minority was a novel and therefore stressful experience.

Many of the stressors that affect working women, such as overrepresentation in lower level jobs and lack of access to training and promotion opportunities, also apply to minority workers (Morrison & Von Glinow, 1990). Some studies have examined stressors unique to minority groups. For example, one study found that minority home-care workers were often confronted with racist attitudes on the job (Bartoldus, Gillery, & Sturges, 1989). James, Lovato, and Khoo (1994) also reported that greater perceived differences in values between minority workers and their majority supervisors was negatively related to minority workers' health.

Type A Behavior Pattern

An individual difference variable that has received considerable attention in recent years is the Type A behavior pattern (TABP). Type As are identified by certain personality traits, such as impatience, competitiveness, and hostility. Essentially, Type A may operate as a moderator variable such that Type A individuals perceive some stimuli as more stressful (e.g., waiting in a long line) or perhaps less stressful (e.g., having to meet a time deadline) than non–Type A individuals. Also, in the face of perceived stress, the level/severity of outcomes such as physiological reactions may be heightened in Type A individuals compared to others. For instance, given their experience of work and life stress, Type A individuals have a greater propensity for developing coronary heart disease (CHD).

Defining TABP. The initial interest in Type A originated in the 1950s with the clinical observations of two cardiologists, Drs. Friedman and Rosenman. Over the years of their medical practice, they had noticed distinct behavior differences between patients with heart disease and those without.

Friedman and Rosenman defined *Type A behavior pattern* as "an action-emotion complex that can be observed in any person who is aggressively involved in a chronic, incessant struggle to achieve more and more in less and less time, and if required to do so, against the opposing efforts of other things or persons" (1974, p. 76). They found that a constellation of behaviors distinguishes the CHD patient: an exaggerated sense of time urgency, excessive competitiveness and achievement striving, and hostility and aggressiveness. Other descriptors of Type A that have been used include tense, preoccupied with deadlines, work-oriented, impatient, and control-oriented.

The non–Type A person was described as the polar opposite of these characteristics and called Type B. The Type B person was recognized as being able to relax without feeling guilty and to have fun for its own sake, not turning every opportunity into a competition. The story behind the adoption of these terms (i.e., Type A or B) is an interesting one and grew out of Friedman's and Rosenman's frustration at having grant proposals rejected because they used the term "emotional stress" as a label for these behavioral tendencies (Friedman & Ulmer, 1984).

In addition to these core behavioral characteristics, Type As differ from Type Bs on a number of physical, psychological, and other behavioral dimensions. In general, Type As have higher cholesterol levels, greater blood clotting, higher triglyceride (fat) levels, and greater sympathetic nervous system arousal than Type Bs (Lovallo & Pishkin, 1980). Type A women are more likely to have high blood pressure, although that relationship is not consistent in men (Rosenman & Friedman, 1961). Type As also report higher levels of stress (Dearborn & Hastings, 1987; Gamble & Matteson, 1992; Jamal & Baba, 1991), increased physical health problems (Kirkcaldy & Martin, 2000), and greater dissatisfaction with their jobs (Dearborn & Hastings, 1987; Gamble & Matteson, 1992) than Type Bs. Not surprisingly, Type As set higher performance standards (Grimm & Yarnold, 1984), actually perform better (C. Lee, 1992), are more job-involved (Jamal & Baba, 1991), have higher self esteem, achievement, and power needs (Schaubroeck & Ganster, 1991), engage in fewer leisure activities (Kirkcaldy, Shepard, & Cooper, 1993), and smoke more and exercise less (Howard, Cunningham, & Rechnitzer, 1976) than Type Bs. Also, compared to Type Bs, Type As may commit greater numbers of aggressive acts toward other employees (Baron, Neuman, & Geddes, 1999).

The Type A person can be distinguished on some demographic characteristics. In particular, Type A appears to be an affliction of success and youth: The prevalence of Type A increases with socioeconomic status and decreases with age (Schaubroeck & Ganster, 1991; Shekelle, Schoenberger, & Stamler, 1976). Type A behavior pattern was also once believed to be a man's disease, but scientists now know that third variables, such as employment and martial status masked the prevalence of Type A in women in early research: Married people in high-status jobs also tend to be men.

TABP and Heart Disease. Although we have conceptualized TABP as a moderator in the stress process, TAPB can also have an effect on outcomes like CHD through mediating variables such as cognitive appraisal. To date, much of the Type A research has considered the relationship between TABP and CHD. Some large-scale prospective (longitudinal) studies have investigated the link between Type A and heart disease across a variety of people and settings.

Perhaps the most well-known of these studies is the Western Collaborative Group Study (Rosenman et al., 1975). This study was the first prospective research designed to assess the relationship between heart disease and TABP in men. Potential confounding variables were controlled by using a double-blind design (i.e., ensuring that the investigators had no knowledge of the health status or Type A scores of the men they assessed). Traditional risk factors for heart disease (obesity, high blood pressure, smoking) were also measured and controlled in the statistical analyses. The study participants were tracked for 8 1/2 years and then assessed for evidence of coronary heart disease. The results showed that the Type A men had a risk ratio for heart disease of more than 2 to 1, even after other risk factors were considered (Brand, 1978).

The Framingham Heart Study (Haynes & Feinleib, 1982) extended the Western Collaborative Group Study by examining the relationship between heart disease and TABP in both men and women in white- and blue-collar jobs. A prospective design and a follow-up assessment 8 1/2 years later were also used in this research. Again, Type A proved to be an independent predictor of of coronary heart disease in both men and women (Haynes, Feinlaub, & Kannel, 1980).

A few years later, researchers attempted to replicate the results of the original Western Collaborative Study (Stamler, 1980). A research protocol similar to the previous studies was used across eight different data collection sites in the United States. After 7 years, the relationship between TABP and heart disease was assessed. However, in this study, no link between Type A and any type of coronary heart disease was found (Shekelle et al., 1985). These disconfirming data suggested that the way Type A was measured (as a global construct) contributed to the null findings and set the stage for much of the controversy that would follow Type A research for many years. Ganster, Schaubroeck, Sime, and Mayes (1991) pointed out that TABP is a construct with multiple aspects (i.e., a multidimensional construct), and they found that the hostility component of TABP (measured via the structured interview; see following) was a significant predictor of CHD. A second component, achievement striving, was positively related to performance but not to CHD in another study (Edwards & Baglioni, 1991). These findings underscore the difficulties of making global predictions involving TABP, given that it is a multifaceted construct in which different components differentially predict select outcomes.

Measuring TABP.   Because the methods and specific measurement instruments used to assess TABP are at the core of this still ongoing controversy about the relationship between Type A and heart disease, we next examine the specific Type A measures in some detail.

The structured interview (SI), developed in 1960, was used in the Western Collaborative Group Study. A trained interviewer asks respondents to answer a series of approximately 30 structured questions about how they characteristically respond to a variety of common life situations. An interesting aspect of the SI is that the interviewer records the respondent's behavior during the interview, as well as his or her answers to the structured questions. For example, the interviewer may ask a question slowly, noting whether the interviewee interrupts before the question is completed. Both the responses to the structured questions and the behaviors observed during the interview are aggregated to assess the interviewee's degree of impatience, hostility, arousal, and competitiveness. This information is then used to classify the person into one of five categories that place Type A on a continuum.

Most of the remaining methods of measuring Type A are totally self-report. The most widely used self-report instrument is the Jenkins Activity Survey (JAS; C. D. Jenkins, Zyzanski, Rosenman, & Cleveland, 1971). Several forms of the JAS exist. The current form contains 52 multiple-choice items (e.g., "Would people you know well agree that you tend to get irritated easily?" "Would people you know well agree that you tend to do most things in a hurry?"), although subsets of these items are used to form a 21-item global Type A scale, a 21-item speed and impatience scale, a 24-item job involvement scale, and a 20-item hard-driving and competitive scale. The content of all JAS scales was developed to assess the same TABP dimensions measured by the SI.

The Framingham Type A Scale was developed to measure TABP in the Framingham Heart Study (Haynes, Levine, & Scotch, 1978). The current version has 10 items derived from 300 originally used in the study. Two versions of the Framingham scale exist (employed and unemployed persons). The content of the items focuses primarily on time pressure, competition, speed, and impatience. Four of the 10 items are work-related; a 6-item version without the work-related items also exists (Chesny et al., 1981).

Superficially, all Type A instruments appear to be adequately measuring the TABP construct as originally defined by Friedman and Rosenman. However, as mentioned earlier, some studies failed to find expected relationships between Type and coronary heart disease. Edwards (1991) reviewed the measurement properties of the SI, the JAS, the Framingham Scale, and the Bortner Scale (Bortner, 1969; not discussed here).

Summarizing Edward's (1991) review briefly, reliabilities (test–retest and internal consistency) for the SI are acceptable, although the data are quite mixed for the JAS and the Framingham scales. The concurrent and predictive validity evidence (i.e., the relationship between Type A and current health status and between Type A and future health status, respectively) is strong, especially for the SI, the "Gold Standard" of TABP instruments (Dembroski & Czajkowski, 1989). The validity data for the JAS and Framingham scales are more limited but also supportive. However, the interrelationships (correlations) between the SI, JAS, and Framingham measures are low to moderate.

This information is quite significant: Because the three measures of TABP purport to assess the same construct, their correlations should be fairly high.

The lack of convergence among the Type A measures therefore appears to be a primary culprit in producing the mixed results across studies. Because these weak relationships could evolve from the presence of measurement error (low reliability) and/or the multidimensionality of the TABP construct, Edwards recommended that TABP instruments should be subjected to systematic item development/refinement to reduce measurement error and that global measures of Type A be replaced with appropriate dimensional or component measures.

Other studies have confirmed Edwards's (1991) latter recommendation, indicating that the various dimensions of Type A are differentially related to outcomes, such as performance and health. Barling and Charbonneau (1992) examined undergraduate responses to survey measures and performance on a proofreading task in the laboratory. They found that the Type A dimension Achievement Striving was positively related to task performance and grade point average, whereas the dimension Impatience-Irritability predicted self-reported headaches and poor sleep habits. Another study (C. Lee, Ashford, & Jamieson, 1993) reported that Achievement Striving was positively related to class performance, and Anger-Hostility was positively related to anxiety.

So, what conclusion can be drawn about Type A? Two meta-analyses summarized the status of TABP research. Booth-Kewley and Friedman (1987) found a modest but reliable association between Type A and coronary heart disease across 83 studies, although negative affect, particularly depression, was also significantly related to heart disease. They both reported that the SI was clearly superior to the JAS as a predictor of heart disease. Of the JAS dimensions, only the Hard-Driving (Competitive/Aggressive) dimension demonstrated any relationship to disease. Incorporating some methodological improvements and an updated database, Matthews (1988), however, did not find such strong support for the relationship between TABP and heart disease across all types of studies as Booth-Kewley and Friedman had reported. These two reviews clearly indicate that Type A is an independent risk factor for coronary heart disease, although the magnitude of that risk may vary depending on the type of TABP measure or dimension, the type of study design, and the type of subject population under consideration.

Considering the health implications of Type A, various programs have been devised to intervene in the development of heart disease for susceptible persons. Examples of TABP interventions include job and task redesign, job placement, individual counseling, and drug therapy. Because of the scope and number of these interventions, they will be discussed in some detail in Chapter 8.

Hardiness

Defining Hardiness. Another personality variable that has captured the attention of stress researchers over the past 15 years is hardiness. Drawing from existential psychology, Kobasa (1979; Kobasa & Maddi, 1977) defined *hardiness* as a constellation of three interrelated personal attributes: (1) *Control* refers to the belief that one's environment is personally controllable and predictable; (2) *Commitment* is a belief that one should be involved in and believe in the value of certain life domains (work, family, etc.); and (3) *Challenge* refers to the belief that change in life is normal and can lead to personal growth and development. Kobasa conceived of hardiness as a personal characteristic that provides a source of psychological resilience against stress and resulting illness. All three of the interrelated dispositions are believed to serve adaptive functions both in the perception of and response to life stressors.

In the initial research, Kobasa and her colleagues (1979; Kobasa, Hilker, & Maddi, 1980; Kobasa, Maddi & Kahn, 1982) collected data on the stressful life events, health status, and personality characteristics of several hundred middle- and upper-level managers over a 5-year interval. The researchers identified a portion of these managers who had experienced intense stress in their lives. They then divided this group into two groups, one of that had also experienced many health problems and one that had experienced few health problems. Kobasa and her colleagues found that the two groups differed on three dimensions: Relative to the high-stress, high-illness group, the managers in the high-stress, low-illness group reported that they exerted greater control over their lives, felt a deeper sense of commitment to various aspects of their lives (both work and nonwork), and actively welcomed challenge and change in their lives. Thus, the "hardy" manager views and interacts with life differently from the "nonhardy" manager, which translates into "...accumulated skills and resources for dealing with stress" (Kobasa et al., 1980, p. 13).

Subsequent studies have generally confirmed the positive effects of hardiness on stress and health. Specifically, hardiness has demonstrated negative relationships with self-reported illness and burnout, and hardy persons are more apt to interpret stressors as controllable and positive (Blaney & Ganelllen, 1990; Hull, Van Treuren, & Virnelli, 1987; Wiebe, 1991). The concept of hardiness has also been expanded to examine its effects on outcomes other than health. In a longitudinal study, Westman (1990) examined the effects of the stressfulness of army training for Israeli defense forces cadets. She found that the stress of training predicted performance decrements but only for cadets low in hardiness. However, Bohle (1997) reported that hardiness was a very poor predictor of shift work tolerance in a sample of nurses.

Critique of Hardiness Research. Hardiness has not escaped criticism from stress researchers. The first concern involves the specific self-report scales that have been used to assess hardiness. The five-scale composite self-report measure originally developed by Kobasa, Maddi, and Kahn (1982) and two abridged versions of the original (see Ouellette, 1993) have sometimes demonstrated low (internal consistency) reliabilties, especially for the challenge dimension (e.g., Hull, Van Treuren & Virnelli, 1987); the challenge dimension has also sometimes failed to show the expected positive correlations with the other hardiness dimensions (e.g., Magnani, 1990). These problems, in combination with other measurement deficiencies in the scales (Ouellette, 1993) led to the development of the Personal Views Survey (Maddi, 1987; 1990). To date, this new composite scale and a slightly modified version (Bartone, Ursano, Wright, & Ingraham, 1989) seem to have addressed the problems with the old scales (e.g., Parkes & Rendall, 1988), although the challenge dimension still does not consistently function as expected (Ouellette, 1993).

The second concern involves the generality of the hardiness construct. To date, few attempts (cf., Westman, 1990) have been made to link hardiness to specific organizational outcomes, such as turnover, layoffs, and mergers, or to other stress-related variables (e.g., coping, affective responses; Blaney & Ganellen, 1990).

Third, the theoretical role of hardiness in the stress process has not been clarified. Kobasa suggested that hardiness functions as a moderator variable in the stress process: Stress predicts the development of strain (illness) only for those those low in hardiness. She also proposed, however, that hardiness has a direct effect on strain: Hardy people report less illness regardless of the stressor-strain relationship (Kobasa, 1982b). Interestingly, a review of the empirical research on hardiness (Hull et al., 1987) concluded that the model that treats hardiness as having a direct effect on strain has the most support.

Rush, Schoel, and Barnard (1995) investigated the process by which hardiness affected stress-related variables in a sample of 325 senior-level public-sector employees experiencing pressures for change in the aftermath of organizational restructuring. They tested a model of hardiness and stress in which hardiness directly influences coping and perceived stress and indirectly influences stress through coping. In turn, stress affects withdrawal intentions directly and through job satisfaction. (Figure 6.4). Specifically, the researchers predicted that hardy employees would experience less stress and use less escapist (escape or emotion-oriented) coping and more proactive (problem-oriented or control) coping (Chapter 7). In addition to the direct effect of hardiness on stress, the use of more control and fewer escape coping strategies by the hardy employee should further reduce experienced stress. Because the hardy employee experiences less stress, he or she should report higher job satisfaction and therefore be less inclined to seek employment elsewhere.

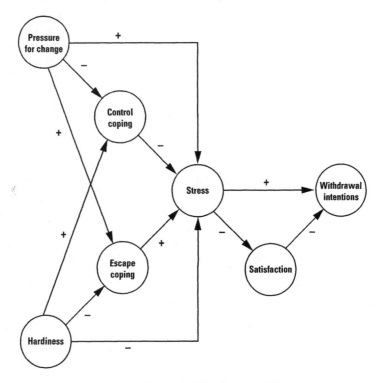

Figure 6.4 A Model of Hardiness and Stress

Consistent with prior research (see Hull et al., 1987), Rush and his colleagues found a direct assocation between hardiness and both stress and satisfaction, such that hardy persons experienced less stress and reported greater satisfaction than their non-hardy counterparts. There was little support for the indirect effects of hardiness on stress through coping strategies. They concluded that hardiness, incorporating a sense of control, commitment and challenge, seems to be a significant counterforce to organizational stressors encountered during downsizing and restructuring.

If, as Kobasa (1982b) has indicated, hardiness is a trainable concept, then such an approach may help to alleviate the stress associated with the organizational change that has become so prevalent in modern work environments. Maddi (1987, 1990) developed the Hardiness Institute to accomplish this end. We will have more to say about this endeavor in Chapter 8.

Culture

Modern technology is rapidly guiding nations toward a global economy. Communications between distant colleagues or clients is now almost instantaneous, enabling professional relationships to develop that would have been difficult a decade ago. Consequently, today's organizations have a real need to understand cultural differences that may influence the conduct of business. In response to this need, organizational stress researchers have explored cultural differences in work stress over the past decade.

Although there are some exceptions (cf. Jamal, 1999b), research has generally shown that cultural differences in organizational stress do exist. For example, comparing British and German managers, Kirkcaldy and Cooper (1992) found significant differences between these two groups on home/work interface and other stressors, as well as differences on several types of coping behaviors. Peterson et al. (1995) found cross-cultural effects for middle managers across 21 countries on work-role conflict, ambiguity, and overload. Bhagat et al. (1994) found cultural differences in managers and their staff across 7 countries in work-role variables, work overload, decision latitude, and problem- and emotion-focused coping. Finally, Kirkcaldy, Brown, and Cooper (1994) reported that senior police officers in Berlin experienced higher levels of stress and engaged in greater numbers of coping behaviors than their counterparts in Northern Ireland.

More recently, Yang, Chen, Choi, and Zou (2000) reported an interesting comparative study on work–family conflict. They hypothesized that Americans experience greater family demands, which have a greater impact on work–family conflict than work demands; the Chinese experience greater work demands, which have a greater impact on work–family conflict than family demands. Their rationale was guided by Hofstede's (1980) notion of individualism versus collectivism. In individualistic countries such as the United States, a career or work emphasis implies the satisfaction of personal ambition and achievement, often at the expense of personal and family life. However, in collectivist countries such as China, career and work signify sacrifice for the good of the family. That is, extra work should bring prosperity and honor to the family. The researchers collected relevant data from Chinese and U. S. industrial workers. They mostly confirmed their predictions, although the data did not fully support the work priority prediction in the Chinese sample.

On the surface, large cultural differences in job-related stress appear to exist. However, in many cases, these differences are accompanied by similarities (e.g., Lu, Kao, Cooper, & Spector, 2000). On a more general level, all cultures experience work stress in the form of common organizational stressors, such as overload and work–family conflict. All cultures respond to these stressors by using common types of coping behaviors. Continuation of these stressors and maladaptive coping behaviors will undoubtedly culminate in decreased physical and/or psychological health. So, although relative differences do exist, the stress *process* is highly similar across cultures.

CONCLUSIONS

We have covered considerable ground in this chapter, concentrating on the strain component of stressor-strain relationships and on the individual difference variables that can influence or moderate stressor-strain relationships. Interestingly, much of the current research dealing with health strains has been guided by a plethora of methodological issues. Nowhere is that more obvious than in the stressful life events research.

The fact that SLEs have demonstrated only a small relationship with health outcomes led researchers to explore other options. Dohrenwend, Krasnoff, Askenasy, and Dohrenwend (1982) developed a more comprehensive list of events and consideration of such factors as the setting and persons involved in the event. Naismith (1975) also created a stressful life events scale that pertains only to the job setting (e.g., a new boss, job transfer). At this time, however, neither scale has been widely used by stress researchers.

The daily hassles approach developed out of researchers' disenchantment with SLEs. Indeed, the minor, annoying events captured in the hassles scales do seem to independently predict the development of disease better than SLEs (e.g., Kanner et al., 1981). Conceptually, these findings make sense: People who have experienced a major life event (e.g., divorce) are more likely to become stressed from any of life's common inconveniences (e.g., traffic), which may lead to other hassles (e.g., argument with neighbor) and possibly another SLE (e.g., personal injury). However, the hassles scale is beset with methodological problems, most notably the lack of clear construct definition (validity). The revised hassles scale (DeLongis et al., 1988) was developed to address these criticisms, but the scales are still plagued by some measurement problems (Hahn & Smith, 1999). So, the true contribution of daily hassles in the prediction of health status has yet to be realized.

Despite the volumes of published studies, the conceptual underpinnings of job attitudes and performance research are underdeveloped compared to health. The moderate bivariate correlations between stress and job-related attitudes have often masked more complex and indirect relationships between these variables: The Bedeian and Armenakis (1981) model and variations of it are, to our knowledge, the only approaches to consider these more complex relationships.

The relationship between stress and job performance is even less understood. Because the bivariate correlation between stress and performance is frequently very low, researchers have examined the possibility that the relationship is nonlinear (inverted-U). The evidence for this nonlinearity is limited, at best (Jamal, 1984). Sullivan and Bhagat (1992) offered some thoughts on the inconsistent stress-performance relationship: Different results may be obtained depending on when performance is measured. For example, short-term (single measurement) performance may be increased under high stress levels, while longer-term performance (multiple measurements over time) may be negatively affected. Such possibilities remain to be tested.

Of all the topics discussed in this chapter, burnout has perhaps generated the most interest among researchers and the general public. In an effort to determine how burnout develops, researchers have proposed different models of the burnout process. However, no consensus has been reached regarding the sequential ordering of the three burnout components. In their meta-analysis of the burnout dimensions, Lee and Ashforth (1996) found support for Leiter's (1991, 1993) contention that emotional exhaustion and depersonalization develop independently of personal accomplishment. Because the meta-analytic results only show the strength of the relationships among the burnout dimensions, the specific sequential ordering of variables in the models (Do emotional exhaustion and personal accomplishment develop in parallel rather than accomplishment following from exhaustion?) could not be determined. So, the definitive "best" model could not be chosen. However, Lee and Ashforth (1996) did reconfirm that emotional exhaustion is the most important dimension. The relative roles of the other two dimensions will probably not be clarified until the model is expanded to incorporate stress, coping, and adjustment variables. Only within this larger framework can the full extent of the complex process called burnout be understood.

Type A behavior pattern, like burnout, has been subjected to considerable scientific scrutiny. Other parallels can be drawn between Type A and burnout research. Both concepts developed out of clinical or nonempirical observation of phenomena in the real world. Because of their health-related implications, both concepts also captured the attention of practitioners and the general public. Consequently, the constructs of Type A and burnout and related theory (if any) developed post hoc. This sequence of events (unsystematic or changing construct definition and development) often presents measurement problems, as it did for both TABP and burnout researchers. Indeed, the inconsistent findings of the several large-scale studies investigating TABP and heart disease appear to be largely due to variability in the manner Type A was measured.

Two recent meta-analyses (Booth-Kewley & Friedman, 1987; Matthews, 1988) determined that TABP is an independent risk factor for heart disease, although they disagreed on the magnitude of the effect. Clearly, however, Type A is a multidimensional construct, in which the hostility and negative affect components are related to disease, while other components (e.g., achievement striving) are related to different outcomes (e.g., performance).

Although Type A is an individual difference variable (admittedly a multifaceted one), relatively little research has considered the role of TABP as a moderator variable; most has examined only the direct relationship of TABP and strain (Kahn & Byosiere, 1992). The same allegation could be made regarding the research on gender and ethnicity. Concentration on main or direct effects of these individual differences on stress responses or strains (cf., Martocchio & O'Leary's 1989 review of gender differences in stress responses) has undoubtedly obscured any complex relationships. More hypotheses-driven research needs to be conducted on these individual differences variables to determine their true role in the stress process.

Hardiness is a recent addition to the several individual difference variables believed to influence the experience of stress. After some early measurement problems and the development of a new scale, hardiness seems to have a promising future (Ouellette, 1993). The available research does indicate that hardy individuals (high perceived control, commitment, and challenge) are more resistant to stress and disease, and that the effect is a direct one: Hardy people experience less stress and illness regardless of their life situations. However, at this time, little is known about the relationship between hardiness and job-related variables. Perhaps, as the sophistication of organizational stress theories and the methods to test them grow, hardiness will find a permanent place in the stress process along with other related constructs. For example, it is conceivable that the hardy worker might also be less likely to be Type A, report burnout, experience multiple daily hassles, perform poorly on the job, or suffer from low work morale.

The only contextual variable discussed in this chapter, culture, captured the attention of organizational stress researchers only within the past decade. As we discussed earlier, we know that specific types of stressors and coping behaviors differ across many cultures. However, these findings do not obscure the fact that the overall process of work stress appears to be highly similar across cultures. So, while experts may elect to target different stressors across cultures for study or intervention, the impact of these stressors should be quite consistent (e.g., decreased well-being, job atttitudes) regardless of context.

Finally, the reader may have noticed that we did not consider the role of coping or the availability of social support as potentially important moderators. This omission should not be interpreted to mean that we view coping or social support as unimportant variables in the stress process. In fact, the opposite is true—they are critically important variables deserving a comprehensive and critical treatment. Accordingly, the next chapter focuses exclusively on the role of coping and social support in the stress process.

CHAPTER 7

COPING WITH WORK STRESS

The focus of this chapter is a topic that has generated considerable interest among organizational researchers, the media, and the general public: coping with work stress. Needless to say, as public concerns about work stress have increased, the media have increasingly turned their attention to the topic of work stress and, more specifically, the topic of coping with work stress. This media attention has led to an even greater public awareness of the dangers associated with work stress, and has helped to fuel a mini-industry of popular press books on the topic of coping with stress at work (e.g., Atkinson, 1988).

Within the academic research community, there has been a steady upsurge of interest in coping as well For instance, scholarly journals are devoting an increasing number of pages to issues relating to job-related coping. Although some of the earlier stress models do not explicitly acknowledge the role of coping in the stress process (e.g., Karasek, 1979), coping has become a key variable in many stress models (e.g., Greenhaus & Parasuraman, 1987; Ratsoy, Sarros, & Aidoo-Taylor, 1986).

This popular and academic interest in coping leads to a series of inevitable but critical questions: (a) What is meant by "coping"? (b) How do we measure coping efforts? (c) Which types of coping strategies do people choose? and (d) Which coping strategies are most effective for managing stress at work? These questions and their tentative answers form the substance of this chapter.

THE MEANING OF COPING

As you might imagine, psychologists have had a long-standing interest in the subject of coping. The very act of survival is inextricably tied to successfully coping with challenges and threats emanating from the environment. Of course, psychologists have historically operated within a number of different paradigms, which has led to a number of different perspectives on the meaning of coping. What follows next are various definitions of coping arising from alternative psychological perspectives.

Psychoanalytic Perspective

One of the earliest psychological perspectives on coping is the psychoanalytic perspective (McCrae, 1984). Here, coping is conceptualized as actions taken by the ego (i.e., defense mechanisms) to protect itself from internal unconscious conflicts.

Thus, for example, the unconscious mind may be pressuring a child to steal some candy from a store. The child may cope with the resulting pressure (or stress) by acknowledging that Mommy will buy the candy so there is really no need to take it! Of course, the primary problem with this approach from a scientific perspective lies in the inability to empirically test predictions derived from the theory. After all, because the stress is presumed to be unconscious, how can it be assessed? If the child were to indicate that he is not experiencing stress, we could simply say "You are, you just do not realize it!" In sum, no way exists to directly observe and measure the ostensible unconscious processes that are supposed to give rise to coping.

Behavioristic Perspective

The behavioristic perspective dominated American psychology for roughly 40 years (approximately 1920–1960). The behaviorist would conceptualize coping as a series of learned behaviors that serve to remove or lessen the effects of aversive environmental stimuli. Consider the classic negative reinforcement situation in which an animal learns to remove an aversive stimulus, such as an electric shock, by pressing a lever. To the behaviorist, the animal's lever-pressing behavior is an example of coping, and coping is the end product of learning.

Humans also engage in this form of coping; for example, people quickly learn to carry umbrellas to avoid getting wet and control their driving speed (sometimes!) to avoid the stress of an encounter with a highway patrol officer.

Physiological Perspective

Previously, we considered the early work of Cannon and Selye Researchers adopting a physiological approach to the study of stress are likely to explain coping in physiological terms. Indeed, the general adaptation syndrome considered earlier can be thought of as the body's attempts to cope with an unwanted agent or situation.

As an example of this perspective, some research has examined how corticosteroid levels in the blood diminish as animals gain mastery over threatening events (Steptoe, 1989). Successful coping, then, might be conceptualized in terms of reductions in corticosteroid output. Similarly, in humans, reductions of various physiological indices have been observed as the novelty of the stressor diminishes, and individuals have the opportunity to cope with the stressor (cf. Balick & Herd, 1986).

Evolutionary/Biological Perspective

From an evolutionary standpoint, coping is understood in terms of adaptation to the environment. Thus, some organisms adapted or coped more effectively with environmental challenges, and these organisms stood a greater chance of surviving and genetically transmitting to their offspring the propensity to behave in similar ways. Coping therefore represents adaptive behaviors, which evolved to solve specific problems. That is, these behaviors are thought to have evolved over time to enable organisms to maximize their ability to cope with environmental stressors (Buss & Kenrick, 1998).

Cognitive Perspective

The cognitive perspective represents the most recent perspective for understanding the meaning of coping. Since Lazarus (1966) published his seminal book on coping, much of the literature has assumed a "cognitive flavor," whereby the individual is seen as an active agent who cognitively appraises her situation. She decides whether the presence of a stressor is bothersome and, if so, on the possible courses of action to cope with the stressor. This approach stands in stark contrast to earlier ones in which coping falls largely outside the province of conscious awareness.

The cognitive approach, then, views the individual as a decision maker who engages in two forms of appraisal: primary appraisal and secondary appraisal (Folkman, 1984; Folkman & Lazarus, 1980; Lazarus & Folkman, 1984). As we discussed earlier (Chapter 1), *primary appraisal* essentially involves determining whether and the extent to which a stressor is perceived as a threat, loss, or challenge (Lazarus & Launier, 1978). *Secondary appraisal* is the process of deciding upon potential responses—coping strategies—to deal with the stressor.

DEFINITIONS OF COPING

The psychological perspectives mentioned earlier offer quite distinct conceptualizations concerning the meaning of coping. Specific conceptual definitions have proliferated over the past few decades, leading to several conceptual definitions in the research literature. Moreover, some of these definitions combine elements from alternative perspectives, especially the cognitive and behavioral perspectives.

For example, Pearlin and Schooler (1978) defined coping as "... any response to external life-strains that serves to prevent, avoid, or control emotional distress" (Pearlin & Schooler, 1978, p. 2). This response may be either behavioral (e.g., taking action) or cognitive (e.g., looking for the "silver lining") More recently, Dewe and Guest (1990) offered a similar definition, combining cognitive and behavioral elements: Coping is any cognitive and/or behavioral response to internal/external demands imposed by the stressful situation.

Latack and Havlovic (1992) summarized a number of conceptual definitions of coping found both in the life stress and job stress literatures; a few of these are presented in Table 7.1. Notice that while many of these definitions are similar, a fair degree of diversity exists in the way coping is conceptualized.

TABLE 7.1   EXAMPLES OF COPING DEFINITIONS

Coyne, Aldwin, & Lazerus (1981)	*"Coping refers to efforts, both cognitive and behavioral and internal demands and conflicts affecting an individual that tax or exceed that person's resoources."*
Folkman and Lazerus (1980)	*"Coping is defined as the cognitive and behavioral efforts made to master, tolerate, or reduce external and internal demands and conflictsamong them."*
Latack (1986)	*"...coping is defined in this study as a response to situations characterized by uncertainty and important consequences."*
Osipow and Spokane (1984)	*"Coping responses, when they exist in adequate proportion, permit human beings not only to deal with a stress, but to increase their adaptive capacities as a consequence."*
Pearlin and Schooler (1978)	*"...the concept is being used here to reer to any response to external life strains that serves to prevent, avoid, or sontrol emotional distress."*

The diversity of definitions for coping is not a unique phenomenon in the area of job stress; indeed, we have already discussed this diversity in the definitions of stress itself. The lack of a common definition, however, creates problems inasmuch as researchers would like to be able to consolidate research with the goal of arriving at some general conclusions about what coping is and how its effectiveness can be maximized.

Schuler's (1985) Process Model of Coping

One approach that holds considerable promise for arriving at a common understanding of coping is Schuler's (1985) *integrative transactional process model of coping*. This model is quite similar to Beehr and Shuler's (1982) transactional process model of stress we examined earlier in Chapter 2 (Figure 2.4).

Coping as a Dynamic Process. Schuler conceptualizes coping as a process rather than as a defined set of physiological, psychological, and/or behavioral responses. Although a detailed exposition of the model is beyond the scope of this chapter, we would like to highlight some of the most important features of the model.

The model attempts to trace over time (hence the term *process model*) how an individual copes once he encounters a stressor and deems it to be stressful. This realization that a stressor is bothersome is the "coping trigger" that begins the coping process.

The coping trigger leads to both primary and secondary appraisal. These cognitive appraisals are central features of the model and underscore the influence of Lazarus's work. Primary appraisal involves answering a series of questions, such as "What is the relevant stressor?" "Where is the uncertainty?" and "Is it important?" (Schuler, 1985). Only if the stressor is deemed to be important does secondary appraisal begin. For example, if a worker is instructed to complete a complex task with no assistance, she may first determine that fear of not completing the task on time is stressful. Moreover, the worker may feel *uncertain* that she possesses the requisite skills to successfully complete the task and may deem failure to complete the task as extremely *important* from the standpoint of job security.

Secondary appraisal begins by asking why the stressful situation is considered important by focusing on how the situation affects needs/values (Schuler, 1985). Through this self-analysis, a person may determine that the stressor is no longer important and the process is thus terminated. If, however, the situation is still deemed important, the final component of secondary appraisal begins: the selection of specific coping strategies.

A number of factors are assumed to influence the choice of specific coping strategies (e.g., seek help from others, engage in relaxation techniques), including: (a) a cost/benefit analysis of each strategy, (b) readiness to engage in the strategy (e.g., quitting a job), (c) the availability of any needed support, and (d) individual differences, such as problem-solving ability.

An example may help to clarify these concepts. Suppose a person is faced with the potential prospect of an impending layoff. Whether coping efforts include looking for new work may depend on a host of considerations, including whether there is time for a job search, and whether the person is prepared to quit his current job (given that the layoff may be a long time coming or may never occur). Also, level of self-confidence is relevant because he may or may not be confident that a position can be found and, if found, whether there is a realistic chance of securing the new position.

Following implementation, specific strategies must be evaluated for their effectiveness, which may be assessed using a variety of cues, that may be physiological, psychological, or behavioral in nature (Schuler, 1985). Once effectiveness has been analyzed, the individual has valuable feedback that allows him to determine whether further action is necessary. This feedback will also be helpful for modifying existing strategies or selecting new ones as necessary.

In sum, the model is not linear but involves reciprocal influence (hence, the term *transactional model*).

Implications of Schuler's Model. One implication of the model derives from the premise that preferred coping strategies depend on individual difference variables such as self-efficacy. This has potentially important implications when designing organizational interventions to deal with work stress. For example, Schaubroeck, Jones, and Xie (2001) suggested that increasing the amount of job control to deal with job demands may not be successful (and may in fact be counterproductive) if individuals are low in self-efficacy and do not perceive they truly have control over their work environment.

Schuler's (1985) transactional process model also represents an important contribution in clarifying the meaning of coping. Here, coping is conceptualized as a process (much like stress). However, as we noted previously, models are not presented as "statements of truth." Rather, they serve as useful blueprints or frameworks for guiding further research. As research evidence accumulates, the model may be abandoned or, more likely, modified to accommodate new information.

For example, as researchers come to better understand the differences between *acute* (e.g., being fired at work) and *chronic* (e.g., daily monotonous work tasks) stressors (cf. Anshel,2000; Eulberg, Weekley, & Bhagat, 1988; Hahn & Smith, 1995; Pratt & Barling, 1988), they may need to expand the coping process model to address potential differences in how individuals cope with these stressors over time.

Beyond the theoretical contributions, the transactional process model of coping also makes an important contribution by aiding in the development of strategies to measure how work stress is managed. One obvious implication of the model from a measurement standpoint is that coping is a longitudinal process that should be assessed over time (cf. Kasl, 1983). For example, individuals may keep a "coping diary," which traces the process by which they coped with a stressful situation In addition, detailed analyses of the diary contents may help to bolster support for the transactional model if the types of appraisals predicted by the model are recorded. For instance, the diary entries may suggest that a person engaged in a sequence of cognitive appraisals as specified by the model. It would be important, however, to capture coping activities from the outset (as soon as the situation is appraised as stressful), so that data collection does not begin from some arbitrary starting point (Kasl, 1983).

Such a longitudinal approach may also lead to some fruitful theoretical contributions. As an example, one issue previously addressed in the coping literature is whether certain individuals have a more varied coping repertoire, in which they tend to select from a wide variety of specific strategies (Pearlin & Schooler, 1978; C. S. Smith & Sulsky, 1995). Building on this notion, a longitudinal analysis may uncover whether and the extent to which a person attempts one or more strategies at a given point in time. Some people may prefer to attempt one strategy at a time, while others adopt more of a "clustering strategy," such that alternative strategies are adopted concurrently.

The analysis may also shed light on whether some people prefer to begin their coping efforts by choosing strategies aimed at eliminating the stressor (proactive, action-oriented control strategies) before turning to other strategies that do not address the stressor directly, such as cognitively altering the meaning of the stressor through primary appraisal. Indeed, evidence suggests that individuals tend to begin with proactive, action-oriented strategies aimed at directly controlling the stressor. Later, more palliative indirect strategies aimed at making them feel better may be attempted as the direct activities fail over time (Overmier & Hellhammer, 1988; Parkes, 1984; Schuler, 1985).

In fact, a *learned helplessness model* may best explain how the choices of coping strategies change over time (Peterson & Seligman, 1984). Figure 7.1 presents a graph illustrating how the number of direct action-oriented control strategies aimed at removing/attenuating a given stressor may decrease as the number of experiences with the stressor increase over time in spite of the coping attempts. For example, a student continually may be stressed by ongoing family problems that she believes is affecting her school performance. She makes every effort to solve the problems through discussions with family members. As the family arguments persist (in spite of efforts to ameliorate the situation), she may begin to resign herself to a fate of endless battles and cease any attempts to end the fighting.

Of course, rather than repeated exposures to a stressor, one single stressful encounter may be perceived as sufficiently bothersome. Learned helplessness would still be expected to provide a realistic account of coping behavior directed toward the single encounter if the stressor is not removed and remains bothersome over time. As an illustration, a man discovers he is HIV positive. This news triggers a series of active coping attempts, including the adoption of a physical exercise program and meetings with medical professionals to gather pertinent information. If these activities do not lower perceived stress, however, he might become less active and severely depressed Eventually, he may just give in to his illness.

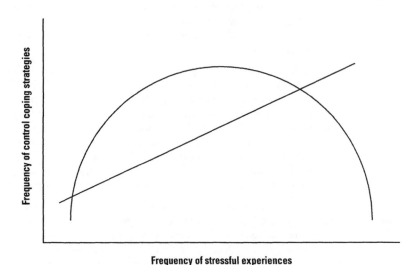

Frequency of control coping strategies

Frequency of stressful experiences

Figure 7.1 Using a Learned Helpfulness Model to Explain How Coping Changes Over Time

In summary, the meaning of coping is not necessarily straightforward, and alternative conceptualizations have been proposed that are quite distinct in some cases. Nonetheless, conceptualizing coping as a process, typified by Schuler's (1985) transactional process model of coping, holds promise for both its potential theoretical and methodological contributions to the study and understanding of coping with work stress.

Before turning our attention to how coping is measured, note that Schuler's model is not unique in that other process models considering coping have been proposed as well. For example, Edwards's (1992) cybernetic theory of stress and coping considers the process of coping (also see Chapter 2). However, Edwards's model is not, strictly speaking, exclusively a coping model; it is a model of the overall stress process, which considers coping a subset of the overall process. What distinguishes Schuler's model, therefore, is the exclusive focus on coping. Clearly, the development of additional models focused specifically on coping is needed, which will almost certainly be realized as coping research progresses. In particular, models focusing on the coping process in specific occupational groups represent an important contribution, insofar as they capture the unique coping challenges inherent in specific occupations (see Anshel, 2000, for a discussion of the coping process in the context of police work).

THE MEASUREMENT OF COPING

The measurement of coping involves recording the actual coping activities undertaken by an individual confronting a situation perceived to be stressful. Ideally, for any coping definition, there should be a close correspondence between the conceptual and operational definitions. That is, the conceptual definition should lead directly to the development of measures. These measures, in turn, should reflect the conceptual definition that gave rise to the measures in the first place.

Consider the psychoanalyst who understands coping as the interplay of internal unconscious psychic forces. She would assess coping by first choosing measures or procedures (e.g., projective tests, dream analysis) that help her glimpse into the unconscious mind.

Unfortunately, the measurement of coping has not always followed closely from any defined theory or conceptual definition. This situation has led to a plethora of coping typologies and measures for assessing these typologies. Without a theoretical context that clearly ties the coping measures to a conceptual definition of coping, interpretation of any coping data derived from these measures becomes somewhat tenuous. F. Cohen (1987) concluded that no real tangible progress has been made in the measurement of coping. Although somewhat dated, that statement is still largely true today. With that somewhat pessimistic appraisal, we now turn to a brief outline of some specific coping measures, and consider the issue of convergence between theory and method in the context of some of these measures.

Specific Measures of Coping

Two highly popular measures of coping, the Ways of Coping (WOC) scale (Folkman & Lazarus, 1980) and the revised Ways of Coping questionnaire (WCQ; Folkman & Lazarus, 1985), have been widely adopted in the life stress and work stress literatures. The underlying theoretical framework that forms the basis of these measures is Folkman and Lazarus's (1980) conceptual definition of coping, defined as the cognitive and behavioral efforts adopted to deal with internal/external demands (Table 7.1). This definition led to the development of two global types of coping categories: problem-focused coping and emotion-focused coping *Problem-focused coping* is defined as coping aimed at proactively doing something about the stressful situation, while *emotion-focused coping* is defined as the cognitive regulation of stressful emotions. As an example, talking to your supervisor about some negative performance feedback you received would be a problem-focused strategy; deciding that you don't care about what the supervisor thinks would typify an emotion-focused coping response.

This typology led to the development of the WOC scale, a 68-item checklist on which respondents indicate whether or not they adopted a number of distinct coping strategies that are assumed to be either problem-focused or emotion-focused (Folkman & Lazarus, 1980). Folkman and Lazarus (1985) later revised the WOC scale to create the WCQ, a 66-item scale in which respondents are asked to indicate, using a 4-point Likert-type scale, the extent to which they used each item when coping with a given stressful situation under consideration. Thus, unlike the WOC (which requires a "yes" or "no" response to each item), the revised WCQ assesses the *extent* to which each of a number of coping responses were attempted.

A number of psychometric evaluations of the WOC and the WCQ have been undertaken (e.g., Folkman, Lazarus, Dunkel-Schetter, DeLongis, & Gruen, 1986; Vitliano, Russo, Carr, Maiuri, & Becker, 1985), and statistical analyses of the scale data have been used to derive categories of coping. As an illustration, Vitliano and colleagues factor analyzed the WOC and uncovered five primary categorizations instead of the two categories (i.e., problem and emotion-focused) originally proposed. Their analysis revealed a "Problem-Focused" catagory containing *both* proactive behaviors (e.g., "stood my ground and fought for what I wanted") and proactive cognitions (e.g., "concentrated on something good that could come out of the whole thing"). Three categories appear to capture more avoidant type cognitions; for example, a "Blamed Self" category emerged from the analysis An example of an item from this category is "Criticized or lectured yourself." Finally, a "Seeks Social Support" category emerged. For instance, one item from this category is "Talked to someone to find out about the situation." Social support is a critically important coping category, as we will discuss later in this chapter.

A conceptual problem immediately arises when statistical analyses are used to derive conceptual categories. The generation of these categories is data-driven rather than theory-driven, and subjective decisions about how the data should be analyzed and interpreted can lead to very different solutions, possibly suggesting a different set of coping categories. Not surprisingly, the various factor analyses of the WOC and the WCQ have arrived at different solutions with different numbers and types of coping categories. As an example, one factor analysis of the WCQ uncovered eight distinct coping categories (cf. Folkman et al., 1986) The reliance on statistical methods to develop coping typologies underscores the problem introduced earlier: Namely, measures of coping with alternative typologies or categories are not necessarily based on any a priori theory or conceptual definition of coping. Rather, empirically derived scales have been developed that have tenuous connections at best to any conceptualization of coping.

Carver, Scheier, & Weintraub, (1989) expressed a similar concern about the need for theoretically derived coping measures. Accordingly, they developed a multidimensional coping inventory ("COPE") containing 13 distinct coping categories based largely on a number of coping theories, including the theory proposed by Folkman and Lazarus (1980) Carver et al.

also included a category of maladaptive coping behaviors, such as drug use and behavioral withdrawal.

In a similar vein, Endler and Parker (1990) developed a multidimensional coping inventory with three categories (task-oriented, emotion-oriented, and avoidance-oriented coping) called the MCI. By way of comparison with the Folkman and Lazarus (1980) model, task-oriented coping would be the same as problem-focused coping, and emotion-oriented would be the same as emotion-focused coping. Returning now to the earlier example of an employee receiving negative feedback, an example of avoidance-oriented coping would be leaving work early or failing to return to work the next day following the news. Endler and Parker (1990) drew on available theory in developing their coping items, especially the distinction between problem-focused and emotion-focused coping. Also, they questioned the reliability and validity (e.g., low internal consistency, weak evidence for validity) of both the WOC and the WCQ as a central impetus for developing their own scale.

Billings and Moos (1981) developed an alternative coping typology and a set of coping scales that suggest a rather different underlying conceptualization of coping. According to their formulation, there are three categories of coping: (a) active-cognitive (11 items: e.g., "Tried to see the best of the"), (b) active behavioral (13 items: "Talked with friend about the problem"), and (c) avoidance strategies (8 items: "Tried to reduce tension by drinking more"). Here, an explicit attempt is made to acknowledge proactive cognitive coping activities as well as behavioral ones. Thus, cognitive reappraisal through active cognitive coping is viewed as a type of proactive coping response as the information is reevaluated so that it is perceived to be less stressful. Also, the inclusion of the avoidance strategies highlights the fact that coping in this framework is not necessarily considered to be either a positive or helpful enterprise (cf. Tattersall, Bennett, & Pugh, 1999).

Coping Measures Designed for the Work Setting

Additional coping measures and typologies have been developed specifically for the work context. One example is the Personal Resources Questionnaire (PRQ) developed by Osipow and Spokane (1984) and used by Osipow and Davis (1988) in a study examining the possibility that the relationship between perceived stress and subsequent strains is weakened when coping behaviors are used. The PRQ contains four coping categories (e.g., rational-cognitive coping). Available evidence suggests that these categories possess satisfactory levels of internal consistency reliability.

A promising typology of coping with work stress was developed by Latack (1986). Drawing on the earlier conceptual formulations offered by Folkman and Lazarus (1980), as well as Billings and Moos (1981), Latack developed three categories of coping activities: (a) control strategies (17 items), (b) escape strategies (11 items), and (c) symptom management strategies (24 items). *Control strategies* are proactive behaviors and cognitions aimed at either removing (behaviors) or reevaluating (cognitions) the stressful situation (e.g., "Get together with my supervisor to discuss this," "Tell myself that I can probably work things out to my advantage"), while *escape strategies* are avoidant-type behaviors and cognitions (e.g., "Remind myself that work isn't everything," "Separate myself as much as possible from the people who created this situation"). *Symptom management* strategies are a somewhat heterogeneous collection of strategies (e.g., "Take tranquilizers, sedatives, or other drugs," "Do physical exercise...") aimed at attenuating the negative consequences, such as anxiety or tension, associated with stress.

Overall, the psychometric analyses performed on the scales suggest that they are psychometrically sound (Latack, 1986). Statistical analyses of coping data supported the existence of separate control and escape factors; symptom management strategies, however, were not included in the analysis (Leiter, 1991).

Latack's (1986) conceptualization of coping is consistent with other earlier ones; for example, Pearlin and Schooler (1978) suggested that coping may be used to: (a) eliminate/modify stressors, (b) perceptually control the meaning of the stressful situation, and (c) help control emotional consequences. These three functions of coping would be presumably addressed, in turn, by control behaviors, control cognitions, and symptom management, respectively.

For example, a supervisor continually yells at an employee for no obvious reason. The employee may talk about these incidents with the supervisor in hope of ending the outbursts (eliminating the stressor). Alternately, the employee may decide that the boss yells at everyone so it is nothing personal and can be ignored (controlling the meaning of the situation). Finally, the employee may go for a brisk walk to relieve some of the tension (controlling emotional consequences). We will return to Latack's conceptualization when stress management is discussed. We believe that this conceptualization is useful for organizing our thoughts about stress management.

One potential weakness associated with the Latack (1986) typology should be noted at this point. Some of the symptom management items may be considered adaptive (e.g., "Use relaxation training"), while others are arguably maladaptive in nature (e.g., "Take tranquilizers..."). There might be some theoretical as well as practical utility in separating these two classes of items. Other analytical procedures beyond those used by Latack (1986) in deriving her categories (e.g., confirmatory factor analysis) may reveal that the symptom-management category can be subdivided into more than one category.

In a study investigating coping with unemployment, Wanberg (1997) used a scale developed by Kinicki and Latack (1990) based on Latack's conceptualization of control and escape coping. The scale assesses five dimensions of coping activities in the face of job loss (Control Activities: Proactive Search, Nonwork Organization, Positive Self Assessment; Escape

Activities: Distancing from Loss, Job Devaluation). Both Kinicki and Latack (1990) and Wanberg (1997) reported that the scale possesses sound psychometric properties. Wanberg's SEM analyses (Chapter 3), however, suggest that future refinements of the scale may be useful.

Dewe and Guest (1990) attempted to develop a set of coping categories by explicitly *avoiding* reference to any a priori theory. The idea was that imposing a theory would restrict the type of information that might be collected. By asking people how they have coped, without reference to preexisting conceptualizations, a richer array of coping responses might be obtained. Although the intent was not to develop a coping measure per se, their research is thought provoking and quite relevant for inclusion in our discussion of coping measures and categories.

From an epistemological standpoint, their contention was that categories of coping should not be derived through theory. Instead, using an inductive approach of open-ended interviews, coping items were generated and the categories emerged through statistical analyses of the coping data. Overall five categories appeared to capture the data and generalized well across some diverse occupations (e.g., teachers and nurses). The categories identified were (a) "Rational Task-Oriented Behavior," (b) "Emotional Release," (c) "Distraction," (d) "Social Support," and (e) "Passive Rationalization." For example, assume your computer is malfunctioning and you must complete a report within one hour! You may (a) try to repair the computer yourself (task-oriented behavior), (b) kick your favorite chair (emotional release), (c) attempt to think about something else for a while to calm yourself (distraction), (d) call a friend for some consoling (social support), or (e) decide that the report is not that important anyway (passive rationalization).

Although the inductive approach is useful in generating information and developing a conceptual framework or theory of coping, the framework still needs to be tested on future samples. Interestingly, the Dewe and Guest (1990) coping typology includes dimensions similar to those contained in some of the other preceding typologies.

Finally, Beaton, Murphy, Johnson, Pike, and Corneil (1999) developed a coping measure specifically designed for emergency workers (e.g., paramedics): The Coping Responses of Rescue Workers Inventory (CRRWI). A more tailored coping measure may be useful for capturing coping responses idiosyncratic to certain jobs or occupations. We expect to see more of these types of coping measures in the future.

Methodological Issues

Earlier, we discussed the potential usefulness of collecting longitudinal coping data. As the preceding discussion of coping measures suggests, however, these scales have not been designed for collecting longitudinal data. What characterizes these measures is that they are all self-report questionnaires, used to obtain cross-sectional retrospective reports of coping. Typically, individuals are asked how they previously coped with: (a) a specific stressor chosen by the researcher, such as role ambiguity (e.g., Latack, 1986), (b) a self-selected episode that they felt was stressful (e.g., Parkes, 1990), or (c) stress in general without a specific stressor referent (e.g., Carver et al., 1989) .

In spite of some differences in method (i.e., whether the researcher or the subject chooses the stressor referent), all of these studies share a reliance on cross-sectional coping data based on individual, self-reported memories for previously attempted coping activities. This type of approach is certainly "cleaner" from the standpoint of obtaining interpretable quantitative data. However, it fails to capture the inherent richness and complexity of coping as predicted by Schuler's (1985) transactional model. Longitudinal studies of coping are rare (see Holahan, Moos, Holahan, & Cronkite, 1999).

Perhaps more troubling are a series of conceptual and methodological problems associated with the self-report, cross-sectional approach. A number of distinct problems may be raised in this regard. First, self-report measures of coping may potentially suffer from common method variance (Ganster & Schaubroeck, 1991), a topic introduced in Chapter 3. Recall that method variance occurs when the method of measurement (e.g., self-reports) introduces error: for example, when a person provides socially desirable responses. Of course, this is a potential problem associated with any type of self-report data. Thus, longitudinal data may be similarly affected by sources of method variance if the data are based on self-reports.

A second problem directly relevant to the cross-sectional nature of the data is the reliance placed on a respondent's memory when generating coping responses (cf. Stone et al., 1998; see also Chapter 3). This problem is potentially critical because detailed memory of coping-related activities, especially if many assorted specific responses must be recalled, is likely to fade over time. This issue may be especially problematic when the context of the question is something like "How do you cope with everyday stress?" Without a focus or specific context (i.e., a specific stressor) a greater number of activities will have to be retrieved from memory.

The issue of memory decay was considered by Sulsky and Smith (1995), who hypothesized that the number of stressors an individual experienced at work would predict the number of coping strategies reported when they were asked to report how they coped with a *single focal job stressor* chosen by the respondent. Specifically, Sulsky and Smith (1995) adopted the concept of *cognitive schemas* (Alba & Hasher, 1983) as the framework for their study. The concept of a schema derives from cognitive and social-cognitive psychology. In short, schemas are organized bodies of information held in memory that are linked together. A coping schema would thus contain a constellation of assorted coping activities used in the past to deal with various stressful situations (see also Peacock, Wong, & Reker, 1993).

When an individual is asked to recall prior coping activities for one stressor, a memory search of the coping schema(s) would be conducted. Unfortunately, however, an unwanted by-product of this search is that coping strategies attempted for stressors other than the focal stressor under consideration may be retrieved from the schema(s) and reported, thus generating a false positive report. Because people who have experienced more stress in the past are assumed to have more detailed/richer coping schemas, a higher rate of false recognitions on the coping measure would be expected when the self-report coping measure is completed by considering one focal stressor. Overall, Sulsky and Smith (1995) obtained results consistent with this interpretation.

These results make sense intuitively. Assume you have attempted a number of coping strategies in the past to deal with the stress of final exams (e.g., studying all night, discussing the material with classmates). Now, you are asked how you coped with a particular exam last year. You might report that you studied all night for that particular exam whether you did or not. After all, you have coped that way in the past, and it comes to mind when you are asked to remember an event that is then 1 year old.

A third problem with this methodology is conceptual: Self-report scales constrain responses to the sample of items on the scale. Even when an option exists to include additional information (e.g., an open-ended question soliciting additional coping responses not covered by the scale), the rich detail afforded by a more qualitative analysis of coping cannot easily be captured Clearly, information about sequences of activities, time frame, and so on, are lost when the cross-sectional approach is adopted.

Additional problems endemic to the cross-sectional, self-report coping methodology were reviewed by Stone, Greenberg, Kennedy-Moore, and Newman (1991). For example, they noted that scales utilizing an "extent" response key, such as the WCQ scale (e.g., 0 = not used; 3 = used a great deal), lead to problems because the meaning of the term "extent" appears to vary across people and items. As an example, one person may interpret "extent" as the number of times a coping response is enacted, while another interprets "extent" in terms of the amount of effort expended in one coping response. Obviously, this issue raises concerns about measurement reliability. The problem of unreliability was also raised by O'Driscoll and Cooper (1994), who noted the generally poor internal consistency reliability of existing coping measures.

Overall, a confusing array of coping measures exists, some weakly grounded in terms of theory, some of dubious psychometric quality. Myriad concerns about the cross-sectional, self-report methodology that is central to the use of these various measures also exist. On a more positive note, however, the development of Latack's (1986) coping typology is encouraging. This typology, especially the control and escape dimensions, can be highly useful in conceptualizing alternative ways of coping with job stress. In particular, this framework will be very helpful when we provide an organized framework for stress management, which will be both the final topic addressed in this chapter and the focus of the last chapter (Chapter 8).

CHOOSING COPING STRATEGIES: THE TRAIT VERSUS SITUATION DEBATE

Now that we have discussed the meaning and measurement of coping, we can turn our attention to a topic that has generated considerable interest in both the life and job stress literatures. Specifically, what influences the choice(s) of specific coping strategies? At the heart of this issue is the perennial problem raised in discussions of personality: Is personality a trait, state, or an interaction of the two? In the context of coping, an analogue exists: The choice of specific types of coping strategies (e.g., active vs. avoidant strategies) may be determined by (a) certain personality traits, other individual difference variables, or dispositional tendencies, (b) the situation, however "situation" is defined, or (c) the interaction between (a) and (b). As one might imagine, coping research has found support for all three possibilities, which are considered next.

Individual Differences in Coping

We first examined individual differences as they relate to the stress process in Chapter 6. Here, the emphasis is on individual differences as they pertain to coping responses. Considerable research has focused on the idea that the choice of specific coping responses depends on: (a) certain personality traits like locus of control, (b) preferential tendencies, such as generalized preferences for particular types of coping activities, and (c) other individual difference variables, such as gender.

A variety of variables, including socioeconomic status, personality traits, and other individual difference variables (e.g., gender, age, sex-role orientation, availability of social networks) have all been shown to predict choices for alternative types of coping responses (Blanchard-Fields, Sulsky, & Robinson-Whelen, 1991; Gianakos, 2000; Greenglass, Burke, & Ondrack, 1990; Holahan & Moos, 1987; Parkes, 1990). Much of this research has been conducted in the life stress area, although some studies have specifically considered work stress (e.g., Parkes, 1990). For example, research suggests that people with an internal locus of control (i.e., they perceive they have personal control over their environment) tend to adopt more action-oriented strategies compared to those with an external locus of control (i.e., they feel little control over their lives), who tend to opt for more avoidant-type strategies (cf. Folkman, 1984). Holahan and Moos (1987) found that people with family support tended to report more active coping activities compared to others with less support. Dougall, Hyman, Hayward, McFeeley, and Baum (2001)found that an optimistic disposition was associated with greater reported use of problem-focused strategies and less avoidant strategies. Jex, Bliese, Buzzell, and Primeau (2001) suggested that individuals high in self-efficacy may have a propensity to choose control-oriented strategies. Finally, Smith and Sulsky (1995) discovered, across three diverse work samples, a variety of stressors, a general preference for control-type coping strategies at work compared to escape- or symptom-management-type strategies.

Although the preponderance of the evidence across numerous studies and variables supports the importance of individual difference variables as predictors of coping choices, a few caveats are in order. First, a problem arises when respondents are asked to select their own stressful situation as the coping referent (e.g., Parkes, 1990). In this case, the individual difference variable in question (e.g., gender) may predispose the respondent to select a particular *type* of stressor, and this type of stressor, in turn, influences coping responses rather than gender per se. This possibility would support the contention that the *situation* (i.e., the specific stressor) rather than gender influenced coping responses. Asking respondents how they cope in general rather than how they cope with a specific stressor referent would seem to be a preferable strategy for examining the role of individual differences (cf. Carver et al., 1989).

Second, all of the results may be tempered by problems discussed earlier in connection with the self-report coping measures. Problems such as method variance may affect the quality of the self-report data in some cases such that any conclusions should be drawn with some caution.

Situational Influences on Coping Activities

Just as evidence has accumulated suggesting that individual differences predict coping response choices, other evidence points to the importance of situational variables as predictors of choice. For example, Folkman and Lazarus (1980) found that individuals tend to cope differently with family-related issues compared to work issues. Kalichman, Gueritault-Chalvin, and Demi (2000) found that nurses reported different coping strategies conditional on the type of stressors involved. McCrae (1984) reported that different coping patterns were invoked as a function of how the stressful situation is appraised (as a threat, loss, or challenge). Parkes (1986) discovered that coping type varied across five different categories of stressful work episodes.

Intuitively, it makes sense that the situation should influence coping choices Schuler's (1985) transactional model, for example, clearly highlights the importance of situational factors. As discussed earlier, the model posits that the choice of specific coping responses depends on a number of situational variables, including whether resources are available to engage in particular responses. Thus, "situation" is defined more broadly in the model beyond type or class of stressor to include variables such as readiness and available support.

Certainly, the fact that some coping research has been targeted toward such diverse occupations as lawyers (e.g., Kobasa, 1982a), teachers (e.g., Schoenfeld, 1990), police officers (e.g., Anshel, 2000; Beehr, Johnson, & Nieva, 1995; Hart et al., 1995), bus drivers (e.g., Kuhlmann, 1990; Raggatt, 1991), and physicians (Ghosh, 2000) is testimony to the idea that researchers acknowledge the importance of situational factors (e.g., occupational type) in the study of coping.

Overall, both empirical and theoretical support exist for the role of the situation in predicting coping choices. Once again, however, a cautionary note about methodological limitations is in order: Limitations inherent in the self-report approach may call into question some of the preceding findings.

Evidence for Interactive Effects

Do individual difference variables and situational variables interact to predict coping choices? By interaction, we mean that individual differences and the situation work together and cannot be easily separated. A nice illustration of this idea can be found in Schuler's (1985) transactional model in which both types of variables (e.g., cognitive complexity and readiness) are assumed to jointly determine coping choices.

Evidence for the interactionist position is scant, although this could be at least partially explained by the fact that the interactionist position has, relatively speaking, received less attention in the first place. However, available data support the interactionist position. For instance, Parkes (1984) found that locus of control predicted type of coping responses conditional upon controllability. Thus, both the individual difference variable (locus of control) and the situational variable (controllability) were apparently involved in the choice of specific responses. This finding implies, for example, that a person with an internal locus of control may choose an active coping response only if he believes the situation is controllable or can be modified. If he determines there is no chance of removing the stressful situation, active coping is not likely to take plac.e

Likewise, Pearlin and Schooler (1978) presented evidence that both the type of stressful situation (e.g., money problems) and individual difference variables (e.g., socioeconomic status) predict the choices of specific coping responses.

Overall, evidence points to the potential importance of both individual difference and situational variables in the prediction of specific coping responses (Figure 7.2). Although perhaps theoretically important, it is necessary to consider the *practical* importance of this evidence as well. Specifically, how can this evidence be useful when planning stress management interventions? This issue is one of the questions considered in the next chapter.

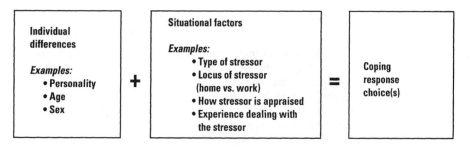

Figure 7.2 Interactionist Perspective on How People Choose Coping Responses

COPING EFFICACY

A question of critical importance to designers of stress management programs is a simple one: Do certain coping strategies work better than others? This question is fundamental inasmuch as stress management should ideally promote coping strategies presumed to be effective. Some research has attempted to address this question, but the results are mixed and difficult to consolidate. What follows is a brief summary of some of these results.

Latack (1986) reported significant negative correlations between control coping and anxiety as well as propensity to quit. A positive correlation between control coping and job satisfaction was also reported. Both escape and symptom management coping were significant predictors of psychosomatic complaints (see also Leiter, 1991) Parkes (1990) found that emotion-focused coping (i.e., using a subscale from the WOC scale) was associated with somatic and affective symptoms. Healy and McKay (2000)found that avoidant coping strategies predicted mood disturbance. However, Kuhlmann (1990) failed to find relationships between problem-focused coping and alternative strain measures.

In some studies, researchers have found interactive effects For example, Osipow and Davis (1988) discovered that use of social support as a coping strategy moderated the stress-strain relationship, such that increasing levels of certain sources of stress were less predictive of increasing strains as levels of social-support increased (see also Parkes, 1990). Other studies, however, have failed to uncover interactive effects (e.g., Aldwin & Revenson, 1987; Shinn, Rosario, Morch, & Chestnut, 1984).

Distilling these diverse results, it is tempting to conclude that control and problem-focused coping are generally better than more avoidant strategies (e.g., escape and certain types of emotion-focused coping). Certainly, this statement makes some intuitive sense. However, with one exception (Aldwin & Revenson, 1987) these studies did not *directly* examine whether coping was successful in attenuating/eliminating the stressful situation. Rather, the researchers inferred success based on correlational/predictive information.

Is the *direct* examination of coping success important? Yes, it is for both methodological as well as theoretical reasons. First, from a methodological standpoint, the correlational strategy is problematic. Respondents are typically asked how they coped with a single stressful episode, and the number of coping responses (e.g., number of specific control coping strategies reported) is correlated with some distal outcome measure like job satisfaction (cf. Latack, 1986).

Why should number of coping responses to *one* stressful situation, however, predict something as global as job satisfaction? The correlation is only interpretable if it is assumed that number of coping responses somehow typifies how people cope in all situations. For example, the respondent would not be expected to engage in much escape-type coping in other situations if he does not report many escape-type responses to the single stressor under consideration. This assumption is tantamount to accepting the proposition that situational variables probably play little or no role in coping response selection.

A second concern is more theoretical. Why should the number of coping responses to a stressful situation, such as the number of reported control coping strategies, predict anything? If the coping was effective in managing the stressful situation, the person would probably end her coping efforts. On the other hand, as the report of control coping responses increases, many specific control strategies probably failed. In short, number of coping responses becomes hopelessly confounded with the issue of whether or not individual coping responses were or were not successful.

Based on the preceding discussion, any examinations of coping efficacy necessitate the examination of coping success *directly* (rather than inferentially through correlational data). Of course, a conceptual definition of success is needed if it is to be measured.

In one study, Aldwin and Revenson (1987) defined success as whether and the extent to which respondents felt they handled the stressful situation well. However, success can be conceptualized more broadly. Thus, success may mean successful removal of a stressor, success in cognitively reappraising a situation, or success in managing stress through exercise and relaxation. In short, rather than stating that a given coping response is inherently "good'" or successful, what the response is trying to accomplish (e.g., managing symptoms) should be considered. Then one should attempt to determine whether and the degree to which the response was successful in meeting its intended result.

The Role of Social Support

Social support, broadly defined here as "the resources provided by other persons" (Cohen & Syme, 1985, p. 4), has probably received more attention from organizational stress researchers in recent years than any other individual or group characteristic. Social support is thought to enable people to cope with life and work stress effectively because, as a consequence of the support, they feel valued and are enmeshed in a network of communication and mutual obligation (House, 1981; Lazarus, 1966; Lazarus & Folkman, 1984). Individuals indicating that they have close, supportive family members, friends, supervisors and/or coworkers, who are available when life is stressful, indeed have reported lower depression (Barrera, 1981; Billings & Moos, 1981; Frese, 1999), physical health problems (Schmieder & Smith, 1996), anxiety (Barrera, 1981; Billings & Moos, 1981; Frese, 1999), use of health services (Broadhead, Gehlbach, DeGruy, & Kaplan, 1989), and health-care costs (Manning, Jackson, & Fusilier, 1996).

Theoretical Models of Social Support.   One important research question concerning social support is whether it directly affects strain levels equally, regardless of how severe the stress is perceived to be, or whether it works best for highly stressed individuals (e.g., Beehr, King, & King, 1990; Ganster, Fusilier & Mayes, 1986; Gore, 1985).

One of the most common effects is a *direct* or *main effect* of social support on strain, which predicts that social support has beneficial effects on strain regardless of the amount of experienced stress (i.e., the severity of the stressors) experienced. In a sample of workers from five different organizations, individuals who reported low supervisor support also reported strains, such as dissatisfaction with work and depression (Beehr, 1976). Another study (Blau, 1981) examined social support in a sample of bus drivers and found that drivers with supportive supervisors and coworkers were more satisfied with their jobs. Last, Zellars and Perrewe (2001) discovered that the availability of emotional social support may have a beneficial effect on burnout, depending on the exact nature of the support.

Other researchers have reported a more indirect link between social support and strain, referred to as the *buffering* or *moderating effect* of social support (e.g., Frese, 1999; Schaubroeck & Fink, 1998; Schmieder & Smith, 1996). The buffering effect posits that the relationship between stress(ors) and strains varies such that social support is effective primarily for those individuals experiencing high stress (Figure 7.3). Social support is assumed to be most effective only at high stress levels because increases in perceived stress are compensated with a mobilization of resources to reduce or manage the perceived threat (Gore, 1985)

Along these lines, House and Wells (1978) studied work-related social support in a sample of chemical plant employees. They found that only the highly stressed employees, who also reported high levels of supervisor support,

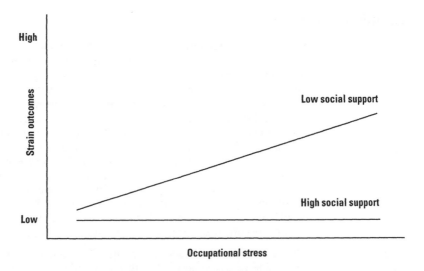

**Figure 7.3 The Interaction Effects of Stress and Social Support Predicted
by the Buffering Hypothesis**

experienced fewer mental and physical health problems (compared to employees with low levels of support). A similar type of relationship also existed between extra-organizational (spouse, family, and friends) support and strain.

Other research, however, has failed to find evidence of a buffering effect (e.g., Beehr, Jex, Stacy, & Murray, 2000). Although Beehr et al. found that social support predicted psychological strains, it did not moderate the stressor-strain relationship.

Interestingly, reverse buffering effects have also been reported. This counterintuitive finding states that social support has a negative effect on strain In a sample of nurses, Kaufmann and Beehr (1986) found that stressor-strain relationships were stronger for those nurses who reported low social support. That is, as the level of stress increased, there was a greater tendency for strains to increase as well when the provision of social support was deemed to be low. More recently, a study examining burnout in nursing-home nurses reported that high levels of coworker support were associated with high levels of emotional exhaustion (Ray & Miller, 1994). Different explanations have been offered for this type of effect. One explanation is that the providers of social support may remind the recipient of the stressful situation (Blau, 1981) or may convince him that the situation is even worse than originally imagined (LaRocco, House, & French, 1980).

So, what can be surmised from these results? When would one expect to find a main effect or a buffering effect for social support? Although the answers are far from definitive at this point, a few generalizations can be offered. Most studies that reported buffering effects have examined health-related strains (e.g., physical well-being, anxiety, depression; Beehr, 1985; Cohen & Wills, 1985; Parkes, Mendham, & von Rabenau, 1994), whereas studies that have found main effects have typically examined job attitudes (Beehr, King, & King, 1990; LaRocco et al., 1980; Parkes et al., 1994). These findings are reasonable because health and well-being should be more affected than attitudinal states in high-stress situations.

Measures of Social Support.   Researchers have also noted differences depending on the type of social support measure used. One type of social support measure, social embeddedness, attempts to describe a person's integration in a social network (how many friends or relatives they have). A second type of social support measure, received (enacted) support, assesses what people do when they seek support from others (whom they have asked for help in the recent past). Neither social embeddedness nor received support measures have consistently shown health-protective effects. In the case of social embeddedness, the measures really do not describe the process by which support influences stress and strain (Gottlieb, 1983), so a relationship between them would not be expected. The received support measures, on the other hand, seem to be associated with ineffective coping: That is, people often seek help from others when they are unable to deal with a stressful situation (Kaufmann & Beehr, 1986; Rosenberg, 1987).

The most commonly used measure of social support is perceived support, or the support perceived to be available but not yet received. This type of social support measure has shown the most consistent relationships with stress and health strains and is thought to be health-protective (House & Wells, 1978; Wethington & Kessler, 1986). The health-protective effects of perceived support presumably arise because, if a person perceives that he has potential support from others, he is less likely to appraise a situation as stressful (Wethington & Kessler, 1986).

Social support researchers have called for an expanded conceptualization, not only of the type (e.g., received or perceived) of social support measures, but also of the form or content (Barling, Bluen, & Fain, 1987). Typically, social support measures have assessed the emotional or instrumental (i.e., providing money or goods) components. Fenlason and Beehr (1994) examined job-related social support in a heterogeneous sample of female office workers using the traditional emotional and instrumental social support measures and more focused or specific measures of verbally transmitted work support (e.g., "We talk about how we dislike some parts of our work," "We share interesting ideas about performing our jobs"). They found that the focused measures were more important predictors of strains than the traditional measures. Although these results seem promising, further research is needed to establish the usefulness of these new scales.

New Perspectives on Social Support. In addition to methodological issues, researchers have investigated the boundary conditions under which social support operates in the work environment Etzion (1984) examined the relative effects of both work-related and extra-organizational support on male and female workers. Etzion reasoned that social support may be differentially effective for men and women because women are socialized in childhood to be more relationship-oriented than men. She asked 657 male and female professionals to answer a survey on social support, job and life stressors, and burnout. The women reported experiencing more stress (including burnout) but also more social support than men. Interestingly, her results also suggested that women tended to rely on extra-organizational sources of social support, whereas men tended to rely on work-related sources of social support.

An expanded job demands-control model (J. J. Johnson, 1989; see also Theorell & Karasek, 1996) has also incorporated the notion of social support to more fully explain the relationship between control at work and health. Recall from Chapter 2 that Karasek's (1979) model proposes that job-related stressors are harmful only when combined with low control Johnson (1989) predicted that the *combined* lack of work control and perceived social support has the most harmful effects on health and demonstrated empirical support for his predictions (J. V. Johnson & Hall., 1988). However, other empirical tests of this proposition, which implies a three-way interaction between stress(ors), control, and social support, have not been very supportive (Melamed, Kushnir, & Meir, 1991; Parkes, Mendham, & von Rabenau, 1994; Schmieder, 1994).

Frese (1999) reexamined the buffering effect of social support using both methodological and theoretical improvements over past research. Specifically, using blue-collar workers in the German metal industry, he tested the effects of social support using objective measures (i.e., observations, peer ratings, and self-perceptions of stressors) and a longitudinal design to control for prior psychological dysfunction. Frese also used the Match Hypothesis as a theoretical framework; the Match Hypothesis states that the buffering effect should be strongest when a match exists between coping requirements (e.g., social stressors, such as coworker conflict) and available support (Cohen & Wills, 1985). Extending that hypothesis to the dependent variables, Frese predicted that social support also should show a buffering effect more frequently with social dysfunctions (e.g., social anxiety). He found support for the buffering hypothesis and for the Match Hypothesis and its extension. That is, the social stressors and social dysfunctions (strains) were most often associated with the buffering effects.

Social support researchers have expended much effort over the past couple of decades examining the various methodological and theoretical issues discussed here. Although some of the basic issues have been at least partially resolved (e.g., Under what conditions would the buffering effect be expected and strongest?), some issues loom on the horizon. In particular, seeking social support may serve as a useful coping endeavor to help (a) remove/modify the stressful situation, (b) perceive the situation differently, or (c) manage the consequences of stress. In this way, following Latack (1986), seeking social support can be understood to function as either a behavioral control, cognitive control, or symptom management strategy. The specific function of support in a given situation depends on what type of support is provided and how the support is used (see also Gore, 1985).

To clarify these distinctions, an example might be helpful. Assume you just learned that your credit card has been cancelled due to insufficient payments. First, you might call a friend who can lend you money to enable you to reinstate your card (removing the stressful situation). Alternately, you may contact the friend to seek advice that may lessen your worries about losing the card (perceiving the situation differently). Finally, you may call your friend to ask if she would like to help you eat your way out of misery at the local fast-food outlet (managing the consequences). (Naturally, your friend would pay!)

Support for the idea that social support has potentially multiple points of impact in the stress process was obtained by Viswesvaran et al. (1999). Their meta-analyses suggest that social support was related to reductions in stressors and strains and that social support also moderated the stress-strain relationship. Clearly, social support can influence the stress process in multiple ways.

Finally, evidence suggests that some organizational interventions may help increase the amount of social support that employees receive (Heany, Price, & Rafferty, 1995). For example, interventions aimed at improving the social environment (e.g., increasing group consensus) may attenuate the relationships between work stress and both depression and morale (Bliese & Britt, 2001).

By now, you should begin to understand how conceptually related topics like coping and social support are to the process of stress management. In the following concluding comments, we begin to build the conceptual link between coping and stress management interventions at work. The final chapter provides a detailed treatment of stress management at work.

CONCLUSIONS

To this point, we have attempted to consider the meaning and measurement of coping with work stress. Additionally, we examined some issues that are of concern to coping researchers, such as: (a) What predicts the choice(s) of coping responses? and (b) Are some coping responses more successful than others? Overall, the reader may sense that coping research is in a state of disarray, as both theoretical and methodological problems appear to plague much of the research. We do not wish to paint such a pessimistic portrait, however. In fact, our contention is that theory and empirical research in the area of coping is highly useful for (a) suggesting possible coping responses that may be introduced to workers for stress management on the job, and (b) helping to develop an overall framework for stress management interventions.

Drawing on Latack's (1986) formulation of control, escape, and symptom management coping discussed earlier, it is obvious how some types of coping are highly relevant to the topic of stress management. Coping to manage stress can be expressed in terms of the three broad functions implied by Latack's conceptualization: (a) removal/attenuation of stressors, (b) modifying perceptions about stressors, (c) and removal or attenuation of negative outcomes associated with stress. These strategies may have reciprocal influences on each other.

Suppose you are experiencing stress due to time pressure, so engage in control behavioral strategies, like delegating some work to others. If others do not accept the work, however, you may decide to engage in symptom management coping through exercise to burn off your feelings of stress. While exercising, your thinking may become clearer and control cognitive coping begins. The outcome of this process might be the realization that failing to meet a deadline has few consequences for you. Realizing this, a new control behavioral strategy is initiated, such as talking to your supervisor about a possible time extension.

This hypothetical scenario conveys the potentially intricate link among the various types of coping strategies. More importantly, it serves to highlight the fact that coping is really the act of managing stress at the individual level.

This discussion focuses on the relationship between coping and stress management. *Stress management interventions* (SMIs) at work can be defined as any organizational attempt to: (a) remove/attenuate specific work stressors, (b) reduce levels of perceived stress by altering individual perceptions about stressors, or (c) lessen the psychological, physiological, and behavioral impact of stress through symptom management. SMIs may include one or more of these components. Notice that these three components are identical to those outlined in Figure 7.4. However, the "target of treatment" for SMIs may be the individual, organization, or both, which means that the goal of the SMI may be to help individuals cope by addressing one or more of the components just listed. Additionally, however, SMIs may target the organization by removing/attenuating stressors that are common to groups of workers. In sum, SMIs aimed at assisting individuals in one or more of the three components are essentially organizationally sponsored attempts at teaching effective coping strategies.

Interestingly, the obvious link between coping and SMIs has not really been acknowledged in work-stress research (Kahn & Byosiere, 1992). For the most part, coping and SMI research have progressed quite independently with few attempts to integrate the two. One notable exception is a framework for SMIs proposed by Ivancevich, Matteson, Freedman, and Phillips (1990) (see Figure 7.4). Without providing a detailed explanation of their framework, it is evident that they conceptualize SMIs in terms of three points of intervention that mirror the three components outlined previously. Moreover, although not included in Figure 7.4, the term "coping" appears in their framework, but only to denote activities aimed at helping people manage the consequences of stress.

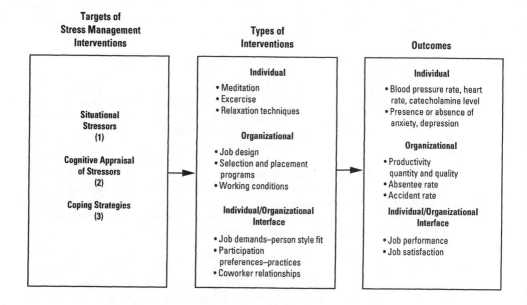

Figure 7.4 Stress Management Interventions: Targets, Types and Outcomes

Other than Ivancevich et al.'s (1990) formulation, the failure to consolidate the coping and SMI literature is unfortunate, especially given that the two topic areas are quite complementary and interconnected. The development of models that consolidate coping with SMIs awaits future research. In the interim, we propose an integrated framework for stress management drawing from both the coping and stress management literatures The outline of such a framework is provided in the following chapter.

Clearly, awareness is increasing on all fronts that stress at work is a ubiquitous phenomenon, which must be addressed in some systematic way. Organizations as well as the employees directly affected by work stress are searching for solutions. Additionally, beyond structured stress management interventions, managers are looking for ways to help their employees on a day-to-day basis. Clearly, much is yet to be learned about coping with job stress and stress management in general. Accordingly, we would like to conclude this discussion by highlighting a few questions that are in need of immediate research attention.

1. *How do individuals cope over time?* As discussed previously, perhaps the greatest weakness of the cross-sectional methodology is its failure to capture the longitudinal nature of coping (Frese, 1999). For example, do most individuals begin with more control-oriented strategies and only move to more sypmtom-management strategies if the control strategies are not effective?

2. *What variables influence choice of coping strategies?* Related to the first question is the issue of whether certain individual difference and/or situational variables influence the choice(s) of specific coping responses. Moreover, under what circumstances do these variables interact? For instance, compared to external locus of control individuals, those with an internal locus of control may prefer to choose control-oriented strategies, although this may only be true when the stressor is acute (e.g., receiving negative feedback for poor performance on a particular task). For chronic stressors, such as a monotonous job, the element of perceived controllability may be low; therefore, more palliative symptom management strategies are chosen instead. The distinction between acute and chronic stressors is important and undoubtedly has important implications for how individuals cope.

3. *What is really meant by coping?* Inherent in the discussion throughout this chapter is the idea that coping is a multifaceted concept. Coping as it has been traditionally defined includes both behavioral and cognitive elements. Additionally, however, coping can be proactive or escapist. This point raises an important theoretical question about the meaning of coping: Are all forms of coping, as we have defined them, really coping? By way of illustration, both physical exercise and smoking may be viewed as behaviorally based symptom management coping strategies, but is the latter really coping? Without a definition of coping effectiveness, this question cannot be answered. Smoking may make the individual feel better after a stressful encounter, although smoking itself can create additional stressors (e.g., interpersonal conflicts) and strains (e.g., physiological effects). Is smoking, then, a coping response or merely a form of maladaptive behavior? Moreover, is this question answerable through scientific investigation or is it ultimately a value judgment?

Given that we have defined stress as a process and not as a single stimulus/stressor or response/strain, any so-called coping response that ultimately contributes to increasing negative outcomes over time does more harm than good. In that sense, maladaptive behaviors/cognitions are probably not conceptually equivalent to other responses included under the rubric of coping. However, this is a question that can be answered through scientific inquiry; it is not merely a question of value judgments concerning particular responses, such as smoking. Through the process of scientific inquiry, coping researchers should reach a better understanding of whether all responses labeled "coping" are actually equivalent from a conceptual standpoint.

STRESS MANAGEMENT

In the previous chapter, stress management was introduced by defining stress management interventions in organizations at both the individual and organizational levels of analysis. In this chapter, we devote our attention to the topic of stress management in organizations.

At the organizational level, stress management involves the identification of stressors common to groups of employees with the goal of eliminating or at least decreasing the level/intensity of the identified stressor(s). At the individual level, organizational stress management can take a number of forms; for example: (a) teaching individuals control-behavioral coping skills designed to remove/attenuate stressors, (b) teaching individuals control-cognitive coping skills to alter perceptions about specific stressors, and (c) promoting symptom management programs aimed at decreasing the negative impact of perceived stress (Cooper & Cartwright, 2001).

We begin our discussion by considering stress management at the organizational level, followed by an examination of programs aimed at the individual. We also briefly discuss some stress management programs with a specific focus (e.g., burnout). Then, we consider some specific organizational "case studies" to hopefully arrive at a greater appreciation of how organizations today are dealing with stress management.

STRESS MANAGEMENT AT THE ORGANIZATIONAL LEVEL

Any type of change in the function or structure of the organization with the goal of alleviating or eliminating job-related stress can qualify as a stress management intervention. In fact, any intervention or change that creates an improved work environment, such as a better selection or performance appraisal system, can be labeled a stress management technique. Because they attempt to actually alter stressful aspects of the work environment, such stress management strategies are often referred to as *primary interventions*. However, these types of changes are usually not considered to be stress management interventions, although they may indeed reduce worker stress.

Elkin and Rosch (1990) summarized several organization-directed strategies to reduce stress: redesign the task, redesign the work environment, establish flexible work schedules, encourage participative management, include the employee in career development, analyze work roles and establish goals, provide social support and feedback, build cohesive teams, establish fair employment policies, and share the rewards. Most of these strategies have the goal of increasing employee participation and autonomy and therefore increasing perceived control at work. Stress researchers have long acknowledged that low perceived control is fundamental to reports of job-related stress (cf., Karasek, 1989; see also Chapter 3). Now we examine some of these strategies and then consider their efficacy as stress management interventions.

Role Stress and Group Conflict

When conflict arises within a work group because members are unclear about work roles, a technique called role analysis (Dayal & Thomas, 1968; W. L. French & Bell, 1984) can be helpful. The purpose of role analysis is to clarify the role expectations and obligations of work group members. Initially, a group coordinator or consultant asks the worker (or a representative of a group of workers in similar jobs) to list the duties, behaviors, responsibilities (e.g., balance the budget, meet with upper management, supervise clerical staff), and position (e.g., middle management) in the organization that he or she perceives as defining the work role. The focal work role is discussed in the group until consensus is reached. The end product of this discussion is the *role profile*, a document that defines the work role in terms of duties, behaviors, and responsibilities. This exercise often dramatically clears up confusion about why someone is not doing his or her job correctly; the reason is usually inconsistent perceptions among workers regarding their and others' work-related responsibilities and obligations.

To jointly address the problems of role-conflict and role ambiguity, a well-written and current job description developed from a thorough job analysis can be useful. The job analysis can clarify any misunderstandings between what job incumbents say they do and what their role set members say they should do (Dipboye, Smith, & Howell, 1994). Although a *job analysis* may be helpful in mitigating against role stressors, it has rarely been considered in stress management programs.

Schaubroeck, Ganster, Sime, and Ditman (1993) empirically examined a role-based intervention to specifically address role ambiguity. The researchers experimentally tested an intervention, role clarification, designed to clarify individual work roles with university staff. After a pretest indicated that role stress was a major stressor for these employees, management clarified their respective departmental roles. Supervisors were subsequently trained how to clarify subordinate roles using a dyadic exchange process (role clarification). Employees were then randomly assigned either to participate in a thorough role clarification discussion with their supervisors or to a control group. An assessment a few months after the intervention indicated that role ambiguity and supervisor dissatisfaction were reduced in the experimental group. However, no effects were observed for physical strain (self-reported or absence due to illness). Both the experimental and control groups reported decreased role conflict. Schaubroeck et al. (1993) concluded that the effects of the intervention were weak but promising.

Some exercises also have been proposed to reduce conflict between or among different work groups (e.g., marketing and production). The *organizational mirror technique* (W. L. French & Bell, 1984) is a set of activities in which a work group receives feedback from one or more groups about how the group is perceived. For practical reasons, representatives of each group, rather than the whole group, meet with a group coordinator. During the meeting, one of the groups "fishbowls" to discuss the issues; the fishbowl is composed of an inner circle of people who talk and an outer circle of people who only listen and observe. The outside circle cannot interrupt the inner circle for any reason. Then, the groups reverse positions. The total group finally reforms with both work groups, discusses the dialogue, and charts a course of action for solving the identified problem(s).

Structural Changes

Another type of stress management intervention reduces stress by actually changing the structure of the organization or the nature of jobs and work within the organization. Similar to the group-level interventions, structural changes are often implemented to increase worker productivity or general functioning. However, they also frequently decrease stress and increase satisfaction.

A commonly used structural intervention is a *quality circles program,* a specific type of participative management (i.e., worker input into managerial decision making). This program is a specialized type of participative management because it targets the enhancement of product quality, such as making a better automobile or providing improved service to clients. A quality circles group is typically composed of 10 or fewer employees from a work group that meets regularly to analyze production or performance-related problems. Their recommendations are forwarded to management for support and/or assistance in carrying out the recommendations. Many organizations have reported dramatic increases in product quality and organizational effectiveness after implementing such a program. As a consequence of their participation in the program, workers also typically feel more invested and involved in their job and the organization.

Several years ago, one of us had the opportunity to design and implement such a program for a social services agency in a large city in the southwestern United States. Both short-term and long-term (i.e., 6 months–2 years) assessments indicated that social-service caseworkers and their support staff perceived decreased job-related stress and increased positive work attitudes as a consequence of the quality circles intervention.

Other types of structural changes in the organization can be used to reduce job-related stress. *Job* or *task redesign* is one such technique. Many jobs can be changed to increase, for example, the amount of variety, skill, and significance the worker experiences. For instance, an assembly-line worker's job might be changed so that she receives additional training to work on two or three different assembly tasks.

Evaluation Research

Of course, the important question is: Do these primary (stressor reduction) interventions work? Although little hard assessment data exist for primary stress interventions, some evidence suggests that they can be effective (R. J. Burke, 1993). For example, Heaney, Price, and Rafferty (1995) trained human-service workers how to mobilize available support from others in their work environment and how to use participatory problem-solving techniques to enhance work team and organizational functioning. Results indicated that the training improved work team climate and reduced depressive symptoms and somatization (psychological distress as indicated by perceptions of bodily dysfunctions, such as being out of breath and heaviness in the limbs) in those workers most at risk for quitting their jobs. Perceptions of increased supervisor support and coping abilities at work were also noted in some of the program participants.

May and Schwoerer (1994) used a team-based approach to target unsafe aspects of the work environment in a large meatpacking plant in the Midwest. Joint management-labor teams with representation from each department in the plant were formed and trained in team-building and job redesign techniques. Using a variety of sources, such as a physical symptoms survey, OSHA logs for cumulative trauma disorders (CTDs), observations, and employee interviews, the teams prioritized jobs for redesign and developed and implemented solutions. Redesign recommendations included adjusting workstation heights to reduce bending, redesigning tool handles to improve wrist position, and providing floor mats to reduce fatigue. The job redesign efforts resulted in reduction in CTDs, lost production time, and restricted duty days. This study is an example of research that did not focus specifically on stress reduction at work, but rather on "bottom-line" issues, such as production and health-related absences. The reduction of stress in the redesigned jobs represents an obvious, although unmeasured, variable.

Unfortunately, attempts at alleviating stress through primary interventions at work are not always successful. Landsbergis and Vivona-Vaughan (1995) developed an intervention for a public health agency based on organizational development, action research, and Karasek's (1979) demands-control model. Unlike most other studies that have used primary interventions, this research was predicated on the concept of job-related stress reduction: Physicians conducting employee medical examinations noted that many of the presenting symptoms seemed to be stress related, and the framework for the intervention was drawn directly from organizational stress theory.

Employee committees were involved in the action research, which consisted of problem diagnosis, action planning, and action taking. The problem-solving committees in two departments identified several stressors (e.g., uneven and repetitive workload, poor communication) and implemented relevant interventions (e.g., changes in the distribution and variety of work activities and regular staff meetings). For both departments, control and intervention groups were compared at 1 and 17 months postintervention on job satisfaction and psychological and physical strain. Results indicated a mixed effect of the interventions in one department and a negligible or perhaps negative effect in the other department. Landsbergis and Vivona-Vaughn (1995) concluded that obstacles to effective implementation of the interventions, such as a major reorganization of the agency during the assessment phase and a lack of management commitment to the change process, were instrumental in producing these outcomes.

What conclusions can be drawn across these studies? Of the primary intervention studies we reviewed, two were successful and one was not. This success rate seems to be fairly representative of the small body of published research on primary interventions. However, many assessments have used a case study approach or provide primarily anecdotal evidence of intervention efficacy. Others provide only weak inference data because of a lack of experimental control and long-term intervention assessments (Ivancevich & Matteson, 1986; L. R. Murphy, 1988). Indeed, the research on primary interventions differs little from the voluminous literature on the effects of organizational change and development, particularly regarding the difficulty encountered in conducting well-designed assessments.

We offer a systematic approach to stress management at the organizational level with the stress audit (Cartright, Cooper & Murphy,

1995), which its developers designed to identify chronic stressors. These stressors can then be removed or controlled through intervention strategies specifically tailored to the identified stressor(s). This approach is discussed next.

The Stress Audit

Imagine waking up in the morning, only to remember you have a critically important meeting for which you are ill-prepared. How will you cope with this situation? Next, you arrive at work, only to discover that someone has stolen $100 from your desk! Now, what will you do? As you call security, you discover a huge tear in your new jacket. The "day from hell," indeed; and it has only just begun!

This chain of events might be understood as Murphy's Law applied to stress: If something stressful can happen, it will. What this horror story hopefully conveys is that it would be virtually impossible to anticipate every possible stressor in advance and have a planned coping response. Life is simply too complex and unpredictable. Nonetheless, there may be certain chronic stressors that are both predictable and common to a number of coworkers. These stressors may be identifiable and targeted for either removal or attenuation. After all, borrowing from the medical dictum, if you want to treat the disorder, you must identify and treat the underlying cause(s) rather than focusing on the symptoms. In a similar vein, is it not preferable to target SMIs at the source of the stress—the stimuli that create perceived stress in the first place?

As reasonable as this argument may sound, this type of intervention in industry has been the exception rather than the rule. Perhaps due to the fact that most practitioners in the business of stress management have mental-health or medical backgrounds, their underlying philosophy is to fit the individual to the environment rather than the environment to the individual (Cooper & Cartright, 1994). From this perspective, it makes sense to help people manage the symptoms of stress such that the target of treatment becomes the individual rather than the organization at large. A number of scholars, however, have raised the point that the underemphasis on treating the organization as "patient" is unfortunate (e.g., Handy, 1986; Kolbell, 1995): Treating the organization as the patient implies that the organization, not the individual worker, may need treatment or modification in some way.

A second potential reason for the underemphasis on stress management programs aimed at directly controlling stressors is the belief that stress is a unique experience; thus it will be difficult if not impossible to isolate common stressors across individuals. That is, it would be prohibitively costly for an organization to assist in the control of a myriad of stressors that are unique to specific individuals. Of course, whether communality exists in stressors across individuals is an empirical question that can be answered only through the process of scientific inquiry.

Such a process was proposed by Cartright, Cooper, and Murphy (1995), who introduced the idea of a *stress audit*. Simply, a stress audit is designed to identify chronic stressors that afflict groups of individuals. Once identified, these stressors may be removed or at least controlled through an intervention strategy specifically tailored to the stressor(s) in question. So, if a commonly reported stressor for a specific work group or department is the inability to manage time effectively, a time-management program may be introduced to deal with this particular source of stress.

Cartright et al. (1995) recommended the use of a self-report index, the Occupational Stress Indicator (Cooper, Sloan, & Williams, 1988), to identify potential sources of stress. Although this instrument and other self-report stress inventories, such as the Job Stress Index (JSI; Sandman, 1992), require respondents to report the existence of potential stressors, the stressors tend to be rather generic. The JSI, for instance, is comprised of 11 distinct subscales including items examining lack of feedback and physical demands and dangers. These subscales may be applied to a variety of different jobs.

Certainly, administering such scales as part of a stress audit may provide useful and important information. These scales, however, will likely fail to capture the existence of stressors that are more unique: those that may only apply to the particular job(s) under consideration. To investigate these more specialized stressors, a self-report inventory may need to be developed that focuses on potential stressors unique to the job(s). An example of this type of scale for nurses was discussed in Chapter 4.

A portion of a specialized self-report scale for control-room operators is contained in Table 8.1. The scale was developed as part of a consulting project for the management of a pulp mill; they were interested in lowering stress levels within the organization's control rooms. Although management initially wanted immediate assistance in the form of relaxation training and other symptom-management approaches, they were amenable to proceeding with a stress audit, particularly given the intuitive appeal of such a process.

To develop this scale, it is useful to follow a three-step process, which was used in the development of the control-room scale. First, a task-based job analysis (Harvey, 1991) and an ergonomic analysis must be conducted. A *task-based job analysis* involves identifying the key job tasks performed on the job under consideration. To obtain this information, a variety of techniques might be used, including the examination of existing job descriptions, observations, interviews, and questionnaires. The analysis should uncover tasks that are frequently performed on the job. The ergonomic analysis focuses on the physical work environment, including the lighting, temperature, office layout, and workstation design.

TABLE 8.1   SELF-REPORT SCALE FROM A STRESS AUDIT FOR
CONTROL ROOM OPERATORS

The Work Environment	Yes	No	?
1. Monitor is positioned too high or too low.	1	2	3
2. Monitor is positioned too close or too far away.	1	2	3
3. Monitor is not height adjustable.	1	2	3
4. Monitor is difficult to to see/read.	1	2	3
5. Surrounding light is bright or too dim.	1	2	3
6. Task lighting is needed but unavailable.	1	2	3
7. Glare is visible on the monitor.	1	2	3
8. Seating lacks a backrest that is separate from the seat pan.	1	2	3
9. Seating lacks adequate/adjustable lumbar support.	1	2	3
10. The control room is not properly ventilated.	1	2	3

The second step is to conduct structured interviews (Chapter 3) and focus groups with individuals who both perform and supervise the work; these data may then be used to identify potential stressors associated with both the various tasks and the physical work environment. At this point, other stressors not anticipated by the specific tasks may also emerge from these discussions.

The third and final step is to select potential stressors for inclusion in the self-report inventory, decide on a response format, and develop schemes for scoring and interpreting the data to follow. Notice that the items in Figure 8.1 do not require respondents to indicate the severity of each stressor, which, however, could have been a feature of the scale. Given that severity ratings on a 5- or 7-point scale for many items may have taken too long to complete, respondents were instead asked to indicate, for each predetermined grouping of items, the three most bothersome stressors in rank order. One advantage of creating such a "top 3" list is that severity ratings do not always clearly indicate which stressors are perceived as most bothersome. Thus, for example, two items may both receive the highest severity rating, yet the subjective experience of stress associated with one of the items may be much higher (cf. Dewe & Brook, 2000).

	Yes	No	?
1. There is insufficient training for start-ups or shut-downs	1	2	3
2. There is a lack of computer simulation training.	1	2	3
3. Some individuals lack training on how field jobs operate.	1	2	3
4. Some individuals lack knowledge about specific field jobs.	1	2	3
5. There is a lack of ongoing field training.	1	2	3
6. There is insufficient training on how to handle emergency situations.	1	2	3

* Taken from a stress audit of pulp mill operators.

Figure 8.1 Sample Items from a Stress Audit Survey

Ideally, the scale should then be administered to workers and supervisors who did not participate in earlier phases of the development process. This step creates greater levels of overall participation across employees and helps to ensure that the results are not circular or necessarily redundant across the interviews, focus groups, and the questionnaire. Guarantees of participant anonymity and confidentiality are critical for this phase of the audit because each participant is reporting information about what he/she finds to be personally stressful.

Identifying the salient stressors that appear to be common to groups of employees becomes the end point of the stress audit. Of course, deciding on what constitutes a "common and serious stressor" is subject to judgment and interpretation. Just as accounting audits are fraught with some levels of subjectivity, so too is the stress audit. Carefully conducted, however, the audit is arguably the best first point of attack in the battle against stress at work.

The results of the stress audit may be used to develop specific action plans to either eliminate or at least control/attenuate the stressors identified. These action plans may run the gamut from job redesign, developing new selection, training, or performance appraisal systems, to the development of workshops designed to optimize leadership performance and group decision-making skills. The introduction of improved lighting, equipment, or even the purchase of ergonomically designed office chairs may also be the end result. This rather heterogeneous array of potential action plans suggests that expertise may be required in a number of related fields, including industrial-organizational psychology, organizational behavior, human resource management, and human factors/ergonomics. The management of job stress is one unique area that invites interdisciplinary collaboration. For us, this represents one of the most exciting aspects of working in stress management.

After action plans are developed and executed, the interventions should be evaluated through a systematic process of program evaluation. This evaluation requires more than the collection of testimonials and anecdotal accounts. The results of this research may bolster claims of success or suggest the need to improve existing interventions, and/or develop new action plans.

Of course, practical constraints (e.g., it is too time-consuming or costly to develop a survey) or other factors (e.g., a task analysis has been previously conducted) may necessitate a modification or even elimination of some of the stress audit components. For example, Luck (2000) used an interview process exclusively to generate a list of salient stressors for a group of physicians.

At this juncture, it is important to note that organizational stress researchers do not unanimously agree that organizational-level interventions are necessarily going to lead to positive and intended effects (cf. Kompier, Guerts, Grundemann, Vink, & Smulders, 1998). In a thought-provoking paper, Briner and Reynolds (1999) argued that very little evidence exists that organizational-level interventions have a positive causal impact on either organizational or personal outcomes. Moreover, they suggested that simply introducing an intervention does not mean that there will not be some unintended negative effects.

For example, assume a stress audit is conducted and the decision is reached that some job redesign is needed to address stressors relating to monotony/boredom. Perhaps the new job will increase skill variety and reduce boredom; however, the new job may lead to unintended levels of role ambiguity, or stress created because of insufficient skills to perform the work.

Implicit in the stress audit approach is the notion that the intervention will remove/attenuate the stressor assumed to be the cause of one or more negative outcomes (e.g., absenteeism). Thus, following this logic, the intervention should have a positive impact on the outcome(s)and we should see some improvement (e.g., reduced absenteeism). Although this point might make sense at the level of logical argument, it may be tantamount to wishful thinking in many instances because we are only *assuming* a causal link, and many other factors may be the real causal agents affecting the outcome(s) of interest. For example, changing the work hours (assumed to be linked to absenteeism) may not change absenteeism rates if the rates are *really* affected by worker motivation and job attitudes, not the job stressor.

Of course, the stress audit process may prove to be highly beneficial if it targets sources of stress that are highly salient to many workers. Assume that the overall process as described is initiated in an organization, and all indications from evaluation studies are that the action plans were successful in eliminating a variety of salient work stressors. Does this fact obviate the need for other approaches or strategies? Our response would be absolutely not! It is useful to think about SMIs in the broadest of terms, implying that other interventions should be considered, such as programs designed to enhance the use of control-coping strategies and to ameliorate the negative consequences of stress through symptom management. These alternative but complementary approaches to stress management are considered next.

STRESS MANAGEMENT AT THE INDIVIDUAL LEVEL

Throughout this book, the following point has been made repeatedly: All human beings will not face the same stressors or perceive the same situations as equally stressful. Given that the experience of stress is often highly individualistic, the organizational level of analysis may be highly useful, but still somewhat limited. To complement organizationally sponsored attempts at *removing* perceived stressors common to multiple individuals, individual-level stress management becomes important. In the following sections, we closely examine the topic of individual-level stress management in organizations.

Teaching Effective Control-Coping Skills

One potentially viable approach to stress management in work organizations is the promotion of programs aimed at helping individuals to cope with daily stress. Arguably, this goal is best achieved by their seeking assistance from qualified mental-health practitioners, such as psychologists or social workers, who provide individual-level psychotherapy. Of course, people can seek this assistance on their own. However, organizations may facilitate the link between their workforce and the mental-health community.

Employee Assistance Programs (EAP). Emplyee Assistance Programs (EAPs) can be defined as organizationally sponsored programs designed to assist employees who are encountering personal problems (Macdonald, Shain, & Wells, 1993). However, the scope of EAP programs has broadened greatly over time; Table 8.2 illustrates some of the changes between typical, present-day EAPs and those that existed over 50 years ago. Notwithstanding the information contained in the table, American EAP programs are often more restrictive than programs in some other countries (e.g., Canada). That is, many American programs are primarily concerned with drug/alcohol-related issues (Macdonald et al., 1993; Mullady, 1991).

Although some organizations undoubtedly care about the physical and mental health of their employees, the organizational interest in EAPs often arises from the realization that employees' personal problems can adversely affect work performance. Developing and establishing an EAP can foster and enhance goodwill between employees and management. Moreover, given the traditional interest of labor unions in employees' welfare, EAPs can facilitate cooperation and enhanced relations between labor and management. The popularity of EAPs in North America is not surprising, given the general upsurge of interest in work stress and stress management. Indeed, a scientific journal exists that is entirely dedicated to EAP research, *Employee Assistance Quarterly.*

TABLE 8.2   SOME TRENDS ON HOW EAPS HAVE CHANGED IN THE PAST 50 YEARS

EAPs in the 1940's	Modern Day EAPs
U. S. Programs	Worldwide in developed countries
Alchohol specific problems only	Broad brush (i.e. wide range of problems such as marital, emotional work problems, drugs and alcohol, etc.)
Supervisors identify alcohol problems	Supervisors identify work problems
On-site treatment	Off-site treatment
Mandatory referral	Voluntary referral
Little confidentiality of treatment	Confidential
Management program	Management and union program
Informal policy	Policy in writing

Adapted from: S. MacDonald, M. Shain, & S. Wells, (1993), *Effectiveness of EAPs*. Addiction Research Foundation.

EAPs can take on many forms (Masi, 1984). For example, some are conducted in-house, staffed by organizational employees. Alternatively, organizations often build a network with external agencies and formal ties with diverse professionals, such as addiction specialists and clinical psychologists. EAPs may also be designed so that referrals are made by immediate supervisors; other EAPs include coworker and/or family referrals (Feuer, 1983). Finally, the scope of EAPs can vary; for example, some deal exclusively with chemical dependence, while others are broad-brush and may deal with a variety of issues (e.g., personal problems, financial problems, legal difficulties; Berman, Sulsky, Pargament, Balzer, & Kausch, 1991).

Given the diversity in the types of EAP programs, it is generally recommended that any organization contemplating the introduction of an EAP first conduct a *Needs Assessment* to help determine the best program, given the characteristics, problems, and resources of the organization

(Berman et al., 1991). According to Berman et al., a needs assessment should be conducted to (1) identify the types/severity of problems affecting employees, (2) identify community agencies/professionals who might be included in an EAP network of services, (3) identify employee perceived barriers to using an EAP, including financial costs for the employee, concerns about confidentiality, and location of services, (4) examine organizational characteristics, such as communication systems, employee-management relationships, and financial resources for setting up an EAP, and (5) examine the relationship between self-reports of stress/personal difficulties and indicators of work performance (e.g., performance quality, absenteeism).

Although potentially expensive and time-consuming in the beginning, a needs analysis can be extremely important in tailoring an EAP to the needs of the organization in question (Balzer & Pargament, 1987). The analysis can reveal whether the EAP should focus on a particular area, or whether a general or broad-brush program is indicated. Moreover, employee-perceived barriers to use (e.g., fear that confidentiality will breached or that they will be labeled as "weak" or "sick" by coworkers or management) can initially be addressed in the design of the EAP process. Certainly, development of any EAP should be a joint venture between management and the employees who will ostensibly benefit from the EAP. By including employee's input and giving them a key role in the formative stages of program development, employee concerns (first identified in the needs analysis) can be addressed, and employees will likely feel a greater sense of ownership in the EAP initiative. This perception of ownership should then translate into greater acceptance of the resulting program and likely increased employee participation in the program as well.

Regardless of the upsurge of interest in EAPs, research evaluating the quality of EAPs has been fraught with a series of problems. According to Macdonald et al. (1993), a number of problems associated with research evaluating EAP effectiveness exist. First, EAPs vary greatly across organizations; therefore, results of a study conducted on a single EAP may not generalize to other EAP programs. Second, it is difficult to consolidate research because the outcome variables used across studies varies greatly. For example, some studies use employee well-being as the focal criterion, while others focus on indicators of work performance/productivity. Third, confidentiality safeguards built into EAP programs can make it impossible to collect important data, such as who are the EAP users and performance data. Inability to collect the latter information makes it impossible to examine performance changes following the introduction of an EAP program. Fourth, few studies evaluating EAPs have included control groups and have opted instead for a pretest/intervention/posttest design. This type of nonexperimental design does not control for confounds that may provide alternative explanations for why posttest scores are different from pretest scores (see also Chapter 3).

As an illustration, assume job performance is measured prior to the introduction of an EAP (i.e., the pretest), and then the EAP is introduced (i.e., the intervention). After a few years, performance is assessed again (i.e., the posttest). If performance has improved over time, can the improvements be unambiguously ascribed to the EAP? Of course not! The improvements might have stemmed from a host of factors, including changes in employee job satisfaction over time, increased job experience, and employee attrition. Without the inclusion of a control group, establishing cause and effect link between EAP programs and valued organizational outcomes becomes impossible. Finally, most of the evaluation studies that have been conducted with EAPs tend to focus on substance abuse. Relatively little evaluative research examining broad-brush EAP programs has been conducted, which might include psychological counseling, substance abuse, and a potential array of other issues. Of course, including psychotherapy or psychological counseling under the "evaluation umbrella" raises the issue of the effectiveness of psychotherapy in general as a therapeutic tool.

In addition, it can be difficult to determine which components of an EAP program are really successful, because the separate program components are not isolated and studied separately (Cartright, Cooper, & Murphy, 1995). Generally, success is defined as whether participants report higher job satisfaction and lower stress as a result of the EAP. However, other dimensions exist on which EAP success may be examined. For example, one criterion of EAP success might be whether workers who may benefit from the assistance actually seek it out. To help in this regard, managers can be trained to identify potentially "troubled employees" (Atkinson, 1989). Whether and the extent to which these training programs can turn managers into diagnosticians is questionable, however. So, a second criterion of EAP success might be the extent to which managers successfully identify potentially troubled employees for possible intervention.

Regardless of how EAPs vary in their operation and structure, the therapeutic value of one-on-one clinical interventions, a mainstay of the EAP, holds promise as a mechanism for improving individual coping skills (cf. Pelletier & Lutz, 1991). The real challenge is in the development of an effective EAP that can: (a) help in the identification of individuals who may benefit from an intervention, and (b) provide the necessary mechanisms to ensure that the intervention is delivered in a confidential, cost-effective, and timely manner.

Therapists may have particular clinical orientations (e.g., humanistic vs. psychodynamic). Workers seeking help in managing stress might consider therapists who operate from a cognitive, behavioral, or cognitive-behavioral perspective. Many people do not realize that it is appropriate to ask a prospective therapist his or her clinical biases. For instance, a cognitively oriented therapist likely concentrates on developing control-cognitive coping strategies, or strategies designed to help people rethink their problems and cognitively alter their perceived stress. One therapeutic approach in this category is rational-emotive therapy (Ellis, 1978). Here, the focus is on altering irrational thinking through self-talk and careful scrutiny of the entire thinking and decision-making process.

A more behaviorally oriented therapist may be most helpful in developing control-behavioral coping responses. A typical intervention would probably involve a series of steps, teaching the client to: (a) clarify the problem, (b) generate alternative courses of action, (c) evaluate alternatives and select particular responses, (d) initiate responses and evaluate success with the need for possible strategy revisions (Weiten, Lloyd, & Lashley, 1991).

As EAPs gain in exposure and popularity, concerns about legal issues regarding EAPs inevitably surface, especially in the United States. For example, Nye (1990) wrote an entire book addressing legal issues relating to EAPs. Nye considers such issues as how cases of malpractice can arise from an EAP, whether an EAP should have written policies/procedures, and what constitutes professional liability.

As EAPs proliferate, professional organizing bodies will continue to emerge. At the time of this writing, two professional organizations concerned with EAPs can be identified: The Employee Assistance Professionals Association (EAPA), and the Employee Assistance Society of North America (EASNA). These groups provide guidance on the development of EAPs and publish guidelines relating to the development and maintenance of effective EAP initiatives. For example, the EAPA has developed "Program Standards," while the EASNA has published guidelines around program philosophy and suggested procedures for "best practice" (Employee Assistance Program of North America, 1990).

Relating EAPs to the broader topic of stress management, it is obvious that they represent just one of several approaches organizations may adopt in developing stress management programs. Although EAPs have been discussed here in the context of teaching effective coping skills, EAPs can also assist individuals in alleviating the adverse consequences of stress. We now turn to this topic.

Alleviating the Consequences of Stress

Without a doubt, most applied SMIs would fall into the general category of "symptom management programs," those aimed at reducing the adverse psychological, physiological, and behavioral consequences associated with stress. The popularity of SMIs that adopt this focus is verified by some statistics. For instance, one report (Pelletier & Lutz, 1991) indicates that an astonishing 50% of worker absenteeism could be avoided through stress management intervention! Further, the estimated cost for medical treatment and loss of worker productivity due to heart disease in the United States was $110 billion for one year (Gebhardt & Crump, 1990). In light of the constant barrage of data linking stress to lost dollars and reduced worker satisfaction and morale, organizations have increasingly turned to SMIs, which are relatively easy to implement and not too costly up front. Compared to the stress audit with its associated action plans, and the development of potentially costly EAPs, symptom management programs make both practical and fiscal sense to many organizations.

These SMI programs vary across organizations according to their specific components and the number of components included. Some of the more popular components include Jacobsen's progressive relaxation, the relaxation response, autogenic training, clinical biofeedback, meditation, and visualization therapies (Pelletier & Lutz, 1991). In addition to these components, general wellness and fitness components are often integrated as well, including exercise and dieting programs (Gebhardt & Crump, 1990). Some of these types of interventions are next examined in more detail.

Relaxation/Meditation Techniques. The techniques to which we refer are structured relaxation or meditation exercises, not simply resting or thinking pleasant thoughts. The history of these techniques dates back to antiquity: In the sixth century B.C. Eastern scriptures mention mental and physical relaxation achieved through meditative practices. One of the most well-known forms of meditation today, *transcendental meditation* (TM), gained recognition in this country when the Maharishi Mahesh Yogi introduced it to the United States in the early 1960s. TM is a simple type of meditation that requires minimal instruction, although it does have a spiritual emphasis.

Secular or nonspiritual techniques have also been popularized. One of the most widely used secular techniques is the *relaxation response* (Benson, 1975). Herbert Benson, a Harvard cardiologist, developed the relaxation response for his patients by distilling the essential components of TM, which he claims produces the same effects as TM. These essential components are given in Table 8.3.

Meditative and relaxation practices differ not only in the amount of spiritual or religious emphasis, but also in the amount and focus of the training. Many (e.g., TM) require some degree of formal training and others, such as the relaxation response, can be self-taught. Some, such as TM and the relaxation response, primarily emphasize mental relaxation. Others, such as a technique known as *progressive relaxation*, emphasize physical and muscular relaxation. The first secular technique, progressive relaxation was developed by Jacobson (1929), a physician, to treat anxiety. Mastering this technique requires formal instruction in the sequential tensing and releasing of 16 skeletal muscle groups identified by Jacobson. The end result should be the achievement of profound muscle relaxation in all major muscle groups in the body. Progressive relaxation may be particularly helpful for those individuals who manifest stress through muscular tension in the head, neck, and back.

Relaxation training is one of the most popular topics in organizational stress management workshops and seminars. For example, New York Telephone Company and Metropolitan Life Insurance Company regularly provide relaxation or meditation exercises in the stress management training they offer their employees.

TABLE 8.3   HOW TO BRING FORTH THE RELAXATION RESPONSE

1. **A Quiet Environment**

   Ideally, you should choose a quiet, calm environment with as few distractions as possible.

2. **A Mental Device**

   To shift the mind from logical, externally oriented thought, there should be a constant stimulis; a sound, work or phrase repeated silently or aloud; or fixed gaze at an object.

3. **A Passive Attitude**

   When distracting thoughts occur, they are to be disregarded and attention redirected to the repitition or gazing; you should not worry about how well you are performing the technique.

4. **A Comfortable Position**

   A comfortable posture is important so that there is no undue muscular tension.

Biofeedback. Biofeedback involves the electronic measurement of physiological (body) processes, which can be converted to light or sound signals to provide sensory feedback on how these processes function. For example, a person hooked up to a biofeedback machine can receive information about the muscle tension in his neck or forehead in the form of soft tones. Using this auditory feedback, he can then learn through repeated trials to control the tension in his forehead or neck by controlling the pitch of the tones. Hopefully, after considerable practice, he can control his muscle tension without the biofeedback machine. Given that biofeedback therapy requires expensive equipment, a trained technician, and a considerable time investment, it is rarely the first avenue of attack against stress. Biofeedback is typically used in conjunction with other approaches, such as relaxation exercises and therapy, particularly when a single approach appears to be insufficient.

Exercise. The last couple of decades of the 20th century could be called the health era. One of the consequences of this health consciousness is that people of all ages and lifestyles incorporated exercise programs into their daily or weekly routines. Many organizations, such as Coors Brewing Company, Kennicott Copper, Hewlett-Packard, and Johnson & Johnson, followed suit by developing exercise programs and providing modern, well-equipped in-house exercise facilities. Some organizations (e.g., Mesa Petroleum) have even offered incentives in the form of cash and fringe benefits to employees who use their facilities on a regular basis (Bailey, 1990). These fitness centers are also frequently an integral part of a corporate wellness program (e.g., Coors Brewing Co.), which we discuss in detail at the end of this chapter.

Beyond the overall health benefits, does the personal and organizational emphasis on physical fitness have any merit as a stress-reduction aid? The answer appears to be a definite yes! Physical fitness experts agree that a consistent exercise routine is one of the easiest and most reliable methods to reduce the harmful effects of stress as well as to achieve physical fitness. These beneficial effects can include both increased physical and mental health.

Positive outcomes are most clearly observed when the exercise is aerobic. *Aerobic exercise* is any physical activity that produces an elevated respiration, heart rate, and metabolic rate for 20-30 minutes. Examples of aerobic exercise include jogging, swimming, tennis, and bicycling. The reason aerobic exercise is effective seems almost paradoxical: Both the experience of stress and vigorous exercise increase physiological activation (e.g., elevated heart rate, metabolism) and hormonal activation (e.g., elevated adrenaline levels). However, physically fit people show lower physiological and hormonal activation at rest and under stress (Falkenberg, 1987; Selye, 1974). In other words, the bodies of physically fit people usually maintain a much lower baseline of arousal and depart relatively less from their (lower) baseline than less fit people. Engaging in aerobic exercise soon after experiencing stress also seems to have additional benefits: One of the immediate effects of vigorous exercise is to metabolize or burn off the harmful by-products of the stress response quickly (Falkenberg, 1987).

The reasons behind the mental health benefits, however, are less obvious. The mental health of the individual who exercises may improve because exercise often serves as a break or diversion in the day's activities. Also, she may feel that she is doing something positive for her health. Some research by Plante and his colleagues (Plante, Chizmar, & Owen, 1999; Plante, Lantis, & Checa, 1998) supports this latter prediction. They demonstrated that perceived fitness (i.e., a person's self-perception of his or her fitness) was associated with both the psychological and physiological benefits of exercise.

Another explanation for the mental effects of exercise is the presence of endorphins, which are naturally occurring painkillers produced by the brain. Scientists have measured significant elevations of endorphins in the bloodstream of people who were exercising vigorously. Increases in endorphin levels are also believed to be related to the phenomena of "runner's high" and "getting a second wind," which are frequently reported by athletes (Falkenberg, 1987).

The positive benefits of exercise have also been linked to organizationally relevant outcomes, such as task performance—although scant research has been conducted (Falkenberg, 1987). Evidence also exists that employees' job satisfaction may be improved when companies invest in on-site exercise facilities (Taylor, 2000). People who exercise regularly seem to perform better on some physical and cognitive tasks, especially under stressful conditions. The rationale is that they are generally less physiologically aroused. This finding is particularly applicable if performance decreases when a person is excessively aroused. Also, fit people recover from stressful events more rapidly. In situations in which a person must make judgments or decisions under stress, the ability to recover from the harmful effects of stress quickly may be a crucial determinant of performance.

A variety of individual-level interventions have now been considered. Admittedly, we were somewhat selective in our choices and certainly were not able to present a comprehensive list of interventions. Nonetheless, we did attempt to introduce you to the most commonly used interventions in work organizations. In the next section, we discuss research examining the effectiveness of individual-level interventions for attenuating or removing the negative effects associated with the stress process.

Evaluation Research.   Again, the now-familiar question is posed: Do individual-level interventions work? A larger amount of assessment data exist for individual stress interventions compared to organizational-level interventions. However, the nature of the data that do exist often precludes drawing definite conclusions regarding their efficacy.

In the now-classic evaluation study of a well-developed stress management intervention and assessment, Ganster and his colleagues (Ganster, Mayes, Sime, & Tharp, 1982) warned against being overly optimistic about the effectiveness of these programs. They assessed the effectiveness of 8 weeks of stress management training, which consisted of cognitive behavioral therapy and progressive relaxation exercises, in a group of public-agency employees. Using a true experimental design, the researchers randomly assigned employees to either a control or experimental (treatment) group. Physiological (urine samples of adrenaline and noradrenaline) and psychological (self-reported depression, anxiety, irritation, and body complaints) measures were teken immediately before and after the training and at 4 months posttraining. Although some decreases in both physiological and psychological stress responses were found in the experimental relative to the control group, the researchers judged these effects to be of minimal practical value, particularly over time. They suggested that, instead of training employees to better endure stress at work, a potentially healthier and more ethical approach would be to make the organizational environment less stressful.

In the years since Ganster et al.'s (1982) study, stress management training and assessment has been studied further. According to Ganster (1995), these programs may produce short-term changes in various outcome variables (e.g., blood pressure), although there is little research examining the long-term benefits of these programs. Also, Ganster pointed out that little research has linked these programs to organizational outcomes, such as productivity and absenteeism. Thus, the financial impact of these programs are uncertain.

Peters and Carlson (1999) examined a stress management intervention/health promotion program using a controlled group design and found effects of the intervention on some of the physical and health attitude measures. However, they found no effects on organizational outcome variables such as decreased absenteeism and increased job satisfaction.

Overall, Pelletier and Lutz (1991) argued that the data examining stress management programs are mixed, and Ivancevich et al. (1990) noted that while the research has improved, the research designs are still generally weak. Finally, Cartwright et al. (1995) pointed to a lack of control groups in many studies, and a reliance on cross-sectional rather than longitudinal designs (cf. Munz & Kohler, 1997).

A recent meta-analysis of 48 studies examining stress management interventions (van der Klink, Blonk, Schene, & van Dijk, 2001) found generally small to moderate effects, depending on the specific intervention (e.g., relaxation techniques). Their analysis, however, highlighted that these interventions may be more successful for some outcomes (e.g., perceived work life quality) compared to others. Last, Rowe (2000) found that including refresher sessions at specific intervals improved the effectiveness of an intervention program. Thus, an important parameter of intervention success may be the degree to which programs are on-going versus one-time events.

Perhaps one of the most fundamental questions surrounding these programs is, which components should be included and why? For example, is there any *incremental* benefit to providing training in progressive relaxation if cognitive behavioral therapy is included? Also, would the inclusion of some components invite problems of attrition and noncompliance? As an illustration of this, it has been estimated that only 15–30% of white-collar employees participate in fitness programs (Gebhardt & Crump, 1990). In addition, will individuals continue to practice these techniques once the program is completed (cf. Ivancevich et. al., 1990)?

Bruning and Frew (1987) attempted to address the relative effectiveness of 8–10 hours each of three different types of common stress management training—cognitive behavioral skills, exercise, and meditation—in a longitudinal field experiment. They assigned workers from a hospital-equipment facility to one of the three treatment groups or a control group. Each group was also later trained in the other interventions to assess the effectiveness of dual-combination strategies (e.g., exercise and meditation). Physiological measures (pulse rate, blood pressure, and galvanic skin or sweating response) were assessed at 2-week intervals for 6 months. Results indicated that each type of intervention was individually effective in reducing blood pressure and pulse rate. Dual-combination strategies also showed decreases in pulse rate but no single combination appeared to be superior to any others.

Since Bruning and Frew's study, the available data suggest that there may indeed be some incremental utility in combining some of these components into one SMI. Based on meta-analytic data, Lehrer, Carr, Sargunaraj, and Woolfolk (1994) suggested that components like biofeedback and progressive relaxation have different effects. This finding implies that the choice of components should be guided by some theoretical framework, in which specific intended effects (e.g., muscle relaxation vs. reducing arousal) inform the selection of particular components. If two components are redundant, there is no need to include both. Along these lines, Forbes and Pekala (1993) discovered that both progressive relaxation and hypnosis were associated with similar psychophysiological reactions. Therefore, including both of these in one SMI may be unnecessary.

So, why did Bruning and Frew not find differential effects for the different treatments or combinations of treatments? Their experimental design required the loss of a control group early in the evaluation process to ensure that all subjects received all treatments. They also used only physiological outcome variables. Both factors may have seriously restricted their ability to detect measurable group differences. Unfortunately, most evaluation studies are sufficiently different from one another that these differences might explain the conflicting results. On balance, however, these types of interventions seem to have some effectiveness in reducing psychological and physiological stress indicators, and particular combinations may be relatively more effective in some cases.

STRESS MANAGEMENT FOR SPECIFIC PURPOSES

We have covered the various approaches to stress management, from changing the organization using interventions such as job redesign and participative management, to changing the person using techniques such as meditation and exercise programs. However, some interventions target specific areas of concern. We now discuss interventions for three areas of special concern, burnout, Type A behavior, and job loss.

Reducing Burnout

Because burnout is typically perceived to develop from a susceptible person interacting with a particularly stressful work environment (Shirom, 1989), various interventions focusing on both the person and the work environment have been proposed.

Pines (1982) cited two organizational stressors, work overload and excessive paperwork and red tape, as contributors to the development of worker burnout. The obvious solution to these stressors (i.e., redistribute the workload or hire additional employees and re-evaluate job-related procedures and rules) may be impractical or impossible in the age of the "lean and mean" philosophy of management. However, other organizationally based approaches have been suggested. For example, professional training seminars and workshops and orientation programs have been suggested to circumvent burnout. Training seminars and workshops can be particularly helpful when workers have varied educational and job-related backgrounds. Orientation programs, such as one discussed by Cherniss (1993), in which a novice spent two months "shadowing" an experienced colleague before assuming full professional responsibilities, are another option. A somewhat different approach is a *realistic job preview (RJP)* or work socialization program (Wanous, 1976).

Realistic job previews attempt to provide the prospective employee with a balanced picture of his or her future job, with the specific intent of dispelling any unrealistic job-related expectations. Kramer (1974) developed a type of RJP program specifically designed for nurses, which she claimed reduced unrealistic expectations associated with the daily activities of nursing and therefore decreased the incidence of burnout. As opposed to dealing with job-related burnout after it develops, this intervention aims to prevent its occurrence. The program consists of four phases (Table 8.4).

TABLE 8.4   REALISTIC JOB PREVIEW FOR NURSING JOBS

Phase 1:   **Introduction of Actual Job Incidents**
            Example: Interpersonal conflicts with doctors

Phase 2:   **Methods to Deal with Phase 1 Incidents**
            Example: Discussing conflictual situations with nursing supervisor

Phase 3:   **Presentations by Nursing Supervisors, Administrators, and Veteran Nurses**
            Example: Communication of specific expectations for the novice's behavior in their professional interactions with doctors

Phase 4:   **Presentation of Behavioral Skills to Manage Job Incidents**
            Example: Skill-based training on conflict resolution and communication

Adapted from *Reality Shock: Why Nurses Leave Nursing*, by M. Kramer, 1974, St. Louis, MO: Moby Press

How effective are such socialization programs? Because these programs make sense intuitively, it is surprising that evaluations of RJPs have not been uniformly positive (e.g., Guzzo, Jette, & Katzell, 1985). However, most RJPs involve only the first one or two phases of Kramer's program, so a direct comparison between RJPs and Kramer's anticipatory socialization program for nurses is not possible.

Performance feedback is another organizational intervention for burnout that has been widely embraced (Maslach & Jackson, 1982). In many jobs with high levels of human contact, particularly in the health-care field, employees rarely hear positive feedback: Clients continue to use the services only because they are still ill or distressed. Therefore, workers often develop a distorted sense of their work effectiveness. A well-developed performance-appraisal system using realistic performance standards and frequent performance feedback can do much to alleviate this distortion (Cherniss, 1993; Maslach & Jackson, 1982).

Social support groups represent yet another approach to alleviating job-related burnout (Winnubst, 1993). Considerable research has shown that social support is inversely related to burnout (i.e., low levels of social support are associated with high burnout; e.g., Constable & Russell, 1986; Davis-Sacks, Jayarante, & Chess, 1985), so social support would seem to be both an intuitive and practical burnout intervention. Although such an approach has been widely touted by burnout experts (e.g., Corrigan et al., 1995), systematic assessments of social support groups as a burnout intervention are rare.

One such study (Kobell, 1995) compared the efficacy of a social support group against a meditation group and a control (no intervention) group in alleviating burnout in 38 employees of a children's services center. Kobell found no differences among the groups in any of three burnout dimensions (personal achievement, emotional exhaustion, and depersonalization). However, the social support intervention (a social support group of unreported composition that met daily in the workplace for 20 minutes) was assessed after only 1 month, a small number of employees participated in the study, and, according to the author, the organizational environment was extremely stressful. Kobell concluded that "...a strategy that seeks to modulate the stress response of individuals is insufficient in the face of these organizational factors..." p. 41.

Van Dierendonck, Schaufeli, & Buunk (1998) examined the effectiveness of a cognitive restructuring intervention on burnout and other select outcomes (e.g., absenteeism). Specifically, employing a sample of 149 professionals working with mentally disabled clients, they predicted that the intervention should increase perceptions of equity (i.e., fairness) because employees in this line of work often feel that the organizational returns (e.g., pay) are not commensurate with their contributions and efforts. Results suggested that, compared to control condition participants, those receiving the cognitive restructuring training demonstrated lower levels of emotional exhaustion posttraining. Other components of burnout were not affected, thus reinforcing the case for the multidimensionality of burnout (Chapter 6). Moreover, the existence of social support did not moderate the effects. That is, those intervention participants receiving higher levels of social support did not experience significantly lower levels of burnout.

Westman and Eden (1997) examined the effects of vacation time on burnout in a sample of 90 clerical employees. Using a sophisticated longitudinal design, they found that, indeed, burnout decreased during vacation time, although it returned when employees returned to work. Westman and Eden suggested that burnout is not necessarily a constant: It can be removed through intervention. However, because vacations cannot occur frequently, they suggested other types of respites, such as time off for exercise. The researchers also remarked that the effect of any respites will be temporary. Thus, ways to prolong the positive effects of any respites introduced into the workplace must be sought.

So what can be concluded about organizational burnout interventions? Because the locus of burnout is typically the job, a number of organizational interventions have been proposed that should alleviate the burnout process in susceptible workers, although, with the exception of a few studies (e.g., Kramer, 1974), the effectiveness of these interventions has not been adequately tested. Individually oriented interventions, such as cognitive restructuring and respites (e.g., vacations) show some promise for ameliorating the effects of burnout. Hopefully, future research will provide more options for organizations concerned with the problem of burnout.

Managing Type A Behavior

Like burnout, Type A behavior has been the focus of interventions to ameliorate its negative effects. Unlike burnout, however, many of these efforts have specifically targeted the person, undoubtedly because of the direct health effects of Type A in the form of cardiovascular disease. Friedman and Rosenman, the developers of TABP, and their colleagues have proposed guidelines for lifestyle and attitude change (M. Friedman & Rosenman, 1983; M. Friedman & Ulmer, 1984; Table 8.5). Friedman et al. (1984) claimed success in reducing Type A behaviors and cardiovascular disease: Compared to the control group (N = 270), the patients in the experimental group (N = 592) who received Type A behavior counseling showed a 43.8% reduction in Type A behavior over a three-year period. Over the same time interval, the experimental group also had a cumulative cardiac recurrence rate of 7.2% compared to 13% in the control group.

Other researchers have reported success in reducing Type A behaviors through, for example, cognitive-behavioral strategies (Roskies, Seraganian, & Oseasohn, 1986) and combinations of relaxation and stress-reducing imagery training (Suinn, 1975). Roskies et al. (1986) developed an eight-part program to modify TABP, composed largely of self-monitoring, problem-solving, relaxation exercises, and cognitive-behavioral training. She assessed the efficacy of this intervention by randomly assigning 107 disease-free Type

A managers to one of three groups: weight training, aerobic exercise, and the Type A modification program. Compared to the other two groups, participants in the modification program showed a significant decrease (13–23%) in several Type A behaviors, although no group differences were noted in measures of physiological arousal (heart rate, blood pressure). Finally, social support and social network interventions (e.g., group counseling), commonly prescribed for recovering heart attack victims, has also shown promise for reducing TABP (Bruhn, 1996).

As knowledge of TABP has evolved, researchers have concluded that TABP is a multidimensional construct and not all components are necessarily associated with negative outcomes (Chapter 6). Thus, interventions should ideally be targeting negative components (e.g., hostility) for health and well-being.

The hostility component of TABP seems to be specifically associated with the development of cardiovascular disease (also see Chapter 6). Therefore, programs that target anger reduction (e.g., Abernethy, 1995) should be particularly effective in reducing the TABP health risks. P. Bennett, Wallace, Carroll, and Smith (1991) randomly assigned 44 unmedicated, mildly hypertensive Type A men to one of three conditions: standard stress management training or one of two Type A management training programs. The stress management intervention covered education about stress and its effects, relaxation training, cognitive restructuring, and meditation. The first Type A intervention group focused on the modification of time-urgent behavior, anger control, and assertiveness skills. Because the second Type A group was simply a delayed intervention group that received the TABP training at a later time, it served as a control group for the initial assessments. The Type A management training proved to be superior to the stress management training in reducing the hostility component of TABP, as well as blood pressure.

The programs just described require major philosophical and lifestyle changes and, as a consequence, typically capture the attention of Type As only after they have experienced some type of major health crisis, such as a heart attack. One school of thought maintains that TABP should be treated as a chronic illness that cannot be cured, only controlled (Roskies, 1978). As discussed in Chapter 5, Type A behaviors (e.g., competitiveness, aggressiveness) are valued and reinforced in contemporary society, so any typical prevention efforts (e.g., therapy) are not likely to be well received. Consequently, the chronic disease model prescribes the reduction of tension and anger through activities such as exercise and hobbies and the control of physiological reactivity through medication that inhibits the sympathetic nervous system (e.g., beta-blockers). Another school of thought maintains that these personal interventions may be ineffective unless aspects of the larger environment (cultural, family, and work) that trigger Type A are addressed (e.g., the cultural value of competitiveness). According to Suinn, Brock, & Edie, (1975) one approach is to counteract these learned (and reinforced) behaviors through anxiety management and controlled imagery training.

Consistent with Suinn et al.'s (1975) environmental emphasis, Matteson and Ivancevich (1982) proposed yet another approach to TABP management. One goal of personnel or human resource departments is to optimize the person-environment fit (i.e., find the right person for the job) by matching various attributes of the person to organizational characteristics. They reasoned that organizations can be and often are described using typical TABP terms (e.g., time-urgent, competitive, aggressive), and certain individual and organizational TABP profiles may be particularly problematic. Specifically, they hypothesized that Type B workers in Type B organizations would suffer the least health problems, while Type A workers in Type A organizations the most. Their rationale was that a person–environment match would exaggerate individual personality characteristics, bringing out the A or B characteristics in the worker (As an aside, in terms of P–E fit theory, a Type A person should "fit" well in a Type A environment. However, their theoretical position was at odds with this claim). All other groups—Type A workers in Type B organizations and Type B workers in Type A organizations—were expected to fall between these two extremes.

After assessing both the work environment and individual workers on TABP dimensions in a sample of medical technologists, Matteson and Ivancevich (1982) confirmed both hypotheses. At least in terms of health, the maximal person–environment fit in some cases has its costs. As intriguing as these findings are, however, they were not tied to any measures of cardiovascular functioning.

What is the current status of TABP treatment and intervention? Given the rather positive results reported in many controlled studies, the reader may assume that Type A interventions have successfully addressed an important risk factor in the development of cardiovascular disease. However, Roskies (1990) voiced concern that although the various treatment interventions had been successful in affecting Type A behaviors, few had been successful in modifying physiological reactivity to stress, the presumed link between Type A and cardiovascular disease. The one exception was the intervention program developed by Friedman and his colleagues (Friedman et al., 1984). But, Roskies (1990) questioned whether the modification of TABP specifically or other components of their intervention (e.g., social support) may have influenced their results.

In the intervening years, Friedman and his colleagues (Friedman, 1996; Friedman et al., 1984) have continued to demonstrate success in identifying and treating TABP. However, Type A is a multidimensional construct and the interventions developed to treat it are equally multifaceted. So, exactly which components of the interventions are effective is unclear. Hopefully, future research will unravel this mystery.

Dealing with Job Loss

In Chapter 5, we discussed the growing research literature on downsizing and job loss. From these studies, behavioral scientists have learned much about how people deal with job change and loss. However, beyond the efforts of career guidance counselors and outplacement firms, relatively little is known about the most effective strategies to seek new employment. A notable exception is the longitudinal research of Caplan, Vinokur and their colleagues (e.g., Caplan, Vinokur, Price, & van Ryn, 1989; Vinokur, Price, Caplan, van Ryn, & Curran, 1995; Vinokur, Schule, Vuori, & Price, 2000; Vinokur, van Ryn, Gramlich, & Price, 1991).

In their initial study, Caplan et al. (JOBS I; 1989) randomly assigned 928 recently unemployed adults obtained through state employment compensation offices to either experimental or control conditions. The control condition consisted of providing participants only with an informational booklet on job seeking. The experimental group was a multicomponent intervention that focused on training in job seeking using a problem-solving orientation. The intervention attempted to establish trust and rapport between the trainers and participants, enhance job-seeking performance through increasing individual motivation to seek employment and building job-seeking skills, teaching inoculation against setbacks by anticipating problems and practicing coping skills to deal with them, and providing social support from peers and trainers. Compared to pretest measures, posttests at 1 and 4 months after the intervention demonstrated that participants in the intervention condition had higher quality reemployment (i.e., earnings and job satisfaction). For those individuals who remained unemployed across conditions, participants in the intervention group demonstrated a higher motivational level. Vinokur, van Ryn, Gramlich, and Price (1991) tracked the program over a 2 1/2 year period to assess its long-term effectiveness. Their results were consistent with those found by Caplan et al. (1989) at the 1- and 4-month posttreatment assessments. Specifically, participants who received the intervention continued to report higher monthly earnings and level of employment, and fewer job changes. Vinokur et al. (1991) also calculated a benefit-cost analysis of the intervention using standard economic guidelines (i.e., from the perspectives of the participants and the federal and state governments). After 32 months, the total net gain was determined to be $5392, $720, and $308 per participant for the average participant and for the federal and state governments, respectively.

Recently, Vinokur et al. (2000) published a 2-year follow-up to a diverse community sample of 2,005 recently unemployed workers who participated in an earlier intervention (JOBS II; Vinokur, Price, & Schul, 1995). This sample was demographically similar to the population of unemployed job seekers in the United States, so it provided an optimal means for studying the long-term health effects of unemployment in this country. At the 2-year follow-up, the researchers reported that the group that had received the experimental intervention had higher levels of reemployment and income, lower levels of depressive symptoms, and better emotional functioning than the control group.

An assessment of another intervention program targeting outplaced employees was undertaken by one of the largest outplacement firms in the United States (Maysent & Spera, 1995). The program focused on five areas: (1) defining/understanding and assessing stress; (2) managing stress by managing thought processes (i.e., cognitive behavioral techniques); (3) managing stress by reducing its impact through relaxation and visualization techniques; (4) managing stress by increasing personal control through learning to evaluate and cope with stressors; and (5) learning to incorporate stress management techniques into everyday life. These five modules were presented as two three-hour classes to approximately 100 clients of the outplacement firm in the treatment group. Approximately 50 clients participated in the control group.

Compared to the premeasures, participants in the treatment condition showed comparable levels of strain and coping resources at the postintervention assessment 1 week later. However, the control group showed higher levels of strain and decreased coping resources between the pre- and postassessments. Unfortunately, the researchers did not provide any assessment data beyond the immediate postintervention period to determine if these trends remained or changed over time.

The preceding job-loss interventions suffer from some obvious weaknesses. Because both interventions had several components, perhaps the most critical weakness is that the researchers were unable to determine if one, some, or all of the components contributed to the study results. Caplan et al. (1989) acknowledged this problem, but indicated that their self-report assessments were uniformly high across dimensions. Unfortunately, individual component assessments may be impractical in field tests of interventions because they require complex experimental designs, which would require a large number of participants and extra experimental and control groups (e.g., the Solomon 4-group design). One helpful strategy is to develop the intervention from an a priori conceptual framework using components of proven validity. Caplan et al. (1989) developed such a framework and refined it further in Vinokur, Price, Caplan, van Ryn, and Curran (1995). The limited intervention studies have also not targeted specific occupational groups or types of unemployed people (e.g., professional workers, factory workers), so the relative effectiveness of the interventions across groups is unknown. Finally, the role of the displaced worker's family and significant others in the coping process has remained relatively unexplored, although prior research (Vinokur & Caplan, 1987) has shown that spouses can provide an important source of instrumental and emotional support.

So, do stress and coping interventions targeting unemployed workers achieve their goals of helping the participants cope with the stress of unemployment and achieving reemployment? Our review suggests they do appear to achieve at least some of their goals, although no predictions can be offered regarding which intervention components are the most helpful and which groups profit most from participating in such interventions. From societal, organizational, and personal perspectives, these questions are important ones that will follow workers well into the 21st century. Hopefully, future research will tackle these unanswered questions.

APPLICATION: PROGRAMS IN INDUSTRY

Wellness Programs

Earlier in this chapter, we discussed employee assistance programs (EAPs), which are organizationally sponsored programs that provide employees with access to counseling from mental health professionals for a variety of problems, such as substance abuse, depression, and interpersonal conflict. However, within the last couple of decades, organizations have embraced the larger concept of health promotion or wellness programs. These broad-brush programs may incorporate some type of EAP program but also offer health assessments and screening, as well as, for example, independent programs on exercise, nutrition, weight management, smoking cessation, parenting, and stress management (cf. Danna & Griffin, 1999). Wellness programs usually offer stress management training as only one component of a series of programs, all united with the single goal of improving the mental and physical health of employees and their families. Because the improvement of workers' physical and emotional health can indeed influence how they perceive and manage stress in their environment, we briefly review a few of the more successful wellness programs in industry, followed by a short discussion about programs that have only focused on stress management.

Johnson & Johnson's Live for Life Program. Probably the most well known wellness program was developed by Johnson & Johnson. Johnson & Johnson (J&J) specializes in behavior change programs that focus on increasing the quality of life for its employees. J&J claims to have the most comprehensive selection of programs that can be customized to fit individual needs. In fact, Johnson & Johnson has been so successful in the health promotion field that it is among a small group of companies marketing their services (i.e., designing and implementing customized wellness programs) to other organizations. According to their Health Care Systems, Inc., the first step in creating a wellness program in any organization involves systematic planning and analysis. Specifically, some of the questions to be initially considered are: What type of wellness programs are needed? Does management support the creation and continuation of such programs? How can employee participation be ensured? How will program success be assessed? Using qualitative and quantitative techniques, these questions and others should be addressed before any type of program development.

The most well known component of the Johnson & Johnson system is the Live for Life program, a high intensity approach to lifestyle and health status management. The Live for Life modules include smoking cessation, cholesterol and blood pressure screening and management, medical information (especially cancer awareness and prevention), nutritional guidance, weight management, exercise programs, auto and work safety, and stress management. They are presented in both library (written) and video formats. They may be used by the individual employee or incorporated into a training program. Theey provide specific action steps and interactive exercises and require participants to individually pace themselves to achieve optimum benefit.

Other Johnson & Johnson programs include Health Risk Assessments, which use algorithms to provide individualized health profiles, the Health Response System 3000, a computer response terminal that delivers educational and motivational feedback to participants on a wide range of health-related topics, and Impact, a program that is geared toward the provision of customized services to high-health-risk employees. Two other specialized modules are Fitness and Ergonomics. The Fitness program aids in the development of customized fitness centers, from the design of the facility and exercise equipment to customized exercise programs for employees. The Ergonomics program provides training kits, which educate employees and their supervisors on workplace hazard identification, prevention, and change. Other Ergonomics modules focus on the prevention of workplace injuries caused by repetitive tasks, strenuous work, or long periods of sitting or standing through customized exercise or behavior change programs.

Does the Johnson & Johnson system work? Almost 15 years ago, Bly, Jones, and Richardson (1986) published an evaluation of two groups of J&J employees (N = 5, 192 & N = 3,259) exposed to the Live for Life Program compared to a control group (N = 2,955) over 5 years. Even after accounting for group baseline differences, mean annual inpatient cost increases were $43 and $42 for the Live for Life groups and $76 for the control group. The two Live for Life groups also had lower rates of increases in hospital admissions and stays. More recently, Jones, Bly, and Richardson (1990) examined absenteeism in two groups of J&J employees over 3 years. Employees in the Live for Life program at four sites (N = 1,406) were compared to a control group at five sites (N = 487). After controlling for group baseline differences in demographic characteristics and absenteeism, wage earners' mean absenteeism levels in the Live for Life groups declined over the study period and were lower than the control group's mean absenteeism level. However, no comparable group differences were obtained for salaried employees.

Yes, according to Johnson & Johnson's data, their program does work. However, the health-care giant does have to toil diligently to maintain program success. For example, J&J offered high-risk employees (e.g., smokers) $500 discounts on their insurance premiums if they would have their blood pressure, cholesterol, and body-fat levels checked and respond to a health-risk questionnaire. The company sends high-risk workers letters urging them to join diet and exercise programs. If the employees refuse, they lose the insurance discount. J&J claims success with this new incentive program: 96% of their 35,000 U. S. employees completed the health assessments in 1995, compared to 40% prior to the discount offer (Jeffrey, 1996). Other incentives include free laundry service after a workout in the fitness center: Employees can dump their dirty exercise clothes in a basket, and the company will wash and return their clothes at no charge. J&J also provides towels and personal grooming items. Although these services seem minor, they undoubtedly contribute to the high employee participation rate in the Live for Life program (Verespej, 1993).

AT&T's Total Life Concept Program. AT&T launched their wellness program in 1983, guided by two fundamental goals: (1) to create a corporate culture that encourages healthy behavior, and (2) to find the best combinations of interventions to reduce employee health risks (Bellingham, Johnson, McCauley, & Mendes, 1987). Although the impetus for this wellness program was originally to help employees deal with divestiture, AT&T soon realized that such a program could have broader corporate benefits through reductions in absenteeism, disability payments, and insurance premiums. In May 1983, employees participating in a pilot test of the program at two sites were given an orientation session, health-risk appraisals, supportive activities (e.g., support groups), and the option of enrolling in three of nine 4- to 12-week health programs.

Because one of the program goals was to alter corporate culture to be more receptive to positive health practices, the communications giant facilitated several changes: (1) Vending machines were stocked with fruit and juice, not just candy bars and chips; (2) Magazines and nutritional bulletins were sent to program participants to augment the training from the modules; (3) In addition to obtaining union support, an advisory committee was formed composed of upper AT&T management; and (4) Leadership committees, consisting entirely of program participants, were formed to encourage employee participation and program ownership, as well as to provide feedback and creative ideas on the program itself. These leadership committees were independent of the internal support groups that had been created to aid in the achievement of health goals (e.g., weight-loss groups).

The second goal of the program was to provide the best possible interventions to reduce health risks. To accomplish this, assessment of program efficacy was vital. Therefore, one year later (May 1984), 745 (62%) of those who originally participated in one or more modules from the Total Life Concept were reassessed at the two pilot test sites. (Data were also collected from five sites that served as controls.) The results indicated that significant reductions in health risks occurred at one or more pilot sites. Across all modules, participants' blood pressure and cholesterol levels decreased. The exercise module was the most popular; the participants in this module showed significant reductions in both body fat and blood pressure (systolic and diastolic). The average Total Life Concept participant lost 10 pounds in the 12-week weight control module. Of the participants in the smoking cessation program, 53% were still not smoking 6 months later. Participants who completed the stress management and interpersonal skills programs also reported reduced levels of stress (60% and 41% at the two sites) and improvements in their work and personal relationships (50%), respectively.

Five years later (1988), AT&T's Total Life Concept program was reevaluated (Holt, McCauley, & Paul, 1995). Unfortunately, only 31% of the original participants across multiple sites were assessed, and this group was demographically different from the original participants (e.g., a greater percentage of minorities and higher paid workers). The 1988 participants had lower high-density lipoprotein (a cardiovascular health indicator; higher is better), although the other medical indices remained the same or worsened. However, health-related behaviors generally improved: Alcohol consumption, smoking, and Type A behavior decreased since 1983. Comparison of the 1988 pilot group with the 1988 control group also did not fare as expected: For example, the pilot group had higher blood pressure and cholesterol values.

The 5-year assessment concluded that, for those 1983 participants who returned for the 1988 measurement, very limited evidence existed for any positive effects on health-risk indicators (e.g., cholesterol), while health-related attitudes and behaviors appeared to improve. In particular, decreases in alcohol consumption and smoking seem to be attributed to the program. However, the researchers assumed that the low response rate and lack of comparability of the control group limited their ability to conclude that study outcomes were caused by the Total Life Concept Program. The reevaluation was cited as an excellent example of the difficulty of conducting longitudinal research in dynamic work settings, even when the initial design is sound and significant efforts are made to retain study and comparison group participants (Holt et al., 1995, p. 425).

Coors Brewing Company's LifeCheck Program. Since the early 1980s, Coors Brewing Co. has developed and maintained a highly successful wellness program. The guiding force behind this program is the brewing company's CEO and chairman, William Coors, who first envisioned the corporate wellness concept before it became faddish. In 1981, the company opened its 25,000-square-foot wellness facility, which offers aerobics and strength training, cardiovascular equipment, and an indoor jogging track. In 1984, the company also began to offer personal health-risk assessments or Health Hazard Appraisal (HHA); some of the guidelines to determine risk are provided by hypertension and cholesterol asseessments and employee characteristics (smoking status, weight, and level of physical activity) (Verespej, 1993).

Beyond Mr. Coor's personal commitment to health, however, in 1987 the Coors Company began to encounter costs associated with aging and disabled employees. Although this trend is reflected in the general U. S. working population, Coors starting experiencing the "graying" of its workforce even earlier due to low turnover within the company. To meet this challenge, the LifeCheck Program was born in 1990. LifeCheck was established specifically to stall the onset of and severity of cardiovascular disease among employees, thereby reducing corporate disability and medical costs. After the health-risk assessment, participants in the Lifecheck Program were given time from their jobs to meet with Coors's wellness counselors, who reviewed participants' health profiles and offered suggestions for improving health-related behaviors. Often these suggestions included participation in health-improvement classes, such as those dealing with issues of cholesterol, nutrition, smoking cessation, hypertension, and exercise. These classes were held in the work area during all shifts to accommodate all employees. Wellness specialists were also always available, as well as "talk-to-the-doc" sessions, in which participants could meet personally with Coors's staff cardiologist. Exercise equipment was even moved from the Wellness Center and placed on the plant floor, thus allowing employees to use the equipment at their convenience (Caudron, 1990, 1991).

The Coors staff developed subtle and not-so-subtle reminders and incentives to encourage employees to keep their LifeCheck commitments. Posters, table tents, tray mats, and electronic messages scattered throughout the work areas served as frequent LifeCheck reminders. Participants were also given key chains, water bottles, and T-shirts to advertise the program. Competitions among work units were held to encourage physical activity; for example, prizes were awarded to the units that increased their overall minutes or miles of physical exercise by the greatest amount. Finally, employees who maintained a healthy lifestyle received a 5% reduction in their health insurance copayment.

How did LifeCheck fare? According to LifeCheck data, 90% of participants in the original intervention (N = 692) had one or more cardiovascular risk factors. Of those who completed the exit screening (72%), the changes included lower systolic blood pressure, reduced body weight, lower cholesterol, and increased physical exercise. An independent cost-benefit analysis by researchers at the University of Oregon indicated that Coors's wellness program was definitely cost beneficial; specifically, for each dollar spent on the program, Coors may have received a return ranging from $1.24 to $8.33 (Terborg, 1988). The wellness program's continuing success has enabled Coors to offer it to a larger number of employees and expand the wellness facilities in recent years.

Does the wellness concept work? The foregoing discussion of three well-conceived and maintained programs housed in large corporations demonstrates that wellness programs can and do succeed in their goal of producing (and maintaining) healthier employees. However, the success of these programs has typically been achieved through considerable commitment in money, resources, and personnel, a commitment that many organizations are unable or unwilling to make. AT&T's difficulty in making sense of the 5-year assessment of its Total Life Concept Program nicely illustrates the obstacles involved in maintaining such programs, even with strong corporate commitment.

Stress Management Programs

Although the ultimate organizational goal with wellness programs is to reduce or contain health-care costs, side benefits of such programs hopefully include the development of more productive, well-adjusted, and less stressed workers. However, some programs have been created specifically to reduce stress and its effects. For example, B.F. Goodrich developed a program, Manage Your Stress, designed specifically for its employees. The 9-hour program was tailored to each participant because it focused on the identification of personal stress responses and a plan to manage these responses. Metropolitan Life's stress management program was so successful that the company even marketed it to other companies. This program has a varied format, emphasizing stress reduction through such techniques as communication skills training, time management, and relaxation exercises.

One of the most committed efforts at organizational stress management came from ICI-Zeneca Pharmaceuticals, a European firm (Teasdale & McKeown, 1994). In the mid-1980s to early 1990s, the company's medical officers noted a steadily increasing referral load of stress-related illness. The organization had undergone major changes, which undoubtedly contributed to employee distress. Among these changes, Zeneca separated from ICI in 1993 to become its own company. The pharmaceutical industry is also an extremely competitive, research-oriented enterprise that depends heavily on a high level of scientific creativity and commitment to expensive product development ventures. In addition, Zeneca manufactured products in 17 countries and sold these products in 130 countries. Its 13,000 employees were located primarily in the United Kingdom, western Europe, the United States, and Japan. All of these factors depicted an international organization that demanded considerable time, commitment, and expertise from its employees, all of which set the stage for high levels of job-related stress.

The company made a commitment to attack the stress at its doorstep by developing a six-level strategy. The first and second levels of interventions were the treatment of stress-related problems and the identification of emerging stress-related problems within the organization. The third level attempted to legitimize stress disorders through the education and involvement of senior management. The fourth and fifth levels resembled the only step most organizations take—specifically, increasing companywide awareness of stress-related problems through education and training (e.g., stress management workshops). The sixth level attempted to change the total organizational culture through the acceptance of new norms (e.g., taking more time for family and leisure activities, decreasing job-related demands).

Zeneca's stress management workshop incorporated some interesting approaches and is worth a closer look. The idea behind their workshop was that stress is a normal part of life but that it can (and often does) get out of control. It is therefore important to be able to recognize when stress levels are becoming too high and also to have the skills to deal with it. The workshop lasted for 2 days, with a follow-up half-day session 2 months later. In the first exercise, participants pair off and spend 5 minutes telling their partner what stresses them; after one person finishes, the process is repeated with the other person. This exercise relaxes everyone and helps them frame the group's mission. The total group then holds a brainstorming session on "what stresses me." Finally, customized videos illustrate the wrong and right ways of dealing with stress in the organization, followed by a brief introduction to relaxation techniques.

Did Zeneca's approach work? They did track the outcome of their efforts. Both before and after they attended stress management workshops, employees responded to a self-report health measure; a 15–20% improvement on distress scores was documented. A decrease in referrals to mental health or medical services also occurred after the workshops (Figure 8.2).

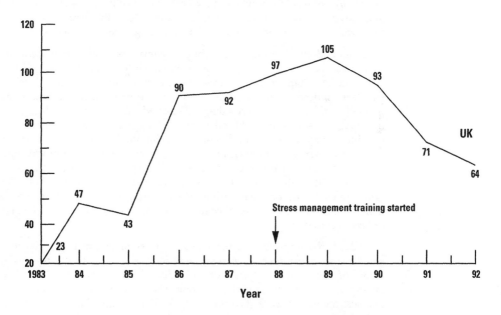

Figure 8.2 Referrals to Psychiatrists or Psychologists; Attendance at Zeneca Pharmaceuticals Medical Centers or Family Doctors' Clinics

Zeneca's experience with organizational stress managment is indeed encouraging. However, we must voice a caveat. The pharmaceutical giant made a considerable commitment in time, personnel, and resources to create this success. This type of commitment is extremely rare. More commonly, organizations attempt to handle only job-related stress (and distress) through generic, one-shot stress management workshops delivered by a consultant who is unfamiliar with the organization and its employees. Such programs have questionable impact beyond their entertainment value. We have more to say about this in our conclusions.

CONCLUSIONS

In this chapter, we reviewed stress management from several different perspectives. We examined the various organizational techniques (e.g., task redesign, quality circles) and personal techniques (e.g., relaxation, exercise) used to achieve stress reduction. We also looked at stress management for specific purposes, such as dealing with job loss and burnout. In addition to EAPs, some well-known programs in industry, both the broad-based wellness programs as well as programs that have stress management as their primary goal, were examined. In most cases, our assessment was, at the very least, guardedly optimistic. So, why did a recent review of the organizational stress and stress management literature (Kahn & Byosiere, 1992) call organizational stress management "disappointing in several respects"?

Kahn and Byosiere's first criticism of organizational stress management is that it has been concentrated disproportionately on reducing the effects of stress rather than reducing stress in the environment (i.e., job-related stressors). Indeed, as discussed previously, stress management programs have focused primarily on providing distressed individuals with general information about stress, a broad array of coping skills (e.g., communication training, cognitive-behavioral coping techniques) and some form of systematic relaxation training. However, most programs have not attempted to alleviate the actual source of individual distress. Similarly, their second criticism is that the focus of stress management has been the individual rather than the job or organization. The enduring theme is that, if only the individual can become stress-resistant, the stressful environment can be more or less tolerated.

Indeed, the individual as the focus of stress management is even more pervasive than previous discussions indicated. We certainly did not review many of the alternate forms of individual intervention that have been attempted to manage job-related stress. One current trend is the use of massage therapy at work (Overman, 1993). For example, the Calvert Group in Bethesda, Maryland, provided message therapy for its 200 employees as part of the benefits package: One day each week employees could receive a

15-minute neck, shoulder, and back message while seated. Other companies, such as Cable Midlands, have offered their stressed employees hypnosis training, as well as aromatheraphy and reflexology (a type of foot and hand massage) (Butler, 1996).

Another personal-level intervention that has long been used in academic jobs is the sabbatical (Bachler, 1995; Romano, 1995b). Corporate sabbaticals originated in the 1970s and have remained in some form. These sanctioned leaves may or may not be paid, offered after a certain length of employment, intended for specific purposes (education or personal development), or guarantee the same or a similar job upon return. For example, Apple has offered 6 weeks at full pay after 5 years of employment, Xerox, up to 1 year at full pay after 3 years, and AT&T, 9 to 24 months at no pay but full benefits after 5 years. Proponents of the sabbatical as a stress management tool claim that it defuses stress, particularly for employees in high-pressure research and development and consulting jobs. Another use of sabbaticals has emerged in the downsizing era when the workforce needed to be reduced. Corporations, such as AT&T and Bell Atlantic, have used sabbaticals to temporarily reduce their workforce (and, of course, their payroll).

Third, Kahn and Byosiere (1992) maintained that too few stress management programs have been adequately evaluated, a criticism that was also raised earlier in this chapter. Fourth, they claim that the content of most programs reflect the preferences and training of the stress management consultants more than the needs of the organization and its employees. As discussed earlier, we definitely concur that far too many stress management workshops are one-shot, prepackaged programs that offer little more than an afternoon's entertainment. However, Kahn and Byosiere also offer words of encouragement, as we did at the beginning of this section, by concluding that the meager evidence does suggest that stress management can work, at least with white-collar and managerial workers. Unfortunately, virtually nothing is known about organizational stress management for blue-collar workers or special groups, such as minority or disabled employees, although we conjecture that their needs would differ.

A few closing comments are in order. It is clear that there is no one best way to manage stress in organizations. All other things being equal, it is preferable to intervene in all phases of the stress process. Thus, identifying and removing/controlling stressors where possible, promoting the use of clinical interventions where necessary (e.g., through EAPs), and providing interventions to help manage stress symptoms are all potentially useful. However, as mentioned repeatedly in this chapter, the vast majority of stress management interventions in industry have focused solely on the individual. That fact has prompted organizational stress researchers (e.g., Cartwright, Cooper, & Murphy, 1995; Ganster, 1995), ourselves included, to voice the following sentiment: Instead of training employees to better endure stress at work, a potentially healthier and more ethical approach would be to make the organizational environment less stressful. It makes little sense to place skilled, motivated workers in a dysfunctional workplace and expect positive outcomes, regardless of the "stress-resistant" bag of tricks they might acquire.

Of course, as noted earlier, identifying stressors that are common to a sufficiently large group of workers to warrant an organizational-level intervention might be extremely difficult. Intuitively, it is reasonable to assume that stressors related to the work environment, such as poor lighting, faulty equipment, or uncomfortable chairs, will often be perceived as stressful to all employees experiencing these stressors. Psychosocial stressors, however, such as interpersonal conflict, role ambiguity, or inadequate assistance from coworkers, may or may not emerge as sufficiently general to warrant an organizational intervention. A stress audit is a wise time and cost investment to determine whether and the extent to which consensus exists concerning one or more stressors that can be targeted for intervention.

Perhaps the concept of the stress audit underscores the idea that many organizational interventions that are generally not conceived as stress management programs can be properly conceptualized within the umbrella of stress management. For example, developing a new performance appraisal system may seem far removed from the province of stress management. If, however, the system is developed to address perceived stress regarding perceptions of unfair promotions, inadequate feedback, and so on, it is clearly sensible to conceptualize the appraisal system development from the standpoint of stress management.

Many researchers and practitioners in the fields of industrial and organizational psychology and organizational behavior often do not readily associate job stress with traditional areas of inquiry, such as personnel selection, training, performance appraisal, work motivation, or leadership. The material presented in this book, and particularly the information concerning stress management, hopefully conveys the inherent link between work stress and other topics of interest. In closing, we offer some unanswered research questions that link the topic of stress management to other topics that traditionally have interested behavioral scientists.

1. Is it possible to identify individuals who are skilled at managing stress? Moreover, should this skill be used as a selection criterion for some jobs? Complicating this question, however, is the issue that some level of stress (arousal) may be beneficial, especially when performance must be optimized (Chapter 6).

2. Is it useful for organizations to include information about common job-related stressors and methods of coping with them during realistic job previews?

3. Should performance appraisal systems include an assessment of how individual workers cope with their own stress, and/or whether they help coworkers in their own coping efforts?

4. Which coping strategies do top leaders use, including CEOs, presidents, and high-level politicians? Is the ability to effectively manage stress a necessary skill for effective leadership in these jobs?

In conclusion, the topic of stress management is extremely broad and vitally important to both the health of individual workers and the organizations employing them. Hopefully, the material in this chapter highlights both the challenges and opportunities facing researchers as they attempt to develop strategies aimed at managing stress at work.

REFERENCES

Abernethy, A. D. (1995). The development of an anger management training program for law enforcement personnel. In L. R. Murphy, J. J. Hurrell Jr., S. L. Sauter, & G. P. Keita (Eds.), *Job stress interventions* (pp. 21–30). Washington, DC: American Psychological Association.

Abramis, D. J. (1994). Work role ambiguity, job satisfaction, and job performance: Meta-analyses and review. *Psychological Reports, 75* (3), 1411–1433.

Adams, J. D. (1988, August). A healthy cut in costs. *Personnel Adminstrator,* 42–47.

Agervold, M. (1976). Shiftwork: A critical review. *Scandinavian Journal of Psychology, 17,* 181–188.

Aiello, J. R., & Kolb, K. J. (1995). Electronic performance monitoring: A risk factor for workplace stress. In S. L. Sauter & L. R. Murphy (Eds.), *Organizational risk factors for job stress.* Washington, DC: American Psychological Association.

Aiello, J. R., & Shao, Y. (1993). Electronic performance monitoring and stress: The role of feedback and goal setting. In G. Salvendy & M. Smith (Eds.), *Human computer interaction: Software and hardware interfaces.* Amsterdam: Elsevier.

Akerstedt, T. (1985). Adjustment of physiological circadian rhythms and the sleep-wake cycle to shiftwork. In S. Folkard & T. H. Monk (Eds.), *Hours of work: Temporal factors in work-scheduling.* New York: Wiley.

Alba, J. W., & Hasher, L. (1983). Is memory schematic? *Psychological Bulletin, 93*(2), 203–231.

Aldwin, C. M., & Revenson, T.A. (1987). Does coping help? A reexamination of the relation between coping and mental health. *Journal of Personality and Social Psychology, 53,* 337–348.

Alexander, F. (1950). *Psychosomatic medicine: Its principles and application.* New York: Norton.

Alfredsson, L., Karasek, R., & Theorell, T. (1982). Myocardial infarction risk and psychosocial work environment: An analysis of the male Swedish working force. *Social Science and Medicine, 16,* 463–467.

Allen, T. D., Freeman, D. M., Russell, J. E. A., Reizenstein, R. C., & Rentz, J. O. (2001). Survivor reactions to organizational downsizing: Does time ease the pain? *Journal of Occupational and Organizational Psychology, 74,* 145–164.

Allen, T. D., Herst, D. E. L., Bruck, C. S., & Sutton, M. (2000). Consequences associated with work-to-family conflict: A review and agenda for future research. *Journal of Occupational Health Psychology, 5,* 278–308.

Amick, B. C., III, & Smith, M. J. (1992). Stress, computer-based work monitoring and measurement systems: A conceptual overview. *Applied Ergonomics, 23,* 6–16.

Angersbach D., Knauth, P., Loskant, H., Karvonen, M. J., Undeutsch, K., & Rutenfranz, J. (1980). A retrospective cohort study comparing complaints and diseases in day and shift workers. *International Archives of Occupational and Environmental Health, 45,* 127–140.

Anshel, M. H. (2000). A conceptual model and implications for coping with stressful events in police work. *Criminal Justice & Behavior, 27,* 375–400.

Applebaum, S. H., Simpson, R., & Shapiro, B. T. (1987). The tough test of downsizing. *Organizational Dynamics, 16*(2), 68–79.

Appley, M. H., & Trumbull, R. (1967). On the concept of psychological stress. In M. Appley & R. Trumbull (Eds.), *Psychological stress.* New York: Appleton-Century-Crofts.

Arndt, S., Clevenger, J., & Meiskey, L. (1985). Students' attitudes toward computers. *Computers and the Social Sciences, 1,* 181–190.

Arnetz, J. E., Arnetz, B. B., & Petterson, I. (1996). Violence in the nursing profession: Occupational and liefstyle risk factors in Swedish nurses. *Work and Stress, 10,* 119–127.

Arsenault, A., Dolan, S. L., & Van Ameringen, M. R. (1991). Stress and mental strain in hospital work: Exploring the relationship beyond personality. *Journal of Organizational Behavior, 12,* 483–493.

Ashby, W. R. (1966). *An introduction to cybernetics.* New York: Wiley.

Ashford, S. J. (1988). Individual strategies for coping with stress during organizational transitions. *Journal of Applied Behavioral Science, 24*(1), 19–36.

Astrand, P., & Rodahl, K. (1986). *Textbook of work physiology* (3rd ed.). New York: McGraw-Hill.

Astrom, S., Nilsson, M., Norberg, A., Sandman, P., & Winblad, B. (1991). Staff burnout in dementia care: Relations to empathy and attitudes. *International Journal of Nursing Studies, 28,* 65–75.

Atkinson, J. M. (1988). *Coping with stress at work*. London: Thorsons.

Averill, J. (1973). Personal control over aversive stimuli and its relationship to stress. *Psychological Bulletin, 80*, 286–303.

Ax, A. F. (1953). *Psychosomatic Medicine, 15*, 433–442.

Bacharach, S., & Bamberger, P. (1992). Causal models of role stressor antecedents and consequences: The importance of occupational differences. *Journal of Vocational Behavior, 41*, 13–34.

Bachler, C. J. (1995, January). Workers take leave of job stress. *Personnel Journal*, 38–48.

Badura, B. (1984). Life-style and health: Some remarks on different viewpoints. *Social Science and Medicine, 19*, 341–347.

Baglioni, A. J., Cooper, Cary L., & Hingley, Peter. (1990). Job stress, mental health and job satisfaction among UK senior nurses. *Stress Medicine, 6*(1), 9–20.

Bagozzi, R. (1981). Attitudes, intentions, and behavior: A test of some key hypotheses. *Journal of Personality and Social Psychology, 41*, 607–627.

Bailey, C. N. (1990, November). Wellness programs that work. *Business and Health, 8*, 28–40.

Bakker, A. B., & Schaufeli, W. B. (2000). Burnout contagion processes among teachers. *Journal of Applied Social Psychology, 30*, 2289–2308.

Balick, L. R., & Herd, J. A. (1986). Assessment of physiological indices related to cardiovascular disease as influenced by job stress. *Journal of Organizational Behavior Management, 8*, 103–115.

Balzer, W. K., & Pargament, K. (1987). The key to designing a successful employee assistance program. *Personnel, 64*, 48–56.

Barling, J., Bluen, S. D., & Fain, R. (1987). Psychological functioning following an acute disaster. *Journal of Applied Psychology, 72*, 683–690.

Barling, J., & Charbonneau, D. (1992). Disentangling the relationship between the achievement striving and impatience-irritability dimensions of Type A behavior, performance, and health. *Journal of Organizational Behavior, 13*, 369–377.

Barmack, J. E. (1937). Boredom and other factors in the physiology of mental effort: An exploratory study. *Archives of Psychology*, 218, 1–83.

Baron, R. A., Neuman, J. H., & Geddes, D. (1999). Social and personal determinants of workplace aggression: Evidence for the impact of perceived injustice and the Type A behavior pattern. *Aggressive Behavior, 25*, 281–296.

Bartoldus, E., Gillery, B., & Sturges, P. J. (1989). Job-related stress and coping among home-care workers with elderly people. *Health and Social Work, 14*, 204–210.

Bartone, P. T., Ursano, R. J., Wright, K. M., & Ingraham, L. H. (1989). The impact of a military air disaster on the health of assistance workers. *Journal of Nervous and Mental Disease, 17*, 317–328. Beaton, R., & Murphy, S. (1993). Sources of occupational stress in firefighters/EMTs and firefighter/paramedics and correlations with job-related outcomes. *Prehospital and Disaster Medicine, 8*, 140–150.

Beaton, R., Murphy, S., Johnson, C., Pike, K., & Corneil, W. (1999). Coping responses and posttraumatic stress symptomatology in urban fire service personnel. *Journal of Traumatic Stress, 12*, 293–308.

Beaton, R., Murphy, S., Pike, K., & Jarrett, M. (1995). Stress-symptom factors in firefighters and paramedics. In S. L. Sauter & L. R. Murphy (Eds.), *Organizational risk factors for job stress.* Washington, DC: American Psychological Association.

Bedeian, A. G., & Armenakis, A. A. (1981). A path analytic study of the consequences of role conflict and ambiguity. *Academy of Management Journal, 24*, 417–424.

Beehr, T. A. (1976). Perceived situational moderators of the relationship between subjective role ambiguity and role strain. *Journal of Applied Psychology, 61*, 35–40.

Beehr, T. A. (1985). Organizational stress and employee effectiveness: A job characteristics approach. In T. A. Beehr & R. S. Bhagat (Eds.), *Human stress and cognition in organizations.* (pp. 57–81). New York: Wiley Interscience.

Beehr, T. A., & Franz, T. M. (1987). The current debate about the meaning of job stress. In J. Ivancevich & D. Ganster (Eds.), *Job stress: From theory to suggestions.* New York: Hawthorne Press.

Beehr, T. A., Jex, S. M., Stacy, B. A., & Murray, M. A. (2000). Work stressors and coworker support as predictors of individual strain and job performance. *Journal of Organizational Behavior, 21*, 391–405.

Beehr, T. A., Johnson, L. B., & Nieva, R. (1995). Occupational stress: Coping of police and their spouses. *Journal of Organizational Behavior, 16*, 3–25.

Beehr, T. A., King, L. A., & King, D. W. (1990). Social support and occupational stress: Talking to supervisors. *Journal of Vocational Medicine, 36*, 61–81.

Beehr, T. A., & Newman, J. E. (1978). Job stress, employee health, and organizational effectiveness: A facet analysis, model, and literature review. *Personnel Psychology, 31*, 665–699.

Beehr, T. A., & Schuler, R. S. (1982). Current and future perspectives on stress in organizations. In Rowland & Ferris (Eds.), *Personnel management: New perspectives.* Boston: Allyn & Bacon.

Begley, T. M., & Czajka, J. M. (1993). Panel analysis of the moderating effects of commitment on job satisfaction, intent to quit, and health following organizational change. *Journal of Applied Psychology, 78*, 552–556.

Bellingham, R., Johnson, D., McCauley, M., & Mendes, T. (1987). Projected cost savings from AT&T Communications Total Life Concept (TLC) Process. In Projected cost savings from AT&T Communications Total Life Concept (TLC) Process. J. O. (Ed.), Stevens Point, WI: National Wellness Institute/Association Publication. (pp. 35–42).

Benight, C., Swift, E., Sanger, J., Smith, A., & Zeppelin, D. (1999). Coping self-efficacy as a mediator of distress following a natural disaster. *Journal of Applied Social Psychology, 29*(12), 2443–2464.

Bennett, N., Martin, C. L., Bies, R. J., & Brockner, J. (1995). Coping with a layoff: A longitudinal study of victims. *Journal of Management, 21,* 1025–1040.

Bennett, P., Wallace, L., Carroll, D., & Smith, N. (1991). Treating Type A behaviours and mild hypertension in middle-aged men. *Journal of Psychosomatic Research, 35,* 209–233.

Benson, H. (1975). *The relaxation response.* New York: Avon Books.

Berman, P. S., Sulsky, L. M., Pargament, K., Balzer, W. K., & Kausch, D. (1991). The role of needs assessment in the design of employee assitance programs: A case study. *Employee Assistance Quarterly, 6,* 21–35.

Berridge, J., & Cooper, C. L. (1993). Stress and coping in U.S. organizations: The role of the Employee Assistance Programme. *Work and Stress, 7,* 89–102.

Bhagat, R. S. (1983). Effects of stressful life events on individual performance effectiveness and work adjustment processes within organizational settings: A research model. *Academy of Management Review, 8,* 606–671.

Bhagat, R. S. et al. (1994). Organizational stress and coping in seven national contexts: A cross-cultural investigation. In G. P. Keita & J. J. Hurrell, Jr. (Eds.), *Job stress in a changing workforce,* 93–105. Washington DC: American Psychological Association.

Bhagat, R. S., & Allie, S. M. (1989). Organizational stress, personal life stress, and symptoms of life strains: An examination of the moderating role of sense of competence. *Journal of Vocational Behavior, 35,* 231–253.

Bhagat, R. S., McQuaid, S. J., Lindholm, H., & Segovis, J. (1985). Total life stress: A multimethod validation of the construct and its effects on organizationally valued outcomes and withdrawal behaviors. *Journal of Applied Psychology, 70,* 202–214.

Billings, A., & Moos, R. H. (1981). The role of coping reponses and social resources in attenuating the stress of life events. *Journal of Behavioral Medicine, 4,* 157–189.

Binning, J. F., & Barrett, G. V. (1989). Validity of personnel decisions: A conceptual analysis of the inferential and evidential bases. *Journal of Applied Psychology, 74,* 478–494.

Blanchard-Fields, F., Sulsky, L., & Robinson-Whelen, S. (1991). Moderating effects of age and context on the relationship between gender, sex role differences, and coping. *Sex Roles, 25,* 645–660.

Blaney, P. H., & Ganellen, R. J. (1990). Hardiness and social support. In B. R. Sarason, I. G. Sarason, & G. R. Pierce (Eds.), *Social support: An interactional view* (pp. 297–318). New York: Wiley.

Blau, G. J. (1981). An empirical investigation of job stress, social support, and job strain. *Organizational Behavior and Human Performance, 27,* 279–302.

Bliese, P. D., & Britt, T. W. (2001). Social support, group consensus and stressor-strain relationships: Social context matters. *Journal of Organizational behavior, 22,* 425–436.

Bliese, P. D., & Jex, S. M. (1999). Incorporating multiple levels of analysis into occupational stress research. *Work and Stress, 13,* 1–6.

Bliss, E. L., Migeon, C. J., Branch, C. H., & Samuels, L. T. (1956). Reaction of the adrenal cortex to emotional stress. *Psychosomatic Medicine, 18, 56.*

Bloom, J. D. (1989). The character of danger in psychiatric practice: Are the mentally ill dangerous? *Bulletin of the American Academy of Psychiatry and the Law, 17, 241–255.*

Bly, J. L., Jones, R. C., & Richardson, J. E. (1986). Impact of worksite health promotion on health care costs and utilization: Evaluation of Johnson & Johnson's Live for Life program. *Health Promotion, 256* (23), 3235–3240.

Boggild, H., Knutsson, A. (1999). Shift work, risk factors and cardiovascular disease. *Scandinavian Journal of Work, Environment & Health, 25*(2), 85–99.

Bohle, P. (1997). Does "hardiness" predict adaptation to shiftwork? *Work and Stress, 11, 369–376.*

Bohle, P., & Tilley, A. J. (1998). Early experience of shiftwork: Influences on attitudes. *Journal of Occupational and Organizational Psychology, 71, 61–79.*

Booth-Kewley, S., & Friedman, H. S. (1987). Psychological predictors of heart disease: A quantitative review. *Psychological Bulletin, 101, 343–362.*

Bortner, R. W. (1969). A short rating scale as a potential measure of pattern A behavior. *Journal of Chronic Diseases, 22, 87–91.*

Bosma, H., Stansfeld, S. A., & Marmot, M. G. (1998). Job control, personal characteristics, and heart disease. *Journal of Occupational Health Psychology, 3, 402–409.*

Bourbeau, J., Brisson, C., & Allaire, S. (1996) Prevalence of the sick building syndrome symptoms in office workers before and after being exposed to a building with an improved ventilation system, *Occupational and Environmental Medicine, 53, 204–210.*

Bowers, K. S. (1973). Situationalism in psychology: An analysis and a critique. *Psychological Review, 80, 307– 336.*

Boyd, A. (1997). Employee traps—corruption in the workplace. *Management Review, 86, 9.*

Brand, R. (1978). Coronary-prone behavior as an independent risk factor for coronary heart disease. In T. M. Dembroski (Ed.), *Coronary-prone behavior.* New York: Springer-Verlag.

Braverman, M. (1999). *Preventing workplace violence: A guide for employers and practitioners.* Thousand Oaks, CA: Sage.

Breaugh, J. A., & Colihan, J. P. (1994). Measuring facets of job ambiguity: Construct validity evidence. *Journal of Applied Psychology, 79, 191–202.*

Brett, J. M., Stroh, L. K., & Reilly, A. H. (1990). *Impact of societal shifts and corporate changes on employee relocation.* Washington, DC: Employee Relocation Council.

Brett, J. M., Stroh, L. K., & Reilly, A. H. (1992). What is it like being a dual-career manager in the 1990s? In S. Zedeck (Ed.) *Work, families, and organizations.* San Francisco: Jossey-Bass.

Brief, A. P., Burke, M. J., George, J. M., Robinson, B. S., & Webster, J. (1988). Should negative affectivity remain an unmeasured variable in the study of job stress? *Journal of Applied Psychology, 73, 193–198.*

Brief, A. P., & George, J. M. (1991). Psychological stress and the workplace: A brief comment on Lazarus' outlook. Special issue: Handbook on job stress. *Journal of Social Behavior and Personality, 6*(7), 15–20.

Brief, A. P., Schuler, R. S., & Van Sell, M. (1981). *Managing job stress.* Boston: Little, Brown.

Briner, R., & Hockey, R. J. (1988). Operator stress and computer-based work. In C. L. Cooper & R. Payne (Eds.), *Causes, coping, and consequences of stress at work.* New York: Wiley.

Briner, R. B., & Reynolds, S. (1999). The costs, benefits, and limitations of organizational level stress interventions. *Journal of Organizational Behavior, 20,* 647–664.

Broadbent, D. (1976). Noise and the details of experiments: A reply to Poulton. *Applied Ergonomics, 7,* 231–235.

Broadbent, D. (1978). The current state of noise research: Reply to Poulton. *Psychological Bulletin, 85,* 1052–1067.

Broadhead, W. E., Gehlbach, S. H., DeGruy, F. V., & Kaplan, B. (1989). Functional versus structural social support and health care utilization in a family medicine outpatient practice. *Medical Care, 27,* 221–223.

Brock, D. B., & Sulsky, L. M. (1994). Attitudes toward computers: Construct validations and relations to computer use. *Journal of Organizational Behavior, 15,* 17–35.

Brockner, J. (1985). The relation of trait self-esteem and positive inequity to productivity. *Journal of Personality, 53,* 517–529.

Brockner, J. (1990). Scope of justice in the workplace: How survivors react to co-worker layoffs. *Journal of Social Issues 46*(1), 95–106.

Brockner, J., Davy, J., & Carter, C. (1985). Layoffs, self-esteem, and survivor guilt: Motivational, affective, and attitudinal consequences. *Organizational Behavior and Human Decision Processes, 36,* 229–244.

Brockner, J., Grover, S. L., & Blonder, M. D. (1988). Predictors of survivors' job involvement following layoffs: A field study. *Journal of Applied Psychology, 73,* 436–442.

Brockner, J., Grover, S., Reed, T. F., & Dewitt, R. L. (1992). Layoffs, job insecurity, and survivors' work effort: Evidence of an inverted-U relationship. *Academy of Management Journal, 35*(2), 413–425.

Brockner, J., Tyler, T. R., & Cooper-Schneider, R. (1992). The influence of prior commitment to an institution on reactions to perceived unfairness: The higher they are, the harder they fall. *Administrative Science Quarterly, 37,* 241–261.

Brockner, J., Wiesenfeld, B. M., & Martin, C. L. (1995). Decision frame, procedural justice, and survivors' reactions to job layoffs. *Organizational Behavior and Human Decision Processes, 63,* 59–68.

Bruhn, J. G. (1996). Social support and heart disease. In C. L. Cooper (Ed.), *Handbook of stress, medicine, and health* (pp. 253–268). Boca Raton, FL: CRC Press.

Bruning, N. S., & Frew, D. R. (1987). Effects of exercise, relaxation and management skills training on physiological stress indicators: A field experiment. *Journal of Applied Psychology, 72,* 515–521.

Burke, M. J., Brief, A. P., & George, J. M. (1993). The role of negative affectivity in understanding relations between self-reports of stressors and strains: A comment on the applied psychology literature. *Journal of Applied Psychology, 78,* 402–412.

Burke, P. M., Reichler, R. J., Smith, E., Dugaw, K., McCauley, E., & Mitchell, J. (1985). Correlation between serum and salivary cortisol levels in depressed and non-depressed children and adolescents. *American Journal of Psychiatry, 142,* 1067–1076.

Burke, R. J. (1988). Some antecedents and consequences for work-family conflict. *Journal of Social Behavior and Personality, 3,* 287–302.

Burke, R. J. (1993). Organizational-level interventions to reduce occupational stressors. *Work and Stress, 7,* 77–88.

Burke, R. J., & Greenglass, E. R. (1987). *Work and the family.* Unpublished manuscript, York University, Toronto.

Burton, G. D., Keels, J. K., & Shook, C. L. (1996). Downsizing the firm: Answering the strategic questions. *Academy of Management Executive, 10,* 38–45.

Butler, S. (1996, May 16). Alternative ways to take out stress. *People Management,* 43–44.

Cambronne, D., Shih, J., & Harri, K. (1999). Innovative stress management for financial service organizations. In J. M. Oher (Ed.), *The employee assistance handbook* (pp. 361–386). New York: Wiley.

Campbell, D. T., & Fiske, D. W. (1959). Convergent and discriminant validity by the multitrait-multimethod matrix. *Psychological Bulletin, 56,* 81–105.

Campbell, S. (1995, June). Better than the company gym. *HR Magazine,* 108–112.

Campion, M., & Lord, R. (1982). A control system conceptualization of the goal-setting and changing process. *Organizational Behavior and Human Performance, 30,* 265–287.

Cannon, W. B. (1922). New evidence for sympathetic control of some internal secretions. *American Journal of Psychiatry, 2,* 15.

Cannon, W. B. (1929). *Bodily changes in pain, hunger, fear, and rage.* Boston: C. T. Branford.

Cannon, W. B. (1932). *The wisdom of the body.* New York: Norton.

Cannon, W. B. (1939). *The wisdom of the body* (2nd ed.). New York: Norton.

Caplan, R. (1971). *Organizational stress and individual strain: A social psychological study of risk factors in coronary heart disease among administrators, engineers, and scientists.* Ann Arbor, MI: Research Center for Group Dynamics.

Caplan, R. D. (1983). Person-environment fit: Past, present, and future. In C. Cooper (Ed.), *Stress research.* Chichester, England: Wiley.

Caplan, R. D., Cobb, S., French, J. R. P., Jr., Van Harrison, R., & Pinneau, S. R. (1975). *Job demands and worker health* (NIOSH Research Report, #75–160). Washington, DC: National Institute for Occupational Safety and Health.

Caplan, R. D., Cobb, S., French, J. R. P., Jr., Harrison, R. V., & Pinneau, S. R. (1980). *Job demands and worker health: Main effects and occupational differences*. Ann Arbor, MI: Institute for Social Research.

Caplan, R. D., Vinokur, A. D., Price, R. H., & van Ryn, M. (1989). Job seeking, reemployment, and mental health: A randomized field experiment in coping with job loss. *Journal of Applied Psychology, 759–769*.

Carayon, P., & Zijlstra, F. (1999). Relationship between job control, work pressure and strain: Studies on the USA and in the Netherlands. *Work and Stress, 13,* 32–48.

Carmel, H., & Hunter, M. (1991). Psychiatrists injured by patient attack. *Bulletin of the American Academy of Psychiatry and the Law, 19,* 309–316.

Carson, J., Maal, S., Roche, S., Fagin, L., DeVilliers, N., O'Malley, P., Brown, D., Leary, J., & Holloway, F. (1999). Burnout in mental health nurses: Much ado about nothing? *Stress Medicine, 15,* 127–134.

Cartwright, S., & Cooper, C. L. (1994). The human effect of mergers and acquisitions. In C. L. Cooper & D. M. Rousseau (Eds.), *Trends in organizational behavior* (pp. 47–62). New York: Wiley.

Cartwright, S., Cooper, C. L., & Murphy, L. R. (1995). Diagnosing a health organization: A proactive approach to stress in the workplace. In L. R. Murphy, J. J. Hurrell, Jr., S. L. Sauter, & G. P. Keita (Eds.), *Job stress interventions* (pp. 217–234). Washington, DC: American Psychological Association.

Carver, C. S., Scheier, M. F., & Weintraub, J. K. (1989). Assessing coping stategies: A theoretically based approach. *Journal of Personality and Social Psychology, 56*(2), 267–283.

Caudron, S. (1990, July). The wellness payoff. *Personnel Journal, 69*(5), 55–62.

Caudron, S. (1991, February 4). *Wellness works. Industry Week, 240*(3), 22–26.

Caudron, S. (1992, February). A low-cost wellness program. *Personnel Journal, 71*(2), 34–38.

Cavanaugh, M. A., Boswell, W. R., Roehling, M. V., & Boudreau, J. W. (2000). An empirical examination of self-reported work stress among U.S. managers. *Journal of Applied Psychology, 85,* 65–74.

Cervinka, R. (1993). Night shift dose and stress at work. *Ergonomics, 36,* 155–160.

Chacko, T. I. (1983). Job and life satisfaction: A causal analysis of their relationships. *Academy of Management Journal, 26,* 163–169.

Champoux, J. E. (1978). Perceptions of work and nonwork. *Sociology of Work and Occupations, 5,* 402–422.

Charmot, D. (1987). Electronic work and the white-collar employee. In R. E. Kraut (Ed.), *Technology and the Transformation of White-Collar Work* (pp. 23–34). Hillsdale, NJ: Erlbaum.

Chatman, J. A. (1989). Improving interactional organizational research: A model of person-organization fit. *Academy of Management Review, 14*(3), 333–349.

Chen, P. Y., & Spector, P. E. (1991). Negative affectivity as the underlying cause of correlations between stressors and strains. *Journal of Applied Psychology, 76,* 398–407.

Cherniss, C. (1980). *Professional burnout in human service organizations.* New York: Praeger.

Cherniss, C. (1993). Role of professional self-efficacy in the etiology and amelioration of burnout. In W. B. Schaufeli, C. Maslach, & T. Marek (Eds.), *Professional burnout: Recent developments in theory and research* (pp. 135–149). Washington, DC: Taylor & Francis.

Cherrington, D. J., & England, J. L. (1980). The desire for an enriched job as a moderator of the enrichment-satisfaction relationship. *Organizational Behavior and Human Performance, 25,* 139–159.

Chesney, M. A., Sevelius, G., Black, G., Ward, M., Swan, G., & Rosenman, R. (1981). Work environment, Type A behavior, and coronary heart disease risks. *Journal of Occupational Medicine, 23,* 551–555.

Chiriboga, D. A., & Bailey, J. (1986). Stress and burnout among critical care and medical surgical nurses: A comparative study. *Critical Care Quarterly, 9,* 84–92.

Cobb, S., & Rose, R. M. (1973). Hypertension, peptide ulcer, and diabetes in air traffic controllers. *Journal of the American Medical Association, 224,* 489–492.

Cohen, F. (1987). Measurement of coping. In S. V. Kasl & C. L. Cooper (Eds.), *Stress and health: Issues in research methodology* (pp. 283–305). Chichester, England: Wiley.

Cohen, S. (1980). After-effects of stress on human performance and social behavior: A review of research and theory. *Psychological Bulletin, 88,* 82–108.

Cohen, S., & Syme, S. L. (1985). *Social support and health.* San Diego, CA: Academic Press.

Cohen, S., & Wills, T. A. (1985). Stress, social support and the buffering hypothesis. *Psychological Bulletin, 98*(2), 310–357.

Colquhoun, W. P., & Rutenfranz, J. (1980). *Studies of shiftwork.* London: Taylor & Francis.

Constable, J. F., & Russell, D. W. (1986). The effect of social support and the work environment upon burnout among nurses. *Journal of Human Stress, 12,* 20–26.

Cook, T. D., Campbell, D. T., & Peracchio, L. (1990). Quasi-experimentation. In M. D. Dunnette & L. M. Hough et al. (Eds.), *Handbook of industrial and organizational psychology,* (2nd ed., Vol. 1, pp. 491–576). Palo Alto, CA: Consulting Psychologists Press.

Cooley, E., & Yovanoff, P. (1996). Supporting professionals-at-risk: Evaluating interventions to reduce burnout and improve retention of special educators. *Exceptional Children, 62*(4), 336–355.

Cooper, C. L. (1980). Dentists under pressure: A social psychological study. In C. L. Cooper & J. Marshall (Eds.), *White collar and professional stress.* New York: Wiley.

Cooper, C. L., & Cartwright, S. (1994). Healthy mind, healthy organization: A proactive approach to occupational stress. National Institute for Occupational Safety and Health Conference (1992, Washington, DC). *Human Relations, 47,* 455–471.

Cooper, C. L., & Cartwright, S. (2001). A strategic approach to organizational stress management. In P. A. Hancock, & P. A. Desmond, (Eds.) *Stress, workload, and fatigue: Human factors in Transportation* (pp. 235–248). Mahwah, NJ: Erlbaum .

Cooper, C. L., & Davidson. M. J. (1982). The high cost of stress on women managers. *Organizational Dynamics, 10,* 44–53.

Cooper, C. L., & Marshall, J. (1976). Occupational sources of stress: A review of the literature relating to coronary heart disease and mental health. *Journal of Occupational Psychology, 49,* 11–28.

Cooper, C. L., & Roden, J. (1985). Mental health and satisfaction among tax officers. *Social Science and Medicine, 21,* 747–751.

Cooper, C. L., Sloan, S. J., & Williams, S. (1988). *Occupational stress indicator management guide.* Oxford, England: NFER-Nelson.

Cooper, C. L., Watts, J., Baglioni, A. J., Jr., & Kelly, M. (1988). Occupational stress amongst general practice dentists. *Journal of Occupational Psychology, 61,* 163–174.

Coping with uncertainty. (1995, June 29). *People Management, 1*(13), 23–24.

Corcoran, K. J. (1986). Measuring burnout: A reliability and convergent validity study. *Journal of Social Behavior and Personality, 1,* 107–112.

Corcoran, K. J. (1995). Measuring burnout: An updated reliability and convergent validity study. In R. Crandall & P. Perrewe (Eds.), *Occupational stress: A handbook* (pp. 263–268). Philadelphia, PA: Taylor and Francis.

Corneil, W., Beaton, R., Murphy, S., Johnson, C., & Pike, K. (1999). Exposure to traumatic indcidents and prevalence of posttraumatic stress symptomatology in urban firefighters in two countries. *Journal of Occupational Health Psychology, 4,* 131–141.

Corrigan, P. W., Holmes, E. P., & Luchins, D. (1995). Burnout and collegial support in state psychiatric hospital staff. *Journal of Clinical Psychology, 51,* 703–710.

Costa, G. (1996). The impact of shift and night work on health. Applied Ergonomics, 27(1), 9–16.

Costa, G., Folkard S., & Harrington, J. M. (2000). Shiftwork and extended hours of work. In *Hunter's diseases of occupations,* P. J. Baxter, P. H. Adams, T. C. Aw, A. Cockcroft, & J. M. Harrington (Eds.), (pp. 581–589). London: Edward Arnold.

Cox, T. (1978). *Stress.* Baltimore: University Park Press.

Cox, T. (1985). The nature and measurement of stress. *Ergonomics, 28,* 1155–1163.

Cox, T., Kuk, G., & Schur, H. (1991). *The meaningfulness of work to professional burnout.* Unpublished manuscript, University of Nottingham.

Coyne, J. C., Aldwin, C., & Lazarus, R. S. (1981). Depression and coping in stressful episodes. *Journal of Abnormal Psychology, 90,* 439–447.

Coyne, J. C., & Holroyd, K. (1982). Stress, coping, and illness: A transactional perspective. In T. Millon, C. Green, & R. Meagher (Eds.), *Handbook of clinical health psychology.* New York: Plenum.

Creativity, strategy needed in work/life program management. (1995, September). *Employee Benefit Plan Review, 50*(3), 40–41.

Creed, F. (1985). *Psychosocial variables and appendicitis.* Unpublished master's thesis, University of Cambridge, England.

Crosby, F. (1984). Job satisfaction and domestic life. In M. D. Lee & R. N. Kanurgo (Eds.), *Management of work and personal life.* New York: Praeger.

Crosby, F. (1985). *Divorce in corporate America.* Unpublished manuscript, Smith College, North Hampton, MA.

Crouter, A. C. (1984). Spillover from family to work: The neglected side of work-family interface. *Human Relations, 37,* 425–552.

Cummings, N., & VandenBos, G. (1981). The twenty-year Kaiser-Permanente experience with psychotherapy and medical utilization. *Health Policy Quarterly, 1*(2).

Czeisler, C. A., Moore-Ede, M. C. & Coleman, R. M. (1982). Rotating shift work schedules that disrupt sleep are improved by applying circadian principles. *Science, 217,* 460–463.

Dalton, D. R., & Mesch, D. J. (1990). The impact of flexible scheduling on employee attendance and turnover. *Administrative Science Quarterly, 35,* 370–387.

Danna, K., & Griffin, R. W. (1999). Health and well-being in the workplace. *Journal of Management, 25,* 357–384.

Davidson, M. J., & Cooper, C. L. (1987). Female managers in Britain: A comparative perspective. *Human Resource Management, 26,* 217–242.

Davidson, M. J., & Veno, A. (1980). Stress and the policeman. In C. L. Cooper & J. Marshall (Eds.), *White collar and professional stress.* New York: Wiley.

Davidson, R., & Henderson, R. (2000). Electronic performance monitoring: A laboratory investigation of the influence of monitoring and difficulty on task performance, mood state, and self-reported stress levels. *Journal of Applied Social Psychology, 30,* 906–920.

Davies, D. & Jones, D. (1982). Hearing and noise. In W. T. Singleton (Ed.), *The body at work.* New York: Cambridge University Press.

Davis-Sacks, M. L., Jayarante, S., & Chess, W. A. (1985). A comparison of the effects of social support on the incidence of burnout. *Social Work, 30*(3), 240–244.

Davy, J. A., Kinicki, A. J., & Scheck, C. L. (1991). Developing and testing a model of survivor responses to layoffs. *Journal of Vocational Behavior, 38,* 302–317.

Dayal, I., & Thomas, J. M. (1968). Operation KPE: Developing a new organization. *Journal of Applied Behavioral Science, 4,* 473–506.

Dearborn, M. J., & Hastings, J. E. (1987). Type A personality as a mediator of stress and strain in employed women. *Journal of Human Stress, 13,* 53–60.

Decker, P. J., & Borgen, F. H. (1993). Dimensions of work appraisal: Stress, strain, coping, job satisfaction, and negative affectivity. *Journal of Counseling Psychology, 40,* 470–478.

DeFrank, R. S., & Ivancevich, J. M. (1986). Job loss: An individual level review and model. *Journal of Vocational Behavior, 28,* 1–20.

De Haus, P., & Diekstra, R. F. (1999). Do teachers burn out more easily? A comparison of teachers with other social professions on work stress and burnout symptoms. In R. Vandenberghe & M.A. Huberman (Eds.), *Understanding and preventing teacher burnout: A sourcebook of international research and practice* (pp. 269–284). New York: Cambridge University Press.

Dekker, I., & Barling, J. (1998). Personal and organizational predictors of workplace sexual harassment of women by men. *Journal of Occupational Health Psychology, 3,* 7–18.

DeLongis, A., Coyne, J. C., Dakof, G., Folkman, S., & Lazarus, R. S. (1982). Relationship of daily hassles, uplifts, and major life events to health status. *Health Psychology, 1,* 119–136.

DeLongis, A., Folkman, S., & Lazarus, R. S. (1988). The impact of daily stress on health and mood: Psychological and social resources as mediators. *Journal of Personality and Social Psychology, 54,* 486–495.

Dembroski, T. M., & Czajkowski, S. M. (1989). Historical and current developments in coronary-prone behavior. In T. M. Dembroski (Ed.), *In search of coronary-prone behavior: Beyond Type-A.* Hillsdale, NJ: Erlbaum.

Demerouti, E., Bakker, A. B., Nachreiner, F., & Schaufeli, W. B. (2001). The job demands-resources model of burnout. *Journal of Applied Psychology, 86*(3), 499–512 .

de Rijk, A. E., Le Blanc, P.M., Schaufeli, W. B., & de Jong, J. (1998). Active coping and need for control as moderators of the job demand-control model: Effects of burnout. *Journal of Occupational & Organizational Psychology, 71,* 1–18.

Dewe, P., & Brook, R. (2000). Sequential tree analysis of work stressors: exploring score profiles in the context of the stressor-strain relationship. *International Journal of Stress Management, 7,* 1–18.

Dewe, P., & Guest, D. (1990). Methods of coping with stress at work: A conceptual analysis and empirical study of measurement issues. *Journal of Organizational Behavior, 11,* 135–150.

Dierendonck, D. V., Schaufeli, W. B., & Buunk, B. P. (2001). Toward a process model of burnout: Results from a secondary analysis. *European Journal of Work and Organizational Psychology, 10,* 41–52.

Dignam, J. T., Barrera, M., West, S. G. (1986). Occupational stress, social support, and burnout among correctional officers. *American Journal of Community Psychology 14*(2), 177–193.

DiMatteo, M. R., Shugars, D. A., & Hays, R. D. (1993). Occupational stress, life stress and mental health among dentists. *Journal of Occupational and Organizational Psychology, 66,* 153–162.

Dimsdale, J. & Herd, J. A. (1982). Variability of plasma lipids in response to emotional arousal. *Psychosomatic Medicine, 44,* 413–430.

Dinman, B., Stephenson, R., Horvath, S., & Colwell, M. (1974). Work in hot environments: I. Field studies of work load, thermal stress, and physiologic response. *Journal of Occupational Medicine, 16,* 785–791.

Dipboye, R. L., Smith, C. S., & Howell, W. (1994). *Understanding industrial and organizational psychology: An integrated approach.* Fort Worth: Harcourt Brace.

Dohrenwend, B. S., Dohrenwend, B. P., Dodson, M., & Shrout, P. E. (1984). Symptoms, hassles, social supports, and life events: Problem of confounded measures. *Journal of Abnormal Psychology, 93,* 222–230.

Dohrenwend, B. S., Krasnoff, L., Askenasy, A. R., & Dohrenwend, B. P. (1982). The Psychiatric Epidemiology Research Interview life events scale. In L. Goldberger & S. Bresnitz (Eds.), *Handbook of stress: Theoretical and clinical aspects.* New York: The Free Press.

Dohrenwend, B., Pearlin, L., Clayton, P., Hanburg, B., Riley, R., & Rose, R. M. (1982). Report on stress and life events. In G. Elliott and C. Eisdorfer (Eds.), *Stress and human health.* New York: Springer.

Dohrenwend, B. P., Raphael, K. G., Schwartz, S., Stueve, A., & Skodol, A. (1993). The structured event probe and narrative rating method for measuring stressful life events. In L. Goldberger and S. Breznitz (Eds.), *Handbook of stress: Theoretical and clinical aspects* (pp. 174–184). New York: The Free Press.

Dohrenwend, B. P., & Shrout, P. E. (1985). Hassles in the conceptualization and measurement of life stress variables. *American Psychologist, 40,* 780–785.

Dolan, S. L. (1995). Individual, organizational, and social determinants of managerial burnout: Theoretical and empirical update. In R. Crandall & P. L. Perrewe (Eds.), *Occupational stress: A handbook* (pp. 223–238). Washington, DC: Taylor & Francis.

Dompierre, J., & Lavoie, F. (1994). Subjective work stress and family violence. In G. P. Keita & J. J. Hurrell Jr. (Eds.), *Job stress in a changing workforce: Investigating gender, diversity, and family issues* (pp. 213–227). Washington, DC: American Psychological Association.

Dougall, A. L., Hyman, K. B., Hayward, M. C., McFeeley, S., & Baum, A. (2001). Optimism and traumatic stress: The importance of social support and coping. *Journal of Applied Social Psychology, 31,* 223–245.

Duff, W. R., & Lipscomb, H. S. (1973). A health testing concept: Simple-by-design. In D. Davies & J. Tchobanoff (Eds.), *Health evaluation: An entry intro the health care system.* New York: Intercontinental Medical Book.

Duxbury, L. E., & Higgins, C. A. (1991). Gender differences in workfamily conflict. *Journal of Applied Psychology, 76,* 60–74.

Dworkin, A. G., Haney, C. A., & Telschow, R. L. (1988). Fear, victimization, and stress among urban public school teachers. *Journal of Organizational Behavior, 9,* 159–171.

Earnshaw, J., & Cooper, C. L. (1994). Employee stress litigation: The UK experience. *Work and Stress, 8,* 287–295.

Eaton, J. W. (1980). Stress in social work practice. In C. L. Cooper & J. Marshall (Eds.), *White collar and professional stress*. New York: Wiley.

Eckenrode, J. (1984). Impact of chronic and acute stressors on daily reports of mood. *Journal of Personality and Social Psychology, 46*, 907–918.

Edwards, J. R. (1991). The measurement of Type A behavior pattern: An assessment of criterion-oriented validity, content validity, and construct validity. In C. L. Cooper & R. Payne (Eds.), *Personality and stress: Individual differences in the stress process* (pp. 151–180). Chichester, England: Wiley.

Edwards, J. R. (1992). A cybernetic theory of stress, coping, and well-being in organizations. *Academy of Management Review, 17*, 238–274.

Edwards, J. R. (1996). An examination of competing versions of the person-environment fit approach to stress. *Academy of Management Journal, 39*, 292–339.

Edwards, J. R., & Baglioni, A. J. (1991). Relationship between Type A behavior pattern and mental and physical symptoms: A comparison of global and component measures. *Journal of Applied Psychology, 76*, 276–290.

Edwards, J. R., & Baglioni, A. J. (1993). The measurement of coping with stress: Construct validity of the ways of coping checklist and the Cybernetic Coping Scale. *Work and Stress, 7*(1), 17–31.

Edwards, J. R., & Cooper, C. L. (1990). The person-environment fit approach to stress: Recurring problems and some suggested solutions. *Journal of Organizational Behavior, 11*, 293–307.

Edwards, J. R., & Rothbard, N. P. (1999). Work and family stress and well being: An examination of person-environment fit in the work and family domains. *Organizational Behavior and Human Decision Processes, 77*, 85–129.

Edwards, J. R., & Rothbard, N. P. (2000). Mechanisms linking work and familiy: Clarifying the relationship between work and family constructs. *Academy of Management Review, 25*, 178–199.

Elkin, A. J., & Rosch, P. J. (1990). Promoting mental health at the workplace: The prevention side of stress management. *Occupational Medicine: State of the Art Review, 5*(4), 739–754.

Elliott, G. R., & Eisdorfer, C. (1982). *Stress and human health: Analysis and implications for research*. New York: Springer.

Ellis, A. (1978). What people can do for themselves to cope with stress. In C. L. Cooper & R. Payne (Eds.), *Stress at work* (pp. 209–222). New York: Wiley.

Elmadjian, F. (1955). Adrenocortical function of combat infantrymen in Korea. *Ciba Foundation Colloquia on Endocrinology, 8*, 627.

Employee Assistance Society of North America. (1990, Spring). What are the program issues between EASNA and EAPA? *The Source, 5*(1).

Endler, N. S. & Parker, J. D. A. (1990). Multidimensional assessment of coping: A critical evaluation. *Journal of Personality and Social Psychology, 58*(5), 884–854.

Erfurt, J. C., Foote, A., & Heirich, M. A. (1992). The cost-effectiveness of worksite wellness programs for hypertension control, weight loss, smoking cessation, and exercise. *Personnel Psychology, 43,* 5–27.

Eschenbrenner, A. J. (1971). Effects of intermittent noise on the performance of a complex psychomotor task. *Human Factors, 13*(1), 59–63.

Estrers, S. D. (1997). Risk management beats lawsuits on RSI threat. *National Underwriter, 10,* 9–12.

Etzion, D. (1984). Moderating effect of social support on the stress-burnout relationship. *Journal of Applied Psychology, 69,* 615–622.

Eulberg, J. R., Weekley, J. A., & Bhagat, R. S. (1988). Models of stress in organizational research: A metatheoretical perspective. *Human Relations, 41,* 331–350.

Evans, G. W., Johansson, G., & Rydstedt, L. (1999). Hassles on the job: A study of a job intervention with urban bus drivers. *Journal of Organizational Behavior, 20,* 199–208.

Evans, G. W., & Johnson, D. (2000). Stress and open-office noise. *Journal of Applied Psychology, 85,* 779–783.

Evans, P., & Bartolome, F. (1984). The changing pictures of relationships between career and family. *Journal of Occupational Behavior, 5,* 921.

Falkenberg, L. E. (1987). Employee fitness programs: Their impact on the employee and the organization. *Academy of Management Review, 12,* 511–522.

Fenlason, K. J., & Beehr, T. A. (1994). Social support and occupational stress: Effects of talking to others. *Journal of Organizational Behavior, 15*(2), 157–175.

Feuer, B. (1983). A peer referral model that works. *EAP Digest, 3,* 36–37.

Fimian, M. J., & Fastenau, P. S. (1990). The validity and reliability of the Teacher Stress Inventory: A re-analysis of aggregate data. *Journal of Organizational Behavior, 11,* 151–157.

Firth, H., & Britton, P. (1989). Burnout, absence, and turnover amongst British nursing staff. *Journal of Occupational Psychology, 62,* 55–59.

Firth-Cozens, J. (2001). Interventions to improve physicians' well-being and patient care. *Social Science and Medicine, 52,* 215–222.

Fisher, C. D. (1993). Boredom at work: A neglected concept. *Human Relations, 46*(3), 395–417.

Fisher, C. D., & Gittleson, R. (1983). A meta-analysis of the correlates of role conflict and ambiguity. *Journal of Applied Psychology, 68,* 320–333.

Fisher, G. G., Hoffman, J. R., Lin, L. F., Fuller, J. A., & Laber, M. (2000). Defining work/life balance. In G.G. Fisher and M.A. Hemingway (Co-chairs), *Is there more to life than work and family?* Symosium presented at the 15th annual conference of the Society for Industrial and Organizational Psychology, New Orleans, LA.

Fisher, S. (1985). Control and blue collar work. In C. L. Cooper, & M. J. Smith (Eds.), *Job stress and blue collar work.* New York: Wiley.

Flannery, R. B., Jr. (1986). Major life events and daily hassles in predicting health status: Methodological inquiry. *Journal of Clinical Psychology, 42,* 485–487.

Fleming, I., & Baum, A. (1987). Psychobiological assessment. In J. Ivancevich & D. Ganster (Eds.), *Job stress: From theory to suggestion.* New York: The Hawthorne Press.

Fleming, R., Baum, A., & Singer, J. (1984). Toward an integrative approach to the study of stress. *Journal of Personality and Social Psychology, 46,* 939–949.

Fletcher, B. C., & Jones, F. (1993). A refutation of Karasek's demand-discretion model of occupational stress with a range of dependent measures. *Journal of Organizational Behavior, 14,* 319–330.

Flynn, G. (1995, February). Companies make wellness work. *Personnel Journal,* 64–66.

Folkard, S. (1990). Circadian performance rhythms: Some practical and theoretical implications. *Philosophical Transactions of the Royal Society of London: Biological Sciences, 327,* 543–553.

Folkard, S., Minors, D., & Waterhouse, J. (1985). Chronobiology and shift work: Current issues and trends. *Chronobiologica, 12,* 31–54.

Folkman, S. (1984). Personal control and stress and coping processes: A theoretical analysis. *Journal of Personality and Social Psychology, 46,* 839–852.

Folkman, S., & Lazarus, R. S. (1980). An analysis of coping in a middle-aged community sample. *Journal of Health and Social Behavior, 21,* 219–239.

Folkman, S., & Lazarus, R. S. (1985). If it changes it must be a process: A study of emotion and coping during three stages of a college examination. *Journal of Personality and Social Psychology, 48,* 150–170.

Folkman, S., Lazarus, R. S., Dunkel-Schetter, C., DeLongis, A., & Gruen, R. J. (1986). Dynamics of a stressful encounter: Cognitive appraisal, coping, and encounter outcomes. *Journal of Personality and Social Psychology, 50,* 992–1003.

Fong, J. Y. (1995). Patient assaults on psychologists: An unrecognized occupational hazard. In S. L. Sauter & L. R. Murphy (Eds.), *Organizational risk factors for job stress.* Washington, DC: American Psychological Association.

Forbes, E. J., & Pekala, R. J. (1993). Psychophysiological effects of several stress management techniques. *Psychological Reports, 72,* 19–27.

Ford, D. L. (1980). Work, job satisfaction, and employee well-being: An exploratory study of minority professionals. *Journal of Social and Behavioral Sciences, 26,* 70–75.

Ford, D. L. (1985). Facets of work support and employee work outcomes: An exploratory analysis. *Journal of Management, 11,* 5–20.

Ford, J. D., & Ford, L. W. (1995). The role of conversations in producing intentional change in organizations. *Academy of Management Review, 20,* 541–570.

Foret, J., Bensimon, G., Benoit, O., & Vieux, N. (1981). Quality of sleep as a function of age and shift work. In A. Reinberg, N. Vieux, & P. Andlauer (Eds.), *Night and shift work: Biological and social aspects.* Oxford: Pergamon Press.

Fox, M. L., Dwyer, D. J., & Ganster, D. G. (1993). Effects of stressful job demands and control on physiological and attitudinal outcomes in a hospital setting. *Academy of Management Journal, 36,* 289–318.

Frankenhaeuser, M. (1991). The psychophysiology of workload, stress, and health. Comparisons between the sexes. *Annals of Behavioral Medicine, 13*(4), 197–204.

Frankenhaeuser, M., Lundberg, U., & Chesney, M. (1991). *Women, work, and health: Stress and opportunites.* New York: Plenum Press.

Frankenhaeuser, M., Lundberg, U., Fredrikson, M., Melin, B., Tuomisto, M., & Myrsten, A. (1989). Stress on and off the job as related to sex and occupational status in white-collar workers. *Journal of Organizational Behavior, 10,* 321–346.

Frankenhaeuser, M., Nordheden, B., Myrsten, A. L., & Post, B. (1971). Psychophysiological reactions to understimulation and overstimulation. *Acta Psychologica, 35,* 298.

Frankenhaeuser, M., & Rissler, A. (1970a). Catecholamine output during relaxation and anticipation. *Perceptual and Motor Skills, 30,* 745.

Frankenhaeuser, M., & Rissler, A. (1970b). Effects of punishment on catecholamine release and efficiency of performance. *Psychopharmacologia, 17,* 378.

Frazer, H. T. (1998). RMs can curb indoor air-pollution. *National Underwriter Property & Casualty-Risk Benefits management, 102,* 23, 78.

French, J. R. P., & Caplan, R. D. (1973). Organizational stress and individual strain. In A. J. Marrow (Ed.), *The failure of success.* New York: AMACOM.

French, J. R. P., Jr., Caplan, R. D., & Harrison, R. V. (1982). *The mechanisms of job stress and strain.* London: Wiley.

French, J. R. P., Jr., Rodgers, W. L., & Cobb, S. (1974). Adjustment as person-environment fit. In G. Coelho, D. Hamburg, & J. Adams (Eds.), *Coping and adaptation.* New York: Basic Books.

French, W. L., & Bell, C. H. (1984). *Organization development: Behavioral science interventions for organization improvement.* Englewood Cliffs, NJ: Prentice-Hall.

Frese, M. (1999). Social support as a moderator of the relationship between work stressors and psychological dysfunctioning: A longitudinal study with objective measures. *Journal of Occupational Health Psychology, 4,* 179–192.

Frese, M., & Okonek, K. (1984). Reasons to leave shiftwork and psychological and psychosomatic complaints of former shiftworkers. *Journal of Applied Psychology, 69,* 509–514.

Frese, M. & Zapf, D. (1988). Methodological issues in the study of work stress: Objective vs. subjective measurement of work stress and the question of longitudinal studies. In C. Cooper & R. Payne (Eds.), *Causes, coping, and consequences of stress at work.* Chichester, England: Wiley.

Frese, M., & Zapf, D. (1999). On the importance of the objective environment in stress and attribution theory. Counterpoint to Perrewé and Zellars. *Journal of Organizational Behavior, 20,* 761–765.

Frew, D. R., & Bruning, N. S. (1987). Perceived organizational characteristics and personality measures as predictors of stress/strain in the workplace. *Journal of Management, 13,* 633–646.

Fried, Y., Ben-David, H. A., Tiegs, R. B., Avital, N., & Yeverechyahu, U. (1998). The interactive effect of role conflict and role ambiguity on job performance. *Journal of Occupational and Organizational Psychology, 71,* 19–27.

Fried, Y., Rowland, K. M., & Ferris, G. R. (1984). The physiological measurement of work stress: A critique. *Personnel Psychology, 37,* 583–615.

Friedman, I. (2000). Burnout in teachers: Shattered dreams of impeccable professional performance. *Journal of Clinical Psychology, 56,* 595–606.

Friedman, M. (1996). *Type A behavior: Its diagnosis and treatment.* New York: Plenum Press.

Friedman, M., & Rosenman, R. H. (1974). *Type A behavior and your heart.* New York: Random House.

Friedman, M., Thoresen, C. E., Gill, J. J., Powell, L. H., Ulmer, D., Thompson, T., Price, V. A., Rabin, D. D., Breall, W. S., Dixon, T., Levy, R., & Bourg, E. (1984). Alteration of type A behavior and reduction in cardiac recurrences in postmyocardial infarction patients. *American Heart Journal, 108*(2), 237–248.

Friedman, M., & Ulmer, D. (1984). *Treating type A behavior and your heart.* New York: Knopf.

Froberg, J., Karlsson, C. G., Levi, L., & Lidberg, L. (1971). Physiological and biochemical stress reactions induced by psychosocial stimuli. In L. Levi (Ed.), *Society, stress and disease* (Vol. 1). New York: Oxford University Press.

Frone, M. R. (1990). Intolerance of ambiguity as a moderator of the occupational role stress-strain relationship: A meta-analysis. *Journal of Organizational Behavior, 11,* 309–320.

Frone, M. R. (2000). Interpersonal conflict at work and psychological outcomse: Testing a model among young workers. *Journal of Occupational Health Psychology, 5,* 246–255.

Frone, M. R., & McFarlin, D. (1989). Chronic occupational stressors, self-focused attention, and well-being: Testing a cybernetic model of stress. *Journal of Applied Psychology, 74*(6), 876–883.

Frone, M. R., Russell, M., & Barnes, G. M. (1996). Work-family conflit, gender, and health-related outcomes: A study of employed parents in two community samples. *Journal of Occupational Health Psychology, 1,* 57–69.

Frone, M. R., Russell, M., & Cooper, M. L. (1992). Antecedents and outcomes of work-family conflict: Testing a model of the work-family interface. *Journal of Applied Psychology, 77,* 65–78.

Frost, P. J., & Jamal, M. (1979). Shift work, attitudes, and reported behavior: Some associations between individual characteristics and hours of work and leisure. *Journal of Applied Psychology, 64,* 77–81.

Funkenstein, D. H. (1955). The physiology of fear and anger. *Scientific American, 192*(5), 74–80.

Furnham, A., & Hughes, K. (1999). Individual difference correlates of nightwork and shift-work rotation. *Personality & Individual Differences, 26,* 941–959.

Gadbois, C. (1981). Women on night shift: Interdependence of sleep and off-the-job activities. In A. Reinberg, N. Vieux, & P. Andlauer (Eds.), *Night and shift work: Biological and social aspects.* Oxford: Pergamon Press.

Gallatin, L. (1989). *Electronic monitoring in the workplace: Supervision or surveillance.* Boston: Massachusetts Coalition on New Office Technology.

Galpin, T. J. (1996). *The human side of change: A practical guide to organization redesign.* San Francisco, CA: Jossey-Bass.

Gamble, G. O., & Matteson, M. T. (1992). Type A behavior, job satisfaction, and stress among Black professionals. *Psychological Reports, 70,* 43–50.

Ganster, D. C. (1989). Worker control and well-being: A review of research in the workplace. In S. Sauter, J. Hurrell, & C. Cooper (Eds.), *Job control and worker health.* Chichester, England: Wiley.

Ganster, D. C. (1995). Interventions for building healthy organizations: Suggestions from the stress research literature. In L. R. Murphy, J. J. Hurrell, Jr., S. L. Sauter, & G. P. Keita (Eds.), *Job stress interventions* (pp. 323–336). Washington, DC: American Psychological Association.

Ganster, D. C., Fox, M. L., & Dwyer, D. J. (2001). Explaining employees' health care costs: A prospective examination of stressful job demands, personal control, and physiological reactivity. *Journal of Applied Psychology, 86,* 954–964.

Ganster, D. C., & Fusilier, M. R. (1989). Control in the workplace. In C. Cooper & I. Robertson (Eds.), *International review of industrial and organizational psychology.* Chichester, England: Wiley.

Ganster, D. C., Fusilier, M. R., & Mayes, B. T. (1986). Role of social support in the experience of stress at work. *Journal of Applied Psychology, 71,* 102–110.

Ganster, D. C., Mayes, B. T., Sime, W. E., & Tharp, G. D. (1982). Managing organizational stress: A field experiment. *Journal of Applied Psychology, 67,* 533–542.

Ganster, D. C., & Schaubroeck J. (1991). Work stress and employee health. *Journal of Management, 17,* 235–271.

Ganster, D. C., Schaubroeck, J., Sime, W. E., & Mayes, B. T. (1991). The homological validity of the Type A personality among employed adults. *Journal of Applied Psychology, 76,* 276–290.

Garden, A. (1989). Burnout: The effect of psychological type on research findings. *Journal of Occupational Psychology, 62,* 223–234.

Garst, H., Frese, M., & Molenaar, P. C. (2000). The temporal factor of change in stressor-strain relatioships: A growth curve model on a longitudinal study in East Germany. *Journal of Applied Psychology, 85,* 417–438.

Gebhardt, D. L., & Crump, C. E. (1990). Employee fitness and wellness programs in the workplace. *American Psychologist, 45,* 262–272.

Geiser, D. S. (1989). Psychosocial influences on human immunity. *Clinical Psychology Review, 9,* 689–715.

Ghosh, A. (2000). Occupational stress, strain, and coping in physicians and executives. *Journal of Personality & Clinical Studies, 16,* 9–15.

Gianakos, I. (2000). Gender roles and coping with work stress. *Sex Roles, 42,* 1059–1079.

Gilbert, E. (1990, December 10). Family benefits are no "soft" issue: J&J official. *National Underwriter, 15,* 21.

Ginexi, E. M., Howe, G. W., & Caplan, R. D. (2000). Depression and control beliefs in relation to reemployment: What are the directions of effect? *Journal of Occupational Health Psychology, 5,* 323–336.

Glass, C. G., & Singer, J. E. (1972). Behavioral after effects of unpredictable and uncontrollable aversive events. *American Scientist, 60,* 457–465.

Glowinkowski, S. P., & Cooper, C. L. (1986). Managers and professional in business/industrial settings: The research evidence. In J. M. Ivancevich & D. C. Ganster (Eds.), *Job stress: From theory to suggestions.* New York: The Hawthorne Press.

Goddard, S. (1996, September 23). Stressed workers find little support. *Business Insurance, 30*(39), 13, 17.

Goldenhar, L. M., Swanson, N. G., Hurrell, Jr., J. J., Ruder, A., & Deddens, J. (1998). Stressors and adverse outcomes for female construction workers. *Journal of Occupational Health Psychology, 3,* 19–32.

Golembiewski, R. T., & Munzenrider, R. F. (1988). *Phases of burnout: Developments in concepts and applications.* New York: Praeger.

Golembiewski, R. T., & Proehl, C. W. (1978). A survey of the empirical literature on flexible work hours: Character and consequences of a major innovation. *Academy of Management Review, 3,* 823–853.

Gore, S. (1985). Social support and styles of coping with stress. In S. Cohen & L. Syme (Eds.), *Social support and health* (pp. 263–278). Orlando: Academic Press.

Gorter, R. C., Albrecht, G., Hoogstraten, J., & Eijkman, M. A. (1999). Factorial validity of the Maslach burnout inventory—Dutch version (MBI-NL) among dentists. *Journal of Organizational Behavior, 20,* 209–217.

Gottlieb, D. E. (1983). Defensiveness and social support: Two ways chronic patients reduce strain. *Dissertation Abstracts International* 43(10-B), 3361.

Grandey, A. A., & Cropanzano, R. (1999). The conservation of resources model appled to work-family conflict and strain. *Journal of Vocational Behavior, 54,* 350–370.

Gray, J. (1978). *The psychology of fear and stress.* New York: McGraw-Hill.

Greenglass, E. R., Burke, R. J. & Ondrack, M. (1990). A gender role perspective of coping and burnout. *Applied Psychology: An International Review, 39*(1), 5–27.

Greenglass, E. R., Fiksenbaum, L., & Burke, R. J. (1995). The relationship between social support and burnout over time in teachers. In R. Crandall & P. L. Perrewe (Eds.), *Occupational stress: A handbook* (pp. 239–248). Philadelphia, PA: Taylor & Francis.

Greenglass, E. R., Pantony, K. L., & Burke, R. J. (1988). A gender-role perspective on role conflict, work stress, and social support. *Journal of Social Behavior and Personality, 3,* 317–328.

Greenhaus, J. J., & Beutell, N. J. (1985). Sources of conflict between work and family roles. *Academy of Management Review, 10,* 76–88.

Greenhaus, J. H., & Parasuraman, S. (1987). A work-nonwork interactive perspective of stress and its consequences. *Journal of Organizational Behavior Management, 8*(2), 37–60.

Greller, M. M., Parsons, C. K., & Mitchell, D. R. D. (1992). Additive effects and beyond: Occupational stressors and social buffers in a police organization. In J. C. Quick, L. R. Murphy, & J. J. Hurrell, Jr. (Eds.), *Stress and well-being at work.* Washington, DC: American Psychological Association.

Grimm, L. G., & Yarnold, P. R. (1984). Performance standards and the Type A behavior pattern. *Cognitive Therapy and Research, 8,* 59–66.

Grosch, J. W., & Murphy, L. (1998). Occupational difference in depression and global health: Results from a national sample of U.S. workers. *Journal of Occupational and Environmental Medicine, 40,* 153–164.

Gross, N., Mason, W. S., & McEachern, A. W. (1958). *Explorations in role analysis: Studies of the school superintendent role.* New York: Wiley.

Gupta, N., & Beehr, T. A. (1981). Relationships among employee's work and nonwork responses. *Journal of Occupational Behavior, 2,* 203–209.

Gutek, B. A., Repetti, R. L., & Silver, D. L. (1988). Nonwork roles and stress at work. In C. L. Cooper & R. Payne (Eds.), Causes, coping, and consequences of stress at work. New York: Wiley.

Gutierres, S. E., Saenz, D. S., & Green, B. L. (1994). Job stress and health outcomes among White and Hispanic employees: A test of the person-environment fit model. In G. P. Keita & J. J. Hurrell, Jr. (Eds.), *Job stress in a changing workforce.* Washington, DC: American Psychological Association.

Guzzo, R. A., Jette, R. D., & Katzell, R. A. (1985). The effects of psychologically based intervention programs on worker productivity: A meta-analysis. *Personnel Psychology, 38,* 275–292.

Haaga, D. A. F., Davison, G. C., Williams, M. E., Dolezal, S. L., Haleblian, J., Rosenbaum, J., Dwyer, J. H., Baker, S., Nezami, E., DeQuattro, V. (1994). Mode-specific impact of relaxation training for hypertensive men with type A behavior pattern. *Behavior Therapy, 25,* 209–223.

Hackman, J. R., & Oldham, G. R. (1980). *Work Redesign.* Reading MA: Addison-Wesley.

Hahn, S., & Smith, C. S. (1999). Daily hassles and chronic stressors: Conceptual and measurement issues. *Stress Medicine, 15,* 89–101.

Hahn, S. E., & Smith, C. S. (1995). *Hassles and chronic stressors: What should we really be measuring?* Paper presented at the APA-NIOSH conference, Washington, DC.

Hale, H. B., Kratochvil, C. H., & Ellis, J. R. (1958). Plasma corticosteroid levels in aircrewmen after long flights. *Journal of Clinical Endocrinology & Metabolism, 18,* 1440.

Hall, D. T. (1990). Promoting work/family balance: An organization-change approach. *Organizational Dynamics, 18*(3), 4–18.

Hamilton, C. A. (April, 1987). Telecommuting. *Personnel Journal,* 91–101.

Hamilton, V. L., Broman, C. L., Hoffman, W. S., & Renner, D. S. (1990). Hard times and vulnerable people: Initial effects of plant closing on autoworkers' mental health. *Journal of Health and Social Behavior, 31,* 123–140.

Hammen, C., Davila, J., Brown, G., Ellicott, A., & Gitlin, M. (1992). Psychiatric history and stress: Predictors of severity of unipolar depression. *Journal of Abnormal Psychology, 101,* 45–52.

Hammer, L. B., Allen, E., & Grigsby, T. D. (1997). Work-family conflict in dual-earner couples: Within-individual and crossover effects on work and family. *Journal of Vocational Behavior, 50,* 185–203.

Hancock, P. A., & Vasmatzidis, I. (1998). Human occupational and performance limits under stress: The thermal environment as a prototypical example. *Ergonomics, 41,* 1169–1191.

Handy, J. (1986). Considering organizations in organizational stress research: A rejoinder to Glowinkowski and Cooper, and to Duckworth. *Bulletin of the British Psychological Society, 39,* 205-210.

Harris, M. M., Heller, T., & Braddock, D. (1988). Sex differences in psychological well-being during a facility closure. *Journal of Management, 14,* 391–402.

Harrison, R. V. (1978). Person-environment fit and job stress. In C. Cooper & R. Payne (Eds.), *Stress at work.* New York: Wiley.

Harrison, R. V. (1985). The person-environment fit model and the study of job stress. In T. Beehr & R. Bhagat (Eds.), *Human stress and cognition in organizations.* New York: Wiley.

Hart, P. M. (1999). Predicting employee life satisfaction: A coherent model of personality, work and nonwork experiences, and domain satisfactions. *Journal of Applied Psychology, 84,* 564–584.

Hart, P. M., Wearing, A. J., & Headey, B. (1995). Police stress and well-being: Integrating personality, coping, and daily work experiences. *Journal of Occupational and Organizational Psychology, 68,* 133–156.

Harvey, R. J. (1991). Job analysis. In M. D. Dunnette & L. M. Hough (Eds.), *Handbook of industrial and organizational psychology* (2nd ed., Vol. 2, pp. 71–163). Palo Alto, CA: Consulting Psychologists Press.

Hatfield, M. O. (1990). Stress and the American worker. *American Psychologist, 45,* 1162–1164.

Haydon, D. F., Murray, T. D., & Edwards, T. L. (1986, October). Texas employee health and fitness program: An example of unique legislation. *Journal of Physical Education, Recreation, and Dance*, 28–32.

Haynes, S., LaCroix, A., & Lippin, T. (1987). The effect of high job demands and low control on the health of employed women. In J. C. Quick, R. Bhagat, J. Dalton, & J. D. Quick (Eds.), *Work stress: Health care systems in the workplace*. New York: Praeger.

Haynes, S. G., & Feinleib, M. (1982). Type A behavior and the incidence of coronary heart disease in the Framingham Heart Study. In H. Denolin (Ed.), *Psychological problems before and after myocardial infarction. Advances in cardiology* (Vol. 29). Basel, Switzerland: Karger.

Haynes, S. G., Feinleib, M., & Kannel, W. B. (1980). The relationship of psychosocial factors to coronary heart disease in the Framingham study: Eight-year incidences of coronary heart disease. *American Journal of Epidemiology*, 37–58.

Haynes, S. G., Levine, S., & Scotch, N. (1978). The relationship of psychosocial factors to coronary heart disease in the Framingham study: I. Methods and risk factors. *American Journal of Epidemiology, 107*, 362–381.

Healy, C. M., & McKay, M. F. (2000). Nursing stress: The effects of coping strategies and job satisfaction in a sample of Australian nurses. *Journal of Advanced Nursing, 31*, 681–688.

Heany, C. A., Price, R. A., & Rafferty, J. (1995). Increasing coping resources at work: A field experiment to increase social support, improve work team function, and enhance employee mental health. *Journal of Organizational Behavior, 16*, 335–352.

Hedge, A. (1984). Suggestive evidence for a relationship between office design and self-reports of ill-health among office workers in the United Kingdom. *Journal of Architectural Planning and Research, 1*, 163–174.

Hedge, A., Erickson, W. A., & Rubin, G. (1992). Effects of personal and occupational factors on sick building syndrome reports in air-conditioned offices. In J. C. Quick, L. R. Murphy, & J. J. Hurrell, Jr. (Eds.), *Stress and well-being at work*. Washington, DC: American Psychological Association.

Heiman, M. F. (1975). The police suicide. *Journal of Police Science and Administration, 3*, 267–273.

Hemingway, M. A., & Smith, C. S. (1999). Organizational climate and occupational stressors as predictors of withdrawal behaviors and injuries in nurses. *Journal of Occupational and Organizational Psychology, 72*, 285–299.

Hendrix, W. H., Ovalle, N. K., & Troxler, R. G. (1985). Behavioral and physiological consequences of stress and its antecedent factors. *Journal of Applied Psychology, 70*, 188–201.

Herbert, A. (1983). The influence of shift work on leisure activities: A study with repeated measures. *Ergonomics, 26*, 565–574.

Hildebrandt, G. & Stratman, I. (1979). Circadian system response to night work in relation to the individual circadian phase position. *International Archives for Occupational and Environmental Health, 3*, 73–83.

Hill, E. J., Miller, B. C., Weiner, S. P., & Colihan, J. (1998). Influences of the virtual office on aspects of work and work/life balance. *Personnel Psychology, 51,* 667–683.

Hill, T., Smith, N. D., & Mann, M. F. (1987). Role of efficacy expectations in predicting the decision to use advanced technologies: The case of computers. *Journal of Applied Psychology, 72,* 307–313.

Hipwell, A. E., Tyler, P. A., & Wilson, C. M. (1989). Sources of stress and dissatisfaction among nurses in four hospital environments. *British Journal of Medical Psychology, 62*(1), 71–79.

Hobfoll, S. E. (1988). *The ecology of stress.* New York: Hemisphere.

Hobfoll, S. E. (1989). Conservation of resources: A new attempt at conceptualizing stress. *American Psychologist, 44,* 512–524.

Hobfoll, S. E. (2001). Conservation of resources: A rejoinder to the commentaries. *Applied Psychology: An International Review, 50,* 419–421.

Hobfoll, S. E., & Shirom, A. (2001). Conservation of resources theory: Applications to stress and management in the workplace. In R. T. Golembiewski (Ed.), *Handbook of organizational behavior* (2nd ed., pp. 57–80). New York: Marcel Dekker.

Hofstede, G. (1980). *Cultural consequences: International differences in work-related values.* Beverly Hills, CA: Sage.

Holahan, C. J., & Moos, R. H. (1987). Personal and contextual determinants of coping strategies. *Journal of Personality and Social Psychology, 52*(5), 946–955.

Holahan, C. J., Moos, R. H., Holahan, C. K., & Cronkite, R. C. (1999). Resource loss, resource gain, and depressive symptoms: A 10-year model. *Journal of Personality and Social Psychology, 77,* 620–629.

Holahan, C. K., & Holahan, C. J. (1987). Life stress, hassles, and self-efficacy in aging: A replication and extension. *Journal of Applied Social Psychology, 17,* 574–592.

Holahan, C. K., Holahan, C. J., & Belk, S. S. (1984). Adjustment in aging: The roles of life stress, hassles, and self-efficacy. *Health Psychology, 3*(4), 315–328.

Holmes, T. H., & Rahe, R. H. (1967). The social readjustment rating scale. *Journal of Psychosomatic Research, 11,* 213–218.

Holt, M. C., McCauley, M., & Paul, D. (1995). Health impacts of AT&T's Total Life Concept (TLC) program after five years. *American Journal of Health Promotion, 9*(6), 421–425.

House, J. S. (1981). *Work stress and social support.* Reading, MA: Addison-Wesley.

House, J. S., & Wells, J. A. (1978). Occupational stress and health. In *Reducing occupational stress: Proceedings of a conference.* Cincinnati, OH: National Institute for Occupational Safety and Health.

Howard, G. S. (1994). Why do people say nasty things about self-reports? *Journal of Organizational Behavior, 15,* 399–404.

Howard, J. H., Cunningham, D. A., & Rechnitzer, P. A. (1976). Health patterns associated with Type A behavior: A managerial population. *Journal of Human Stress, 2,* 24–28.

Howard, J. H., Cunningham, D. A., & Rechnitzer, P. A. (1986). Role ambiguity, Type A behavior, and job satisfaction: Moderating effects on cardiovascular and biochemical responses associated with coronary risk. *Journal of Applied Psychology, 71,* 95–101.

Howell, W. C. (1991). Human factors in the workplace. In M. D. Dunnette, & L. M. Hough (Eds.), *Handbook of industrial and organizational psychology* (2nd ed., Vol. 2, pp. 209–269). Palo Alto, CA: Consulting Psychologist Press.

Hull, J. G., Van Treuren, R. R., & Virnelli, S. (1987). Hardiness and health: A critique and alternative approach. *Journal of Personality and Social Psychology, 53,* 518–530.

Hunter, J. E. & Schmidt, F. L. (1990). *Methods of meta-analysis: Correcting error and bias in research findings.* Newbury Park, CA.

Hurrell, J. J. (1977). *Job stress among police officers: A preliminary analysis* (NIOSH Publication No. 7604228). U.S. Department of Health, Education, and Welfare. Cincinnati, OH: U.S. Government Printing Office.

Hurrell, J. J., Nelson, D. L., & Simmons, B. L. (1998). Measuring job stressors and strains: Where have we been, where we are, and where we need to go. *Journal of Occupational Health Psychology, 3,* 368–389.

Hyland, M. E. (1987). Control theory interpretation of psychological mechanisms of depression: Comparison and integration of several theories. *Psychological Bulletin, 102,* 109–121.

Irving, R. H., Higgins, C. A., & Safayeni, F. R. (1986). Computerized performance monitoring systems: Use and abuse. *Communications of the ACM, 29,* 794–801.

Ivancevich, J. M. (1986). Life events and hassles as predictors of health symptoms, job performance, and absenteeism. *Journal of Occupational Behavior, 7,* 39–51.

Ivancevich, J. M., & Matteson, M. T. (1980). *Stress and work.* Glenville, IL: Scott Foresman.

Ivancevich, J. M., Matteson, M. T., Freedman, S. M., & Phillips, J. S. (1990). Worksite stress managment interventions. *American Psychologist, 45,* 252–261.

Ivancevich, J. M., & Matteson, M. T. (1986). Organizational level stress management interventions: A review and recommendations. *Journal of Organizational Behavior Management, 8*(2), 229–248.

Ivancevich, J. M., & Matteson, M. T. (1988). Type A behaviour and the healthy individual. *British Journal of Medical Psychology, 61*(1), 37–56.

Iverson, R. D., Olekalns, M., & Erwin, P. (1998). Affectivity, organizational stressors and absenteeism: A causal model of burnout and its consequences. *Journal of Vocational Behavior, 52,* 1–23.

Jackson, S. E. (1983). Participation in decision-making as a strategy for reducing job-related strain. *Journal of Applied Psychology, 68,* 3–19.

Jackson, S. E., & Schuler, R. S. (1985). A meta-analysis and conceptual critique of research on role ambiguity and role conflict in work settings. *Organizational Behavior and Human Decision Processes, 36,* 16–28.

Jackson, S. E., Turner, J. A., & Brief, A. P. (1987). Correlates of burnout among public service lawyers. *Journal of Occupational Behavior, 8,* 339–349.

Jackson, S. E., Zedeck, S., & Summers, E. (1985). Family life disruptions: Effects of job-induced structural and emotional interference. *Academy of Management Journal, 28,* 574–586.

Jacobson, E. J. (1929). *Progressive relaxation.* Chicago: University of Chicago Press.

Jamal, M. (1984). Job stress and job performance controversy: An empirical assessment. *Organizational Behavior and Human Performance, 33,* 1–21.

Jamal, M. (1999a). Job stress and employee well-being: A cross-cultural empirical study. *Stress Medicine, 15,* 153–158.

Jamal, M. (1999b). Job stress, Type A behavior, and well-being: A cross-cultural examination. *International Journal of Stress Management, 6*(1), 57–67.

Jamal, M., & Baba, V. V. (1991). Type A behavior, its prevalence and consequences among women nurses: An empirical examination. *Human Relations, 44,* 1213–1228.

James, K., Lovato, C., & Khoo, G. (1994). Social identity correlates of minority workers' health. *Academy of Management Journal, 37,* 383–396.

Janis, I. (1951). *Air war and emotional stress.* New York: McGraw-Hill.

Janis, I. (1958). *Psychological stress.* New York: Wiley.

Janis, I., & Mann, L. (1977a). *Decision-making: A psychological analysis of conflict, choice, and commitment.* New York: Free Press.

Janis, I., & Mann, L. (1977b, June). Emergency decision making: A theoretical analysis of responses to disaster warnings. *Journal of Human Stress,* 35–48.

Janssen, P. M., Schaufeli, W. B., & Houkes, I. (1999). Work-related and individual determinants of three burnout dimensions. *Work and Stress, 13,* 74–86.

Jeffrey, N. A. (1996, June 20). "Wellness plans" try to target the not-so-well. *The Wall Street Journal,* pp. A1–A2.

Jenkins, C. D., Zyzanski, S. J., Rosenman, R. H., & Cleveland, G. L. (1971). Association of coronary-prone behavior scores with recurrence of coronary heart disease. *Journal of Chronic Diseases, 24,* 601–611.

Jenkins, S., & Calhoun, J. F. (1991). Teacher stress: Issues and intervention. *Psychology in the Schools, 28,* 60–70.

Jensen, R. (1983, September). Workers' compensation claims attributed to heat and cold exposure. *Professional Safety,* 19–24.

Jex, S. M., & Beehr, T. A. (1991). Emerging theoretical and methodological issues in the study of work-related stress. *Research in Personnel and Human Resources Management, 9,* 311–365.

Jex, S. M., Beehr, T. A., & Roberts, C. K. (1992). The meaning of occupational stress items to survey respondents. *Journal of Applied Psychology, 77,* 623–628.

Jex, S. M., Bliese, P. D., Buzzell, S., & Primeau, J. (2001). The impact of self-efficacy on stressor-strain relations: Coping style as an explanatory mechanism. *Journal of Applied Psychology, 86*, 401–409.

Jex, S. M., & Elacqua, T. C. (1999). Self-esteem as a moderator: A comparison of global and organization-based measures. *Journal of Occupational and Organizational Psychology, 72*, 71–81.

Jex, S. M., & Spector, P. E. (1996). The impact of negative affectivity on stressor-strain relations: A replication and extension. *Work and Stress, 10*, 36–45.

Jick, T. D., & Mitz, L. F. (1985). Sex differences in work stress. *Academy of Management Review, 10*, 408–420.

Johns, G. (1981). Difference score measures of organizational behavior variables: A critique. *Organizational Behavior and Human Performance, 27*, 443–463.

Johnson, A. K., & Anderson, E. A. (1990). Stress and arousal. In J. T. Cacioppo & L. G. Tassinary, et al. (Eds.), *Principles of psychophysiology: Physical, social, and inferential elements* (pp. 216–252). NewYork: Cambridge University Press.

Johnson, J. J. (1989). Female clerical workers' perceived work and nonwork stress and dissatisfaction as predictors of psychological distress. *Women & Health, 15*(4), 61–76.

Johnson, J. V. (1989). Control, collectivity, and the psychosocial work environment. In S. L. Sauter, J. J. Hurrell, & C. L. Cooper (Eds.), *Job control and worker health* (pp. 55–74). New York: Wiley.

Johnson, J. V., & Hall, E. M. (1988). Job strain, workplace, social support and cardiovascular disease: A cross-sectional study of a random sample of the Swedish working population. *American Journal of Public Health, 78*, 1336–1342.

Jones, R. C., Bly, J. L., & Richardson, J. E. (1990). A study of a work site health promotion program and absenteeism. *Journal of Occupational Medicine, 32*(2), 95–99.

Jones, A. D., & Dallmann-Jones, A. S. (1996). *The essential guide to living a stress free life.* Fond du Lac, WI: Three Blue Herons.

Jonge, J. de, Dollard, M. F., Dormann, C., Blanc, P. M. Le, & Houtman, I. L. D. (2000). The demand-control model: Specific demands, specific control, and well-defined groups. *International Journal of Stress Management, 7*(4), 269–287.

Joreskog, K. G., & Sorbom, D. (1989). *LISREL 7: A guide to the program and applications* (2nd ed.). Chicago, IL: SPSS.

Jose, William, Jr., & Anderson, D. (1991). Control Data's StayWell program: A health cost management strategy. In S. M. Weiss, J. E. Fielding, & A. Baum (Eds.), *Health at work: Perspectives in behavioral medicine* (pp. 49–72). Hillsdale, NJ: Erlbaum.

Judge, T. A., Boudreau, J. W., & Bretz, R. D. (1994). Job and life attitudes of male executives. *Journal of Applied Psychology, 79*, 767–782.

Judge, T. A., Erez, A., & Thoresen, C. J. (2000). Why negative affectivity (and self-deception) should be included in job stress research: Bathing the baby with the bath water. *Journal of Organizational Behavior, 21,* 101–111.

Kagan, A., & Levi, L. (1975). Health and environment-psychosocial stimuli: A review. In L. Levi (Ed.), *Society, stress and disease* (Vol. 2). New York: Oxford University Press.

Kahn, R. L., & Byosiere, P. (1992). Stress in organizations. In M. D. Dunnette & L. M. Hough (Eds.), *Handbook of industrial and organizational psychology* (Vol. 2, pp. 571–650). Palo Alto, CA: Consulting Psychologists Press.

Kahn, R. L., Wolfe, D. M., Quinn, R. P., Snoek, J. D., & Rosenthal, R. A. (1964). Organizational stress: Studies in role conflict and ambiguity. New York: Wiley.

Kaldenberg, D. O., & Becker, B. W. (1992). Workload and psychological strain: A test of the French, Rodgers, and Cobb hypothesis. *Journal of Occupational Behavior, 13,* 617–624.

Kalichman, S. C., Gueritault-Chalvin, V., & Demi, A. (2000). Sources of occupational stress and coping strategies among nurses working in AIDS Care. *Journal of the Association of Nurses in AIDS Care, 11,* 31–37.

Kanner, A. D., Coyne, J. C., Schaefer, C., & Lazarus, R. S. (1981). Comparison of two modes of stress measurement: Daily hassles and uplifts versus major life events. *Journal of Behavioral Medicine, 4,* 1–39.

Kanter, R. M. (1977). *Work and family in the United States: A critical review and agenda for research and policy.* New York: Russell Sage.

Karasek, R., Jr. (1979). Job demands, job decision latitude, and mental strain: Implications for job redesign. *Administrative Science Quarterly, 24,* 285–308.

Karasek, R. (1989). Control in the workplace and its health-related aspects. In S. L. Sauter, J. J. Hurrell, & C. L. Cooper (Eds.), *Job control and worker health* (pp. 129–159). New York: Wiley.

Karasek, R. (1990). Lower health risk with increased job control among white collar workers. *Journal of Organizational Behavior, 11,* 171–185.

Karasek, R., Theorell, T. (1990). *Healthy work.* New York: Basic Books.

Kasl, S. V. (1983). Pursuing the link between stressful life experiences and disease: A time for reappraisal. In C. C. Cooper (Ed.), *Stress research: Issues for the eighties* (pp. 79–102). Chichester, England: Wiley.

Kasl, S. V. (1996). Theory of stress and health. In C. L. Cooper (Ed.), *Handbook of stress, medicine, and health* (pp. 13–26). Boca Raton, FL: CRC Press.

Kasl, S. (1989). An epidemiological perspective on the role of control in health. In S. Sauter, J. Hurrell, & C. Cooper (Eds.), *Job control and worker health.* Chichester, England: Wiley.

Katkin, E. S., Dermit, S., & Wine, S. K. F. (1993). Psychological assessment of stress. In L. Goldberger & S. Breznitz (Eds.), *Handbook of stress: Theoretical and clinical aspects* (pp. 142–157). New York: Free Press.

Kaufmann, G. M., & Beehr, T. A. (1986). Interactions between job stressors and social support: Some counterintuitive results. *Journal of Applied Psychology, 71,* 522–526.

Kaufmann, G. M., & Beehr, T. A. (1989). Occupational stressors, individual strains, and social supports among police officers. *Human Relations, 42*(2), 285–197.

Kelloway, E. K., & Barling, J. (1994). Stress, control, well-being, and marital functioning: A causal correlational analysis. In G. P. Keita & J. J. Hurrell, Jr. (Eds.), *Job stress in a changing workforce: Investigating gender, diversity, and family issues* (pp. 241–251). Washington, DC: American Psychological Association.

Kelly, K. R., & Stone, G. L. (1987). Effects of three psychological treatments and self-monitoring on the reduction of Type A behavior. *Journal of Counseling Psychology, 34,* 46–54.

Kemery, E. R., Bedeian, A. G., Mossholder, K. W., & Touliatos, J. (1985). Outcomes of role stress: A multi-sample constructive replication. *Academy of Management Journal, 28,* 363–375.

Kemery, E. R., Mossholder, K. W., & Bedeian, A. G. (1987). Role stress, physical symptomatology, and turnover intentions: A causal analysis of three alternative specifications. *Journal of Occupational Behavior, 8,* 11–23.

Keon, T. L., & McDonald, B. (1982). Job satisfaction and life satisfaction: An empirical evaluation of their relationship. *Human Relations, 35,* 167–180.

King, L. A., & King, D. W. (1990). Role conflict and role ambiguity: A critical assessment of construct validity. *Psychological Bulletin, 107*(1), 48–64.

Kingston, P. W. (1988). Studying the work-family connection: A theoretical progress, ideological bias and shaky foundations for policy. *Journal of Social Behavior and Personality 3*(4), 61–90.

Kinicki, A. J. (1985). Personal consequences of plant closings: A model and preliminary test. *Human Relations, 38*(3), 197–212.

Kinicki, A. J., & Latack, J. (1990). Explication of the construct of coping with involuntary job loss. *Journal of Vocational Behavior, 36,* 339–360.

Kinicki, A. J., McKee, F. M., & Wade, K. J. (1996). Annual review, 1991–1995: Occupational health. *Journal of Vocational Behavior, 49,* 190–220.

Kinicki, A. J., Prussia, G. E., & McKee-Ryan, F. M. (2000). A panel study of coping with involuntary job loss. *Academy of Management Journal, 43,* 90–100.

Kinicki, A. J., & Vecchio, R. P. (1994). Influences on the quality of supervisor-subordinate relations: The role of time pressure, organizational commitment, and locus of control. *Journal of Organizational Behavior, 15,* 75–82.

Kirchmeyer, C. (1992). Perceptions of nonwork-to-work spillover: Challenging the common view of conflict-ridden domain relationships. *Basic and Applied Social Psychology, 13,* 231–249.

Kirkcaldy, B. D., Brown, J., & Cooper, C. L. (1994). Occupational stress profiles of senior police managers: Cross-cultural study of officers from Berlin and Northern Ireland. *Stress Medicine, 10,* 127–130.

Kirkcaldy, B. D., & Cooper, C. L. (1992). Cross-cultural differences in occupational stress among British and German managers. *Work and Stress, 6*(2), 177–190.

Kirkcaldy, B. D., & Martin, T. (2000). Job stress and satisfaction among nurses: Individual differences. *Stress Medicine, 16*, 77–89.

Kirkcaldy, B. D., Shepard, R. J., & Cooper, C. L. (1993). Relationships between Type A behaviour, work, and leisure. *Personality and Individual Differences, 15*, 69–74.

Kirkcaldy, B. D., Trimpop, R., & Cooper, G. L. (1997). Working hours, job stress, work satisfaction, an accident rates among medical practitioners and allied personnel. *International Journal of Stress Management, 4*, 79–88.

Kirmeyer, S. L., & Diamond, A. (1985). Coping by police officers: A study of role stress and Type A and Type B behavior patterns. *Journal of Occupational Behavior, 6*, 183–195.

Kivimaeki, M., & Kalimo, R. (1996). Self-esteem and the occupational stress process: Testing two alternative models in a sample of blue-collar workers. *Journal of Occupational Health Psychology, 1*, 187–196.

Kivimaeki, M., & Lindstroem, K. (1995). Effects of private self-consciousness and control on the occupational stress-strain relationship. *Stress Medicine, 11*(1), 7–16.

Kivimaeki, M., Vahtera, J., Koskenvuo, M., Uutela, A., & Pentti, J. (1998). Response of hostile individuals to stressful changes in their working lives: Tests of a psychosocial vulnerability model. *Psychological Medicine, 28*, 903–913.

Kline, M., & Cowan, P. A. (1988). Re-thinking the connections among "work" and "family" and well-being. *Journal of Social Behavior and Personality, 3*(4), 61–90.

Knutsson, A., Akerstedt, T., Jonsson, B., & Orth-Gomer, K. (1986, July 12). Increased risk of ischaemic heart disease in ship workers. *Lancet,* 89–92.

Kobasa, S. C. (1979). Stressful life events, personality, and health: An inquiry into hardiness. *Journal of Personality and Social Psychology, 37*, 1–11.

Kobasa, S. C. (1982a). Commitment and coping in stress resistance among lawyers. Journal of *Personality and Social Psychology, 42*, 707–717.

Kobasa, S. C. (1982b). The hardy personality: Toward a social psychology of stress and health. In G. Sanders & J. Suls (Eds.), *Social psychology of health and illness*. Hillsdale, NJ: Erlbaum.

Kobasa, S. C., Hilker, R. R. J., & Maddi, S. R. (1980). Remaining healthy in the encounter with stress. In J. F. McHan & R. H. Wheater (Eds.), *Stress, work, and health*. Chicago: American Medical Association.

Kobasa, S. C., & Maddi, S. R. (1977). Existential personality theory. In R. J. Corsini (Ed.), *Current personality theories*. Itasca, IL: F. E. Peacock.

Kobasa, S. C., Maddi, S. R., & Kahn, S. (1982). Hardiness and health: A prospective study. *Journal of Personality and Social Psychology, 42*, 168–177.

Kolbell, R. M. (1995). When relaxation is not enough. In L. R. Murphy, J. J. Hurrell, Jr., S. L. Sauter, & G. P. Keita (Eds.), *Job stress interventions* (pp. 31–44). Washington, DC: American Psychological Association.

Koller, M. (1983). Health risks related to shift work: An example of time-contingent effects of long-term stress. *International Archives of Occupational and Environmental Health, 53,* 59–75.

Kompier, M. A. J., Geurts, S. A. E., Gruendemann, R. W. M., Vink, P., & Smulders, P. G. W. (1998). Cases in stress prevention: The success of a participative and stepwise approach. *Stress Medicine, 14,* 155–168.

Koniarek, J., & Dudek, B. (1996). Social support as a buffer in the stress-burnout relationship. *International Journal of Stress Management, 3,* 99–106.

Kop, N., & Euwema, M. C. (2001). Occupational stress and the use of force by Dutch police officers. *Criminal Justice and Behavior, 28,* 631–652.

Kop, N., Euwema, M., & Schaufeli, W. (1999). Burnout, job stress and violent behaviour among Dutch police. *Work and Stress, 13,* 326–340.

Korunka, C. & Vitouch, O. (1999). The effects of implementation of information technology on employees' strain and job satisfaction: A context-dependent approach. *Work and Stress, 13,* 341–363.

Kossek, E. E., & Ozeki, C. (1998). Work-family conflict, policies, and the job-life satisfaction relationship: A review and directions for organizational behavior-human resources research. *Journal of Applied Psychology, 83,* 139–149.

Kramer, M. (1974). *Reality shock: Why nurses leave nursing.* St. Louis, MO: Mosby Press.

Kraut, R. E. (1987). Social issues and white-collar technology. In R. E. Kraut (Ed.) *Technology and the transformation of white-collar work.* Hillsdale, NJ: Erlbaum.

Kuhlmann, T. (1990). Coping with occupational stress amoung urban bus drivers and tram drivers. *Journal of Occupational Psychology, 72,* 377–385.

Kyriacou, C., & Sutcliffe, J. (1978). Teacher stress: Prevalence, sources and symptoms. *British Journal of Educational Psychology, 48,* 159–167.

Lachman, S. (1972). *Psychosomatic disorders: A behavioral interpretation.* New York: Wiley.

Lambert, S. J. (1990). Processes linking work and family: A critical review and research agenda. *Human Relations, 43,* 239–257.

Landon, L. (1990 May). Pump up your employees. *HR Magazine,* 34–37.

Landsbergis, P. A. (1988). Occupational stress among health care workers: A test of the job-demands-control model. *Journal of Organizational Behavior, 9,* 217–239.

Landsbergis, P. A., Schnall, P. L., Schwartz, J. E., Warren, K., & Pickering, T. G. (1995). Job strain, hypertension, and cardiovascular disease: Empirical evidence, methodological issues, and recommendations for future research. In S. L. Sauter and L. R. Murphy (Eds.),

Organizational risk factors for job stress (pp. 97–112). Washington, DC: American Psychological Assocation.

Landsbergis, P. A., & Vivona-Vaughan, E. (1995). Evaluation of an occupational stress intervention in a public agency. *Journal of Occupational Behavior, 16,* 29–48.

Landy, F. J. (1986). Stamp collecting versus science: Validation as hypothesis testing. *American Psychologist, 41,* 1183–1192.

Lang, D., Wittig-Berman, U., & Rizkalla, A. (1992). The influences of role stress, physical symptoms, and job satisfaction on turnover intentions: A two-sample test of a modified Bedeian and Armenakis model. *Journal of Social Behavior and Personality, 7,* 555–568.

LaRocco, J. M., House, J. S. & French, J. R. P., Jr. (1980). Social support, occupational stress, and health. *Journal of Health and Social Behavior, 21,* 202–218.

Latack, J. C. (1986). Coping with job stress; measures and future directions for scale development. *Journal of Applied Psychology, 71,* 377–385.

Latack, J. C., & Havlovic, S. (1992). Coping with job stress: A conceptual evaluation framework for coping measures. *Journal of Organizational Behavior, 13,* 479–508.

Latack, J. C., Kinicki, A. J., & Prussia, G. E. (1995). An integrative process model of coping with job loss. *Academy of Management Review, 20,* 311–342.

Laurig, W., Becker-Biskaborn, G. U., & Reiche, D. (1971). Software problems in analyzing physiological and work study data. *Ergonomics, 14,* 625–631.

Lazarus, R. S. (1966). *Psychological stress and the coping process.* New York: McGraw-Hill.

Lazarus, R. S. (1976). *Patterns of adjustment.* New York: McGraw-Hill.

Lazarus, R. S. (1983). The costs and benefits of denial. In S. Bresnitz (Ed.), *Denial of stress* (pp. 1–30). New York: Guilford.

Lazarus, R. S. (1984). On the primacy of cognition. *American Psychologist, 39,* 124–129.

Lazarus, R. S. (1991). Psychological stress in the workplace. *Journal of Social Behavior and Personality, 6,* 1–13.

Lazarus, R. S. (2001). Conservation of resources theory (COR): Little more than words masquerading as a new theory. *Applied Psychology: An International Review, 50,* 381–391.

Lazarus, R. S., DeLongis, A., Folkman, S., & Gruen, R. (1985). Stress and adaptational outcomes: The problem of confounded measures. *American Psychologist, 40,* 770–779.

Lazarus, R. S., & Folkman, S. (1984). *Stress, appraisal, and coping.* New York: Springer.

Lazarus, R. S., & Launier, R. (1978). Stress-related transactions between person and environment. In L. A. Pervin & M. Lewis (Eds.), *Perspectives in interactional psychology* (pp. 287–327). New York: Plenum.

Leana, C. R., & Feldman, D. C. (1988). Individual responses to job loss: Perceptions, reactions, and coping behaviors. *Journal of Management, 14,* 375–389.

Leana, C. R., Feldman, D. C., & Yan, G. Y. (1998). Predictors of coping behavior after a layoff. *Journal of Organizational Behavior, 19*, 85–97.

Leavenworth, G. (1995). Wellness programs pay dividends. *Business and Health, 13*(3), 23–27.

Lee, C. L. (1987). Professional in medical settings: The research evidence in the 1980's. *Journal of Organizational Behavior Management, 8*, 195–213.

Lee, C. (1992). The relations of personality and cognitive styles on job and class performance. *Journal of Organizational Behavior, 13*, 175–185.

Lee, C. (1991, September). Balancing work and family. *Training, 28*(9), 23–28.

Lee, C., Ashford, S. J., & Jamieson, L. F. (1993). The effects of Type A behavior dimensions and optimism on coping strategy, health, and performance. *Journal of Organizational Behavior, 14*, 143–157.

Lee, R. T., & Ashforth, B. E. (1993). A longitudinal study of burnout among supervisors and managers: Comparisons between Leiter and Maslach (1988) and Golembiewski et al. (1986) models. *Organizational Behavior and Human Decision Processes, 54*, 369–398.

Lee, R. T., & Ashforth, B. E. (1996). A meta-analytic examination of the correlates of the three dimensions of job burnout. *Journal of Applied Psychology, 81*, 123–133.

Leeper, P. (1983). VDTs and vision: Workplace design is the key. *Human Factors Bulletin, 26*, 1–3.

Lehman, E. (1995, February 26). Business must do more for working parents. *Parade Magazine*, 12–14.

Lehrer, P. M., Carr, R., Sargunaraj, D., & Woolfolk, R. L. (1994). Stress management techniques: Are they all equivalent, or do they have specific effects? *Biofeedback and Self Regulation, 19*, 353–401.

Leiter, M. (1991). Coping patterns as predictors of burnout: The function of control and escapist coping behavior. *Journal of Organizational Behavior, 12*, 123–144.

Leiter, M. (1993). Burnout as a developmental process: Consideration of models. In W. B. Schaufeli, C. Maslach, & T. Marek (Eds.), *Professional burnout: Recent developments in theory and research. Series in applied psychology: Social issues and questions.* (pp. 237–250). Washington, DC: Taylor & Francis.

Leiter, M. P., & Durup, M. J. (1996). Work, home, and in-between: A longitudinal study of spillover. *Journal of Applied Behavioral Science, 32*, 29–47.

Leiter, M. P., & Maslach, C. (1988). The impact of interpersonal environment on burnout and organizational commitment. *Journal of Organizational Behavior, 9*, 297–308.

Lemkau, J. P., Rafferty, J. P., Purdy, R. R., & Rudisill, J. R. (1987). Sex role stress and job burnout among family practice physicians. *Journal of Vocational Behavior, 31*, 81–90.

Lennernäs, M.A., Hambræus, L., & Åkerstedt, T. (1994). Nutrient intake in day workers and shift workers. *Work and Stress, 8*, 332–342.

Levenson, J. L., & Bemis, C. (1991). The role of psychological factors in cancer onset and progression. *Psychosomatics, 32*(2), 124–132.

Levi, L. (1972). Stress and distress in response to psychosocial stimuli. *Acta Medica Scandinavica, 528,* 1–166.

Levi, L. (1973). Humanokologie-psychosomatische Gesichtpunkte und Forschungsstrategien. *Psychosomatic Medicine, 5,* 92.

Levi, L. (1974). Stress, distress and psychosocial stimuli. In A. McLean (Ed.), *Occupational stress.* Springfield, IL: Charles C Thomas.

Levi, L. (1990). Occupational stress: Spice of life or kiss of death? *American Psychologist, 45,* 1142–1145.

Levinson, H. (1996, July–August). When executives burn out. *Harvard Business Review, 74*(4), 152–163.

Lewin, K. (1951). *Field theory in social science.* New York: Harper.

Lindell, M. K., & Whitney, D. J. (2001). Accounting for common method variance in cross-sectional research designs. *Journal of Applied Psychology, 86,* 114–121.

Liou, K., Sylvia, R. D., & Brunk, G. (1990). Non-work factors and job satisfaction revisited. *Human Relations, 43,* 77–86.

Locke, E. A. (1976). The nature and causes of job satisfaction. In M. Dunnette (Ed.), *Handbook of industrial and organizational psychology,* (pp. 1297–1349). Chicago: Rand McNally.

London, M., Crandall, R., & Seals, G. W. (1977). The contribution of job and leisure satisfaction to the quality of life. *Journal of Applied Psychology, 62,* 328–334.

Lovallo, W. R., & Pishkin, V. (1980). Type A behavior, self-involvement, autonomic activity, and the traits of neuroticism and extraversion. *Psychosomatic Medicine, 42,* 329–334.

Lu, L., Kao, S. F., Cooper, C. L., & Spector, P. E. (2000). Managerial stress, locus of control and job strain in Taiwan and UK: A comparative study. *International Journal of Stress Management, 7,* 209–226.

Luck, C. (2000). Reducing stress among junior doctors. *British Medical Journal, 321,* n.p.

Luecken, L. J., Suarez, E. C., Kuhn, C. M., Barefoot, J. C., Blumenthal, J. A., Siegler, I. C., & Williams, R. B. (1977). Stress in employed women: Impact of marital status and children at home on neurohormone output and home strain. *Psychosomatic Medicine, 59,* 352–359.

Lundberg, U. (1999). Stress responses in low-status jobs and their relationship to health risks: Musculoskeletal disorders. *Annals of the New York Academy of Sciences, 896,* 162–172.

Lundberg, U., & Frankenhaeuser, M. (1999). Stress and workload of men and women in high-ranking positions. *Journal of Occupational Health Psychology, 4,* 142–151.

Lundberg, U., & Johansson, G. (2000). Stress and health risks in repetitive work and supervisory monitoring work. In R. W. Backs and W. Boucsein (Eds.) *Engineering psychophysiology: Issues and applications* (pp. 339–359). Mahwah, NJ: Erlbaum.

Macdonald, S., Shain, M., & Wells, S. (1993). *Effectiveness of EAPs.* Addiction Research Foundation.

Maddi, S. R. (1987). Hardiness training at Illinois Bell Telephone. In J. P. Opatz (Ed.), *Health Promotion Evaluation.* Stevens Point, WI: National Wellness Institute.

Maddi, S. R. (1990). Issues and interventions in stress mastery. In H. S. Friedman (Ed.), *Personality and Disease.* New York: Wiley.

Magnani, L. E. (1990). Hardiness, self-perceived health, and activity among independently functioning older adults. *Scholarly Inquiry for Nursing Practice: An International Journal, 4,* 171–184.

Manning, M. R., Jackson, C. N., & Fusilier, M. R. (1996). Occupational stress, social support, and the costs of health care. *Academy of Management Journal, 39,* 738–750.

Many, C. (1995, June 26). Beyond drug and alcohol abuse. *Business Insurance, 29*(26), 3–4.

Margolis, B. L., Kroes, W. H., & Quinn, R. P. (1974). Job stress: An unlisted occupational hazard. *Journal of Occupational Medicine, 16,* 654–661.

Marks, M. L., & Mirvis, P. L. (1985). Merger syndrome: Stress and uncertainty. *Mergers & Acquisitions, 20,* 50–55.

Marshall, J. (1978). Stress amongst nurses. In C. L. Cooper & J. Marshall (Eds.), *White collar and professional stress.* New York: Wiley.

Martin, R., & Wall, T. D. (1989). Attentional demand and cost responsibility as stressors in shopfloor jobs. *Academy of Management Journal, 32,* 69–86.

Martocchio, J. J., & O'Leary, A. M. (1989). Sex differences in occupational stress: A meta-analytic review. *Journal of Applied Psychology, 74,* 495–501.

Masi, D. (1984). *Designing employee assistance programs.* New York: American Management Association.

Maslach, C. (1982). Burnout: The cost of caring. Englewood Cliffs, NJ: Prentice Hall.

Maslach, C. (1993). Burnout: A multidimensional perspective. In W. B. Schaufeli, C. Maslach, & T. Marek (Eds.), *Professional burnout: Recent developments in theory and research. Series in applied psychology: Social issues and questions* (pp. 19–32). Washington, DC: Taylor & Francis.

Maslach, C. (1999). Progress in understanding teacher burnout. In R. Vandenberghe & M.A. Huberman (Eds.). *Understanding and preventing teacher burnout: A sourcebook of international research and practice* (pp. 211–222). New York: Cambridge University Press.

Maslach, C., & Jackson, S. E. (1981). The measurement of experienced burnout. *Journal of Occupational Behavior, 2,* 99–113.

Maslach, C., & Jackson, S. E. (1982). Burnout in health professions: A social psychological analysis. In G. Sanders & J. Suls (Eds.), *Social psychology of health and illness* (pp. 227–251). Hillsdale, NJ: Erlbaum.

Maslach, C., & Jackson, S. E. (1984). Patterns of burnout among a national sample of public contact workers. Journal of Health and Human Resources Administration, 7, 189–212.

Maslach, C., & Jackson, S. E. (1986). The Maslach Burnout Inventory: Manual (2nd ed.). Palo Alto, CA: Consulting Psychologists Press.

Maslach, C., & Schaufeli, W. B. (1993). Historical and conceptual development of burnout. In W. B. Schaufeli, C. Maslach, & T. Marek (Eds.), Professional burnout: Recent developments in theory and research (pp. 1–16). Washington, DC: Taylor & Francis.

Mason, J. C. (1993, July). Working in the family way. Management Review (25–28).

Mason, J. W. (1971). A re-evaluation of the concept of non-specificity in stress theory. Journal of Psychiatric Research, 8, 323.

Mason, J. W. (1972). Organization of psychoendrocrine mechanisms. In J. Greenfield & R. Sternbach (Eds.), Handbook of psychophysiology. New York: Holt, Rinehart & Winston.

Mason, J. W. (1975a). A historical view of the stress field. Journal of Human Stress, 1(2), 22–36.

Mason, J. W. (1975b). A historical view of the stress field (Part II). Journal of Human Stress, 1(3), 22–26.

Mason, J. W. (1975c). Emotion as reflected in patterns of endocrine integration. In L. Levi (Ed.), Emotions: Their parameters and measurement. New York: Raven Press.

Mason, J. W., Sachar, E. J., Fishman, J. R., Hamburg, D. A., & Handlon, J. H. (1965). Corticosteroid responses to hospital admission. Archives of General Psychiatry, 13, 1.

Mathews, K., Cottington, E., Talbott, E., Kuller, L., & Siegel, J. (1987). Stressful work conditions and diastolic blood pressure among blue collar factory workers. American Journal of Epidemiology, 126, 280–291.

Matteson, M. T., & Ivancevich, J. M. (1982). Managing job stress and health. New York: Free Press.

Matthews, K. A. (1988). Coronary heart disease and Type A behaviors: Update on and alternative to the Booth-Kewley and Friedman (1987) quantitative review. Psychological Bulletin, 104, 373–380.

Matthews, K. A., & Rodin, J. (1989). Women's changing work roles: Irnpact on health, family, and public policy. American Psvchologist, 44, 1389–1393.

Maume, D. J., & Houston, P. (2001). Job segregation and gender differences in work-family spillover among white-collar workers. Journal of Family and Economic Issues, 22, 171–189.

May, D. R., & Schwoerer, C. E. (1994). Employee health by design: Using employee involvement teams in ergonomic job redesign. Personnel Psychology, 47, 861–875.

Maysent, M., & Spera, S. (1995). Coping with job loss and career stress: Effectiveness of stress management training with outplaced employees. In L. R. Murphy, J. J. Hurrell, Jr., S. L. Sauter, & G. P. Keita (Eds.), Job stress interventions (pp. 159–170). Washington, DC: American Psychological Association.

McClary, C., Combs, A., Abell, R., & Henshaw, E. (1990, August/September). University heartwalk: A campus walking program. *Journal of Physical Education, Recreation, and Dance, 70*–72.

McClay, C. J. (1998). The development of work-at-home safety programs. *Professional Safety, 43,* 39–41.

McCrae, R. R. (1984). Situational determinants of coping responses: Loss, threat, and challenge. *Journal of Personality and Social Psychology, 46,* 919–928.

McGee, M. K. (1996, March 4). Burnout! *Informationweek, 569,* 34–40.

McGrath, J. E. (1976). Stress and behavior in organizations. In M. Dunnette (Ed.), *Handbook of industrial and organizational psychology* (pp. 1351–1395). Chicago: Rand McNally.

McGrath, J. E., & Beehr, T. A. (1990). Time and the stress process: Some temporal issues in the conceptualization and measurement of stress. *Stress Medicine, 6,* 93–104.

McMichael, A. J., & Hartshorne, J. M. (1980). Cardiovascular disease and cancer mortality in Australia, by occupation, in relation to drinking, smoking, and eating. *Community Health Studies, 4,* 76–80.

Mechanic, D. (1978). *Students under stress.* Madison, WI: University of Wisconsin Press.

Meier, S. T. (1984). The construct validity of burnout. *Journal of Occupational Psychology, 57,* 211–219.

Meijman, T. F., van Dormolen, M., Herber, R. F. M., Rongen, H., & Kuiper, S. (1995). Job strain, neuroendocrine activation, and immune status. In S. L. Sauter and L. R. Murphy (Eds.), *Organizational risk factors for job stress* (pp. 113–126). Washington, DC: American Psychological Association.

Melamed, S., Fried, Y., & Froom, P. (2001). The interactive effect of chronic exposure to noise and job complexity on changes in blood pressure and job satisfaction: A longitudinal study of industrial employees. *Journal of Occupational Health Psychology, 6,* 182–195.

Melamed, S., Ben-Avi, I., Luz, J., & Green, M. S. (1995). Objective and subjective work monotony: Effects on job satisfaction, psychological distress, and absenteeism in blue-collar workers. *Journal of Applied Psychology, 80,* 29–42.

Melamed, S., Kushnir, T., & Meir, E. (1991). Attenuating the impact of job demands: Additive and interactive effects of percieved control and social support. *Journal of Vocational Behavior, 39,* 40–53.

Mendell, M., & Smith, A. (1990). Consistent pattern of elevated symptoms in air-conditioned office buildings: A reanalysis of epidemiologic studies. *American Journal of Public Health, 80,* 1193–1199.

Mendelson, M. B., Catano, V. M., & Kelloway, K. (2000). The role of stress and social support in sick building syndrome. *Work and Stress, 14,* 137–155.

Merton, R. K. (1957). *Social theory and social structure.* Glencoe, IL: Free Press of Glencoe.

Mikhail, A. (1985). Stress: A psychophysiological conception. In A. Monat & R. Lazarus (Eds.), *Stress and coping: An anthology* (2nd ed). New York: Columbia University Press.

Miller, K., Greyling, M., Cooper, C., Lu, L., Sparks, K., & Spector, P. E. (2000). Occupational stress and gender: A cross-cultural study. *Stress Medicine, 15*, 271–278.

Miller, R. L., Griffin, M. A., & Hart, P. M. (1999). Personality and organizational health: The role of conscientiousness. *Work and Stress, 13*, 7–19.

Miller, S. M. (1979). Controllability and human stress: Method, evidence, and theory. *Behavior Research and Therapy, 17*, 287–304.

Miller, T. W. (1993). The assessment of stressful life events. In L. Goldberger & S. Breznitz (Eds.), *Handbook of stress: Theoretical and clinical aspects* (2nd ed.) (pp. 161–173). New York: The Free Press.

Mintzberg, H. (1973). *The nature of managerial work.* New York: Harper & Row.

Mishel, M. H. (1984). Perceived uncertainty and stress in illness. *Research in Nursing and Health, 7*, 163–171.

Mishra, A. K., & Spreitzer, G. M. (1998). Explaining how survivors respond to downsizing: The roles of trust, empowerment, justice, and work redesign. *Academy of Management Review, 23*, 567–588.

Mitchell, J., & Bray, G. (1990). *Emergency service stress.* Englewood Cliffs, NJ: Prentice Hall.

Mitchelson, J. K., & Burns, L. R. (1998). Career mothers and perfectionism: Stress at work and at home. *Personality & Individual Differences, 25*, 477–485.

Molhave, L. (1989). The sick building and other buildings with indoor climate problems. *Environment International, 15*, 65–74.

Moller, A. T., & Botha, H. C. (1996). Effects of a group rational-emotive behavior therapy program on the Type A behavior pattern. *Psychological Reports, 78*, 947–961.

Monat, A., & Lazarus, R. (1985). *Stress and coping: An anthology* (2nd ed). New York: Columbia University Press.

Monk, T. H. (1988). Coping with the stress of shiftwork. *Work and Stress, 2*, 169–172.

Monk, T. H. (1989). Human factors implications of shiftwork. *International Review of Ergonomics, 2*, 111–128.

Monk, T. H., & Embrey, D. E. (1981). A field study of circadian rhythms in actual and interpolated task performance. In A. Reinberg, N. Vieux, & P. Andlauer (Eds.), *Night and shift work: Biological and social aspects.* Oxford: Pergamon Press.

Monk, T. H., & Folkard, S. (1985). Shiftwork and performance. In S. Folkard & T. Monk (Eds.), *Hours of work: Temporal factors in work-scheduling.* Chichester, England: Wiley.

Monk, T. H., & Folkard, S. (1992). *Making shiftwork tolerable.* London: Taylor & Francis.

Moog, R. (1993). Optimization of shift work: Physiological contributions. *Ergonomics, 36,* 1249–1259.

Morrison, A., & Von Glinow, M. (1990). Women and minorities in management. *American Psychologist, 45,* 200–208.

Motowidlo, S. J., Packard, J. S., & Manning, M. R. (1986). Occupational stress: Its causes and consequences for job performance. *Journal of Applied Psychology, 71,* 618–629.

Mullady, S. F. (1991). The champion paper company EAP and major issues for Employee Assistance Programs in the 1990's—Managed care and aging. *Employee Assistance Quarterly, 6,* 37–50.

Munz, D. C., & Kohler, J. M. (1997). Do worksite stress management programs attract the employees who need them and are they effective? *International Journal of Stress Management, 4,* 1–10.

Murphy, L. R. (1988). Workplace interventions for stress reduction and prevention. In C. L. Cooper & R. Payne (Eds.), *Causes and consequences of stress at work* (pp. 88–114). Chichester, England: Wiley.

Murphy, L. (1991). Job dimensions associated with severe disability due to cardiovascular disease. *Journal of Clinical Epidemiology, 44*(2), 155–166.

Murphy, L. R. (1995). Managing job stress: An employee assistance/human resources management partnership. *Personnel Review, 24*(1), 41–50.

Murphy, L. R., DuBois, D., & Hurrell, J. J. (1986). Accident reduction through stress management. *Journal of Business and Psychology, 1*(1), 5–18.

Murphy, S., Beaton, R., Cain, K., & Pike, K. (1994). Gender differences in firefighter job stressors and symptoms of stress. *Women and Health, 22,* 55–69.

Murray, H. (1938). *Explorations in personality.* New York: Oxford University Press.

Nahorney, D. J. (1995, November). A matter of focus. *Managers,* 16–19.

Naismith, D. (1975). *Stress among managers as a function of organizational change.* Unpublished doctoral dissertation, George Washington University, Washington, DC.

Narayanan, L., Menon, S., & Spector, P. E. (1999). Stress in the workplace: A comparison of gender and occupations. *Journal of Organizational Behavior, 20,* 63–73.

National Institute for Occupational Safety and Health (NIOSH). (1986). *Occupational exposure to hot environments, Revised Criteria.* Washington, DC: U.S. Department of Health and Human Services.

Netemeyer, R., Johnston, M., & Burton, S. (1990). Analysis of role conflict and role ambiguity in a structural equations framework. *Journal of Applied Psychology, 75,* 148–157.

9 to 5, Working Women Education Fund. (1990). *Stories of mistrust and manipulation: The electronic monitoring of the American workforce.* Cleveland, OH: Author.

Nisbett R., & Ross, L. (1980). *Human inference: Strategies and shortcomings of social judgment.* Englewood Cliffs, NJ: Prentice Hall.

Nolan, R. L., & Croson, D. C. (1995). *Creative destruction: A six-stage process for transforming the organization*. Boston: Harvard Business School Press.

Norman, D. A. (1984). Stages and levels in human-machine interaction. *International Journal of Man Machine Studies, 21,* 365–375.

Nye, S. G. (1990). *Employee assistance law answer book*. Greenvale, NY: Panel Publisher.

O'Driscoll, M. P., & Beehr, T. A. (1994). Supervisor behaviors, role stressors and uncertainty as predictors of personal outcomes for subordinates. *Journal of Organizational Behavior, 15,* 141–155.

O'Driscoll, M. P., & Cooper, C. L. (1994). Coping with work related stress: A critique of existing measures and proposal for an alternative methodology. *Journal of Occupational and Organizational Psychology, 67,* 343–354.

Office of Technology Assessment, U.S. Congress. (1991, September). *Biological rhythms: Implications for the worker* (OTA-BA-463). Washington, DC: U.S. Government Printing Office.

Ogus, E. D. (1995). Burnout and coping strategies: A comparative study of ward nurses. In R. Crandall & P. L. Perrewe (Eds.), *Occupational stress: A handbook* (pp. 249–261). Philadelphia, PA: Taylor & Francis.

Olson, M. H. & Primps, S. B. (1984). Working at home with computers: Work and nonwork issues. *Journal of Social Issues 40,* 97–112.

O'Neill, H. M., & Lenn, J. (1995). Voices of survivors: Words that downsizing CEO's should hear. *Academy of Management Executive, 9,* 23–34.

Orpen, C., & Welch, M. (1989). Stress and work attitudes among Australian nurses: An empirical study. *Psychological Studies, 34* (3), 214–215.

Osipow, S. H., & Davis, A. S. (1988). The relationship of coping resources to occupational stress and strain. *Journal of Vocational Behavior, 32,* 1–15.

Osipow, S. H., & Spokane, A. R. (1984). Measuring occupational stress, strain and coping. *Applied Social Psychology Annual, 5,* 67–86.

Ouellette, S. C. (1993). Inquiries into hardiness. In L. Goldberger & S. Breznitz (Eds.), *Handbook of stress: Theoretical and clinical aspects* (2nd ed., pp. 77–100). New York: Free Press.

Overman, S. (1993, May). A real pain-in-the-neck benefit. *HR Magazine,* 66–67.

Overmier, J. B., & Hellhammer, D. H. (1988). The learned helplessness model of human depression. In P. Simon, P. Soubrie, & D. Wildlocher (Eds.), *Animal Models of Psychiatric Disorders* (Vol. 2., pp. 177–202). Basel, Switzerland: Karger.

Parker, S. R. (1967). Industry and the family. In S. R. Parker, R. K. Brown, J. Child, & M. A. Smith (Eds.), *The sociology of industry*. London: Allen & Unwin.

Parker, V. A., & Hall, D. T. (1992). Conclusion: Expanding the domain of family and work issues. In S. Zedeck (Ed.) *Work, families, and organizations*. San Francisco, CA: Jossey-Bass.

Parkes, K. R. (1984). Locus of control, cognitive appraisal, and coping in stressful episodes. *Journal of Personality and Social Psychology, 46,* 655–664.

Parkes, K. R. (1986). Coping in stressful episodes: The role of individual differences, environmental factors and situational characteristics. *Journal of Personality and Social Psychology, 19,* 1277–1292.

Parkes, K. R. (1990). Coping, negative affectivity, and the work environment: Additive and interactive predictors of mental health. *Journal of Applied Psychology, 75,* 399–409.

Parkes, K. R. (1999). Shiftwork, job type, and the work environment as joint predictors of health-related outcomes. *Journal of Occupational Health Psychology, 4,* 256–268.

Parkes, K. R., Mendham, C. A., & von Rabenau, C. (1994). Social support and the demand-discretion model of job stress: Tests of additive and interactive effects in two samples. *Journal of Vocational Behavior, 44,* 91–113.

Parkes, K. R., & Rendall, D. (1988). The hardy personality and its relationship to extraversion and neuroticism. *Personality and Individual Differences, 9,* 785–790.

Parsons, T. (1951). *The social system.* Glencoe, IL: Free Press of Glencoe.

Patterson, J. (October, 1994). Welcome to the company that isn't there. *Business Week,* pp. 86–87.

Payne, R. L. (1959). Tracking performance as a function of thermal balance. *Journal of Applied Physiology, 14,* 387–389.

Payne, R. L. (1988). Individual differences in the study of occupational stress. In C. L. Cooper & R. Payne (Eds.). *Causes, coping, and consequences of stress at work.* Chichester, England: Wiley.

Payne, R. L. (2000). Comments on "Why negative affectivity should not be controlled in job stress research: Don't throw out the baby with the bath water." *Journal of Organizational Behavior, 21,* 97–99.

Payne, R. & Fletcher, B. (1983). Job demands, supports, and constraints as predictors of psychological strain among schoolteachers. Journal of Vocational Behavior, 22, 136–147.

Peacock, E. J., Wong, P. T. P., & Reker, G. (1993). Relations between appraisals and coping schemas: Support for the congruence model. *Canadian Journal of Behavioral Science, 25*(1), 64–80.

Pearlin, L. I., & Schooler, C. (1978). The structure of coping. *Journal of Organizational Behavior, 19,* 2–21.

Pelletier, K. R., & Lutz, R. (1989). Mindbody goes to work: A critical review of stress management programs in the workplace. *Advances, Institute for the Advancement of Health, 6,* 28–34.

Pelletier, K. R., & Lutz, R. W. (1991). Healthy people—healthy business: A critical review of stress management programs in the workplace. In S. M. Weiss, J. E. Fielding, & A. Baum (Eds.), *Perspectives in behavioral medicine: Health at work* (pp. 189–204). Hillsdale, NJ: Erlbaum.

Perrewé, P. L., & Hochwarter, W. A. (2001). Can we really have it all? The attainment of work and family values. *Current Directions in Psychological Science, 10,* 29–33.

Perrewé, P. L., & Zellars, K. L. (1999). An examination of attributions and emotions in the transactional approach to the organizational stress process. *Journal of Organizational Behavior, 20,* 739–752.

Persinger, M. A., Tiller, S. G., & Koren, S. A. (1999). Background sound pressure fluctuations (5 dB) from overhead ventilation systems increase subjective fatigue of university students during three-hour lectures. *Perceptual & Motor Skills, 88,* 451–456.

Peters, K. K., & Carlson, J. G. (1999). Worksite stress management with high-risk maintenance workers: A controlled study. *International Journal of Stress Management, 6,* 21–44.

Peterson, C., & Seligman, M. E. P. (1984). Causal explanations as a risk factor for depression: Theory and evidence. *Psychological Review, 91,* 341–374.

Peterson, M. F. et al. (1995). Role conflict, amibiguity, and overload: A 21-nation study. *Academy of Management Journal, 38,* 429–452.

Pfeffer, J., & Ross, J. (1982). The effects of marriage and a working wife on occupational and wage attainment. *Administrative Science Quarterly, 27,* 66–80.

Phillips, B. N., & Lee, M. (1980). The changing role of the American teacher: Current and future sources of stress. In C. L. Cooper & J. Marshall (Eds.), *White collar and professional stress.* New York: Wiley.

Pick, D., & Leiter, M. (1991). Nurses' perceptions of the nature and causes of burnout: A comparison of self reports and standardized measures. *Canadian Journal of Nursing Research, 23,* 33–48.

Piltch, C. A., Walsh, D. C., Mangione, T. W., & Jennings, S. E. (1994). Gender, work, and mental distress in an industrial labor force: An expansion of Karasek's job strain model. In G. P. Keita & J. J. Hurrell Jr. (Eds.), *Job stress in a changing workforce: Investigating gender, diversity, and family issues* (pp. 39–54). Washington, DC: American Psychological Association.

Pines, A. (1982). Changing organizations: Is a work environment without burnout an impossible goal? In W. S. Paine (Ed.), *Job stress and burnout.* Beverly Hills, CA: Sage.

Pines, A., & Aronson, E. (1988). *Career burnout: Causes and cures* (2nd ed.). New York: Free Press.

Pines, A., Aronson, E., & Kafry, D. (1981). *Burnout: From tedium to personal growth.* New York: Free Press.

Piotrkowski, C. S. (1978). *Work and the family system: A naturalistic study of working-class and lower-middle-class families.* New York: Free Press.

Piotrkowski, C. S. (1998). Gender harassment, job satisfaction, and distress among employed white and minority women. *Journal of Occupational Health Psychology, 3,* 33–43.

Plante, T. G., Chizmar, L., & Owen, D. (1999). The contribution of perceived fitness to physiological and self-reported responses to laboratory stress. *International Journal of Stress Management, 6,* 5–20.

Plante, T. G., Lantis, A., & Checa, G. (1998). The influence of perceived versus aerobic fitness of psychological health and physiological stress responsivity. *International Journal of Stress Management, 5,* 141–156.

Potosky, D., & Bobko, P. (2001). A model for predicting computer experience from attitudes toward computers. *Journal of Business and Psychology, 15,* 391–404.

Poulton, E. C. (1976). Continuous noise interferes with work by masking auditory feedback and inner speech. *Applied Ergonomics,7,* 79–84.

Poulton, E. C. (1977). Continuous intense noise masks auditory feedback and inner speech. *Psychological Bulletin, 84,* 977–1001.

Poulton, E. C. (1978). Blue collar stressors. In C. L. Cooper & R. Payne (Eds.), *Stress at work.* New York: Wiley.

Powell, G. N., & Mainiero, L. A. (1999). Managerial decision making regarding alternative work arrangements. *Journal of Occupational and Organizational Psychology, 72,* 41–56.

Powell, L. H., Friedman, M., Thoresen, C. E., Gill, J. J., & Ulmer, D. K. (1984). Can the Type A behavior pattern be altered after myocardial infarction? A second year report from the recurrent coronary prevention project. *Psychosomatic Medicine, 46*(4), 293–313.

Pratt, L. I., & Barling, J. (1988). Differentiating between daily events, acute and chronic stressors: A framework and its implications. In J. J. Hurrell, Jr., L. R. Murphy, S. L. Sauter, & C. L. Cooper (Eds.), *Occupational stress: Issues in research and development.* Philadelphia: Taylor & Francis.

Pretty, G. M., McCarthy, M. E., & Catano, V. M. (1992). Psychological environments and burnout: Gender considerations within the corporation. *Journal of Organizational Behavior, 13,* 701–711.

Prussia, G. E., Kinicki, A. J., & Bracker, J. S. (1993). Psychological and behavioral consequences of job loss: A covariance structure analysis using Weiner's (1985) attribution model. *Journal of Applied Psychology, 78,* 382–394.

Quick, J. C., & Gavin, J. H. (2001). Four perspectives on Conservation of Resources theory: A commentary. *Applied Psychology: An International Review, 50,* 392–400.

Quick J. C., & Quick, J. D. (1984). *Organizational stress and preventive management.* New York: McGraw-Hill.

Quick, J. C., Quick, J. D., Nelson, D. L., & Hurrell, J. J. (1997). Preventive stress management for healthy organizations. In *Preventive stress management in organizations* (pp. 277–299). Washington, DC: American Psychological Association.

Rabkin, J. G. (1980). Stressful life events and schizophrenia: A review of the research literature. *Psychological Bulletin, 87,* 408–425.

Radmacher, S. A., & Sheridan, C. L. (1995). An investigation of the demand-control model of job strain. In S. L. Sauter and L. R. Murphy (Eds.), *Organizational risk factors for job stress* (pp. 127–138). Washington, DC: American Psychological Association.

Rafaeli, A. (1986). Employee attitudes toward working with computers. *Journal of Occupational Behavior, 7*, 89–106.

Rafferty, J. P., Lemkau, J. P., Purdy, R. R., & Rudisill, J. R. (1986). Validity of the Maslach Burnout Inventory for family practice physicians. *Journal of Clinical Psychology, 42,* 488–492.

Raggatt, P. T. F. (1991). Work stress amoung long distance coach drivers: A survey and correlational study. *Journal of Organizational Behavior, 12,* 565–579.

Rahe, R. H. (1974). A model for life changes and illness research: Cross-cultural data from the Norwegian Navy. *Archives of General Psychiatry, 31,* 172–177.

Rahe, R. H. (1989). Recent life change stress and psychological depression. In T. W. Miller (Ed.), *Stressful life events* (pp. 5–11). Madison, CT: International Universities Press.

Rahe, R. H., Mahan, W. J., & Arthur, R. J. (1970). Prediction of near-future health change from subjects' preceding life changes. *Journal of Psychosomatic Research, 13,* 401–405.

Rain, J. S., Lane, I. M., & Steiner, D. D. (1991). A current look at the job satisfaction/life satisfaction relationship: A review and future considerations. *Human Relations, 44, 287–307.*

Ramos, A. A. (1975). The relationship of sex and ethnic background to job related stress of research and development professionals. *Dissertation Abstracts International, 9,* 1862A.

Ramsey, J., & Kwon, Y. (1988). Simplified decision rules for predicting performance loss in the heat. *Proceedings on heat stress indices.* Luxembourg: Commission of the European Communities.

Ratsoy, E. W., Sarros, J. C., & Aidoo-Taylor, N. (1986). Organizational stress and coping: A model and empirical check. *The Alberta Journal of Educational Research, 32*(4), 270–285.

Ray, E. B., & Miller, K. I. (1994). Social support, home/work stress, and burnout: Who can help? *Journal of Applied Behavioral Science, 30*(3), 357–373.

Rees, D., & Cooper, C. (1992). Occupational stress in health service workers in the UK. *Stress Medicine, 8,* 79–90.

Revicki, D. A., & May, H. J. (1985). Occupational stress, social support, and depression. *Health Psychology, 4,* 61–77.

Revicki, D. A., & Whitley, T. W. (1995). Work-related stress and depression in emergency medicine residents. In S. L. Sauter & L. R. Murphy (Eds.), *Organizational risk factors for job stress.* Washington, DC: American Psychological Association.

Revicki, D. A., Whitley, T. W., Gallery, M.E., & Allison, A. J. (1993). Organizational characteristics, occupational stress, and depression in rural emergency medicine technicians. *Journal of Rural Health, 4,* 73–83.

Rice, R. W., Near, J. P., & Hunt, R. G. (1980). The job satisfaction/life satisfaction relationship: A review of empirical research. *Basic and Applied Social Psychology, 1,* 37–64.

Richard, G. V., & Krieshok, T. S. (1989). Occupational stress, strain, and coping in university faculty. *Journal of Vocational Behavior, 34,* 117–132.

Riley, M. W., & Cochran, D. J. (1984). Dexterity performance and reduced ambient temperature. *Human Factors, 26,* 207–214.

Rissen, D., Melin, B., Sandsjo, L., Dohns, I., & Lundberg, U. (2000). Surface EMG and psychophysiological stress reactions in women during repetitive work. *European Journal of Applied Physiology, 83,* 215–222.

Rizzo, J. R., House, R. J., & Lirtzman, S. I. (1970). Role conflict and ambiguity in complex organizations. *Administrative Science Quarterly, 125,* 150–163.

Roberts, S. (1993, September 27). Balancing work, family. *Business Insurance, 3,* 20.

Robertson, I. T., Cooper, C. L., & Williams, J. (1990). The validity of the occupational stress indicator. *Work and Stress,* 4(1), 29–39.

Rodin, J., & Langer, E. (1977). Long term effects of control-relevant interventions with institutionalized aged. *Journal of Personality and Social Psychology, 35,* 897–902.

Romano, C. (1995a, July). Managing change, diversity, and emotions. *Management Review,* 84(7), 6–7.

Romano, C. (1995b, January). Time out. *American Management Association,* 26–29.

Ronen, S. (1981). Arrival and departure patterns of public sector employees before and after implementation of flexitime. *Personnel Psychology, 34,* 817–822.

Ronen, S. (1991). *Flexible working hours: An innovation in the quality of work life.* New York: McGraw-Hill.

Rosenberg, M. R. (1987). Social support: Mechanisms of action and stressor-support specificity. *Dissertation Abstracts International,* 47(7-B), 3124.

Rosenman, R. H., Brand, R. J., Jenkins, D., Friedman, M., Straus, R., & Wurm, M. (1975). Coronary heart disease in the Western Collaborative Group study: Final follow-up experience of 8 1/2 years. *Journal of the American Medical Association, 233,* 872–877.

Rosenman, R. H., & Friedman, M. (1961). Association of specific behavior pattern in women with blood and cardiovascular findings. *Circulation, 24,* 1173–1184.

Roskies, E. (1978). Changing the coronary-prone (Type A) behavior pattern. *Journal of Behavioral Medicine, 1,* 201–216.

Roskies, E. (1990). Type A intervention: Where do we go from here? *Journal of Social Behavior and Personality,* 5(1), 419–438.

Roskies, E., & Carrier, S. (1994). Marriage and children for professional women: Asset or liability? In G. P. Keita & J. J. Hurrell, Jr. (Eds.), *Job stress in a changing workforce: Investigating gender, diversity, and family issues* (pp. 269–282). Washington, DC: American Psychological Association.

Roskies, E., Seraganian, P., & Oseasohn, R. (1986). The Montreal Type A intervention project: Major findings. *Health Psychology, 5*, 45–69.

Roskies, E., Seraganian, P., Oseasohn, R., Hanley, J. A., Collu, R., Martin, N., & Smilga, C. (1986). The Montreal Type A intervention project: Major findings. *Health Psychology, 5*, 45–69.

Roskies, E., Seraganian, P., Oseasohn, R., Smilga, C., Martin, N., & Hanley, J. A. (1989). Treatment of psychological stress responses in healthy Type A men. In R. W. J. Neufeld (Ed.), Advances in the investigation of psychological stress (pp. 284–304). New York: Wiley.

Roskies, E., Spevack, M., Surkis, A., Cohen, C., & Gilman, S. (1978). Changing the coronary-prone (Type A) behavior pattern in a nonclinical population. *Journal of Behavioral Medicine, 1*(2), 201–216.

Ross, E. (1993). Preventing burnout among social workers employed in the field of AIDS/HIV. *Social Work in Health Care, 18*, 91–108.

Rothausen, T. J. (1999). "Family" in organizational research: A review and comparison of definitions and measures. *Journal of Organizational Behavior, 20*, 817–836.

Rowe, M. M. (2000). Skills training in the long-term management of stress and occupational burnout. *Current Psychology: Developmental, Learning, Personality, Social, 19*, 215–228.

Ruben, R. T., Gunderson, E. K. E., & Arthur, R. J. (1971). Life stress and illness patterns in the U.S. Navy, IV: Environmental and demographic variations in relation to illness onset in a battleship's crew. *Journal of Psychosomatic Research, 15*, 221–227.

Rush, M. C., Schoel, W. A., & Barnard, S. M. (1995). Psychological resiliency in the public sector: "Hardiness" and pressure for change. *Journal of Vocational Behavior, 46*, 17–39.

Russell, D. W., Altmaier, E., & VanVelzen, D. (1987). Job-related stress, social support, and burnout among classroom teachers. *Journal of Applied Psychology, 72*, 269–274.

Rutenfranz, J., Knauth, P., & Angersbach, D. (1981). Shiftwork research issues. In L. C. Johnson, D. I. Tepas, W. P. Colquhoun, & M. J. Colligan (Eds.), Advances in sleep research: Vol. 7. *Biological rhythms, sleep and shift work*. New York: Spectrum.

Sadu, G., Cooper, C., & Allison, T. (1989, August). A post office initiative to stamp out stress. *Personnel Management*, 40–45.

Salanova, M., & Schaufeli, W. B. (2000). Exposure to information technology and its relation to burnout. *Behaviour and Information Technology, 19*, 385–392.

Sales, S. M. (1969). Organizational role as a risk factor in coronary heart disease. *Administrative Science Ouarterly, 14*, 325–336.

Sanders, M. S., & McCormick, E. J. (1993). *Human factors in engineering and design* (7th ed.). New York: McGraw-Hill.

Sandman, B. A. (1992). The measurement of job stress: Development of the Job Stress Index. In C. Cranny, P. Smith, & E. Stone (Eds.), *Job satisfaction: How people feel about their jobs and how it affects their performance*. New York: Lexington Books.

Saunders, M. N., & Thornhill, A. (1999). The development and application of a diagnostic tool to help manage survivors of organizational change over time. In R. M. Afzalur & R. T. Golembiewski (Eds.), *Current topics in management* (Vol. 4, pp. 137–153). Stamford, CT: Jai Press.

Sauter, S. L. (1989). NIOSH studies of control and worker well-being: Moderating effects of job control on health complaints in office work. In S. Sauter, J. Hurrell, & C. Cooper (Eds.), *Job control and worker health*. Chichester, England: Wiley.

Sauter, S. L., Hurrell, J. J., Jr., & Cooper, C. L. (1989). *Job control and worker health*. New York: Wiley.

Savicki, V., & Cooley, E. J. (1994). Burnout in child protective service workers: A longitudinal study. *Journal of Organizational Behavior, 15,* 655–666.

Schat, A. C. H., & Kelloway, K. (2000). Effects of perceived control on the outcomes of workplace aggression and violence. *Journal of Occupational Health Psychology, 5,* 386–402.

Schaubroeck, J. (1999). Should the subjective be the objective? On studying mental processes, coping behavior, and actual exposures in organizational stress research. *Journal of Organizational Behavior, 20,* 753–760.

Schaubroeck, J., & Fink, L. S. (1998). Facilitating and inhibiting effects of job control and social support on stress outcomes and role behavior: A contingency model. *Journal of Organizational Behavior, 19,* 167–195.

Schaubroeck, J., & Ganster, D. C. (1991). The role of negative affectivity in work-related stress. Special Issue: Handbook on job stress. *Journal of Social Behavior and Personality, 6,* 319–330.

Schaubroeck, J., Ganster, D. C., & Fox, M. L. (1992). Dispositional affect and work-related stress. *Journal of Applied Psychology, 77,* 322–335.

Schaubroeck, J., Ganster, D. C., Sime, W. E., & Ditman, D. (1993). A field experiment testing supervisory role clarification. *Personnel Psychology, 46,* 1–25.

Schaubroeck, J., Jones, J. R., & Xie, J. L. (2001). Individual differences in utilizing control to cope with job demands: Effects on susceptibility to infectious disease. *Journal of Applied Psychology, 86,* 265–278.

Schaufeli, W. B., & Enzmann, D. (1998). *The burnout companion to study and practice: A critical analysis*. London: Taylor & Francis.

Schaufeli, W. B., Enzmann, D., & Girault, N. (1993). Measurement of burnout: A review. In W. B. Schaufeli, C. Maslach, & T. Marek (Eds.), *Professional burnout: Recent developments in theory and research* (pp. 199–215). Washingon, DC: Taylor & Francis.

Schein, V. E., Maurer, E. H., & Novak, J. F. (1977). Impact of flexible working hours on productivity. *Journal of Applied Psychology, 62,* 463–465.

Schleifer, L. M., Galinsky, T. L., & Pan, C. S. (1992, November). *Mood disturbance and musculoskeletal discomfort: Effects of electronic performance monitoring in a VDT data entry task*. Paper presented at the meeting of the American Psychological

Association/National Institute of Occupational Safety and Health, Washington, DC.

Schmieder, R. A. (1994). *Construct validity of worker control and an assessment of an expanded job demands-control model.* Unpublished doctoral dissertation, Bowling Green State University, Bowling Green, OH.

Schmieder, R. A., & Smith, C. S. (1996). Moderating effects of social support in shiftworking and non-shiftworking nurses. *Work and Stress, 10,* 128–140.

Schmitt, N. (1994). Method bias: The importance of theory and measurement. *Journal of Organizational Behavior, 15,* 393–398.

Schneider, B. (1987). The people make the place. *Personnel Psychology, 40,* 437–453.

Schneiderman, N., Weiss, S. M., & Kaufmann, P. G. (Eds.) (1989). *Handbook of research methods in cardiovascular behavioral medicine.* New York: Plenum Press.

Schoenfeld, I. S. (1990). Coping with job related stress: The case of teachers. *Journal of Occupational Psychology, 63,* 141–149.

Schuler, R. S. (1980). Definition and conceptualization of stress in organizations. *Organizational Behavior and Human Performance, 25,* 184–215.

Schuler, R. S. (1982). Definition and conceptualization of stress in organizations. *Organizational Behavior and Human Performance, 24,* 115–130.

Schuler, R. S. (1985). Integrative transactional process model of coping with stress in organizations. In T. Beehr & R. Bhagat (Eds.), *Human stress and cognition in organizations: An integrated perspective* (pp. 347–374). New York: Wiley.

Schultz, D., & Schultz, S. E. (1998). *Psychology and Work Today: An Introduction to Industrial and Organizational Psychology.* Upper Saddle River, NJ: Prentice Hall.

Schwartz, N. (1999). Self-reports: How questions shape the answers. *American Psychologist, 54,* 93–105.

Schwarzer, R. (2001). Stress, resources, and proactive coping. *Applied Psychology: An International Review, 50,* 400–407.

Seligman, M. E. P. (1975). *Helplessness: On depression, development, and death.* San Francisco, CA: W. H. Freeman.

Selye, H. (1950). *Stress.* Montreal: Acta Inc.

Selye, H. (1956). *The stress of life.* New York: McGraw-Hill.

Selye, H. (1974). *Stress without distress.* Philadelphia, PA: Lippincott.

Selye, H. (1976). *The stress of life* (2nd ed.). NewYork: McGraw-Hill.

Selye, H. (1978). The stress of police work. *Police Stress, 1*(1), 7–8.

Shekelle, R. B., Hulley, S. B., Neaton, J. D., Billings, H., Borhani, N. O., Gerace, T. A., Jacobs, D. R., Lasser, N. L., Mittlemark, M. B., & Stamler, J. (1985). The MRFIT behavior pattern study: II. Type A behavior and incidence of coronary heart disease. *American Journal of Epidemiology, 122,* 559–570.

Shekelle, R. B., Schoenberger, J. A., & Stamler, J. (1976). Correlates of the VAS Type A behavior pattern score. *Journal of Chronic Diseases, 29,* 381–394.

Shinn, M., Rosario, M., Morch, H., & Chestnut, D. (1984). Coping with job stress and burnout in the human services. *Journal of Personality and Social Psychology, 46,* 864–876.

Shirom, A. (1989). Burnout in work organizations. In C. L. Cooper & I. Robertson (Eds.), *International review of industrial and organizational psychology* (pp. 25–48). Chichester, England: Wiley.

Shirom, A., Melamed, S., & Nir-Dotan, M. (2000). The relationships among objective and subjective environmental stress levels and serum uric acid: The moderating effect of perceived control. *Journal of Occupational Health Psychology, 5,* 374–385.

Shouksmith, G., & Burrough, S. (1988). Job stress factors for New Zealand and Canadian air traffic controllers. *Applied Psychology: An International Review, 37*(3), 263–270.

Silverman, M. K., & Smith, C. S. (1995). The effects of human versus computer monitoring of performance on physiological reactions and perceptions of stress. In S. L. Sauter & L. R. Murphy (Eds.), *Organizational risk factors for job stress.* Washington, DC: American Psychological Association.

Sinclair, M. A. (1986). Ergonomic aspects of the automated factory. *Ergonomics, 29,* 1507–1523.

Singer, J. A., Neale, M. S., & Schwartz, G. E. (1989). The nuts and bolts of assessing occupational stress: A collaborative effort with labor. In L. R. Murphy & T. F. Schoenbord (Eds.), *Stress management in work settings* (pp. 3–30). New York: Praeger.

Sinks, T., Mathias, C., Halpern, W., Timbrook, C., & Newman, S. (1987). Surveillance of work-related cold injuries using worker's compensation claims. *Journal of Occupational Health and Safety, 29,* 505–509.

Skinner, H. A., & Lei, H. (1980). Differential weights in life change research: Useful or irrelevant? *Psychosomatic Medicine, 42,* 367–370.

Smith, A. (1989). A review of the effects of noise on human performance. *Scandinavian Journal of Psychology, 30,* 185–206.

Smith, C. S., Reilly, C., & Midkiff, K. (1989). Evaluation of three circadian rhythm questionnaires with suggestions for an improved measure of morningness. *Journal of Applied Psychology, 74*(5), 728–738.

Smith, C. S., Reilly, C., Moore-Hirschl, S., Olsen, H., & Schmieder, R. (1989). *The shiftworker's guide to a good night's sleep.* Bowling Green, OH: Bowling Green State University Press.

Smith, C. S., Robie, C., Folkard, S., Barton, J., Macdonald, I., Smith, L., Spelten, E., Totterdell, P., & Costa, G. (1999). A process model of shiftwork and health. *Journal of Occupational Health Psychology, 4,* 207–218.

Smith, C. S., & Sulsky, L. M. (1995). An investigation of job-related coping strategies across multiple stressors and samples. In L. Murphy, J. Hurrell, Jr., S. Sauter, & G. Keita (Eds.), *Job stress interventions.* Washington, DC: American Psychological Association.

Smith, C. S., & Tisak J. (1993). Discrepancy measures of role stress revisited: New perspectives on old issues. *Organizational Behavior and Human Decision Processes, 56,* 285–307.

Smith, C. S., Tisak, J., Hahn, S. E., & Schmeider, R. A. (1997). The measurement of job control. *Journal of Organizational Behavior, 18,* 225–237.

Smith, F. J., Scott, K. D., & Hulin, C. L. (1977). Trends of job-related attitudes of managerial and professional employees. *Academy of Management Journal, 20,* 454–460.

Smith, L., & Folkard, S. (1993). The perceptions and feelings of shiftworkers' partners. *Ergonomics, 36,* 299–305.

Smith, M. J. (1985). Machine-paced work and stress. In C. L. Cooper & M. J. Smith (Eds.), *Job stress and blue collar work.* New York: Wiley.

Smith, M. J., Carayon, P., Sanders, K. J., Lim, S. Y., & LeGrande, D. (1992). Employee stress and health complaints in jobs with and without electronic performance monitoring. *Applied Ergonomics, 23,* 17–28.

Smith, M. J., Colligan, M. J., & Hurrell, J. J., Jr. (1977, November). *A review of NIOSH psychological stress research.* Paper presented at the UCLA Conference on Job Stress, Los Angeles, CA.

Sorenson, G., Pirie, P., Folsom, A., Luepker, R., Jacobs, D., & Gillum, R. (1985). Sex differences in the relationship between work and health: The Minnesota Heart Survey. *Journal of Health and Social Behavior, 26,* 379–394.

Sparks, K., & Cooper, C. L. (1999). Occupational differences in the work-strain relationship: Towards the use of situation-specific models. *Journal of Occupational and Organizational Psychology, 72,* 219–229.

Spector, P. (1987). Interactive effects of perceived control and job stressors on affective reactions and health outcomes for clerical workers. *Work and Stress, 1,* 155–162.

Spector, P. E. (1994). Using self-report questionnaires in OB research: A comment on the use of a controversial method. *Journal of Organizational Behavior, 15,* 385–392.

Spector, P. E., & Brannick, M. T. (1989). To what degree is method variance inflating correlations among organizational variables? Unpublished manuscript.

Spector, P. E., Chen, P. Y., & O'Connell, J. (2000). A longitudinal study of relations between job stressors and job strains whil controlling for prior negative affectivity and strains. *Journal of Applied Psychology, 85,* 211–218.

Spector, P. E., Dwyer, D. J., & Jex, S. M. (1988). Relation of job stressors to affective, health, and performance outcomes: A comparison of multiple data sources. *Journal of Applied Psychology, 73,* 11–19.

Spector, P. E., Zapf, D., Chen, P. Y., & Frese, M. (2000). Why negative affectivity should not be controlled in job stress research: Don't throw out the baby with the bath water. *Journal of Organizational Behavior, 21,* 79–95.

Spelten, E., Barton, J., & Folkard, S. (1993). Have we underestimated shiftworkers' problems? Evidence from a 'reminiscence' study. *Ergonomics, 36,* 307–312.

Staines, G. L. (1980). Spillover versus compensation: A review of the literature on the relationship between work and nonwork. *Human Relations, 33,* 111–129.

Staines, G. L., & Pleck, J. H. (1983). *The impact of work schedules on the family.* Ann Arbor: University of Michigan.

Staines, G. L., & Pleck, J. (1984). Nonstandard work schedules and family life. *Journal of Applied Psychology, 69,* 515–523.

Staines, G. L., Pottick K. J., & Fudge, D. A. (1986). Wives' employment and husbands' attitudes toward work and life. *Journal of Applied Psychology, 71,* 118–128.

Stamler, J. (1980). Type A behavior pattern: An established major risk for coronary heart disease? In E. Rappaport (Ed.), *Current controversies in cardiovascular disease.* Philadelphia, PA: Saunders.

Standen, P., Daniels, K., & Lamond, D. (1999). The home as a workplace: Work-family interaction and psychological well-being in telework. *Journal of Occupational Health Psychology, 4,* 368–381.

Stanton, J. M., & Barnes-Farrell, J. L. (1996). Effects of electronic performance monitoring on personal control, task satisfaction, and task performance. *Journal of Applied Psychology, 81,* 738–745.

Starnaman, S. M., & Miller, K. I. (1992). A test of a causal model of communication and burnout in the teaching profession. *Communication Education, 41,* 40–53.

Steffy, B. D., & Jones, J. W. (1988). Workplace stress and indicators of coronary-disease risk. *Academy of Management Journal, 31,* 686–698.

Stephens, C., & Long, N. (2000). Communication with police supervisors and peers as a buffer of work-related traumatic stress. *Journal of Organizational Behavior, 21,* 407–424.

Steptoe, A. (1989). Coping and psychophysiological reactions. Special issue: The role of individual differences in stress and stress management. *Advances in Behaviour Research & Therapy, 11*(4), 259–270.

Stevenson, M. K., Busemeyer, J. R., & Naylor, J. C. (1990). Judgment and decision-making theory. In M. D. Dunnette & L. M. Hough (Eds.), *Handbook of industrial and organizational psychology* (2nd ed., Vol. 1, pp. 283–374). Palo Alto, CA: Consulting Psychologists Press.

Stokols, D. (1979). A congruence analysis of human stress. In I. Sarason & C. Spielberger (Eds.), *Stress and anxiety.* Washington, DC: Hemisphere.

Stone, A., Greenberg, M., Kennedy-Moore, E., & Newman, M. (1991). Self-report, situation specific coping questionnaires: What are they measuring? *Journal of Personality and Social Psychology, 61,* 648–658.

Stone, A. A., Schwartz, E., Shiffman, S., Marco, C. A., Hickcox, M., Paty, J., Porter, L. S., & Cruise, L. J. (1998). A comparison of coping assessed by ecological momentary assessment and retrospective recall. *Journal of Personality and Social Psychology, 74,* 1670–1680.

Stressed-out employees learn to relax. (1995, May 1). *Workforce, 74*(5), 25–26.

Suinn, R. M. (1975). *Fundamentals of behavior pathology* (2nd ed.). New York: Wiley.

Suinn, R. M., Brock, L., & Edie, C. A. (1975, August). Behavior therapy for Type A patients [Letter to the editor]. *The American Journal of Cardiology,* 269.

Sullivan, S. E., & Bhagat, R. S. (1992). Organizational stress, job satisfaction, and job performance: Where do we go from here? *Journal of Management, 18,* 353–374.

Sulsky, L. M., & Smith, C. S. (1995, October). *Implications of schema-based processing for self-reports of coping with stress.* Paper presented at the annual meeting of the American Psychological Association National Institute of Occupational Safety and Health, Washington, DC.

Sutton, R., & Rafaeli, A. (1987). Characteristics of work stations as potential occupational stressors. *Academy of Management Journal, 31,* 686–698.

Tait, M., Padgett, M. Y., & Baldwin, T. T. (1989). Job and life satisfaction: A reevaluation of the strength of the relationship and gender effects as a function of the date of the study. *Journal of Applied Psychology, 74,* 502–507.

Tattersall, A. J., Bennett, P., & Pugh, S. (1999). Stress and coping in hospital doctors. *Stress Medicine, 15,* 109–113.

Taylor, E., Briner, R. B., & Folkard, S. (1997). Models of shiftwork and health: An examination of the influence of stress on shiftwork theory. *Human Factors, 39,* 67–82.

Taylor, H. (2000). The difference between exercisers and non-exercisers on work-related variables. *International Journal of Stress Management, 7,* 307–309.

Taylor, M. S., Fisher, C. D., & Ilgen, D. R. (1984). Individuals' reactions to performance feedback in organizations: A control theory perspective. In K. Rowland & J. Ferris (Eds.), *Research in Personnel and Human Resources Managment* (pp. 81–124). Greenwich, CT: JAI Press.

Teasdale, E. L., & McKeown, S. (1994). Managing stress at work: The ICI-Zeneca Pharmaceuticals experience 1986–1993. In C. L. Cooper & S. Williams (Eds.), *Creating healthy work organizations* (pp. 133–165). Chichester, England: Wiley.

Teichner, W. H., Arees, E., & Reilly, R. (1963). Noise and human performance: A psychophysiological approach. *Ergonomics, 6,* 83–97.

Tennant, C. C. (1987). Stress and coronary heart disease. *Australian and New Zealand Journal of Psychiatry, 21,* 276–282.

Tepas, D. I. (1985). Flexitime, compressed workweeks and other alternative work schedules. In S. Folkard, & T. H. Monk (Eds.), *Hours of work: Temporal factors in work-scheduling.* New York: Wiley.

Tepas, D. I. (1990). Do eating and drinking habits interact with work schedule variables? *Work & Stress, 4*(3), 203–211.

Tepas, D. I., Armstrong, D. R., Carlson, M. L., & Duchon, J. C. (1985). Changing industry to continuous operations: Different strokes for different plants. *Behavior Research Methods, Instruments, & Computers, 17*(6), 670–676.

Terborg, J. R. (1985). Working women and stress. In T. A. Beehr & R. S. Bhagat (Eds.), *Human stress and cognition in organizations* (pp. 245–286). New York: Wiley.

Terborg, J. R. (1988). The organization as a context for health promotion. In S. Spacapan & S. Oskamp (Eds.), *The social psychology of health* (pp.119–127). Newbury Park, CA: Sage.

Tetrick L., & LaRocco, J. (1987). Understanding, prediction, and control as moderators of the relationships between perceived stress, satisfaction, and psychological well-being. *Journal of Applied Psychology, 72*, 538–542.

Teuchmann, K., Totterdell, P., & Parker, S. K. (1999). Rushed, unhappy, and drained: An experience sampling study of relations between time pressure, perceived control, mood, and emotional exhaustion in a group of accountants. *Journal of Occupational Health Psychology, 4*, 37–54.

The doctor is in your office. (1996, June). *Sales and Marketing Management, 148*(6), 22.

Theorell, T., & Karasek, R. A. (1996). Current issues relating to psychosocial job strain and cardiovascular disease research. *Journal of Occupational Health Psychology, 1*, 9–26.

Thoern, A. (2000). Emergence and preservation of a chronically sick building. *Journal of Epidemiology and Community Health, 54*, 552–556.

Thomas, L. T., & Ganster, D. C. (1995). Impact of family-supportive work variable on work-family conflict and strain: A control perspective. *Journal of Applied Psychology, 80*, 6–15.

Thompson, M. S., & Cooper, C. L. (2001). A rose by any other name... : A commentary on Hobfoll's Conservation of Resources theory. *Applied Psychology: An International Review, 50*, 408–418.

Thurman, C. W. (1985). Effectiveness of cognitive-behavioral treatments in reducing Type A behavior among university faculty: One year later. *Journal of Counseling Psychology, 32*, 445–448.

Tisak, J., & Smith, C. S. (1994). Defending and extending difference score methods. *Journal of Management, 20*, 675–682.

Tombaugh, J. R., & White, L. P. (1989, April). *The effects of organizationally based social support on survivors' perceived stress and work attitudes.* Paper presented at the fourth annual conference of the Society of Industrial and Organizational Psychology, Boston, MA.

Totman, R., Kiff, J., Reed, S. E., & Craig, J. W. (1980). Predicting experimental colds in volunteers from different measures of recent life stress. *Journal of Psychosomatic Research, 24*, 155–163.

Trocki, K. F., & Orioli, E. M. (1994). Gender differences in stress symptoms, stress-producing contexts, and coping strategies. In G. P. Keita & J. J. Hurrell, Jr. (Eds.), *Job stress in a changing workforce: Investigating gender, diversity, and family issues* (pp. 7–22). Washington, DC: American Psychological Association.

Tucker, P., Barton, J., & Folkard, S. (1996). A comparison of 8 and 12 hour shifts: Impacts on health, well-being and on-shift alertness. *Occupational and Environmental Medicine, 53,* 767–772.

Tucker, P., Smith, L., Macdonald, I., & Folkard, S. (1998). The impact of early and late shift changeovers on sleep, health, and well-being in 8- and 12-hour shift systems. *Journal of Occupational Health Psychology, 3,* 265–275.

Tully, S. (1995, June 12). America's healthiest companies. *Fortune, 131*(1), 98–106.

Turnage, J. J. (1990). The challenge of new workplace technology for psychology. *American Psychologist, 45,* 171–178.

U.S. Bureau of Labor Statistics. (1990). *Occupational injuries and illnesses in the United States by industry.* Bulletin 2399. Washington, DC: U.S. Government Printing Office.

U.S. Congress, Office of Technology Assessment. (1987). *The electronic supervisor: New technology, new tensions.* Washington, DC: U.S. Government Printing Office.

U.S. Department of Labor. (1974). *Women's Bureau Bulletin: The myth and the reality.* Washington, DC: U.S. Government Printing Office.

U.S. Department of Labor. (1978). *Women in traditionally male jobs: The experience of ten public utilities companies.* Washington, DC: U.S. Government Printing Office.

van der Doef, M., & Maes, S. (1999). The job demand-control (-support) model and psychological well-being: A review of 20 years of empirical research. *Work & Stress, 13,* 87–114.

van der Klink, J. J., Blonk, R.W., Schene, A.H., & van Dijk, F.J. (2001). The benefits of interventions for work-related stress. *American Journal of Public Health, 91,* 270–276.

Van der Wielen, J. M. M., Taillieu T., Poolman, A. J. & J. van Zuilichem, J. (1995). Telework: Dispersed organizational activity and new forms of spatio-temporal coordination and control. In J. M. Peiro, F. Prieto, J. L. Melia, & O. Luque (Eds.), *Work and organizational psychology: European contributions of the nineties* (pp. 262–280). Mahwah, NJ: Erlbaum.

van Dierdonck, D., Schaufeli, W.B., & Buunk, B.P. (1998). The evaluation of an individual burnout intervention program: the role of inequity and social support. *Journal of Applied Psychology, 83,* 392–407.

Vener, K. J., Szabo, S., & Moore, J. G. (1989). The effect of shift work on gastrointestinal (GI) function: a review. *Chronobiologica, 16,* 421–439.

Verespej, M. A. (January 4, 1993). Health care: Cost controls and quality can coexist. *Industry Week,* 18–19.

Vermeulen, M., & Mustard, C. (2000). Gender differences in job strain, social support at work, and psychological distress. *Journal of Occupational Health Psychology, 5,* 428–440.

Villiers, N., O'Malley, P., Brown, D., Leary, J., & Holloway, F. (1999). Burnout in mental health nurses: Much ado about nothing? *Stress Medicine, 15,* 127–134.

Vincino, F. L., & Bass, B. (1978). Lifespace variables and managerial success. *Journal of Applied Psychology, 63,* 81–88.

Vining, R. F., McGinley, R. A., Maksvytis, J., & Ho, K. (1983). Salivary cortisol: A better measure of adrenal cortical function than serum cortisol. *Annual Clinical Biochemistry, 20,* 329–335.

Vinokur, A. D., & Caplan, R. D. (1987). Attitudes and social support: Determinants of job-seeking behavior and well-being among the unemployed. Journal of Applied Social Psychology, 17, 1007–1024.

Vinokur, A. D., Price, R. H. & Schul, Y. (1995). Impact of the JOBS intervention on unemployed workers varying in risk for depression. *American Journal of Community Psychology, 23,* 39–74.

Vinokur, A. D., Price, R. H., Caplan, R. D., van Ryn, M., & Curran, J. (1995). The Jobs I preventive intervention for unemployed individuals: Short and long-term effects on reemployment and mental health. In L. R. Murphy, J. J. Hurrell, Jr., S. L. Sauter, & G. P. Keita (Eds.), *Job stress interventions* (pp. 125–138). Washington, DC: American Psychological Association.

Vinokur, A. D., Schule, Y., Vuori, J., & Price, R. H. (2000). Two years after a job loss: Long-term impact of the JOBS program on reemployment and mental health. *Journal of Occupational Health Psychology, 5,* 32–47.

Vinokur, A. D., van Ryn, M., Gramlich, E. M., & Price, R. H. (1991). Long-term follow-up and benefit-cost analysis of the jobs program: A preventive intervention for the unemployed. *Journal of Applied Psychology, 76,* 213–219.

Violette, G. R. (1991, June). The benefits of a wellness program. *Journal of Accountancy,* 126–130.

Viswesvaran, C., Sanchez, J. I., & Fisher, J. (1999). The role of social support in the process of stress: A meta-analysis. *Journal of Vocational Behavior, 54,* 314–334.

Vitliano, P. P., Russo, J., Carr, J. E. Maiuro, R. D., & Becker, J. (1985). The ways of coping checklist: Revision and psychometric properties. *Multivariate Behavioral Research, 20,* 3–26.

Walker, J. (1985). Social problems of shiftwork. In S. Folkard, & T. H. Monk (Eds.), *Hours of work: Temporal factors in work-scheduling.* New York: Wiley.

Wall, T. D., Kemp, N. J., Jackson, P. R., & Clegg, C. W. (1986). Outcomes of autonomous workgroups: A long-term field experiment. *Academy of Management Journal, 29,* 280–304.

Wallace, M., & Buckle, P. (1987). Ergonomic aspects of neck and upper limb disorders. In D. J. Oborne (Ed.), *International Reviews of Ergonomics,* 1, 173–200.

Wallace, M., Levens, M., & Singer, G. (1988). Blue collar stress. In C. L. Cooper & R. Payne (Eds.), *Causes, coping, and consequences of stress at work.* Chichester, England: Wiley.

Wanberg, C. R. (1997). Antecedents and outcomes of coping behaviors among unemployed and reemployed individuals. *Journal of Applied Psychology, 82,* 731–744.

Wanous, J. P. (1976). Organizational entry: From naive expectations to realistic beliefs. Journal of Applied Psychology, 61, 327–332.

Wasterlund, D. S. (1998). A review of heat stress research with application to forestry. Applied Ergonomics, 29(3), 179–183.

Watson, D., & Clark L. A. (1984). Negative affectivity: The disposition to experience negative emotional states. Psychological Bulletin, 96, 465–490.

Weaver, C. N. (1980). Job satisfaction in the United States in the 1970s. Journal of Applied Psychology, 65, 364–367.

Weinberg, S., Edwards, G., & Garove, W. E. (1983). Burnout among employees of state residential facilities serving developmentally disabled persons. Children and Youth Services Review, 5(3), 239–253.

Weinstein, M. (1996, August). Stress relief. Risk and Insurance, 24–27.

Weiten, W., Lloyd, M. A., & Lashley, R. L. (1991). Psychology applied to modern life: Adjustment in the 90s (3rd ed.). Pacific Grove, CA: Brooks/Cole.

Wells, J., Hobfoll, S., & Lavin, J. (1997). Resource loss, resource gain, and communal coping during pregnancy among women with multiple roles. Psychology of Women Quarterly, 21(4), 645–662.

Westman, M. (1990). The relationship between stress and performance: The moderating effect of hardiness. Human Performance, 3, 141–155.

Westman, M., & Eden, D. (1996). The inverted-U relationship between stress and performance: A field study. Work and Stress, 10, 165–173.

Westman, M., & Eden, D. (1997). Effects of a respite from work on burnout: Vacation relief and fade-out. Journal of Applied Psychology, 82, 516–527.

Westman, M., & Etzion, D. (1995). Crossover of stress, strain, and resources from one spouse to another. Journal of Organizational Behavior, 16, 169–181.

Wethington, E. & Kessler, R. C. (1986). Perceived support, received support, and adjustment to stressful life events. Journal of Health & Social Behavior, 27(1), 78–89.

Wiebe, D. J. (1991). Hardiness and stress moderation: A test of proposed mechanisms. Journal of Personality and Social Psychology, 60, 89–99.

Wilensky, H. L. (1960). Work, careers, and social integration. International Social Science Journal, 12, 543–560.

Wilkinson, R. T. (1963). Interaction of noise with knowledge of results and sleep deprivation. Journal of Experimental Psychology, 66, 332–337.

Williams, K. J., & Alliger, G. M. (1994). Role stressors, mood spillover, and perceptions of work-family conflict in employed parents. Academy of Management Journal, 37, 873–868.

Williams, K. J., Suls, J., Alliger, G. M., Learner, S. M., & Wan, C. K. (1991). Multiple role juggling and daily mood states in working mothers: An experience sampling study. Journal of Applied Psychology, 76, 664–674.

Williams, L. J., Cote, J. A., & Buckley, M. R. (1989). Lack of method variance in self-reported affect and perceptions at work: Reality or significant problem? *Journal of Applied Psychology, 74*, 462–468.

Winnubst, J. (1993). Organizational structure, social support, and burnout. In W. B. Schaufeli, C. Maslach, & T. Marek (Eds.), *Professional burnout: Recent developments in theory and research* (pp. 151–162). Washington, DC: Taylor & Francis.

Wolf, T. H., Elston, R. C., & Kissling, G. E. (1989). Relationship of hassles, uplifts, and life events to psychological well-being of freshman medical students. *Behavioral Medicine, 37*–45.

Wolff, H. (1953). *Stress and disease.* Springfield, IL: Charles C. Thomas.

Work/life programs on the rise, survey finds. (1996, August 19). *National Underwriter, 100*(34), 9–10.

Workplace prevention: The state of the nation. *Business and Health, 13*(12), 20–23.

Yang, N., Chen, C., Choi, J., & Zou, Y. (2000). Sources of work-family conflict: A Sino-U.S. comparison of the effects of work and family demands. *Academy of Management Journal, 43*(1), 113–123.

Yerkes, R. M., & Dodson, J. D. (1908). The relation of strength of stimulus to rapidity of habit-formation. *Journal of Comparative Neurology and Psychology, 18*, 459–482.

Zajonc, R. B. (1984). On the primacy of affect. *American Psychologist, 39*, 117–123.

Zedeck, S. (1992). Introduction: Exploring the domain of work and family concerns. In S. Zedeck (Ed.), *Work, families, and organizations.* San Francisco: Jossey-Bass.

Zedeck, S., & Mosier, K. L. (1990). Work in the family and employing organization. *American Psychologist, 45*, 240–251.

Zeier, H. (1994). Workload and psychophysiological stress reactions in air traffic controllers. *Ergonomics, 37*(3), 525–539.

Zellars, K. L., & Perrewe, P. L. (2001). Affective personality and the content of emotional social support: Coping in organizations. *Journal of Applied Psychology, 86*, 459–467.

Zohar, D. (1999). When things go wrong: The effect of daily work hassles on effort, exertion and negative mood. *Journal of Occupational and Organizational Psychology, 72*, 265–283.

INDEX

CREDITS

This page constitutes an extension of the copyright page. We have made every effort to trace the ownership of all copyrighted material and to secure permission from copyright holders. In the event of any question arising as to the use of any material, we will be pleased to make the necessary corrections in future printings. Thanks are due to the following authors, publishers, and agents for permission to use the material indicated.